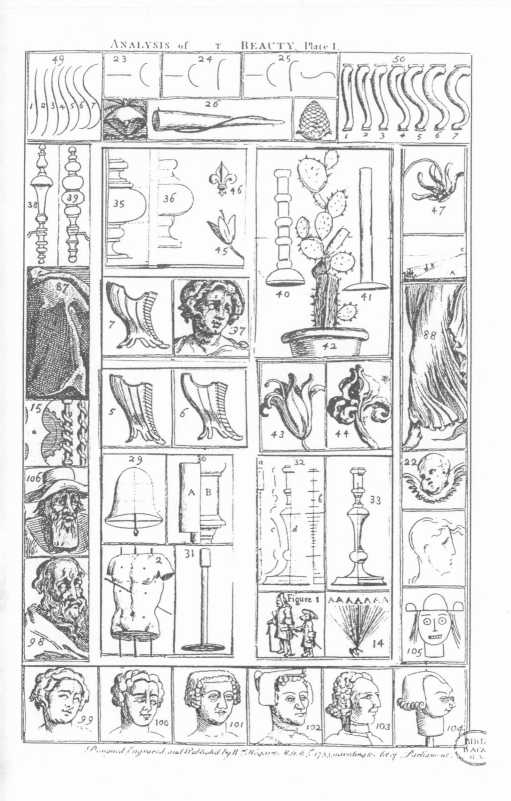

ANALYSIS of т BEAUTY, Plate I.

Designed, Engraved, and Published by W.ᵐ Hogarth, March 5. 1753, according to Act of Parliament.

BODY AND TEXT IN THE

EIGHTEENTH CENTURY

CONTRIBUTORS

Elizabeth Heckendorn Cook

Chris Cullens

Peter de Bolla

Thomas DiPiero

Susan Gustafson

Tassie Gwilliam

Veronica Kelly

Deidre Lynch

Dorothea von Mücke

Neil Saccamano

Helmut J. Schneider

David E. Wellbery

Body & Text in the Eighteenth Century

EDITED BY VERONICA KELLY

AND DOROTHEA VON MÜCKE

STANFORD UNIVERSITY PRESS

Stanford, California 1994

Stanford University Press
Stanford, California
© 1994 by the Board of Trustees
of the Leland Stanford Junior University
Printed in the United States of America

CIP data appear at the end of the book

Stanford University Press publications are
distributed exclusively by Stanford University
Press within the United States, Canada, and
Mexico; they are distributed exclusively by
Cambridge University Press throughout the
rest of the world.

Acknowledgments

The editors extend their deepest appreciation to the contributors, both for their fine essays and for their unflagging cooperation in all aspects of the preparation of this book.

We gratefully acknowledge the American Council of Learned Societies, whose grants for Recent Recipients of the Ph.D. supported both editors during separate stages of this project. We also thank DePaul University's Research Council for its support.

We are indebted to William Warner for his critical and constructive reading of the entire manuscript. Helen Tartar of Stanford University Press provided us with invaluable advice, and her insights provoked important clarifications. We thank Barbara Phillips for her careful and timely editing, Andreas Gailus for compiling the Index, and Diana Reese and Nikolai Borodulin for helping with the proofreading.

We particularly wish to thank Karin Ohme for her visual contribution to our volume. She selected and interpreted the detail from Hogarth's *Analysis of Beauty* that appears on the cover.

Special thanks to Philippe and Miriam, Dan and Claudia.

Contents

PART 3: *The Limits of the Body*

PART 4: *Unnatural Bodies*

REFERENCE MATTER

Contributors

Elizabeth Heckendorn Cook is Assistant Professor of English at Yale University. She is the author of *Fictions in the Republic of Letters* and is currently working on a study of late eighteenth-century natural history, landscape aesthetics, and the novel.

Chris Cullens is an independent scholar and lives in San Francisco. She is the author of *Female Difficulties* and has published articles on women's literature, Kleist, and feminist theory.

Peter de Bolla is Director of English Studies at King's College, Cambridge University. His books include *Harold Bloom: Towards Historical Rhetorics* and *The Discourse of the Sublime*.

Thomas Dipiero is Associate Professor of French and of Visual and Cultural Studies at the University of Rochester. He has published *Dangerous Truths and Criminal Passions: The Evolution of the French Novel, 1569–1791* and numerous articles on psychoanalysis, fiction, and identity politics. He is currently completing a book on whiteness and masculinity.

Susan Gustafson is Assistant Professor of German and a member of the program faculty in Comparative Literature at the University of Rochester. She is the author of *Absent Mothers and Orphaned Fathers: Narcissism and Abjection in Lessing's Aesthetics and Dramatic Production* and articles on Lessing, Goethe, and Kleist.

Tassie Gwilliam teaches English and Women's Studies at the University of Miami and is the author of *Samuel Richardson's Fictions of Gender*. She is currently writing a book on the body in the eighteenth century.

Veronica Kelly is Senior Documentation Specialist at ADAC Laboratories. She lives and writes in Pleasanton, California.

Deidre Lynch is Assistant Professor of English at the State University of New York, Buffalo, and is completing her book *Face Value: The Economy of Character*. She has published articles on eighteenth-century and early nineteenth-century tourism and nationalism.

Dorothea von Mücke is Associate Professor of German at Columbia University and author of *Virtue and the Veil of Illusion: Generic Innovation and the Pedagogical Project in Eighteenth-Century Literature*.

Neil Saccamano is Associate Professor of English at Cornell University and author of *Publication and Poetics in Eighteenth-Century England*. He has published articles on aesthetic theory, satire, and political theory in the eighteenth century.

Helmut J. Schneider is Professor of German Literature at the University of Bonn. He has edited *Idyllen der Deutschen* and *Deutsche Landschaften*. His recent work includes a study of Lessing and Kleist.

David E. Wellbery is Kurrelmeyer Professor of German at Johns Hopkins University. His publications include *Lessing's Lacoon: Semiotics and Aesthetics in the Age of Reason* and a forthcoming study of Goethe's lyrics, *The Specular Moment*.

BODY AND TEXT IN THE

EIGHTEENTH CENTURY

Introduction: Body and Text in the Eighteenth Century

VERONICA KELLY AND

DOROTHEA VON MÜCKE

*T*here is no escaping the body. That, at least, is the conclusion that the body's looming presence in the thought and debate of the past two decades dictates. And with all this publicity there has also inevitably come a new respectability, and the suggestion the body's moment — insofar as critical interest is concerned — is past: that the body has been done. Such cycles characterize our hard-driven academic marketplace. This volume is structured around the perhaps paradoxical thesis that it is a focus on the body in its specific histories that will, at this moment, challenge the vicissitudes of timeliness. The essays collected here examine the body as it is delineated and addressed within eighteenth-century culture. By situating the body in a historical context, this collection not only assumes that a conscious focus on the body is not new but indicates that our study of the body cannot be newly obsolete. It proposes instead that attention to the body and its representations is perennial because fundamental cultural activities are informed by specific versions of the body; because a culture in its moments of heightened self-awareness, when it would understand its own position in history, will also investigate its relationships to the human body.

This volume, then, takes a general interest in the body's resistance to the confident amnesia of intellectual paradigms and its habit of endangering those progressive teleologies that, on the one hand, contain the past in definite histories and, on the other, invoke the new for its radical, transformative power. Far from encouraging us to lay claim to a wholesale topicality, our focus on the body's resistance to forms of closure has demanded that we speak to the complex temporality of the body and its images in history. We have answered this demand by concentrating our essays on the eighteenth century, a period marked by a modernity that, in its precocity, is both alien and familiar. Like our own era in ways that suggest both an origin and a final aberration, the eighteenth century has been the main locus of critical identification, analogy, and analysis in recent discussions of modernity and postmodernity. It has been, in other words, the favorite other. Having been so designated in practice, the period of the eighteenth century becomes crucial to understanding present discussions of the body. We have been struck by the fact that, whether it figures in these discussions as the primal object that conserves civilized society or as the best vehicle for radical social transgression, the body persistently reappears at the center of our love affair with otherness. It is in light of this conjunction between the eighteenth century and the body that we emphasize the otherness of the eighteenth century as an aspect of the current encounter between the body and its histories.

To prevent our emphasis on history from suggesting that the body might be a quiescent object of study, we have found it necessary to introduce the specific roles the body plays in eighteenth-century culture through more general reflections on how corporeality can be thought of in the critique of culture. This has meant situating our volume at the intersections of histories and phenomenologies of the human body, where the body is assumed to be specific and discrete, and of investigations pertaining to semiotic, poetic, and aesthetic operations, which foreground the body's involvement with representation. In what follows, we outline some representative positions within current cultural analyses involving the human body in order to indicate how we organize the rival claims now being made on the body.

In "The Natural and Literary History of Bodily Sensation," Jean Starobinski raises the possibility that the present "infatuation" with the body should be understood in its narcissistic dimension. After tracing medical and philosophical descriptions of cenesthesia, the term coined for a general feeling of "corporeal sensoriality," from the late eighteenth century to Freud, Starobinski concludes his essay by asking: "Where do we draw the line between cenesthesia, which must be a basic assumption of every human existence, and body awareness, which would be the hypochondriacal or perverse consequence of a narcissistic or autoerotic investment?"[1] Starobinski's question not only asks if we can distinguish between two types of the human body, it also implicitly raises the question of our desire to distinguish between them. According to Starobinski, our responses to the body fall into two categories. On the one hand, we all assume the body is a

fundamental given or unproblematic presence that organizes our perceptions and being in the world. This kind of body is the one Merleau-Ponty
describes as "the third term . . . always tacitly understood, in the figure-
background structure, and every figure stands out against the double horizon of external and bodily space" (ibid.). On the other hand, we focus
a conscious, intentional awareness — to the point of obsession — on the
body. Starobinski sees the latter case as a result of a particular crisis, and
suggests that the intense interest in the human body currently displayed by
the human sciences might be understood as partaking in such an "intentional awareness." Indeed, Starobinski views this preoccupation with the
body in terms of a pathology of contemporary Western civilization in
order to disarm any moralistic dismissal of it:

What I devote to an awareness of the body, I subtract from my presence in the
world, from my investment in the other. In a conscious awareness of the body, the
aesthetic element of cenesthesia is in the nature of an instinctual satisfaction undeniably confused with primary physiological information. It is a variation on "turning around upon the subject's own self." There is nothing very bold in drawing the
only superficially banal conclusion that the present infatuation with the different
modes of body consciousness is a symptom of the considerable narcissistic component characteristic of contemporary Western culture. . . . Perhaps one could also
enter a plea on behalf of Narcissus (or at least invoke extenuating circumstances in
his favor). In a world in which technological mastery has made such rapid strides,
can one not understand that the desire to feel — and to feel oneself — should arise as
a compensation, necessary, even in its excesses, to our psychic survival? (ibid.,
pp. 369–70)

Leaving aside the dubious promise of a compensation, Starobinski's
"plea," and its implied warning against the constraining discourse of pathology, pinpoints some of the crucial concerns involved in a critical focus
on the body. With the figure of Narcissus, whose fatal mirror-image fas-
tens us within the primal confusion of "primary physiological information" and an aestheticized bodily awareness, Starobinski foregrounds the
difficulty of positing an empirically given bodily presence onto which a
socially, culturally constructed body would be grafted and from which it
might conceivably be separated. This difficulty is neither a psychological
nor a mythological dead end, but endows the body with a fundamentally
resistive and transgressive force that becomes visible as the body assumes
various figures that are responsive to its cultural context and that make it
possible to examine the relation between the body as discourse and its
scene. Thus Starobinski describes our current obsession with the body,
and the pathological register in which it is manifest, as an effect of our loss

of feeling in a period of rapid technological development. But far from bringing us to a point of self-reflexive compensation, Starobinski's appeal for Narcissus suggests that it is precisely because "an awareness of the body" cannot be purged of an "investment in the other," precisely because we can no longer refer to a separate or a natural body as the critical norm against which we measure the transformations and deformations wrought within civilization, that the body stands out among all other aspects of modern culture as that for which we want to provide a genealogy of its discursive constructedness.

But this "discovery" — that in the technological age we have lost contact with the natural body — cannot simplify the task of describing the body's relation to discourse, since the body is neither simply in discourse nor out of it. This becomes clear as soon as we track the figure of the body in its migrations across recent polemical divides. For example, the body has taken a potentially nostalgic role in the cultural critique of technology, as Starobinski's analysis suggests, while it has often appeared as the aggressor in challenges to the philosophy of consciousness. In addition, within the attack on consciousness, both sophisticated literary appeals to the body, such as Nietzsche's densely worked allusions to the dionysian body, and references to involuntary somatic phenomena like digestion serve equally to undermine the tightly held belief that consciousness simply oversees the body. These appeals to the body for opposing purposes — now against technology, now against consciousness — make it imperative to ask what, if anything, distinguishes the body's wide-ranging role in critical examinations of modernity and rationality. We find that, as against an older tradition of critiques and histories of civilization that focus on the human body (the work of Norbert Elias, for instance), the current concern emphasizes at the same time both the body's discursive character, whereby it is subjected to the orders of civilization and discipline, and its survival within that discursivity as a kinetic potential, inviting transgression against the hegemonic cultures that it elsewhere serves.

In fact, this position of the body precisely at the threshold of cultural activity, of subject formation and signification, has been the common concern of a wide-ranging spectrum of poststructuralist psychoanalytical investigations. For these psychoanalytic approaches, there is no bodily unity before the work of culture. Rather, the work of culture organizes a conflicting conglomerate of physiological information and drives into an individual body, which in turn supports the configuration of the psychical apparatus. Thus Starobinski's diagnosis of a narcissistic fixation on the body can no longer be seen as an occasional, pathological crisis but must be considered a crucial stage of each individual's entry into language. This, at least, is Lacan's model of primary narcissism, a model that emphasizes that the illusion of bodily unity is necessary as the imago or prototype for the development of a psychical identity.[2] Another train of thought within psychoanalytic theory assigns the cultural distinctions of subject/object and of gender to the affective mechanisms of mourning and melancholia operating through a semio-physiological conjunction. For example, Julia Kristeva argues that bodily disgust, as the loathing and rejection of the undifferentiated, provides both the beginning and the support for any oppositional grid of signification.[3] Judith Butler draws on Abraham's and Torok's theory of melancholia in order to model the braiding together of the affective reaction to a fundamental loss with the naturalization or essentialization of a gendered body: "As an antimetaphorical activity, incorporation [i.e., the disavowal of grief, in which the lost object is magically sustained in the body] literalizes the loss on or in the body and so appears as the facticity of the body, the means by which the body comes to bear 'sex' as its literal truth."[4]

Although we cannot do justice to them here, what we can abstract from these complex psychoanalytic models of how processes of identity formation have recourse to specific bodily phenomena is a stronger sense of what psychoanalysis asks of the subject and how the asking of the question places the body at the center of current investigations of the mechanisms of identity formation and discursive practices. Seeking to discover who or what it is that supports the identity of the subject, psychoanalysis traces its object — its "it" — to the human body, where the mythology of abstract knowledge reaches the end of its narrative life in the body's cross-referencing of somatic and semiotic events. In the psychoanalytic analysis, the body refers questions about the truth of psychic identity to language, and questions about linguistic meaning to the impulses of the psyche. This tautology of language and identity relocates the truth of the subject in a human body, which it positions both in discourse and out of it.

The both/and structure of this formulation will disappoint those who secretly expect that the work of research and interpretation will reinstate the rule of an autonomous consciousness over the body and its material histories, even as they pretend otherwise. These expectations linger in part because of the uses to which the psychological disciplines have been put. To the extent that psychology, psychosomatics, and psychoanalysis focus on the body and its potential interference with the social formation of the psyche, the body in question is primarily the private body of an individualized subject. The groundbreaking work of Foucault, particularly his

Discipline and Punish and *History of Sexuality*, reveals the complicity of such disciplines as psychology in the formation of an individualized, sexualized modern subject. As such work indicates, the conceptualization of the body as property owned and operated by an individual is a relatively recent phenomenon of bourgeois culture: it is the paradigm we take for granted, but not the exclusive or uncontested site for a material bodily principle operating as the real subtending reality. It has been easy to misconstrue and underestimate the way that Foucault's work has shaken this paradigm. Curiously enough, rather than obviating the psyche, the charge that the recent articulations of Foucault have been part of our cultural investment in individualism returns to the psyche the full, historically variable powers of specificity and contingency. Likewise, the formulation of the body as both disciplined and transgressive is not a catchall theoretical conundrum, as some have claimed, but a standing refusal of the mind-body hierarchy, a refusal which functions to break that hierarchy regardless of which term is dominant. Both/and is thus not a hypothesis, but a tactical resistance to hypotheses — at least to those dead hypotheses that, like dead metaphors, have lost their rhetorical markers.

Recent examinations of modern civilization that draw attention to another body against which the bourgeois body defines its own classical ideal have worked to recover those markers and, with them, the body's discursivity. Peter Stallybrass and Allon White's *The Politics and Poetics of Transgression*, for example, does not accept the monolithic installation of a unified bourgeois subjectivity supported by its canonical artistic and philosophical masterpieces. Stallybrass and White counter this naturalized bourgeois ideal with the grotesque body described by Bakhtin, in his study of Rabelais, as a material bodily principle contained "not in the biological individual, not in the bourgeois ego, but in the people, a people who are continually growing and renewed," and through whose growth "all that is bodily becomes grandiose, exaggerated, immeasurable."[5] This Bakhtinian body is a body associated with joyful excessivity and collective festivity, with impurity and the socially low: "The openings and orifices of this carnival body are emphasized, not its closure and finish. It is an image of impure corporeal bulk with its orifices (mouth, flared nostrils, anus) yawning wide and its lower regions (belly, legs, feet, buttocks, and genitals) given priority over its upper regions (head, 'spirit', reason)" (ibid., p. 26).

Although they organize their study of the carnivalesque around Bakhtin's analysis of the grotesque body, Stallybrass and White do not simply invert the classical hierarchy to celebrate the people's body as an unproblematic antidote to bourgeois subjectivity. Rather, they argue that

the "carnivalesque" mediates between a classical/classificatory body and its nega-
tions, its Others, what it excludes to create is identity as such. In this process
discourses about the body have a privileged role, for transcodings between different levels and sectors of social and psychic reality are effected through the
intensifying grid of the body. It is no accident, then, that transgressions and the
attempt to control them obsessively return to somatic symbols, for these are ultimate elements of social classification itself. (ibid.)

Stallybrass and White resist this inversion by arguing both that the human
body cannot and must not be analyzed apart from its social context and
that it nevertheless holds a privileged position in the mechanisms of ordering and sense making in European cultures. This position creates a difficult conflict between the rhetorically extravagant claim of these authors
that body images are the "ultimate elements of social classification itself"
and their demand for attention to the contingencies of historical context,
where one imagines that such a claim might be frequently contravened.
But it is important here not to slip back behind the lens of classicism, even
if the authors themselves sometimes do, and instead to emphasize their
somewhat understated point that the privilege held by "somatic symbols"
rests not in an inherent value but in their capacity to translate and intensify otherness. Unlike Bakhtin, for whom the Rabelaisian orifice becomes
very much the locus of a new essentialism, Stallybrass and White place the
body in a position of semiotic privilege, and not at the hypothetical center
but now and again at all the intersections of "social and psychic reality."
There body images function not as the end but as the medium of cultural
differences.

Perhaps because they turn their attention so quickly to the analysis of
image patterns in social history, Stallybrass and White leave largely unan-
swered a question that their own argument raises: What exactly is it (and
indeed how is it) that the "grid of the body" is "intensifying"? A highly
suggestive recent work on this problem is Elaine Scarry's *The Body in
Pain*. Unlike *The Politics and Poetics of Transgression*, which takes the
body's capacity to represent as part of its evidence that the making of
orders and hierarchies is the fundamental cultural activity, *The Body in
Pain* proposes that the fundamental cultural activity of making a world, of
creating artifacts and fictions, takes its genesis in the body's capacity to
suffer. Hence Scarry's study is less interested in "body images" and instead
posits the human body as the source of sentience by which we determine
our access to and engagement with the world.

She sets out from a comparison of the structures of torture and war as
powerful ways of "unmaking the world" through the infliction of pain:
"Pain is exceptional in the whole fabric of psychic, somatic, and percep-

tual states for being the only one that has no object. Though the capacity
to experience physical pain is as primal a fact about the human being as is
the capacity to hear, to touch, to desire, to fear, to hunger, it differs from
these events, and from every other bodily and psychic event, by not having
an object in the external world."[6] Hence the difficulty of articulating and
communicating pain. For the one afflicted it becomes an all-powerful and
at times even exclusive reality, while for the one who merely hears about it
it seems most elusive. It is this dissociation of embodiment, voice, referent,
and representation that is used by torture and war alike: "In both war and
torture, the normal relation between body and voice is deconstructed and
replaced by one in which extremes of the hurt body and unanchored
verbal assertions are laid edge to edge. In each, a fiction is produced, a
fiction that is a projected image of the body: the pain's reality is now the
regime's reality; the factualness of corpses is now the factualness of an
ideology of territorial self-definition" (p. 144).

For Scarry the opposite to pain is not pleasure (the absence of pain and
by extension the absence of the body) but imagining: " 'Pain' and 'imagining' constitute extreme conditions of, on the one hand, intentionality as a
state and, on the other, intentionality as self-objectification; and that between these two boundary conditions all the other more familiar, binary
acts and objects are located. That is, pain and imagining are the 'framing
events' within whose boundaries all other perceptual, somatic, and emotional events occur; thus, between the two extremes can be mapped the
whole terrain of the human psyche" (p. 164). Thus she understands the
"making of the world," all creative, productive, and interactive cultural
activities, as both a form of relief and an extension of the body: "In benign
forms of creation, a bodily attribute is projected into the artifact (a fiction,
a made thing), which essentially takes over the work of the body, thereby
freeing the embodied person of discomfort and thus enabling him to enter
a larger realm of self-extension" (p. 144).

Whereas all these studies are careful to note the problems involved in
positing a naturally given human body and emphasize its implication in
semiotic, coding, metaphorical, and fictionalizing processes, it might very
well be Scarry's book that presses us most to ask the question why above
all things it should be the human body that serves as hinge and anchorage
point for cultural activity. Although she engages in a problematic sub-
sumption of all made objects, ranging from altars, bandages, and baseball
bats to poems and factories, under the rubric of artifact, creation or making, Scarry introduces very fruitful distinctions between various types of
fictions and degrees of making (from making up to making real). Her
discussion of how the body is used in order to substantiate beliefs, fic-

tions, and ideologies points toward formulating if not answering questions mechanistic discourse analyses cannot raise if they merely echo their version of the German ideology: "It's discourse all the way down."

Yet, Scarry's answer — that it is the body in pain that defines the absolute bedrock of the making and unmaking of the world — articulates more of a limit condition than a useful model for why the body provides in the words of Stallybrass and White an "intensifying grid" for the mapping of society. Whereas pain could be described as that kind of "physiological information" that most resists representation, "need" should be understood as the one that is constantly transformed through semiotic processes. Psychoanalysis has drawn our attention to the difficulty of maintaining a clear and simple distinction among pain, pleasure, and desire. By focusing solely on what she calls the "deconstruction" of the "normal relation between voice and body," Scarry makes it impossible to acknowledge that in many cases we might not be able to isolate pain in the "hurt body" or to reduce the "hurt body" to the experience of pain.

The basic premise for this volume, which we hope the above-sketched studies help to illustrate, is that the human body stands in a multiple and complex relation to the limits and centers of the cultural production of meaning. The body provides the "raw material" in the ordering, cathecting, and processing of sensory data, drives, and affects into symbolic systems, but it can also serve as a medium for the transmission of information. Finally, the body becomes a privileged model or model object for the definition and organization of such semiotic events as the distinction between sign and symptom, textual whole and fragment, surface and depth, natural and conventional or artificial, literal and figural, real and imagined. It is primarily in this last function that we understand the human body by calling our anthology *Body and Text in the Eighteenth Century*.

Through this focus on the human body we want to address the current methodological pluralism in the study of European Enlightenment culture, which is marked by the opposing tendencies of, on the one hand, macrohistorical paradigms based on the period's "semiotic deep structure" and, on the other hand, an insistence on the importance of recovering local knowledge and practices. Clearly, there is not just one dominating body image furnishing a model object for eighteenth-century European culture. Rather, in representation, the human body has many historically variable "doubles" which act as master figures to discipline the signifying capacity into systems of meaning and value. In the production of dominant cultural codes, these body doubles both regulate the excesses of signifying practice and define the subjectivity of agents in the semiotic transaction.

The eighteenth century sees both the rise of secular modes of thought founded on the concept of a "natural" body and an intense activity in semiotic theory. In the eighteenth century, the body is increasingly objectified in both scientific and aesthetic analysis. It appears at the center of perceptual philosophies, where the concept of "common sense" naturalizes signifying practices, suggesting that any specific act of writing or reading is grounded in what seems most intimately known, real, or inevitable to us. Yet the eighteenth century continuously debated the nature of language and its origin, the nature of signs, and models for sign production. Even the term "semiotics" was already current. At the close of the *Essay Concerning Human Understanding*, for example, Locke divides "Science" into three parts: Physica or Natural Philosophy, Practica or Ethicks, and Semeiotica or the Doctrine of Signs.[7] In the emerging institution of clinical medicine, to give another example, the term "semeiotic" describes newly codified conventions for interpreting symptoms.[8]

In fact, most disciplines of knowledge in the eighteenth century are marked by fundamental assumptions about (1) the nature of the human body, (2) the nature of the sign and signification, and (3) the role of the body in sign production. At the most general level, eighteenth-century culture can be characterized by a belief in natural language as an episteme of representation.[9] But at the level of local practices this striving for semiotic transparency or "clarity" is contested by partisans of competing knowledge, or is caught up in contradiction and pursued to strange and telling effect. It is in these disjunctions between the culture's dominant paradigms and their aberrations that we can read what is at stake and for whom in cultural representations of the body. To achieve just such readings, we have chosen to organize this volume around those semiotic events that have recourse to the body, but to insist that the specific deployment of the body within aesthetic and semiotic concerns of the century can vary tremendously depending on what exactly is meant by the "human body": whether the body double appears as the physiological organism; the mortal, gendered, classed, or diseased; the erotic or sexual body, dressed or naked, fragmented or whole; a psychological projection; or a rhetorical metaphor.

In recent years the field of eighteenth-century studies has received major new impulses from the application of poststructuralist, feminist, new historical, and cultural materialist questions to this historical period.[10] To the general benefit of the field, this has led both to new ways of reading canonical texts and to the inclusion of previously marginalized or forgotten texts in our study of eighteenth-century culture. As a result, the field of eighteenth-century studies is currently marked by a plurality of competing approaches, each of which asserts its urgency by presenting itself as a precursor to modern subjectivity, or as a key to today's gender or class struggles. Although our volume is informed by the findings of the "new eighteenth-century studies," we do not assume an unbroken continuity between Enlightenment culture and our own. Nor do we assume a clean and simple difference between then and now. Instead, we emphasize the need to read the complex particularities of eighteenth-century culture against the larger paradigms that distinguish the production of meaning in that period from its production in our own. For example, though the human face is conceived as something to be decoded in eighteenth-century physiognomy, this early hermeneutic science produces its own contradictions as it gradually attempts to combine a taxonomic method with the accidents of singularity on the one hand and Enlightenment individualism on the other. Early eighteenth-century poetics uses the dress-body, language-nature analogy and the figure of the "true body" to effectively redefine nature as the ornament of culture and so to consolidate its class interests. In the discourse of eighteenth-century cosmetics, ornaments and paints serve not to enhance the "natural" beauty of the face and figure but to invest them with textuality. For mid-eighteenth-century aesthetics, the body is both the site of ideal beauty and the limit of what can and may be represented.

The essays gathered in this volume demonstrate the multiplicity of the discursive contexts in which the human body is addressed during the eighteenth century. They draw on popular literature, poetics and aesthetics, garden architecture, physiognomy, beauty manuals, pornography, and philosophy as well as on canonical works in the genres of the novel and the drama. In order to further emphasize that our focus in this volume is on the body's place and function in the eighteenth-century semiotic networks rather than on purely thematic assonances, we have organized the essays not thematically but rather in a rough chronological order and according to the function that the body assumes as a model object.

The first three articles all examine texts written during the first half of the eighteenth century and in which the body metaphor is used, not unproblematically, to establish paradigms that we have long associated with the centers of eighteenth-century culture: republican politics and its "individual," neoclassicism, and biography. Elizabeth Heckendorn Cook's "The Limping Woman and the Public Sphere" shows how the human body becomes the model for conceiving a new relationship among author, text, and reading public. Through a close analysis of Montesquieu's *Lettres persanes*, this essay studies how the new communicational ideal of the enlightened Republic of Letters emerges against the declining absolutist culture of spectacle. Although the despotic culture has been organized around the king's body, its end is figured as the disappearance, lack, or feminization of this dual body of father and king, the end of its omnipotence and omnivoyance. In contrast to the king's body a new body makes its appearance, the one of the individual writing subject. This latter body is closely bound up with the then-emerging epistolary genre. Its traces are hallucinated behind the printed letter serving a new model of authentication as opposed to the old one of authorization qua filiation. Yet, the vanishing of the king's body could not be simply replaced by the plenitude or hallucinated presences of the writer's and the Enlightenment critic's body, since ideally the Enlightenment model of a critical, rational exchange of ideas postulates a reading practice that engages with published texts and does not consider the specific biographical position and embodiment of their authors. And yet, the new model of authorship nevertheless needs to rely on a masculine ideal of a republican citizen. Furthermore, the particular handicap of publication, the dissemination of texts under censorship, calls for the wish of not having to hide one's body. In brief, Heckendorn Cook addresses the limits and necessity of the body metaphor as a model for the relationship among author, text, and reading public. Her essay shows that Montesquieu's vision of civic identity in relation to print culture and a republic of letters emerges *ex negativo*, i.e., through the figure of the limping woman (introduced in the novelistic frame) and through the problematic figures of lack within the novelistic fiction itself (eunuchs, slaves, veiled wives, and the impotent despot).

The body, especially the body that can enact and suffer violence, is often invoked in epistemological reflections on wit in the eighteenth century to indicate the threat posed by rhetoric to the century's nascently humanist ideals of communication and meaning. In "Wit's Breaks," Neil Saccamano reads the most sustained critical discourse on wit published during the period, Joseph Addison's series on that topic, which appeared in *The Spectator* from May 7 to May 12, 1711, to analyze the epistemological and political suppositions that determined the treatment of wit as violence in neoclassical theories of language. Saccamano reads Addison's series — in relation to Locke's *Essay*, which excludes wit as the mechanism of epistemological error and even madness — as an apology for wit and literary art generally. Addison reclaims wit by dividing it against itself: true wit maintains the truth of poetry as the truth of metaphor, the visual recognition of a proper body of sense, while the false wit of the letter — of rebuses, puns, and anagrams — is contingent, a chance effect that breaks and mutilates true sense. But, as the case of rhyme shows, Addison's strategy of legitimation does not ensure the corporeal integrity of neoclassical poetry or insulate its sense from contingent forces: neither poems nor bodies can have the formal coherence and integrity of natural objects without a frame to delineate them. Moreover, neoclassical poetics cannot do without the violence that it projects onto "false wit" because, as Addison's remarks on the genesis of poetry show, violence against the natural body is the origin of cultural production and of the ideal of British mercantile culture in particular. Addison's analogy between commerce and wit in *Spectator 69* transfers the figure of the body into a political economy of culture, which rewrites the body-breaking violence of false wit as the transport of merchant "traffic" across nature's dispersed body. In his closing analysis of the political economy of wit, Saccamano shows that neoclassicism depends on the violence it would exclude as false wit: Addison's attempt to use the figure of the body to naturalize cultural artifacts depends on the very violence that he censures in his account of wit and that mercantile ideology celebrates as the labor of commerce.

Because it imagines itself so explicitly as a timely and useful representation of exemplary individuals, eighteenth-century biography is an ideal arena in which to study the reciprocity between conceptions of the subject and technologies of the body. Veronica Kelly's "Locke's Eyes, Swift's Spectacles" looks back from Freud's invention of the unconscious in visual metaphors to an earlier but related moment in the history of the psyche and the technologies that embody it: to the moment when, in the eighteenth century, introspective empirical philosophy and literary biography together focus the subject of consciousness, as if on a lens, in the optical metaphor of a reflective "I." The task of biographical writing as it emerges in the eighteenth century is to visualize and rationalize this virtual consciousness as a body controlled by a perspectival view. Beginning with Johnson's account of Swift's madness in *The Life of Swift*, and analyzing in detail Johnson's claim that Swift went mad because he refused to wear his spectacles, Kelly reads *The Life of Swift* as the limit text of eighteenth-century biography. In the moral spectacle made of Swift's body, biography uses the conventions of optical distance to deny the impossible time of its writing. Kelly moves from an analysis of Johnson on Swift, in which she pays particular attention to Johnson's preoccupation with Swift's Birthday poems and the spectacle of his physical and mental decline, to discuss Locke's theory of consciousness as a perspectival visual technology troubled by the failure of memory and language to maintain the visible distinctions that Locke uses to articulate bodies and identities. In *The Life of*

Swift the biographer would obviate these persistent failures in the moral spectacle of an inarticulate body: it is Swift's refusal to say "I see" that puts his body at the center of Johnson's life writing.

As more than one of the preceding essays have indicated, eighteenth-century theories of meaning and identity depend on the century's philosophical belief that sight was the preeminent bodily sense and on the association of vision and cognition in metaphor. The second group of essays examines the eighteenth-century organization of the field of vision, of seeing and of reading. In "The charm'd eye," Peter de Bolla investigates the cultural production of looking and the cultural manifestations of visuality in mid-eighteenth-century England through an analysis of the bounded space of William Shenstone's garden, the Leasowes. Refuting the assumption that the senses simply perform "naturally," de Bolla uses the architecture of Shenstone's garden, his correspondence, and his "Unconnected Thoughts on Gardening" to ask how were eighteenth-century men and women taught to look? What were they taught to look at, which postures of the body were deemed appropriate for different types of viewing situations? Who legislated and policed the activity of looking, in what service of which ends, which constituencies? The concept of "visuality," which refers to the subject's cultural production through the visual field, allows de Bolla to describe the form and function of the visual for this specific historical moment. Shenstone created a space for looking in his garden within a community of interested individuals, estate owners who were also committed to improving their grounds. The visuality exemplified in Shenstone's garden not only tells us about the nature of the subject as structured by the technologies surrounding this particular instance of the activity of looking, but expands our understanding of what it meant for men and women in mid-eighteenth-century England to look.

The subject of Deidre Lynch's "Overloaded Portraits: The Excesses of Character and Countenance" is the face: in particular, how the face figures in the highly ambivalent thinking that eighteenth-century writers and artists did about bodily surplus and about the possibility that the parts composing what they strove to designate as Human might exceed and devastate the whole. Lynch finds that the overloaded face — for example, the face particularized too much by experience or deformity or, in art, by the overstatements of caricature — served in eighteenth-century debates to mark the boundaries of genres and the point at which culturally legitimate modes of representing personhood shaded into illegitimate or popular modes. The technical questions of exactly how the face should look, or be represented, stood in for questions about personal identity: whether personal identity could be seen, and the extent to which such visualized persons would be subject to the instabilities of literary or artistic genres, with which they would share a medium. Lynch begins her analysis where questions of quantity figure prominently, paradoxically enough, in debates about kind and quality and argues that thinking about the overloaded face allowed for a reworking of the decorums for fleshing out character, for figuring strokes of the pen or paintbrush into life. But in the century's mimetic theory of identity and of art, quantity undermines the positive claims of singularity by threatening inflation: more description and more detail may well define but eventually they disfigure. Added strokes, intended to flesh out a character, turn a portrait into a worthless lampoon or, worse, into something monstrous and unnameable. In addition, the aesthetic judgments of mimesis are troubled by their utilitarian attachments to quantity — to quantities of money, for example, and influence. Lynch reads the production of monsters as an allegory for the eighteenth century's generation of new genres and a new hierarchy. After analyzing the structures of physiognomic and semiotic inflation in Locke's *Essay Concerning Human Understanding* and in the Theophrastan character collections, she turns to two controversies over faces. The first of these debates — manifest in the works of Hogarth and the aesthetic treatises generated by England's Royal Academy of Art — was over the status in visual portraiture of that finishing touch that either finalized a portrait's imitation of a person or pushed it into the debased domain of the outré and the caricatured. The second debate centered on the theatrical style of David Garrick and whether his "grimace" made theater richer or, as his detractors maintained, perverted the legibility of the theatrical body. Lynch shows that as the arts in mid-century wrestled with the question of the "insensible more or less," they displayed the human figure as a mere figure. As new economies of character came into conflict late in the century with Enlightenment pictorialist aesthetics, the face became a figure for disfiguration.

The semiotics of the face is also the subject of Tassie Gwilliam's "Cosmetic Poetics: Coloring Faces in the Eighteenth Century." Moving from mainstream eighteenth-century attacks on cosmetics as the vehicle of disguise and deceit, Gwilliam reads periodical essays and "exotic" advice literature to show us how the dominant, moralized concept of the body in the eighteenth century is challenged from within popular culture by the unstable colors of the female and native bodies that it would rule. Gwilliam focuses on two non-canonical works: *Abdeker: Or the Art of Preserving Beauty*, an English translation of Antoine Le Camus' oriental tale and cosmetic recipe book, and Samuel Jackson Pratt's (unproduced) comedy, *The New Cosmetic, or the Triumph of Beauty*, set in the West Indies. By celebrating the transformation of surface, the treatment of cosmetics in these "low" works explodes the constitution of the self in metaphors of layers and depths. Gwilliam finds that, in the eccentric narratives of *Abdeker* and *The New Cosmetic*, the art of coloring the face moves toward a political poetics that disrupts the century's dominant construction of gender difference and — in the case of *The New Cosmetic* — of the boundaries between races.

During the second half of the eighteenth century the Enlightenment ideal of semiotic transparency found both its culmination and its end with the gradual emergence of Romanticist textual models of expression rather than representation. Certainly, Lessing, Goethe, and Kleist, the authors examined by Dorothea von Mücke, David Wellbery, and Helmut Schneider, cannot be counted among the proponents of a Romanticist cultural program. Yet each of them explores, as these three studies show, the extreme possibilities of an Enlightenment model of representation or — to varying degrees — its transformation through references to the human body. Indeed, Lessing's *Laokoon* is rightfully considered the pivotal text of Enlightenment sign theory. Yet, one aspect that has so far received relatively little attention is the fact that the later chapters in this complex study of the medial differences between painting and poetry shift the attention from a concern with beauty and transparent signification to ugliness and disgust. Von Mücke's "The Powers of Horror and the Magic of Euphemism in Lessing's *Laokoon* and *How the Ancients Represented Death*" demonstrates that this concern with the "mixed sentiments," with semiotic undifferentiation and visceral physical responses on the side of the beholder or recipient, is far from undermining a neoclassicist aesthetics and is, rather, at its very core. Lessing's universalist claims with regard to the "Law of Beauty" depend on the immediate physical response to extremes of ugliness and physicality: disgust or the urge to vomit. Yet, although this involuntary bodily reaction seems to have the advantage of providing Lessing an unquestionable, "natural" means of defining the threshold of representation, the potential loss of body control as well as all the unpleasant aspects of the body as the site of death and decay also provide an obstacle to the Enlightenment project. Lessing was particularly aware of the ideological potential inherent in the depiction of a decaying body as it was exploited by Christianity. In order to understand this dimension of Lessing's concern with the human body and death, von Mücke analyzes the pamphlet *How the Ancients Represented Death*. In this work

Lessing develops a model of how language, particularly the rhetorical strategy of euphemism, allows us to distance ourselves and to gain control over the destabilizing bodily reactions. In brief, her article argues that the Enlightenment utopia of a perfect language, free of opacity and ambiguity, and the aesthetic ideal of poetry as an immaterial medium operating with arbitrary signs that nevertheless approximate the natural accessibility of the signs of painting, ultimately aim at the ability to forget the body as the locus of suffering, pain, and decay.

The overcoming of bodily limitations is also at the center of Goethe's *Werther*, yet here the body is not the one of the beholder or reader of an aesthetic object (as in Lessing) but it is the phantasmatic body created in the textual process itself, a body that serves the radically new aesthetic concretization of subjectivity per se. It is via this phantasmatic body that this novel revolutionizes the epistolary genre and shifts from an aesthetics grounded in a visual representational model to the perceptual register of hearing. Setting out from a close reading of the famous letter that describes how Werther falls in love with Charlotte as they are dancing the then-scandalous new waltz, David Wellbery's "Morphisms of the Phantasmatic Body: Goethe's *The Sorrows of Young Werther*" develops the concept of the phantasmatic body as a body that has neither definite shape nor contours but is accessed or projected through the metamorphoses of desire and anxiety. Wellbery shows how the novel's central model of subjectivity and expression is built on the morphisms of the absolute body. This absolute body is a phantasmatic construct that cancels the Enlightenment model of semiosis as substitution and establishes instead a model of originary metaphorization. Wellbery's essay not only provides a highly refined close reading of the textual, poetic devices of this novel, but it also proposes an innovative way of understanding the mechanisms by which a new, radicalized subjectivity was to guide the emergence of both a new lyricism and ultimately the articulation of Romanticism.

A phantasmatic body not only supports the poetic construction of a new subjectivity but also becomes the focus and the center of a paradigm shift initiated in the second half of the eighteenth century: from Winckelmann to Hegel, the Greek statue provided the prototype of the classicist ideal, as well as the concrete background intuition for the new systemic place of aesthetics within the framework of hermeneutics and *Geschichtsphilosophie*. This imaginary body of the statue served both as the object of empathy and as the source of meaningful expression, which was projected onto the "body" of history at large. What in traditional criticism is called the "symbolic art" of Romanticism is inconceivable without the statue as model object that literally embodied meaning, sense, spirit, and interiority. Helmut Schneider's "Deconstruction of the Hermeneutical Body" analyzes how Kleist's essay on the *Marionettentheater* undermines this "classical body" by on the one hand "exposing" it and, on the other hand, proposing as an alternative an eccentric body of a radical externality. Schneider thus shows (1) how the various models of mechanical, fragmented bodies in Kleist's essay can serve the deconstruction of the paradigm shift initiated in the later eighteenth century, and (2) how Kleist's text reflects on its own rhetorical "positions" and "movements" through a continuous literalization of spatial and corporeal metaphors.

While the previous three essays explore the body as model object in the expansion of the representational paradigms of the Enlightenment, the last three essays in this volume are all concerned with texts of the later eighteenth century in which the body appears as a fundamentally ambiguous phenomenon. In these texts as they try the concepts of the Enlightenment and its social programs, bodies articulate cultural and representational crises, revealing an undifferentiation that ruins the smooth reproduction of subjects and values. Susan Gustafson's "Goethe's *Clavigo*: The Body as an 'Unorthographic' Sign" focuses on one particular phase in German Enlightenment culture, the period that became known as Sturm und Drang, which is marked by a younger generation of poets' impatience with the preceding generation's unadulterated advocacy of rationalism, tolerance, and sensibility. The main focus of this first wave of a critique of Enlightenment culture was an attack on the semiotics of an ideally transparent representation and on the poetics of the bourgeois tragedy. In terms of dramatic technique, those young playwrights aimed at shock, at the radical undermining of whatever had been left of neoclassical notions of decorum. The sexual, grotesque, ugly, and sick body comes back into focus and provides the site for the destabilization of cultural value systems. Gustafson's study examines *Clavigo*'s focus on Marie's sick body. Marie holds the traditional position of the virtuous bourgeois daughter. She is throughout most of the play silent, except for the hysterical symptoms of her body. Thus she invites being constructed into the perfect supplement of her lover or her brother. Yet it is here, as Gustafson shows, that the play uses the sick body to undermine exactly this traditional mechanism. Previously, for the aesthetics and poetics of bourgeois tragedy, the body's gestural language was conceived of as a "natural sign," the vehicle of communicating the "authentic" language of sensibility, but Gustafson's essay demonstrates how in this play the body provides the site for radical semiotic undifferentiation.

Probably no other eighteenth-century writer has explored the subversive potential of the human body to such a degree as the Marquis de Sade. Yet it is far less obvious what exactly was being attacked by his pornographic novels. Thomas DiPiero's "Disfiguring the Victim's Body in Sade's *Justine*" offers a reading that situates *Justine* in the context of the eighteenth-century theory of the novel, the idealizing, if not moralizing, poetics of *vraisemblance*. His close reading of *Justine* investigates the subversive force of Sade's representation of libertine violence. Although libertines mark their victims in order to annihilate them and to experience the burning sensations of pleasure that will allow them to experience total coincidence with nature, Justine's remarkable powers of regeneration thwart libertine mastery. This victim's body, instead of registering the marks of libertine hegemony, resists that inscription and subverts the neat opposition between vice and virtue. The violence and pain Justine undergoes leave no residue attesting to the libertine's superiority, and rather than marking the limits of representation and establishing an unrepresentable zone of political hegemony, pain and violence are textualized. DiPiero shows how Sade's tale of sexual violence, purportedly in the service of virtue, interrogates the cultural foundations of good and evil and initiates a political aesthetic that defies the conventions of eighteenth-century fiction.

In "Mrs. Robinson and the Masquerade of Womanliness," Chris Cullens draws parallels between the life of actress/author Mary Robinson, who is tagged as "Perdita," the lost one, after her affair with the Prince of Wales, and the logic of gender in the transvestite plot of her novel *Walsingham, Or the Pupil of Nature*. Cullens reads both Robinson's *Memoirs* and the historical context in which she is made into a readable sign in and for popular culture against the discourses of masquerade, maternity, and melancholia in *Walsingham*. Organized philosophically around the term "nature," *Walsingham* nevertheless partially de-naturalizes gender by displaying it as a social and pedagogical construct. With the right upbringing, for example, a young woman can masquerade for years with complete success as a man. Organized narratively around cross-dressing and the motif of the masquerade, the novel allows sexual ambiguity to destabilize general semantic codes of self-representation and mutual recognition. But the novel ultimately withdraws from the subversive potential inherent in its plotting of gender as masquerade. For masquerade, whether a masquerade party or the transvestite heroine's extended masquerade, results in *Walsingham* not in carnivalesque exuberance but in gothic horrors. In the end, *Walsingham* can only right the disorder it has uncovered through a hasty, belated reorganization of normative female destiny in the body: around an irre-pressible heterosexual desire and the rehabilitation of proper motherhood. Although in this the novel follows the discursive realignments of its era toward a stricter binarization of gender, Cullens argues that a disfiguring excess of violence and melancholia remains as a symptom of the text's uneasiness about figuration as a process by which the raw material of bodies is pressed into socially and sexually recognizable contours.

Part 1

Discursive Shifts and Realignments

The Limping Woman and the Public Sphere

ELIZABETH HECKENDORN COOK

In the eighteenth century, the writing subject was incorporated at a specific literary site. In epistolary narratives, the letter serves as a metonym of the body of the writing subject, vulnerable like it to markings, invasion, violence of all sorts. The letter-novel's underlying fiction is that implicit in the bound volume one is reading, almost visible through the dark uniform bars of print on the page, are the original documents from which the printed text has been typographically transcribed: handwritten letters, bearing traces of their production in the inkblots, teardrops, scratched-out words, or scriptive tremulousness that signify iconically as well as semantically.[1] While reading, we are intended to imagine a scene of writing: behind the printed page is a manuscript bearing the traces of a bodily origin. Formally as well as thematically, then, the letter constructs the writing subject as corporeal and thus as an already existing object of knowledge that can be mapped by the transparent medium of print. The eighteenth-century epistolary novel gives form to and helps institutionalize a modern understanding of subjectivity as embedded in and inseparable from a discrete body, a notion of individual identity that can be summed up as the body/subject. Subjectivity is thus produced as and in a textual form that articulates the ideologically loaded qualities of discreteness and autonomy assigned to each body/subject.[2]

However, the naturalization of this model of subjectivity in eighteenth-century epistolary narratives was not unremarked or uncontested. The transformations of subjectivity in Montesquieu's *Persian Letters* (1721) anticipate the present ongoing critique of representations of bodies, subjectivity, and power generated by the work of Michel Foucault. Of particular relevance here is Foucault's attention to the metaphor of the body politic: in *Discipline and Punish*, he addresses the analogy between human body and political unit underlying the familiar image of a corporealized state made up of "head," "organs," and "members." The analogy is doubly mystifying: first, it misrepresents the macro-operations of power as emanating from distinct, autonomous sources in conflict with one another; second, it reinforces assumptions about the integrity and autonomy of individuals, relying as it does on the same body/subject model that is incorporated in the epistolary novel. But how could the relation between body and state be conceived differently, and what notion of subjectivity would be implicit in a new model? In response to this question, Foucault proposes a literary genre that would redefine simultaneously the state and the body/subject:

Borrowing a word from Petty and his contemporaries, but giving it a different meaning from the one current in the seventeenth century, one might imagine a political "anatomy." This would not be the study of a state in terms of a "body" (with its elements, its resources and its forces), nor would it be the study of the body and its surroundings in terms of a small state. One would be concerned with the "body politic," as a set of material elements and techniques that serve as weapons, relays, communication routes and supports for the power and knowledge relations that invest human bodies and subjugate them by turning them into objects of knowledge.[3]

In light of the attention to figurations of the civic and sexual body in the *Persian Letters*, I propose that Montesquieu's work is a "political anatomy" in Foucault's sense. Although the interpretive terrain of the conventional epistolary body/subject has shaped its critical history, I will argue in what follows that if some aspects of the *Persian Letters* exploit that model, others deliberately work against it. Specifically, where the letters of many eighteenth-century epistolary fictions generate a phantasmatic erotic body, a kind of prosthetic compensation for an absent lover, Montesquieu's text produces instead a more problematic "body politic." In other words, what is at stake here is the citizen's body. Disturbing the conventional homologies between body and letter and between body and state, Montesquieu invites us to read the Persians' letters not as transparent metonymic containers of authentic selfhood but as materializations of the pervasive and contested effects of power. His strategy of simultaneous disembodiment and disfiguration of the metaphor of the body politic exposes the processes by which subjectivities — and, specifically, gendered subjectivities — are discursively constructed in print.

My analysis will be anchored by two metaphorical bodies that define the symbolic field of early eighteenth-century French absolutism: that of an omnivoyant and omnipotent Father who generates and guarantees language, and that of a silent limping woman, crippled by the public gaze. Between these figures, the *Persian Letters* shapes its readers as politically gendered citizen-critics of the Republic of Letters.

The Father

> The death of the Father would deprive literature of many of its pleasures. If there is no longer a Father, why tell stories?
>
> — Roland Barthes, *The Pleasure of the Text*

> The monarch who reigned for so long is no more. He made people talk a great deal during his life; everyone fell silent on his death.
>
> — *Persian Letters*, Letter XCII

For Barthes, narrative is anchored in the existence of a body — specifically, in the generative capacities of a male body given symbolic and transhistorical status by the initial capital letter of its name. Montesquieu's Persian correspondent, writing after the death of Louis XIV, seems to imply a similar origin for discourse. However, the *Persian Letters*, as distinct from the Persians' letters, can be read so as to provide quite a different response to Barthes's rhetorical question. In contradiction to the idea that narrative always loses meaning in the absence of the Father, the *Persian Letters* suggests that the telling of stories became vastly more important following what could be understood as a kind of cultural paternal death occurring across a specific historical period: the demise of the patriarchal authority structures implicit in absolutist epistemology. In this sense, during the extended transition from absolutism to the modern bureaucratic state undergone by several European nations in the seventeenth and eighteenth centuries, the institutions of print generally and individual works of literature in particular represent efforts to explain and compensate for the effects, whether feared, deplored, or celebrated, of the death of the Father.

In the course of the seventeenth century, the idea of the double monarchical body of the Father-King, the head of the family composed of all his subjects, began to lose its cultural authority. As the analogy implicit in this notion of monarchy between the political and the domestic came undone, public and private emerged as separate spheres demanding different technologies of control. Specifically, although the political fiction of the social contract explained the founding of a civil society of fraternal equals, it did not explicitly address the private domain of the family, for which a different guarantee had to be identified.[4] The question of how to order the private interests and appetites of individual men and women — the problem of the private body — was answered not by political theorists but by writers of what we now call fiction: the novel, and particularly the epistolary novel, developed as a direct response to what could be called an anxiety about the private body at the very heart of the Enlightenment. As that instrument in the private sphere of affective relations analogous to the social contract in the public and civic domain, the literary contract of the epistolary novel produced, socialized, and regulated the postpatriarchal private subject as an inhabitant of the Republic of Letters.

In these early years of the age of mechanical reproduction, then, the social order was being reconstructed by the implications of print, but its effects had not yet been fully internalized or naturalized in the cultural imagination: the book had not yet become transparent. The material forms of books, their surfaces and dimensions, along with the circumstances of their production, were still potentially part of what they could signify. Epistolary novels are particularly directly engaged, both formally and thematically, with material issues of representation: the printed letter, like any text, operates through typographical conventions that assume the transparence of the print character; but it also signifies quasi-iconically, reproducing by exact transcription the shape of an absent originary document and the body/subject that produced it. Yet the editorial apparatus that frames eighteenth-century letter-novels — their prefaces and forewords, epigraphs, footnotes, postscripts — all insist on the novels' participation, indeed their embeddedness, in the forms and institutions of print culture. The editorial frame, directing our attention to the publication history of the letters, to their transformation from private documents into public, published narratives, holds in suspension the double form under which these texts are intended to exist for us: on the one hand, as precious scraps of handwritten paper addressed to a single reader, still bearing their broken seals, scrawled directions, and postmarks; on the other, at the same time, as neatly printed and bound identical volumes circulating within the free-market distribution systems of print capitalism. Because the contradictions between the private document, still linked to the body, and the mechanically mass-produced book are insistently underlined by the conventions of the genre, the letter-novel can be said to allegorize the transitional relation of contemporary readers to modern textuality, and to new models of subjectivity inflected by the modern phenomena of publication and publicity.[5]

The Limping Woman

Mais qui m'expliquera tous ces eunuques?

— Paul Valéry, "Préface aux *Lettres persanes*"

Given this constellation of issues, it is appropriate that the literary-critical history of the *Persian Letters* can be roughly charted as a series of investigations into its bodies. Montesquieu himself proposed an organicist reading of the text in an essay written thirty-three years after its first publication, entitled "Some Reflections on the *Persian Letters*" (1754). Here, retroactively asserting a generic identity for his anomalous text, he writes cryptically of "a secret and, in some sense, obscure chain" buried in the narrative. In search of the secret chain, critics tended to focus on the text's exotic bodies; black and white, veiled and castrated, exiled and imprisoned, the spectacular array seemed to imply a corporeally encoded taxonomy. Paul Valéry's plaintive question quoted above — "But who will explain to me all these eunuchs?" — directed attention to the castrated guards of the harem who mediate between the master and his wives. On the one hand, as the master's surveillance apparatus, disseminating his power even in his absence, the eunuchs are the agents of discipline; they signify the master's phallocentric authority as its lack inscribed on their bodies and affirm his law through their apparent incapacity to transgress it. On the other, however, the famous letter that describes their sexuality as constituting "a third sense" (LIII)[6] allows them simultaneously to be identified with *jouissance*. The rebellious wives are similarly paradoxically engaging: their torrid love letters exalt their husband while their polymorphous sexual transgressions signal the instability of his despotic regime and of the conventional model of the body/subject implicit in the letter-form. In particular the heroic Roxane, a sort of Patrick Henry *avant la lettre*, compels attention; her last defiant message is a stirring articulation of resistance to both sexual and political tyranny.[7]

Despite all this corporeal attention, however, one peculiar body has been overlooked. This may be because it appears neither in the text itself nor in the authoritative 1754 "Reflections," but rather in the original "Introduction" to the *Persian Letters*. From a formalist perspective, the 1721 "Introduction" may seem less interesting than the "Reflections": it makes no insinuating generic claims, promises no satisfying narrative coherence, scales no authorial heights for its survey of the text; indeed, diegetically considered, it locates itself at least partially within the fictional world of the letters' production. Not a famous author but a nameless editor here offers an account of how the letters came to be published, the story of their transformation from private documents into a published book. Nonetheless, this transformation is presided over by a body every bit as strange in its way as the materialized paradox of the eunuch: that of a woman who limps only when someone is looking at her. I choose to focus on the body of the limping woman not as a key to the text's secret chain but, more perversely, because of its radical marginality. As a bridge between the Persians' world, figured by the private letter, and that of Montesquieu's readers, figured by the printed text and located within the imaginary Republic of Letters, the limping woman can be said to operate the exchange between center and margin, local and exotic, public and private, in a text about an Other who is very like ourselves.

The Republic of Letters

> I do not inscribe here a dedicatory letter, nor do I demand any protection for this book; it will be read, if it is good; if it is bad, I don't care whether anyone reads it.
>   I have extracted these first letters to test the public taste. I have many more in my portfolio, which I can give the public later.
>
> — "Introduction" to the *Persian Letters*

Montesquieu's "Introduction" to the *Persian Letters* can be read as a declaration at once triumphal and anxious of the Republic of Letters in Regency France.[8] It proclaims a rupture with the traditional system of court-centered patronage that still sustained much literature, and in its place installs a radically new orientation of the text to its audience. Insisting on the importance of a reading public's judgment of the value of a literary work, its first sentences, quoted above, put the *Persian Letters* squarely in the context of the Enlightenment public sphere. More specifically, they direct our attention to the political and economic realities behind eighteenth-century publication, in transition between the world of courtly patronage and that of market capitalism.[9] We can uncover the infrastructure of this new Republic of Letters in some detail by considering the publishing and distribution network that made the *Persian Letters* available to eighteenth-century French readers.

At the same time that it heralds a new literary order, the "Introduction" reminds us of that order's vulnerability: the sovereignty of the Republic of Letters may be threatened by the interference of other regimes. Under official French censorship, the *Persian Letters* was a banned book. Assuming that the Regency's censors would not approve his highly heterodox manuscript, Montesquieu had gone abroad for a publisher; his book was printed by one of the many French Protestant printers who had settled in Amsterdam, the "central city" of the Republic of Letters, after the revocation of the Edict of Nantes.[10] Intended for illegal distribution in France, the anonymous first edition bears a false printer's name and place of publication, a common evasion that does not prevent present-day historians of print culture from mapping out the transitional Republic of Letters, with capitals at Amsterdam, Rotterdam, Neuchâtel, and Geneva, that shadowed the authorized French publishing industry in the eighteenth century.[11] The occultation of the text's geographical origin on its title page is related to the redefinition of literary values undertaken in the "Introduction." Marking in his first sentence the omission of a dedicatory epistle, the editor goes on to replace the traditional patron with an absolute literary standard independent of patronage: if it is good, his book will be read; if it is not, it will be ignored. Nor does the editor insist on his work's quality; that judgment will be left entirely to his readers. Without protectors or puffers, the text stands on its own. The second sentence further emphasizes this new relation between the reading public and the text, suggesting that the two mutually shape one another: if the publication is a trial-run to determine whether the Persians' letters suit the public taste, at the same time we might infer that public taste itself is being tested, perhaps even being trained, with the *Persian Letters* serving as the instrument of analysis and education.

Such a relation between text and reader diminishes the importance of the editor. Indeed, far from affixing his name to the book, the editor insists on anonymity as the first condition of the letters' publication: "If my name comes to be known, I will be silent from that moment." Secrecy is necessary, he explains, because of the parasitic nature of contemporary literary criticism, which judges a work according to its author's social position rather than by its own inherent value: "If my identity were known, it would be said, 'His book clashes with his character; he should better employ his time; this is not worthy of a serious man.'" By withholding the name of the individual(s) responsible for this publication, the editor not only protects himself but also ensures the text's free operation in the public sphere, independent of its progenitor. In a double sense, Montesquieu as author is refusing what might be called "filiation" as a form of textual legitimation: just as there is no patron-godfather to protect and sponsor these letters, there is no author-father to give them his name.[12] In the absence of that figure, the "Introduction" establishes a dialectical relation between text and reader: the reading public authorizes the text by its approval, "fathering" it in place of both author and patron, but it is also simultaneously the subject on which the text-as-test, as analytical and educational instrument, operates.

The "Introduction" goes on to explore other suggestive ambiguities in the relation between text and reader. For example, the editor's explanation of how the letters came into his hands from his Persian lodgers, who consider him "as someone from another world," implies that where there is such radical cultural difference, the notion of secrecy loses all meaning: "Indeed, people transplanted from so far away could have no more secrets." This comfortable rationalization is contradicted a sentence later, however, when he explains that he has also obtained some letters that the Persians would not have wanted him to see, "so mortifying were they for vanity and jealousy." Despite distance and exoticism, then, there exists a fundamental and universal register of human secrecy, embedded in the cross-cultural truths of the human body, to which this publication will allow us privileged access.[13]

The editor goes on to describe his task as not only to eliminate "Oriental" stylistic points that might bore his French readers but, further, to translate one culture into another, to "adapt the work to our own customs [*moeurs*]." His project, in other words, is to create out of this Persian material what, to echo Said's "Orientalism," might be called "Gallicism."[14] Such an editorial act seems contradictory to the ostensibly ethnographic purpose of publishing the letters: to rewrite the Persians' letters according to French *moeurs* will prevent the reader from obtaining a voyeur's perspective on the exotic Other. But of course, the subject of the *Persian Letters* is not in fact Persia, but contemporary Parisian society. The text ingeniously reverses the structure of cultural voyeurism upon itself in a way that engages Montesquieu's readers as both observing subjects and observed objects, simultaneously critics and the focus of critique.

In the peculiarly everted container of this anonymous text, then, the secrets of the Persian letter-writers are to be exposed, albeit recast in a language and style that are to the reading public's taste. The concept of privacy, however, does not disappear; instead, it is relocated closer to home, "Gallicized" perhaps, in the editor's claim to the anonymity and privacy that he has denied his lodgers. His justification of the decision to suppress his name is summed up in the memorable image of a woman with a problematic relation to publicity, a woman whose body materializes its discomfort with being observed: "I know a woman who walks well enough, but who limps as soon as she is watched." The bizarre figure of this limping woman who is physiologically disconcerted by a gaze generates a series of questions that unite the metaphorics of bodies, print, and power in Montesquieu's text: Why does the limping woman appear here, in the diegetically and ethically slippery frame of this reversible text? What does it mean for the male editor to identify himself with her? How is her body related to the discourses of privacy and the public sphere that preoccupy the "Introduction," and to the other spectacularly deformed bodies of the *Persian Letters*?[15]

Most immediately, of course, this peculiar, feminized image of the author's anonymity calls into question the text's faith in the public sphere, proclaimed in the first two sentences of the "Introduction" examined above. Glossed in relation to the thematics of print culture, the figure of the limping woman implies that publication, under existing social and political conditions, is necessarily related to anonymity and to deformity. In contrast with the emancipated citizens of the Republic of Letters, it seems that the subjects of French absolutism can publish only when hidden from all eyes. This need for concealment, this enforced privacy, links the editor not only to the woman who limps in public but also to the variously veiled, imprisoned, and castrated inhabitants of the Persian harem, who are, like him and her, victims of a deforming gaze.[16]

Gender and Specularity

The French can't imagine that our climate produces men.
— *Persian Letters*, Letter XLVIII

The limping woman directs our attention to the gendered metaphorics of the gaze in this historical context. In the critical history of the *Persian Letters*, the question of gender has too often been treated as though it were relevant only to those letters, produced by a biologically sexed body/subject, that explicitly thematize sexual difference: it is in some contexts essentialized, in some bracketed. However, if gender is understood not merely as a fixed attribute of characterological identity but also as a semiotic category produced by certain modalities of power, it can be seen as organizing the text in quite a different sense. As a "political anatomy," Montesquieu's letter-novel specifically addresses the ways in which gender enters into the encoding of power that radiates from the body of the absolute monarch, ultimately rewriting the construction of gender in the symbolic field of this political system.[17]

Although the text opens with Usbek's voyage to the West, letters to and from his friends, wives, and eunuchs evoke for him and for us the domestic and political domains he is abandoning. Behind its "fatal doors" (II), the unstable kingdom of the harem is ordered by the gaze of the master, for whose scopic pleasure this space and its inhabitants exist. The women enclosed here feel themselves alive only under the desiring eye of the Other, as Zachi's erotically charged account of a spectacular beauty contest in the harem emphasizes.[18] Life at the Persian court is not very different from this, for like the master of the harem, the despotic ruler creates his subjects by his gaze: Usbek's specular metaphor of princely approval — "I found favor in his eyes" (VII) — is not merely "Orientalizing" rhetorical ornamentation.

In his indispensable work on neoclassical constructions of despotism, Alain Grosrichard suggests that the specularity associated with "Oriental" despotism by eighteenth- and nineteenth-century Europeans is a translation of the oculocentrism of absolutist court culture, in which rituals were carefully designed to focus all eyes on the body of the king and to incorporate the subject as spectator into the theater of state.[19] Versailles was orchestrated on precisely these spec(tac)ular terms, as Norbert Elias has shown: the axis of the main entry, passing through a series of narrowing courtyards, channeled the eye to the windows of Louis XIV's "appartements privés," which visually commanded the entire approach. The message is clear: absolute power is both the object of every gaze and is itself all-seeing. Furthermore, Versailles' architectural metaphor for omnivoyance announces the indivisibility of the king's double body: the Sun King, absolute monarch of France, cannot be disentangled from the head of the private (if magnificent) household, the *oikodespotes*. In daily rituals at Versailles, access to the royal body was part of an elaborate, finely graduated system of privilege and exclusion, but there was no moment at which the king was somehow "offstage," a private body. In the context of absolutist monarchy as constructed around and embodied by Louis XIV, the distinction between public and private in the modern sense simply did not exist.[20]

The non-differentiation of public from private spaces was also, of course, the salient feature of the harem in the Enlightenment imagination: precisely what is so exciting about the harem is that it is the most *private* of domains in the political sense, a space deprived of the public rule of law and controlled by the personal will of the master. Thus, the comparison between despotic court and harem, allegorically transposed onto the European absolutist context, sends a clear message — the non-differentiation of political and domestic is inimical to the civic virtue of Louis XIV's subjects. Within the structured field of the absolutist gaze, the hypostatization of the king's body arranges his subjects in undifferentiated subordination. Absolutist topology effectively flattens out other hierarchies, including those inherent in the family. In other words, because the notion of separate and complementary public and private spheres did not exist in Versailles's absolutist culture, the hierarchical subordination of wife to husband and of family to household head was necessarily diminished in significance, thus depriving Louis's male courtiers of any grounds of identity that did not depend on their relation to the monarch's body.[21]

In the *Persian Letters*, an anxiety about the properly gendered identity of the male courtier finds expression in a definition of citizenship as anchored in the male roles of husband and father, precisely those roles thought to be diminished in importance under absolutism as under despotism: Usbek's friend Mirza writes that he undertakes his researches into questions of morality and justice "as a man, as a citizen, and as father of a family" (X). However, he can find no satisfactory answers to his questions in Persia, for despotism, like absolutism, produces courtiers instead of citizens.[22] They also produce unstable political conditions that allow women to govern the ruler through sexual influence; so, as a corollary, the contemporary discourse of citizenship condemned the effeminizing influence of aristocratic women at court and of the *salonnières* in Paris. In the *Persian Letters*, the head eunuch's description of the endless reversals of power in the harem (IX) has a Parisian analogue: Rica marvels naively at the secret power of French women, who form a "new state within the State" (CVII). Under such a "reign of women," citizenship is impossible.[23]

However, if Montesquieu is clear about what conditions *preclude* citizenship, his thoughts on how to *promote* it rely on the somewhat vague category of *moeurs* that we have already encountered: "Customs [*moeurs*] always make better citizens than laws" (CXXIX). To obey the law is good, but self-imposed morality is superior, as we learn in the fable of the Troglodytes who decide after years of self-government that they want a ruler; their tearful king-elect scolds them for such a fall from independent civic virtue (XIV). The Persian domestic parallel to this story also insists that the concept of virtue becomes meaningless under coercion: when Zachi argues that her impeccable behavior entitles her to exemption from the eunuchs' supervision, Usbek responds, "You will perhaps tell me that you have always been faithful to me. Ha! Could you have been otherwise? How could you have deceived the black eunuchs' vigilance? How could you have broken the locks and doors that keep you enclosed? You praise yourself for a virtue that is not voluntary" (XX). Precisely because they are not free, the inhabitants of the harem and the subjects of the despot cannot accurately be described as virtuous; similarly, we infer, the absolutist courtier is outside the domain of *moeurs* in which ideal citizenship can be developed. Under absolutism as under despotism, then, the male courtier is seen as effeminized while women are excessively powerful.[24] The *Persian Letters* implies that this is as true in Paris as it is in Ispahan. Persia is Paris's satiric mirror because in both societies political and domestic spaces are not properly distinguished from one another. Absolutism is only one step removed from despotism and is always in danger of sinking into it, as the cyclical social model illustrated in the Troglodyte fable suggests; thus, it will be almost as difficult to cultivate the ideal citizen in absolutist France as it is at the despot's court or in the harem.

Defiguration

> I have never heard a discussion of public law that didn't begin by carefully researching the origin of societies, which seems ridiculous to me. If men didn't form societies, if they avoided and fled from one another, then it would be necessary to investigate why they kept themselves apart. But they are born bound one to another; a son is born beside his father, and stays there; this is society, and the cause of society.
>
> — *Persian Letters*, Letter XCIV

The figuration of civic inadequacy as bodily lack or deformity or disfigurement — a rhetorical strategy that might technically be described as a *de*figuration — is most explicitly extended to France in the discussion of the effects of disastrous contemporary financial policies.[25] Letters CXXXVIII through CXLVI are all written in 1720, the last year of the Persians' stay in Paris, and they all circle the question of language and its grounding in material referents, investigating what happens when the "natural" connection between signifier and signified is broken. Montesquieu's description of the destruction of the civic body through the inflationary rhetoric of John Law, the adventurer-cum-economist who promoted paper money, further develops the thematics of bodily deformity. Under absolutism, language and money, like gender, are divorced from their original fixed meanings to become sliding registers of value determined by the will of the ruler. Against this gloomy analysis, the peculiar tale of Anaïs recounted in Letter CXLI offers a fantastic deflationary resolution for the state's financial, rhetorical, and corporeal corruption, a resolution enacted by an idealized phallic body.

As the passage quoted above makes clear, Usbek believes that society originates in and is anchored by the father's body. It is not surprising, then, that the Persians' awareness of the instability of registers of value becomes acute with the death of Louis XIV. As described here, the Regency's policies, particularly the financial schemes of John Law, seem designed to destroy the identity of the father as head of the family, as the body generative of meaning and value.[26] France's slide into chaos underlines the etymological and thematic link between *specularity*, the emblem as we have noted of both Persian despotism and French absolutism, and financial *speculation*: Law's arbitrary economic policies create the Gallicized equivalent of Persian despotism, corrupting language along with all other systems of value and thus destroying the conditions necessary to citizenship.

This corruption is depicted in a series of corporeal images that emphasize the materiality and vulnerability of the body. After Louis XIV's death, the civic body is deathly ill: "France, at the death of the late king, was a body stricken with a thousand ills. N—— took up the knife, cut away the useless flesh, and applied some specific remedies. But an inner disease [*vice intérieur*] remained to be cured. A stranger came to undertake the treatment. After many violent remedies, he thought he had restored her healthy plumpness [*embonpoint*], but he had only made her bloated." Inhabiting that deceptively swollen female body, the double meaning of *vice intérieur* suggests the linguistic and moral implications of this illness and false cure. Under Law's economic *Système*, a dynamic of reversibility set up by warring self-interests everts the civic body like a turned coat: "All those who were rich six months ago are presently poor, and those who were without bread are now gorged with wealth. Never before have these two extremes come so close. The stranger turned the state as a tailor turns a coat: he puts above what was beneath, and what was above he puts beneath" (CXXXVIII). The image of deceptive inflation returns in the "Old Mythologist's Fragment" (CLII), which describes Law as the child of Aeolus and a Scottish nymph who stations himself at a crossroads to sell the paternal sacks of wind. He tells those around him that their precious metals are worthless, but that if they follow him to "the Empire of the Imagination" they will be rich beyond belief. His con man's patter exposes the universalized windy insubstantiality on which his *Système* is precariously balanced: "Do you want to be rich? Imagine that I am very wealthy, and that you are too; every morning, convince yourselves that your fortune doubled during the night; then get up, and, if you have creditors, go pay them with what you have imagined, and tell them to imagine in their turn." After appropriating three-quarters of the national wealth, mercantilistically represented as a fixed quantity of gold, he disappears, leaving behind a ruined nation.

This allegorical satire is grimly rewritten in what is chronologically the last letter of the book, as its date indicates, though in the textual sequence it appears before the group of harem letters that conclude the book. Here, France, thinly disguised as "the Indies" (referring to Law's Compagnie des Indes), has been corrupted by its own government. The disease metaphor returns again in the image of an infection spreading throughout the populace, corrupting even "the healthiest members" and destroying the sacred institutions that make up the social fabric, including the family itself: "I have seen faith in contracts banished, the holiest conventions annihilated, all family law overturned." To pay a debt in Law's worthless paper money is literally to murder one's benefactors. As a debtor gloats, "I see that I am settling my affairs. It's true that when I went three days ago to make a payment, I left a whole family in tears, I took away the dowry of two nice girls and the education of a little boy. The father will die of sorrow, the mother of grief." The material aspects of this crime are underlined by a pun on the economist-adventurer's name that brilliantly fixes and condenses the satire: the debtor insists, "I only did what is permitted by the Law" (CXLVI).

In each of these descriptions of the effect of Law's fiscal inflation, the civic body of France and its citizens' bodies are destroyed by the uncoupling of signs from their signifiers. Gold is replaced by paper; *moeurs* and even law itself are superseded by the destructive mandates of (John) Law. However, juxtaposed with these allegories of inflation is a very different story. Zulema's tale, a harem wife's fantasy of a harem reformed, proposes that the destructive effects of linguistic deformity can be reversed by a language grounded in the body. Asked by the other wives about the Moslem tradition "that Paradise is made only for men" (CXLI), Zulema insists that women too will have a paradise, organized around the erotic pleasures provided by harems of supernaturally sexually potent and beautiful men. To illustrate her assertion, she tells the tale of the virtuous Anaïs, who, murdered by her jealous husband Ibrahim, goes to paradise and finds such a harem awaiting her. To avenge herself and her former companions, Anaïs sends one of her heavenly husbands to earth disguised as Ibrahim.

In the real Ibrahim's absence, the divine visitor enters the harem as its master, and his assiduous (implicitly sexual) attentions to the neglected wives win him their favor. They are at first confused by the change in "Ibrahim's" behavior: " 'You don't resemble Ibrahim,' said the wives. 'Say

rather that this impostor doesn't resemble me,' said the triumphant Ibrahim. 'What must one do to be your husband, if what I do doesn't suffice?' "
Obviously, the tale is playing with criteria of identity: in this case, specular evidence contradicts memory and experience, and as a result the grounds for determining identity shift dramatically. The proper name "Ibrahim" slips its link to a specific body/subject and is transferred to the generalized function of "husband" denoting sexual adequacy. "If you aren't Ibrahim," the wives decide, "it's enough for us that you have so well deserved to be him. You are more Ibrahim in a single day than he has been in ten years." Eventually, the real Ibrahim comes home and demands that his wives distinguish the true husband from the false. Confronted with the two men, who look exactly alike but behave very differently indeed, the wives make their choice based on what they now understand by the concept of "husband" — the phallic omnicompetence demonstrated by the false Ibrahim — and assign the title to him who best fulfills the function. The real Ibrahim is declared an impostor and thrown out. When the wives express their fear that they may be deceived in the future, the false Ibrahim reassures them of the incontrovertibility of truth based on the phallic body's testimony: "In the position I occupy in relation to you, one can't sustain himself by trickery." The index of his authenticity is the thirty-six children he sires.

Satirically literalizing the implications of corporeal metaphorics, Zulema's tale makes phallic potency the determining characteristic of the role of "husband," thus re-grounding the signifier in the father's body. Along with the titillation of the double-entendres, however, there is a serious point. The false Ibrahim, whose divine capacities allow him to be a "true" — that is, phallically competent — husband to all of the wives, needs neither the oppressive apparatus of conjugal despotism nor the empty rhetoric of enforced virtue to ensure fidelity. He tears down the walls of the harem, explaining to the wives, "I will never be jealous; I will know how to assure myself of you without constraining you. I have a good enough opinion of my own merit to believe that you'll be faithful to me. If you were not virtuous with me, with whom would you be?" His reforms extend even further: "He dismissed the eunuchs and made his house accessible to all; he didn't even want his wives to veil themselves. It was a rare sight to see them at the banquets, as free as the men around them. Ibrahim thought rightly that the customs [*coutumes*] of the country were not made for citizens like himself." This revolution against merely local practices — another reference to Montesquieu's faith in the efficacy of *moeurs* to create citizens out of subjects — begins with the satiric radicalization of language. If the word "husband" is returned to its original semantic terrain, so that it no longer functions as a code word for "despot," then it follows that the harem as physical space and social construct will no longer be necessary.

In Law's inflationary discourse, words that have gone off the gold standard no longer mean what they say, and as a result the social order collapses. In contrast, that order is satirically restored in Zulema's tale by a deflationary, reductionistic language in which words mean *only* what they say because they are anchored in the bodies that act them out. The reformation of language and society is figured in the sexual equivalent of a social contract that is based on a corporeal arithmetic allowing all men and women as many spouses as they can satisfy sexually. Despite this apparent egalitarianism, however, the tale is by no means a feminist parable; its "resolution" depends on the figuring of women's desire as a potentially dangerous mirror of men's that can only be sated by an angelic phallus. Even as a fantasy, the radical potential of Anaïs's revenge is neutralized by its multiply ironic and misogynistic narrative framing.[27] However, as a monitory fable for Usbek, the message of these paired narratives about linguistic deformity is clear: the dangerous metaphorization of the body must be corrected. Words should remain linked to things: "money" to gold, "husband" to conjugal duty. The fabular social revolution brought about by the false Ibrahim's purifying semiotics is intended to contrast not only with Regency France under Law but also with the situation of Usbek's harem, to which the narrative now turns. The parallel between the real Ibrahim and Usbek, both husbands in name only, is obvious. But the lesson comes too late: Usbek's harem is already irrevocably plunged in chaos.

Disembodiment

> Yesterday a slave came in the middle of the night to tell me that he had found a young man in the harem. I got up, investigated the matter, and found it was a vision.
>
> — *Persian Letters*, Letter CXLIX

Despite the impression they convey as a group, the last fifteen letters (CXLVII–CLXI) document not a violent and precipitate reversal of power but a chain of events extending over three years' time. Their dates allow us to redistribute them in chronological order among the letters we have already read, setting off a revisionary process that also requires us to reconstruct our perceptions of Usbek and to reassess the significance of the text as a whole. Montesquieu carefully exploits the thematic potential of juxtapositions made by letters' dates, so that the reader is actively engaged as interpreter and critic.[28] Once worked out, the redistribution exposes a glaring disjunction between theory and practice: Usbek writes an elegantly reasoned and admirably liberal essay in praise of the sanctity of natural law, identified with "natural" paternal authority against positive laws (*conventions*), which are too often arbitrary, excessive, and parochial, soon after he has unleashed the despotic power of terror by proxy in his own harem. The absolute power Usbek claims over his extended household is an abuse of the principle of paternal authority that he has celebrated as the origin of civil society; his dominion over his wives, in contrast to that of the false Ibrahim, relies on coercive and arbitrary conventions rather than on natural law. Torn apart by warring self-interests that are in Usbek's absence unregulated by either authority or affection, his harem is doomed. Its collapse into the state of nature from which it was only temporarily separated by the unstable structures of despotism will not surprise the reader, who has already been educated in the principles of citizenship by Usbek's own writings.

What does surprise us, however, is the final disposition of the body/subject model within this lurid miniature drama of sex and violence. Here, a disembodiment counters and rewrites the defiguration of Zulema's tale. The sequence of letters begins with the chief eunuch's bombshell describing the wives' insubordination and sexual treachery: Zélis let fall her veil in public; Zachi was found in bed with a slave; a youth in the garden escaped over the wall; and a mysterious letter, with no addressee, is circulating in the harem. Usbek's response to the eunuch's letter is the formal authorization of a reign of terror by proxy, in effect stripping away the harem's ideological veils. The despotic letter literally incarnates the master's will and inscribes it onto the body of the eunuch: "Receive by this letter unbounded power over all the seraglio: command with as great authority as myself. Let fear and terror go with you; run from apartment to apartment bearing punishment and penalties. Let all live in consternation; let all dissolve in tears before you." The harem, functioning synecdochically in these sentences for the women who inhabit it, will be penetrated interrogatively, put under surveillance, and forced to testify about itself: "Interrogate the whole seraglio; begin with the slaves. Don't spare my love: let all undergo your fearsome tribunal. Bring to light the most hidden secrets" (CXLVIII).[29]

Despite this thunderous assertion of omnivoyance and omnipotence, however, the letter exposes the despot's local blindness. Usbek identifies Zélis, the veil-dropper, as the probable source of corruption, while Roxane's brilliant misprision of the metaphorical veil of chastity remains unsuspected. Moreover, the potency of Usbek's mandate of terror is foiled by circumstance. The chief eunuch dies before the letter reaches Ispahan, and, instead of being opened and acted upon, Usbek's letter is reverently encoffered, unread, by his doddering successor. A second letter, reiterating the master's orders, is mysteriously hijacked, diverted from completing the incarnatory chain of command. As a result, it is a full ten months before Usbek's outraged conjugal sovereignty is effectively postally transferred to an appropriate surrogate, the vengeful, bloodthirsty young eunuch Solim. These three final epistolary images of deception and disruption — the literally unauthorized letter circulating in the harem; the fetishized, unread, and therefore impotent letter; and the letter of command mysteriously diverted from its addressee — figure the end of the possibility for rational discourse and reform within the harem. At the same time, they imply the futility of a model of political power based on the letter as a metonym of the autonomous body/subject.

That futility is announced decisively in the book's famous last letter, Roxane's coruscating and celebratory confession. The letter employs both a familiar epistolary rhetoric of female passion descending from Ovid's *Heroides* and the vocabulary of contemporary debates on natural law and individual freedom in the state, a combination that underlines the specific ways in which the harem excludes the political conditions necessary for citizenship. Roxane writes triumphantly, "I have lived in servitude, but I have always been free: I reformed your laws by those of Nature, and my spirit has always maintained itself in independence" (CLXI). However, the letter also forces readers to confront the political implications of how bodies signify in the *Persian Letters*, for it matters whether we read Roxane's letter as a "gender-neutral" political credo generalizable to all subjects or as an articulation of concerns specific to a particular and therefore necessarily gendered subject-position.

While the public discourse of citizenship is ingeniously combined here with the discourse of private passion, the two must not simply be conflated, and given the text's obsession with the politics of sexuality, the two readings cannot be maintained simultaneously. The conclusion of the novel can be construed as a celebration of liberal values only when the literal contents of the letter are ignored, thereby permitting an individual's death to be allegorized as a "universal" political message.[30] To read Roxane's indictment of Usbek's domestic tyranny as a rhetorically successful refutation of political tyranny requires that we ignore the fact that the body behind this letter is already a corpse. Such a reading would efface the inflection of gender as difference in this text, which insists that the specific sexual and economic forms of oppression to which women are subject under domestic despotism are multiply irreconcilable with the citizen's right and duty of participation in public discourse. In other words, whereas the male subject of political despotism can flee the country as Usbek has done, there is no escape for the harem wives, except in the fantasy world of Zulema's tale.[31] In light of her suicide, then, Roxane's letter remains a private declaration of independence, unable to transcend the radically privatized conditions of its original inscription within the walls of the harem.

However, if this letter seems on the one hand to demand its metonymic identification with the specific body/subject that produced it, on the other it simultaneously forecloses the possibility of such an identification by acknowledging that the link between body and subject has already been irrevocably broken before the moment of our reading, and that it only exists in an elegiac past. In the corporeal/epistolary metaphorics of the Persians' letters, then, Roxane's is the most paradoxical body of all, since within the space of the text itself it is made to dissolve. In this sense, the "new language" that Roxane deliberately employs in her indictment directly contradicts the linguistic reform ironically prescribed by Zulema's fantasy, for here the sign is radically disengaged from its signifier. Roxane's letter functions in the plot to signal the ultimate bankruptcy of paternal authority, undermining the despotic conflation of power with the phallic body; at the same time, Montesquieu uses it to dismantle the formal analogy between letter and body and thus the conventional model of the body/subject that produces it. The letter becomes an acknowledgment of the irrecoverable loss of the body/subject and the forms of power it underwrites.

And now we come to the final body of the Persians' letters. As a kind of proleptic postscript, what is chronologically though not textually the book's last-written letter reveals that the destructive effects of despotism in the end undo the autonomy of the despot himself, thus finally disembodying the model of an organicist subjectivity. Usbek will return to Persia to die as a prisoner in the harem he once ruled as a master, a figure more abject than the eunuchs he himself has created: "Wretch that I am, I wish to see my country again, perhaps to become more wretched still. What am I to do there? I will be carrying my head back to my enemies. . . . I am going to enclose myself within walls more terrible for me than for the women who are guarded there." By the end of the text, Usbek himself, in his fear of decollation and his failure of phallic mastery, has become another of the figures of lack who share, in one form or another, the debilitating marks—the veil, the scar, the limp—that signify the effects of the non-differentiation of public from private under absolutism as under despotism. The nightmare conclusion of this private correspondence is a powerfully dramatized argument against the forms of censorship that, to use the gendered language of eighteenth-century political debates, unman the citizen and wound the civic body in its most precious parts. But what model of subjectivity, accommodated by what, if any, metaphorics of the body, can take its place?

From Letters to *Letters*: Writing the Body Politic

The *Persian Letters* is sometimes read as the story of a failure—the failure of Usbek as student of Enlightenment and as master of the harem—that is something of a failure itself, in that it never resolves the problems it exposes, never provides a positive political model as an alternative to the excesses and abuses of Regency absolutism.[32] If we attend only to the narrative contained in the letters, this criticism may seem justified: it is clear that the ideal of civic criticism developed in Usbek's letters home will not be fulfilled by him, for he necessarily remains outside the civic space of French society (as a Persian) and outside the politico-philosophical framework of the Enlightenment (as an unreformed despot). But such an assessment ignores the contemporary understanding of literature as praxis established by the metaphor of the Republic of Letters.[33] If the vulnerability of the public sphere is clearly posed by the figure of the limping woman, so is the possibility of its construction and confirmation through the transformative dialectic between the text and its extra-textual reader. Montesquieu's innovative use of the polyphonic epistolary form makes this dialectic a structural condition, since the project of cultural criticism requires that the reader, actively engaged with the object of the critique, generate comparisons, interpretations, and judgments.[34] In the *Persian Letters*, instead of an authoritative narrator guiding readers through a chronological sequence of events, we encounter a jumble of discrete, sometimes contradictory texts embodying various points of view that must be weighed and interpreted. If the proper activity of a citizen of the Republic of Letters is critique, then the *Persian Letters* not only exposes the conditions that deform and cripple the civic body under absolutism but also seeks its rehabilitation through the construction of its readers as ideal citizen-critics.

This model is initially sketched out, of course, in the "Introduction," which is also where our sense of what constitutes the text itself is established. The idea that the *Persian Letters* never accomplishes the critical project it proposes can be most concisely disputed on the grounds of the crucial difference between the story *in* the letters and the story *of* the letters, a difference set up in the thematization of publication that is specific to the eighteenth-century epistolary form. To treat a letter-novel as only the sum of its parts, as a narrative only incidentally told in letter form, is an occultation of its generic and historic specificity that ignores what Janet Altman has called "epistolarity," defined as "the pressure exerted by form upon meaning."[35] In this context, the distinction between the Persians' letters and the *Persian Letters*, marked by the framing editorial apparatus that recounts the fictionalized publication history of the text, is of the greatest importance. The conventions of the eighteenth-century epistolary genre, fundamentally engaged with the institutions of print culture, paradoxically make this frame central to the work, setting up an oscillation of perspective entirely in keeping with what I have described as the structural eversions and general ontological playfulness of Montesquieu's text.

When the frame of this epistolary narrative is examined in the context of a culture actively redefining its notions of public and private in relation to print culture, the bridge between critique and sociopolitical action that Montesquieu offers his reader becomes evident: it lies in the construction of a critical discursive space, a public sphere of letters (in both senses) that will counterbalance the excesses of absolutism by promoting a discourse of citizenship. We could say, then, taking up Montesquieu's disingenuous critical riddle of 1754 in order to circumvent it, that the "secret chain" of the *Persian Letters* actually lies in its incarnation *as a book*, as a material artifact of the Republic of Letters, that transnational domain taking its visible form in the early eighteenth century in the mass of printed material—pamphlets, ballads, political cartoons, prospectuses, newspapers, novels, broadsheets—produced and consumed by the subjects of Enlightenment print culture. It is precisely as a book in this sense that the *Persian Letters* shapes its readers not as body/subjects but as politically embodied, even politically gendered, citizen-critics.[36]

To return to the text's first body: through the apotropaic figure of the limping woman, the *Persian Letters* articulates civic identity in relation to the construction of a Republic of Letters. Against the political imbalances manifested in the gendered symbolic field of early eighteenth-century French absolutism—that is, the civic lack figured by the limping woman and the anonymous author — Montesquieu brings together the registers of political power, gender, and publication to create simultaneously the discourse of citizenship and the properly male subject who articulates it publicly. Only as a full participant in an uncensored Republic of Letters can the author appear in (his) proper (male) identity, a citizen-critic affirmed rather than physically impaired by the public gaze. As we have seen, the Persians' letters depict the collapse of erotic and political relations where epistolary strategies fail adequately to represent the absent phallus, endlessly reproducing instead the figures of lack that haunt the text (eunuchs, slaves, veiled wives, the impotent despot, the limping woman); they call, albeit ironically, for a return to the Father's body as generator and guarantor of meaning. In contrast, the *Persian Letters* undermines the body/subject metonymy implicit in the letter-form by presenting a series of narratives of disembodiment and defiguration. Montesquieu offers instead an anti-absolutist reconstruction of gender and power relations through the politically gendered citizen-critic. The public sphere, here manifested as "a set of material elements and techniques that . . . invest human bodies," is the real subject of Montesquieu's political anatomy, the "body politic" imagined and produced by the *Persian Letters*.

Wit's Breaks

NEIL SACCAMANO

> *Dennis* the critick could not detest and abhor a pun, or the insinua-
> tion of a pun, more cordially than my father; — he would grow testy
> upon it at any time; — but to be brøke in upon by one, in a serious
> discourse, was as bad, he would say, as a fillip upon the nose; — he
> saw no difference.
>
> — Sterne, *Tristram Shandy*

*T*hrough the ever-philosophical Walter, Laurence Sterne, of course, continually recalls and ridicules in *Tristram Shandy* the danger apparently posed by wit to judgment, a danger signaled most urgently in Locke's *Essay Concerning Human Understanding*. What might not seem a matter of course, however, in Walter's rather familiar castigation of puns is an odd connection that this essay will seek to elaborate: the entangling of language, bodies, and violence. Tristram's father, who at times invokes Locke to repel the errors breaking in upon him, considers a pun "as bad . . . as a fillip" and thereby figures his "serious discourse" as a vulnerable body and this impertinent trope as an offensive gesture; abhorring or shrinking back from puns, he tries to ward off any future violence to the body of philosophical discourse. By specifying the nose as the endangered organ, Sterne not only suggests the phallocentrism of the philosopher, in whom rhetoric induces castration anxiety — a suggestion here supported by the possible puns on testes ("detest," "testy"): as the word "nose" has been "wounded" by association in this novel, Sterne also deprives Walter of the ability to refer unequivocally to a part of his own body.[1] Moreover, in the warmth of his abhorrence Walter himself strikes a blow to his judgment. Since finally "he saw no difference" between puns and fillips, he can no longer tell literal from figurative gestures or, more generally, actual bodies from language. With the disappearance of this difference goes, as well, the philosophical knowledge Walter sought to preserve inviolate from the effects of such species of rhetoric. As a result, he verges on the madness that Locke had diagnosed as arising from mistakes of association and substitution.

This invocation of the body to figure the epistemological threat of rhetoric does not merely exemplify Sterne's fascination with bodily violation in *Tristram Shandy*. Through the Lockean Walter, Sterne directs our attention to a persistent feature of epistemological reflections on wit in the eighteenth century and beyond. In "The Epistemology of Metaphor," for instance, Paul de Man has noted that Locke's frequent recourse to manslaughter, incest, and parricide as examples of mixed modes and abuses of language suggests the ethical stakes of rhetoric, though reminding one more of "a Greek tragedy than the enlightened moderation one tends to associate with the author of *On Government*." De Man remarks that "reflection on the figurality of language" must be begun "if there is to be any understanding," yet "there is no telling where it may lead."[2] In the eighteenth century, the question of wit or figural language often seems to lead to violence. In what follows, I will pursue this question by taking up, however, another of Sterne's suggestions in his comment on Walter. By recalling John Dennis's equally vehement abhorrence of puns, Sterne indicates that puns pose a danger in neoclassical literary discourse comparable to that of rhetoric itself in Locke's philosophy. In other words, Sterne correlates through Walter the exclusionary acts of two discourses: Lockean philosophy's expulsion of all rhetorical figures, and neoclassical criticism's rejection of only certain species of figures, those species Joseph Addison would class under false wit. Although philosophy and literary criticism in general may stipulate their conditions of knowledge and constitute themselves by such acts of exclusion, these two discourses cannot, of course, be conflated in the early eighteenth century, since one takes as a means of knowledge what the other judges the source of error. Nonetheless, Sterne's remark raises a question concerning the function and necessity in neoclassical criticism of the ethically charged figure of bodily violation.

As we shall see, this appeal to the violence of certain tropes that exploit the wit of the letter implicates neoclassical poetics in a political economy, as well as an ethics, of cultural production. Neoclassical inquiries into figural language involve ethics insofar as they consider wit an act performed by a free human agent and a practice regulated by norms of sociality. These inquiries are also connected to a political economy because language is construed not only as a medium of exchange — "exchange" itself setting up an analogical or metaphorical relation between the economic and the linguistic — but as a material to be cultivated or worked into value. In neoclassical literary discourse, the forms and effects of wit are assessed in terms of the productive value of laboring human bodies; not just a moral act, wit is also a cultural production. When it figures as bodily violation, then, the effects of a wit exploiting the materiality of the medium, neoclassical poetics acknowledges an epistemological challenge that extends to notions of moral agency and political-economic value.

Joseph Addison's *Spectator* series on wit is a worthwhile text for examining the entangling of bodies and tropes, and not simply because Addison and Dennis both detest puns. Published from May 7 to May 12, 1711, this group of essays is the most sustained critical discourse on wit to appear in the early eighteenth century. As Addison himself observed, the "so little understood" wit had only occasionally broken in upon serious discourse until then: previous authors had at most "treat[ed] on the Subject as it [had] accidentally fallen in their Way, and . . . without entering into the Bottom of the Matter."[3] Moreover, relying on Locke's epistemology in his account of wit, Addison publishes what amounts to a Lockean apology for figural language.

Readers familiar with the series may find this last claim somewhat overstated, since the way Addison gets to the bottom is not by providing a philosophical exposition of the nature of wit. In fact, most of the essays discuss the various kinds and the "History of false wit" so that Addison can discredit the recent revival of those "antiquated Modes of Wit that have been long exploded out of the Common-wealth of Letters" (1: 245). As a legislator and exemplar of literary culture, Mr. Spectator assumes the task of formulating the principles of taste that should constitute the modern cultured public to which he addresses his writing. The "History of false wit" thus forms part of a project of enlightenment that Addison carries out by aligning the taste, social rank, and historical position of cultured subjects: "The Taste of most of our *English* Poets, as well as Readers," he asserts, "is extremely *Gothic*"; then, quoting Dryden's citation of Segrais on Virgil, he labels "Mob-Readers," the "Rabble of Readers," all those who " 'prefer a Quibble, a Conceit, an Epigram, before solid Sense and elegant Expression' " (1: 269). To cultivate the public and institute a commonwealth of letters is to send both the mob-readers and the rabble-poets of false wit back to a Gothic past that should no longer be present.

That the series on wit consists primarily of a historical presentation of negative rhetorical practices does not prevent it, however, from articulat-

ing a defense of wit; it simply demands a reading alert to the way examples, citations, figures, and allusions operate throughout the text. Such
a reading receives some orientation from the penultimate paper of the
group, *Spectator* 62, in which Addison does explicitly consider the relation between true and false wit that has presumably underwritten the
historical review. And he opens this discussion by citing exactly that passage from the *Essay* (II, xi, 2) where Locke opposes wit and judgment so as
to deny figural language any legitimate epistemological role:

For Wit lying most in the Assemblage of Ideas, and putting those together with
Quickness and Variety, wherein can be found any Resemblance or Congruity
thereby to make up pleasant Pictures and agreeable Visions in the Fancy; Judgment, on the contrary, lies quite on the other Side, In separating carefully one from
another, Ideas wherein can be found the least Difference, thereby to avoid being
misled by Similitude and by Affinity to take one thing for another. This is a Way of
proceeding quite contrary to Metaphor and Allusion. (1: 263–64)

To Locke's "best and most philosophical Account" of wit, Addison says
he wants to add just a "short Explanation" that will enable the definition
to comprehend "most of the Species of Wit, as Metaphors, Similitudes,
Allegories, . . . and all the Methods of Allusion" (1: 264–65). He simply
wants to stress an essential aesthetic component of wit and explain its
formal basis: "In order . . . that the Resemblance in the Ideas be Wit, it is
necessary that the Ideas should not lie too near one another in the Nature
of things; for where the Likeness is obvious, it gives no Surprize" (1: 264).
Yet Addison's apparently minor addendum to the *Essay* performs a telling
revision of Locke's account of wit. By specifying surprise as the characteristic effect of wit and then deriving surprise from the distance between
the ideas assembled, he foregrounds the proximity in the *Essay* of wit to
judgment. For if the ideas associated were not somewhat remote from
each other, only comparison — an act of judgment — would take place.
Addison thus positions Locke's wit next to judgment and extends wit to
include unexpected affinities which at least temporarily depart from the
"obvious," from what is literally "in the way," immediately available to
perception or knowledge. Addison's wit is dilatory; it temporalizes and
temporizes.[4] Most important, however, wit for Addison, like knowledge
for Locke, should always terminate in things. Such surprising figures as
metaphor and allegory may make the congruity of ideas the function of a
remote contiguity, but wit, all the same, issues in cognition because it
remains "in the Nature of things." Locke certainly did not grant wit this
privilege; he asserted that wit assembled ideas according to "*any* Resemblance or Congruity." His indefinite "any" suggests the illimitable power

of wit, its ability to proliferate figures in indifference to the nature of things, appearing perhaps to remain within nature while transgressing or exceeding it.[5] But Addison's seemingly innocuous phrase argues for the cognitive value of figural language in Lockean terms.

Addison's comment on the *Essay*, then, reverses Locke's position on wit while seeming to adhere to it. Invoking later in this *Spectator* paper the authority of Dominique Bouhours in effect to counter Locke's critique, Addison affirms that "it is impossible for any Thought to be beautiful which is not just, and has not its Foundation in the Nature of things: . . . the Basis of all Wit is Truth" (1: 268). Wit adrift from truth is not wit — or, rather, it is the false wit of the letter: true wit "consists in this Resemblance and Congruity of Ideas," whereas false wit lies chiefly "in the Resemblance of Words" and mixed wit, "partly in the Resemblance of Ideas, and partly in the Resemblance of Words" (1: 265). Addison saves wit from Locke's condemnation by tracing at least one kind back to truth. He revises Locke's opposition between wit and judgment in the way that the Neoplatonists recast Plato's opposition between dialectic and rhetoric or poetry: he accepts the criterion that founds the opposition but relocates the opposition within the negative term and thereby manages to sanction a part of what had been excluded.

By dividing wit and introducing a third term into the binary logic of the *Essay*, Addison may affirm what Locke must deny. The question arises, however, whether the affirmation alone of wit's truth suffices to escape the risk of epistemological error that provoked Locke's resistance.[6] A reply to this question requires a fuller understanding of the connection between truth and wit motivating Addison's argument. Since Addison supports his claim about true wit no farther than by an allusion to "the most penetrating of all the French Criticks" (1: 268), we should briefly turn to Dominique Bouhours.

In *La manière de bien penser dans les ouvrages d'esprit*, Bouhours sustains the premise of wit's truth by, in turn, appealing to Aristotle's *Rhetoric*. Aristotle's reduction of "the entire art of thinking wittily to metaphor," Eudoxe contends in the first dialogue, does not demote it to "a kind of deception." Metaphor, instead, "ought to be understood in a good sense [*bon sens*]": "The figural is not false, and metaphor has its truth as well as fiction."[7] Eudoxe concedes the risk of metaphor; he merely isolates its deceptive potential and requests that it be understood in a "bon sens." The truth of wit is then asserted without qualification, as though the other "sens" of metaphor could be blocked and bypassed. In this traditional analysis, metaphor's truth lies, of course, in the resemblance perceived between two entities on the basis of certain properties or predicates that are assumed to be common to both entities and that sanction a transfer of sense. Although any pertinent differences between entities must be suppressed if their names are to be exchanged, metaphor is not (only, simply) false because the common properties are taken to belong to each of the entities before any linguistic intervention. Hence the also traditional characterization of metaphor as an economic comparison: the resemblance between Achilles and a lion explicitly stated in comparison is elided through substitution in the metaphor "This lion sprang forth." Although this phrase "represents to us only one object," the comparison and the subsequent exchange are *understood* — inferred, assumed, and comprehended. The "bon sens" of metaphor depends on the assumption that a substitution nowhere signaled by the metaphor has taken place. Homer's metaphor, Eudoxe continues, "confounds, in a manner of speaking, the lion with Achilles, or Achilles with the lion." But the possibility of confusing the two senses of "lion" in the metaphor already derives from the assumption of substitution; this helps explain why the two entities are only confounded "in a manner of speaking," figuratively, and hence — given the distinction between the perception of things and language that ensures the cognitive status of metaphor — not at all. Metaphor here seems to arise from the assumption of metaphor. As a result, for Bouhours the supposition and recognition of figurality must be considered axiomatic for reading: "These metaphorical ideas deceive no one: one knows what they signify if one has any intelligence, however little." And to underscore the unproblematical cognitive value of figural language, Eudoxe concludes his defense of wit with a comparison that seeks to comprehend metaphor through a hermeneutics of veiling and unveiling: "We may say, then, that metaphors are like transparent veils that let us see what they cover; or like masque-clothes under which we recognize the person who is disguised." Eudoxe's similes want to let us see that true wit lets us see again the familiar body it veils. To recognize a figurative mask is also to recognize the literal face it discovers.

Bouhours's defense of wit against the charge of fraud is encapsulated in this figure of the transparently veiled body. Eudoxe's simile transposes an epistemological investigation of language (the relation between literal and figurative senses) into a perceptual process of recognition grounded in the human body as the sensible condition and preeminent object of knowledge. True wit misleads no one because it always issues from and leads back to a face — as if the very aim of metaphorical exchange were the confirmation of the natural status of the body. But the force of Bouhours's apology should not prevent us from remarking some difficulties with this alliance of wit and perception. In fact, Eudoxe's simile signals at least one difficulty, since through it the body or person comes to designate a linguistic function: in this metaphor for metaphor, the human body is at once an object of perception and a figure for the literal sense of a word; the human face, both itself and its linguistic mask. What this simile lets us read is that the recognizable body guaranteeing the truth of the figure can be yet another figurative disguise. By transposing linguistic categories into corporeal and perceptual ones, Bouhours has wound up drawing into language the very thing supposed to ensure wit's "bon sens." One epistemological consequence of this entangling of language and bodies is that it undercuts the justification of a metaphorical transfer of sense on the basis of a prelinguistic resemblance between entities or ideas. One ethical result is the marked dependence on images of corporeal violence or disfiguration to figure the material character of language.

Relying on the determination of true wit as the recognition of the familiar and proper body of sense, Addison's historical account of the wit of the letter dramatizes these consequences. In the *Spectator*'s classificatory scheme, resemblance — and, with it, the domain of perception that grounds wit in nature — does not disappear entirely from false wit. Instead, the components of language become bodies or objects of perception. False wit consists in the "Resemblance and Congruity . . . of single Letters" (as in anagrams and chronograms), "Syllables" (echoes, doggerel rhymes), "words" (puns), and "whole Sentences or Poems, cast into the Figures of *Eggs*, *Axes*, or *Altars*: Nay some carry the Notion of Wit so far, as to ascribe it even to external Mimickry; and to look upon a Man as an ingenious Person, that can resemble the Tone, Posture, or Face of another" (1: 265). As "external Mimickry," false wit is a perverse *metaphora* that carries things too far by explicitly operating at the level of letters or faces instead of meaning; its substitutions are made possible not by some extra-linguistic perception or cognition but by the perception of marks or sounds "external" to sense though constitutive of representational systems. Hence false wit is not simply artificial or "conventional," possessing no relation to nature, since its mimicry foregrounds resemblance and consequently the "natural" character of language. At least in the case of puns, which may be taken as synecdochal for the genre, false wit too belongs to nature: "Imitation is natural to us, and when it does not raise the Mind to Poetry, Painting, Musick, or other more noble Arts, it often breaks out in Punns and Quibbles." Although, to be sure, an ignoble "Weed" in the garden of rhetoric, punning is nonetheless a growth "which the Soil has a natural Disposition to produce" and which is "impossible to kill." Since the "Seeds of Punning are in the Minds of all Men" naturally, the neoclassical attack on false wit can find no critical leverage in the appeal to natural genealogy. Both true and false wit stem from the same, albeit divided, seed, the seed of imitation (1: 259).

This division or fault in the value of the natural, indicated by the equivocal status of imitation, turns the rhetorical modes associated with false wit into scandalous operations continually requiring suppression. The perversity of wit, its unnatural naturalness or natural unnaturalness, seems to be connected to the peculiar manner in which it obeys (transgresses and exceeds) Horace's dictum, *ut pictura poesis* — the phrase cited by Addison as the motto for his first paper on wit. More generally, false wit's mimesis, whether of letters or faces, is produced in and through the signifying forms of representational systems, which have been relegated to the outside of meaning. It is perhaps for this reason that Addison begins his series by decrying a wit implicated in the spatial relations of signs, a wit deploying written or printed letters as both essential formal elements of linguistic systems and material components of pictorial mimesis. False wit exposes and exploits language as consisting of marks that must be detachable and repeatable, systematically articulated and ordered in some code, and that thus make recognition possible and defer it indefinitely. Indeed, the ironic wit in Addison's citation of "ut pictura poesis erit" as an epigraph for an essay about poems in the shape of objects would not be possible if this line could not be detached from the *Ars Poetica* and translated to the site of *Spectator* 58, where its repetition alters its meaning. But as this phrase had to be already detachable from its most illustrious context and already susceptible there to "external Mimickry," the presumed identity of its meaning in its "first" appearance is also rendered questionable.

Once Addison considers the mimicry of bodies or persons to be not simply analogous to figural language but a signifying practice itself, so that faces become yet another trope, he cannot but stage the effects of "Gothic" false wit as ethically reprehensible, monstrous violence. Throughout the *Spectator* series — though most uncannily in the allegorical dream narrative of paper 63, where "Dwarfs, Cripples, and Scare-Crows" interspersed with six-foot-tall officers in columns are presented as the "disproportioned Persons" forming a "Body of Acrosticks," and where "Men whose Bodies were stuck full of Darts" and "several Monsters of the like Nature" compose mixed wit's army (1: 272, 273) — false wit's figures are themselves figured as grotesquely victimized or deformed bodies. That this move to violent disfiguration motivates Addison's historical review of false wit can be noted in his discussion of typographically shaped, or picture, poems. When Addison at first attributes his inability to translate a Greek poem in the shape of an egg to the fact that "the Author seems to have been more intent upon the Figure of his Poem, than the Sense of it" (1: 246), the lapse of sense seems peculiar to this poem. It is only when he elaborates the genesis of these emblematic poems that the violence characteristic of the genre appears on the scene:

It was impossible for a Man to succeed in these Performances who was not a kind of Painter, or at least a Designer: He was first of all to draw the Out-line of the Subject which he intended to write upon, and afterwards conform the Description to the Figure of his Subject. The Poetry was to contract or dilate itself according to the Mould in which it was cast. In a Word, the Verses were to be cramped or extended to the Dimensions of the Frame that was prepared for them; and to undergo the Fate of those Persons whom the Tyrant *Procrustes* used to lodge in his Iron Bed; if they were too short he stretched them on a Rack, and if they were too long chopped off a Part of their Legs, till they fitted the Couch which he had prepared for them. (1: 247)

Addison generalizes as mutilation the interplay between "Figure" and "Sense" by framing this species of wit in terms of the violence of framing. The metaphor turning a poem into a human body enables Addison to present the dual exigency of picture poems — words must function as both spatially deployable marks and signifying marks — as a willful transgression of a kind of organic unity. False wit does premeditated violence to the integrity and organization of the body. Although the mimesis of letters and syllables is a natural act, the false wit employing these nonsignifying linguistic elements is deemed unnatural and artifactual here: emblematic poems, like disfigured bodies, are made, not found. To stage the genesis of typographical poetry as the work of torture, Addison could not even bring into play the trope of poetic language as a disguise, since this figure would introduce the demands of propriety or decorum. As a kind of dress, poetry would be partly required to abide by the reigning cultural conventions and might therefore appear to be compelled, in Procrustean fashion, to "contract or dilate itself according to the Mould in which it was cast." The figure of poetry as body, however, rejects even the usually benign externality of such cultural conventions, construes them to be arbitrary rules decreed and enforced by a poet-despot, and displaces these constraints onto false wit.

The apology for figural language consists, then, in displacing onto false wit alone the epistemological difficulties posed to cognition or perception by material linguistic conditions. This diversion is accomplished by align-

ing poetry and human bodies within a normative system grounded in the
ethical interaction of individual agents — an ethical grounding that mobi-
lizes humanist sentiment in a denegation of the function and effects of the
materiality of language. Viewing poetic production as an intersubjective
act, Addison can give a moral account of false wit that fully subordinates
language to human practice. And in this ethical accounting, the generation
of typographical poetry can only be construed as the willful disabling of
otherwise normal, proper, fully membered bodies or persons. As the ma-
lign genius morally responsible for such torture, Procrustes, both Elaine
Scarry and Addison might say, confuses the production of artifacts with a
violence that unmakes bodies.[8]

Since this denegation of linguistic materiality still acknowledges a threat
posed to humanist notions of language, however, it enables a different
reading of Procrustes. If typographical poetry discloses a materiality that
resists the reduction of language to a practical instrument and that even
determines cognition, then Procrustes is not just Addison's figure for poets
who abuse or misuse language: he personifies the power language exerts
on human subjects. As if language itself were another subject and as if its
force could only be an act of violence, the torturing artificer stands in for
the contingent effects of language on sense. Having no respect for other
human bodies, Procrustes breaks them on the rack just as material linguistic effects break in upon human subjects presumed to exist before (spatially
and temporally) language. Although such inhuman, linguistic power may
be termed positive insofar as it contributes to the very constitution of
subjects, Addison employs Procrustes to figure this force as the inhumane
negativity of violence that must be ethically disavowed.

But Addison's strategy of legitimation does not ensure the corporeal
integrity of neoclassical poetry or insulate the persons producing it from
this contingent, external force. In fact, as we shall see, neoclassical poetics
cannot itself do without what Addison figures here as violence. The rub is
already there in Addison's reference to "external Mimickry," mimesis as
personation. Although the "ingenious Person, that can resemble the Tone,
Posture, or Face of another" (1: 265) uses no rack or knife, he nonetheless
performs parodic acts that deface bodies precisely in disclosing the re-
producibility of faces or persons. These mimics, who inscribe other faces
on their own, demonstrate that a person is a mask and that bodies may be
recognized as the proper sign of singular persons only if they are reproducible and have been differentiated from other bodies. Addison may ethically censure "external Mimickry" as an abrasive act performed by ingenious wits, but the necessity of mimesis for there to be recognizable

faces — a physiognomic typography of lines and outlines — is not a possibility dependent on the exercise and rectitude of the will.

Despite the effort to shunt the contingencies of the letter to the violence of false wit alone, the *Spectator* series elsewhere allows us to grasp the essential formative role of such external forces. Let us take, for example, Addison's discussion of false wit's rhymes. Figuring typographical poems as mutilated bodies, Addison thereby posits a poetic body of true wit undetermined by any features extraneous to its own composition of sense. Rhyme is one of the features (like metrical quantity or number) that for neoclassical criticism enable a text to be recognized as belonging to poetic discourse. Although considered proper to neoclassical poetry, this device nevertheless has at the same time an external value and hence may be termed a poetic frame or outline. Rhymes are a formal trait essential for the recognition of a poetic body but also susceptible to parodic reproduction and occasioning epistemological mistakes.

Significantly, Addison does not explain the place of rhyme in true wit's body, though he severely criticizes the double rhymes associated with doggerel (e.g., "Ecclesiastick" / "instead of a Stick" [1: 258]) and especially what he introduces as the greatest "Instance of the Decay of Wit and Learning among the French": "*Bouts Rimez*" (1: 256). In the case of double rhymes, banished by Addison without detailed justification, the additional repetition of sound, we may infer, does not so much disfigure sense as it dramatizes the constraint of rhyme generally. Since phonemic resemblances mark no necessary relations among the concepts or objects represented conventionally by language, sound should at most, in Pope's phrase, echo sense. Double rhymes, however, foreground that poetry depends on rhyme and that poets must take their chances with language; they expose the formative effect of a poetic frame supposedly extraneous to sense. Addison's comment on anagrams — "which may change Night into Day, or Black into White, if Chance, who is the Goddess that presides over these sorts of Compositions, shall so direct" (1: 254) — thus applies as well to double rhymes and, indeed, to all forms of wit. These sorts of compositions suggest that poets, needing a break from the goddess, play a hand dealt them by and in language.

Addison's more extensive analysis of *bouts rimés* supports this reading of the perversity of (double) rhyme and indicates what is risked in the lucky stroke or break of wit: the very person of the poet as the agent of linguistic production. *Bouts rimés*, he explains, were "a List of Words that rhyme to one another, drawn up by another Hand, and given to a Poet, who was to make a Poem to the Rhymes in the same Order that they were placed upon the List" (1: 256). What appears unacceptable in *bouts rimés* is not the repetition of sounds but the prior spacing and ordering of rhymed pairs in a list that should then generate a poem. In the genetic frame of Addison's discussion, the priority of such a list "drawn up by another Hand" deprives a poet of the liberty to compose his own thought or to permit thought to clothe itself naturally in an appropriate body. Consequently, the other hand that draws up the rhymes may be compared to the hand of the "Designer" of emblematic poems, and the list, to Procrustes' bed. Indeed, the manner in which an example of *bouts rimés* is presented in *Spectator* 60 stresses the conception of rhyme scheme as a frame. Instead of simply enumerating the *bouts rimés* published in the *Mercure galant*, Addison displays the spatial dimension of the poetic bed by printing the example as follows (1: 257):

> _____ *Lauriers*
> _____ *Guerriers*
> _____ *Musette*
> _____ *Lisette*
>
> _____ *Cesars*
> _____ *Etendars*
> _____ *Houlette*
> _____ *Folette*

Rhymes here form the outline or limit to which a poem must conform. Mere pieces, extremities, ends (*bouts*), rhymes are extrinsic to a poem. And yet this contingent, external limit that breaks a poem defines in that violation the very body of the poem. Alternately conceptualized as internal (echoing or conveying sense, an integral part of the body-poem) and external (mere sound repetition, accidentally related and detachable fragments), rhyme in *bouts rimés* attests to the problematical status of all frames or limits: the contingent limit marked by the frame also constitutes the natural or proper body of the entity. Thus even if *bouts rimés* were drawn up by the same hand that composes the poem, the dependence of poets on the directing chances of rhyme would still dispossess them of the hands with which they write. No hand could draw a limit that would escape this strange logic of a simultaneous internality and externality.

Addison's reaction to Gilles Ménage's submission to such constraints attests to the passage between a violating force and a constitutive power that occurs at the limit: "When a grave Author, like him above-mentioned, tasked himself, could there be any thing more ridiculous? Or would not one be apt to believe that the Author played booty, and did not make his

List of Rhymes till he had finished his Poem?" (1: 258). We may surmise that Addison's suspicion is prompted by his inability to recognize a poem forcibly generated from *bouts rimés* when he sees one; the disfigured and the proper poem, in other words, perfectly mimic each other. His need to assert the posteriority of the rhyme scheme and, more generally, to insist on a proper sequence of verse composition can thus be interpreted as a defense against the uncertainty of temporal priority and, moreover, as a suppression of the possibility that material linguistic relations could govern poetic production. A poem that makes sense, he assumes, cannot have been generated from rhyme, even though nothing in it signals its mode of composition. Just as Swift in *A Tale of a Tub* must parody the dependence of modern writers on citations — "For, what tho' his *Head* be empty, provided his *Common-place-Book* be full"[9] — so must Addison doubt Ménage's account of his own mechanistic and de la Chambre's Shandyesque textual practice, cited in *Spectator* 60:

Monsieur de la Chambre has told me, that he never knew what he was going to write when he took his Pen into his Hand; but that one Sentence always produced another. For my own Part, I never knew what I should write next when I was making Verse. In the first Place I got all my Rhymes together, and was afterwards perhaps three or four Months in filling them up. (1: 257)

Ménage's remarks point not only to the inadequacy of Addison's defense of the cognitive value of wit but also to the consequences of this inadequacy for the perceiving and understanding subject. If writers know what they meant to represent only after and through writing, then the perverse contingency of linguistic materiality constitutes both the poetic body and the person of the writer. For as soon as it is possible for one sentence to produce another and for rhymes to generate poems, then it becomes impossible to tell whether persons or language make sense. The moment that nonsignifying, chance relations of language direct poetic production, the human face of sense seems to become only a figure drawn by language to express its own proper agency. Indeed, confronted with the possibility that human bodies might themselves be the material which language employs to convey its sense, Addison may even find some reassurance in the horrifying but powerful figure of Procrustes. In transposing epistemological questions about wit into an ethical register, this figure at least presents the production of meaning as if it were entirely, indubitably the act of human subjects who can represent their sense as freely as they can obey or transgress moral laws. In what respect could understanding still be deemed possible or even predictable of human subjects if the nature of things depended not on the hand of a person but on the chance of language?

In repudiating, then, the emphasis on spatial figures in picture poems and *bouts rimés* as an arbitrary, willful disfiguration of sense and endowing the poetry of true wit with a body independent of such violent framing, Addison seeks to establish the priority and authority of perceiving subjects as well as to subordinate figural language to their cognition and recognition. I have tried to show, however, that Addison's defense of poetry fails to secure the truth of its figures not just because the analogy itself of poems to bodies turns the supposedly natural or literal face of the cognitive subject into another trope but because the chance material effects that disfigure poetic or human bodies also delineate them. Both internal and external, the *bouts*, lines, and outlines characterizing poems or faces are *de-limiting* — at once making and unmaking an organic unity. To borrow a phrase from Julia Kristeva: the modes of false wit are the "borderline cases" of neoclassical poetics.[10] Symptomatic of a Gothic taste claimed to be regressive, they figure, however, the impossibility of separating decisively the contingent, material elements of language from the sense of nature to which poetry, like philosophy, should always give way. Clinging in the space of letters to the natural body of language which should be effaced so that language might only signify nature as the object and idea of perceiving subjects, and implying that the de-limitation of proper forms of sense also illimitably deforms them, the poets of false wit play on the borders of poetic and human bodies. As precisely the limit case, false wit is incorporated into the cultural commonwealth through the very act of expulsion whereby its borders are drawn.

If space permitted, it would be possible to show that throughout this *Spectator* series Addison's efforts at expulsion simultaneously internalize false wit because its framing effects are constitutive and thus cannot be eliminated without at the same time annihilating bodies themselves. A characteristic rhythm structures the series: at one moment, the contingent or arbitrary traits of false wit must be discredited as a kind of violence; at another, similarly contingent features must be naturalized or incorporated in true wit. Rather than pursue this reading here, however, I will conclude by following out the ethical and political consequences of figuring false wit as an act of corporeal violence. Indeed, as I have already suggested, neoclassical poetics cannot do without this violence because it is the origin of cultural production. The cultural politics of neoclassicism begins with a break.

When he compares the poet of typographical wit to the "Tyrant Procrustes," Addison raises the stakes of his poetics by elevating the torturing Procrustes from a petty highway thief to an absolute monarch (a grand larcenist). The inescapable effects of linguistic materiality are here conceived as the Gothic lawlessness of the morally depraved political ruler who can violate at will the personal property, the natural property in one's person, of his subjects. But this recourse to ethics operates as a ruse of legitimation in Addison. First of all, art in general, including both true and false wit, emerges in Addison's writings precisely through acts of breaking. The necessity of such acts for the appearance of art (and for the subsistence of humanity) can be understood if we return for a moment to the metaphor of art as cultivation. Imitation, we recall, "breaks out in Punns and Quibbles" as naturally as in poetry and "other more noble Arts." Through mimesis, fortunately, nature breaks into forms of art, breaching or parting itself; art is the breaking out of nature. Since both puns and poetry emerge in this breaking of nature, no genealogical strain marks off the noble from the base stock. To argue the illegitimacy of puns, Addison must then align the true and noble with an imperious reason which produces culture by mastering what it cannot kill: "It is indeed impossible to kill a Weed, which the Soil has a natural Disposition to produce. The Seeds of Punning are in the Minds of all Men, and tho' they may be subdued by Reason, Reflection and good Sense, they will be apt to shoot up in the greatest Genius, that is not broken and cultivated by the Rules of Art" (1: 259). As Addison has elaborated this analogy, true wit comes to relate to false wit as art itself relates to nature: false wit, once more, falls back on the natural elements of language while true wit advances toward the rule of reason and "good Sense."

On the one hand, the inconsistency of this analogy — both poetry and puns are arts of language breaking from nature; poetry alone is a rational art superior to merely natural puns — can be explained by the neoclassical premise of a self-regulating unity of nature and reason. As Pope formulates it, the rules of art are "*Nature Methodiz'd*" because "*Nature*, like *Liberty*, is but restrain'd, / By the same Laws which first *herself* ordain'd."[11] The hierarchy of the arts would be founded, then, on the identification of noble poetry with the rule that nature gives to itself. Through human reason, nature, like liberty in liberal politics, legislates to itself; the rules of art are not external, arbitrarily devised, and tyrannically imposed but define, instead, the natural boundaries of cultural products. On the other hand, the violence structuring Addison's analogy — the "natural Disposition to produce" puns must be "subdued," "broken and cultivated" — betrays the need for forceful intervention to curb a natural productivity that can exceed what should be its own limits. Self-legislation must give way to a Procrustean act of domination, the breaking of genius, as the difference made by reason introduces an asymmetry that prevents the assimilation of cultural to natural production. For men and women may naturally imitate what nature supplies, but nature is indiscriminate, promiscuous, indifferent in its excessive production of species to the needs of humanity. Nature lacks a human-oriented principle of production, which art must supply. Hence art, legitimate because descended from nature, must turn against nature and force it into conformity. Nature, like and as false wit, must be "broken" and ruled by culture.

Moreover, the cultural breaking of nature entails a dislocation of what we could justifiably call nature's body. Not just the paradigmatic natural object, the body also figures nature as an organism articulating or breaking itself into segments. Addison invokes nature as an articulated body in the citation from Virgil's *Georgics* introducing *Spectator* 69, devoted to the Royal Exchange (1: 292). In Dryden's translation:

> This Ground with *Bacchus*, that with *Ceres* suits:
> That other loads the Trees with happy Fruits.
> A fourth with Grass, unbidden, decks the Ground:
> Thus *Tmolus* is with yellow Saffron crown'd:
> *India*, black Ebon and white Ivory bears:
> And soft *Idume* weeps her od'rous Tears.
> Thus *Pontus* sends her Beaver Stones from far;
> And naked *Spanyards* temper Steel for War.
> *Epirus* for th' *Elean* Chariot breeds,
> (In hopes of Palms,) a Race of running Steeds.
> This is the Orig'nal Contract; these the Laws
> Impos'd by Nature, and by Nature's Cause,
> On sundry Places.[12]

All species are not producible everywhere and at all times. A law of propriety governs the conditions of natural production: differences in climate and soil divide the earth into parts, places, or nations to which only certain species are suitable. "But e're we stir the yet unbroken Ground," Virgil, according to Dryden, had written just prior to the lines cited by Addison, we should discover "what will thrive and rise, / And what the Genius of the Soil denies."[13] It is nature's self-segmentation that makes it a body — the "particular Care" nature takes, Addison remarks in *Spectator* 69, "to disseminate her Blessings among the different Regions of the World" (1: 294). Addison often refers to the "face" of nature, and Dryden's translation of the *Georgics* continually emphasizes nature's maternal body.

Sometimes Dryden elaborates the body figure by exploiting one sense of a term in Virgil that other translators ignore:

> Nor is the Profit small, the Peasant makes;
> Who smooths with Harrows, or who pounds with Rakes
> The crumbling Clods . . .
> Nor his, who plows across the furrow'd Grounds,
> And on the Back of Earth inflicts new Wounds:
> For he with frequent Exercise Commands
> Th'unwilling Soil, and tames the stubborn Lands.
>
> (bk. 1, ll. 137–44 [bk. 1, ll. 94–99])

In describing the "Profit" gained from breaking and rebreaking ground, Dryden stresses that furrows are the "terga" or back of earth and dramatizes the art of agriculture as the domination through laceration of nature's body. The need to inflict these "Wounds" arises in the *Georgics* when Jove "wills that Mortal Men, inur'd to toil, / Shou'd exercise, with pains, the grudging Soil" and "whet[s] Humane Industry by Care."[14] Before Jove's decree, "no Peasant vex'd [*subigebant* — cultivated or subjugated] the peaceful Ground"; "all was common, and the fruitful Earth / Was free to give her unexacted Birth."[15] But Jove deprived mortals of nature's unbidden plenty and forced them to develop their imperious arts for survival; their plowshares, rakes, and harrows are the "Arms they wield" in an "Iron War" to expel the "proud Foes" subduing the land.[16] Through labor and art, then, the human species must henceforth compel nature to do its bidding and exact what nature would not otherwise yield. Not oriented to human consumption, nature must be profitably broken by the art and technology of agriculture.

Although Virgil's mythological account of the violence of culture cannot, of course, be simply ascribed to Addison, *An Essay on Virgil's Georgics*, first printed with Dryden's translation in 1697, and the several *Spectator* papers headed by citations from the *Georgics* attest to his sustained interest in that work. Moreover, Virgil's text seems to provide Addison with an insistent nexus of terms for describing a political economy of cultural production and for linking wit and the body with commercial exchange. In this instance, it is not a matter of an analogy between language and money as media of exchange, an analogy that would also conjure up the specter of linguistic and financial speculation. In Addison's responses to the *Georgics* we find, rather, an analogy between language and nature as material of production: both must be worked or cultivated for exchange value. In both cases, furthermore, the work of culture is itself an act of substitution or exchange, the violence of which is concealed by the ability to recognize the equivalence this exchange posits and by the aesthetic effect such recognition affords. And since the work of producing equivalent exchange proceeds in the name of nature's own laws — culture being the rule by which nature restrains itself — the attendant violation of natural bodies is hailed as an aesthetic achievement of culture.

Addison's admiration for a particular passage in the *Georgics* may serve to indicate the true wit of a cultural production that naturalizes the violence of exchange and aestheticizes bodily disfiguration. Although Virgil presents agricultural tools as weapons in a war against nature's unruly productivity, he also celebrates grafting, inoculating or budding, and transplanting as technologies that orient nature toward human consumption by mimicking its productive force. Cultural exchange supplements the brutality of war. As in the "external Mimickry" that transplants a face in a body to which it does not properly belong, these techniques of substitution yield monstrous organisms whose foreign or borrowed members, however, are incorporated into their surrogate bodies. Here, in Dryden's words, is Virgil's recommendation for subduing fruitless trees:

> Yet these, receiving Graffs of other Kind,
> Or thence transplanted, change their salvage Mind:
> Their Wildness lose, and quitting Nature's part,
> Obey the Rules and Discipline of Art. . . .
>
> The bat'ning Bastard shoots again and grows:
> And in a short space the laden Boughs arise,
> With happy Fruit advancing to the Skies.
> The Mother Plant admires [*miraturque*] the Leaves unknown,
> Of Alien Trees, and Apples not her own.
>
> (bk. 2, ll. 71–74, 113–17 [bk. 2, ll. 49–52, 80–82])

The figure of a maternal body disciplined by the reproductive technologies of (agri)culture does not provoke moral revulsion or horror. This birth surrogacy that is also a miscegenation — of different species but especially of nature and culture — elicits instead the aesthetic effect of wonder (*mirare*). Standing in for the producers and users of this body, the dismembered and reorganized mother marvels at the bastard limbs and alien fruit, exchanged for her own, that signify her obedience to culture's cause as if it were "Nature's part." Insofar as this reproducing and reproduced maternal body depends on the dismembering practices associated with false wit, such a monstrous figure should be disavowed. The substitution and mixing of kinds resemble the work of Pope's "grotesque painter" who, seeking to "affect the *Marvellous*," masters an "*anti-natural* way of thinking," "mingl[ing] bits of the most various, or discordant kinds, . . . and connect[ing] them with a great deal of flourishing, by heads or tails, as it shall please his imagination."[17] And for Addison in the *Spectator* series on wit, the exchangeability of limbs defines an anagrammatic body: "I remember a witty Author, in allusion to this Kind of Writing, calls his Rival, who (it seems) was distorted, and had his Limbs set in Places that did not properly belong to them, *The Anagram of a Man*" (1: 254). But in his essay on the *Georgics*, Addison praises these same lines from Virgil for eliciting an aesthetic effect he later defines as characteristic of true wit, "that effect which had the most surprise, and by consequence the most to delight in."[18] Although Addison claims that the metaphorical exchanges of true wit are founded on surprising resemblances proper to nature, his response to this uncanny hybrid body suggests that metaphor in fact naturalizes its own forceful operations. By incorporating the alien work of metaphorical exchange, the surprising figure of the grafted maternal body aestheticizes the cultural violence that produced this monster.

When its effects are not aesthetically dissimulated as a marvelous incorporation, the violence of culture is justified in terms of the necessity to transform a recalcitrant nature for human profit. As Jean Baudrillard has argued, however, the need to produce values by subduing a nature also understood as a productive force is the rationale of political economy: "The idea of 'natural Necessity' is only a *moral* idea dictated by political economy" and not "the ontological dimension of man." Necessity is the "philosophical expression of Scarcity" that "arises only in the market economy" as the alibi of economic exchange; only when nature has been objectified does it appear as "an implacable necessity, 'the alienation of man's own body' [Marx's phrase]," which leads to the "operational violence of man against nature" that will come to characterize history.[19] In Addison's biblical version of Virgil's fall into the necessity of cultural labor — "No one of the Sons of *Adam*," he warns in a *Spectator* number with a motto from the *Georgics*, "ought to think himself exempt from that Labour and Industry which were denounced to our first Parent" (4: 592) — the industry that breaks (with) nature and progresses beyond a Gothic condition is precisely the industry essential to Britain's commercial society. Commerce, J. G. A. Pocock has observed, is "the active form of culture itself" in the early eighteenth century.[20] Hence, when elsewhere Addison insists "it is so ordered that nothing valuable can be procured without [labor]," he makes clear that nature must be forcibly cultivated to yield marketable commodities: "Providence furnishes Materials, but expects that we should work them up our selves. The Earth must be laboured before it gives its Encrease, and when it is forced into its several Products, how many Hands must they pass through before they are fit for Use? Manufactures, Trade and Agriculture naturally employ more than nineteen Parts of the Species in twenty" (1: 472). Virgil's Jove made the force of labor and art necessary to survival; Addison's Providence ordains, in addition, commerce necessary for products to become "fit for Use." And this supplement of trade will order in advance the products forced from the earth according to "how many Hands" they can pass through.

In fact, Addison interprets the articulated body of the earth to be the providential cause of commerce, as if market societies were historically entailed in the regional dispersal of nature. In *Spectator* 69, trade is the telos of nature's segmentation: "Nature seems to have taken a particular Care to disseminate her Blessings among the different Regions of the World, with an Eye to this mutual Intercourse and Traffick among Mankind, that the Natives of the several Parts of the Globe might have a kind of Dependance upon one another, and be united by their common Interest" (1: 294–95). The laws imposed by nature on sundry places exist only to be broken by "Traffick." But since breaking these natural limits is necessary to sustain the "Natives of the several Parts," the transgressions of trade should be considered nature's own means of nourishing itself; as Defoe argued, the rivers and roads utilized in trade "are as the Veins and Arteries that Convey Wealth, like the Blood, to all the Parts of the World."[21] Hence the violent defacement reviled in the operations of false wit is celebrated as the commercial cultivation of the "Face of Nature." The following passage from the *Spectator* paper on the Royal Exchange may stand, then, as Addison's georgic:

If we consider our own Country in its natural Prospect, without any of the Benefits and Advantages of Commerce, what a barren uncomfortable Spot of Earth falls to our Share! Natural Historians tell us, that no Fruit grows originally among us . . . ; That our Climate of it self, and without the Assistances of Art, can make no further Advances towards a Plum than to a Sloe . . . : That our Melons, our Peaches, our Figs, our Apricots, and Cherries, are Strangers among us, imported in different Ages, and naturalized in our *English* Gardens; and that they would all degenerate and fall away into the Trash of our own Country, if they were wholly neglected by the Planter, and left to the Mercy of our Sun and Soil. Nor has Traffick more enriched our Vegetable World, than it has improved the whole Face of Nature among us. (1: 295)

Like Defoe's true-born Englishman, the fruit taken to be native to England results from grafts or transplants. Although this produce might seem indigenous, Addison stresses the metaphorical character of the garden of England: commerce translates entities supposedly proper to other regions to the site of England, where these "Strangers" have become "naturalized" so as to mimic a native population. Interpreting this garden as another metaphor of metaphor, we may note that figural or cultural exchange still elicits a surprising recognition. The imports are not quite proper to England; nor are they as utterly alien as false wits, who are " 'a Sort of *French* Huguenots, or *Dutch* Boors, brought over in Herds, but not naturalized' " and who lack " 'Lands of two Pounds *per Annum* in *Parnassus* ' " needed to vote (1: 269). The true English may yet recognize their face in these foreign species because the alien is only a provisionally alienated part of England on the way to being incorporated.

What Addison celebrates in this georgic is the self-engendering work of English culture. As he notes in *Spectator* 583, planting "has something in it like Creation," and "the Pleasure of the one who plants is something like that of a Poet, who, as Aristotle observes, is more delighted with his Productions than any other Writer or Artist whatsoever" (4: 593). Hence he stages the transformation of an originally barren spot of earth into a fruitful garden in order to "trace" the English subject in the "Impressions of his Industry" (4: 595). Aristotle had said: "What is our own is pleasant to all of us, as for instance our own deeds and words"; "it is also pleasant to complete what is defective, for the whole thing thereupon becomes our own work."[22] In improving the "Face of Nature" through culture, we complete and take possession of both nature and ourselves as the product of our own work. In apparently natural objects, we should recognize labor-traces figuring our own values, as we should recognize in poetic language the figure of our own meanings.

Moreover, although poets and planters share a pleasure in objects bearing their signatures, poets resemble merchants in laboring to transport what can be naturalized in different countries. Like linguistic translation for Addison, commerce makes no profit from items whose value is so contingent on their surroundings, so peculiar to their place, that they cannot be equivalently exchanged. The fiction of a universal human need guaranteeing the exchange value of disparate products finds its complement in the fiction of a universality of meaning guaranteeing the truth value of figural language. Hence Addison's test for distinguishing a true from a false piece of wit could also apply to international trade: "translate it"; a pun "vanishes in the Experiment" (1: 263) just as a peculiar commodity resists transport beyond a regional economy. Puns fall outside of language ("a Sound, and nothing but a Sound" [1: 263]) as far as obdurately particular objects fall short of value — neither circulates universally. This imperative to translate indicates that both neoclassical poetics and political economy presuppose a schism between matter or body and value or meaning that organizes exchange: "that is to say," according to Jean-Joseph Goux, "between that aspect of the object (its natural form, its physicality) which resists common denomination and remains *heterogeneous*, external to the very principle of exchange, and what, on the other hand, can be compared, measured, and equated despite differences."[23]

For Addison, the superiority of English literary and commercial culture lies precisely in the ability of metaphorical exchange to efface differences — to break (with) and dematerialize natural bodies — but only insofar as exchange is not symmetrical. If the effects of exchange were considered to be reciprocal, Addison might wonder, in a more troubling sense, whether the incorporation of alien species strikes a blow to the body of England, making it impossible to recognize the very face of the English. As a grafted body that confounds the culturally produced with the properly natural, England might find its literal self engendered by the metaphorical substitutions it claims to naturalize — a body uncannily possessed by the foreign possessions it acquires and requires to reproduce itself. If Addison wondered whether England is itself transported or carried off in its trafficking with others, he might not discover in the work of cultural exchange the signature of English genius.

Hence Addison must insist on the asymmetry of exchange or the unidirectionality, the "bon sens," of metaphor. Since the foreign can only be assimilated to the native that, nonetheless, is engendered by exchange, trade makes the entire earth and its peoples the property of England: "My Friend Sir Andrew calls the Vineyards of *France* our Gardens: the Spice-Islands our Hot-beds; the *Persians* our Silk-Weavers, and the *Chinese* our Potters" (1: 295–96). By "supplying foreign Markets with the Growth and Manufactures of the most distant Regions," Addison remarked in *The Freeholder*, "we receive the same Profit from them, as if they were the Produce of our own Island." And in that same periodical number he expressly promotes the hegemony of trade as a surrogate for military domination: "We reap the Advantages of Conquest, without Violence or Injustice; . . . and, without any Act of Hostility, lay the several Nations, of the World under a kind of Contribution."[24] It is the hegemony of asymmetrical exchange that dissimulates the violence of culture identified with Procrustes' tyrannical acts of disfiguration. Incorporating products from the remotest parts of the earth, England becomes hypertrophically distorted, a marvelously swollen member of a grotesque global body. Such is the political economy of wit in English culture.

Following out Addison's entangling of wit and bodies, my investigation into the epistemology of figural language has ended in an ideology-critique of the ethics and political economy of cultural production. This movement from questions of truth value to those of moral and economic value is performed in Addison's text when the chances or breaks of wit get figured as the violation or breaking of human bodies. In assessing the stakes of this transposition, I have not sought, however, to accuse neo-classical criticism of importing ethical and political-economic concerns and of forcibly imposing or grafting them on an otherwise autonomous, self-sufficient literary domain. That sort of argument would ignore the contingent yet determinant intervention of language, its de-limitation of these distinct fields of value, and the unsettling logic of such acts of grafting. I aimed to show, rather, that by figuring the wit of the letter as a blow to the body, Addison registers something like the productive force of language — its power to constitute the subject presumed to be the agent employing it as a medium for representing knowledge. Bodily violation is an enlightened humanism's figure for the linguistic constitution of the subject. But such a figure invokes moral and political-economic imperatives and thus invites a critique of the ideological contradictions of violence in neoclassical culture.

Yet this superposition of truth, moral, and political-economic values may have its own necessity the moment one attempts to address the material character of language. To account for its effects by affirming that language itself exercises force and that language, not human subjects, literally acts, performs, and produces is to resort to personifying figures that reintroduce the humanism under critique. Insofar as any reference to what language does must rely on such notions of production, action, and performance, this recurrent misfiguration (to distinguish it from disfiguration) is bound to occur. Hence epistemological inquiries into figural language can never break with an ethics and politics of cultural production.

Locke's Eyes, Swift's Spectacles

VERONICA KELLY

> As for the methods of passing his [Swift's] time, I must tell you one
> which constantly employs an hour about noone. He has in his win-
> dow an Orbicular Glass, which by Contraction of the Solar Beams
> into a proper Focus, doth burn, singe, or speckle white, or printed
> Paper, in curious little Holes, or various figures. We chanced to find
> some Experiments of this nature upon the Votes of the House of
> Commons. The name of Tho. Hanmer Speaker was much singed,
> and that of John Barber entirely burn'd out. . . . I doubt not
> but these marks of his are mysticall, & that the Figures he makes
> this way are a significant Cypher to those who have the Skill to
> explain 'em.
>
> —Pope to Dr. Arbuthnot, July 11, 1714

> Adieu bright wit and radiant eyes;
> You must be grave and I be wise.
>
> —Swift, "Stella's Birthday [1725]"

> The Life of Dean Jonathan Swift will never be written.
>
> —Shane Leslie, *The Skull of Swift*

*B*iography, which includes the histories of consciousness and the
body, has responded like a sensitive instrument to perturbations in the
technologies of writing and of seeing. Mapping the unconscious in *The
Interpretation of Dreams,* for example, Freud describes internal perception in the terms of the still-current visual technology of the late nineteenth century, as virtual images: "like the image produced in a telescope
by the passage of light rays."[1] This optical simile, according to Derrida's
"Freud and the Scene of Writing," marks a classical moment in Freud. The
psychographics later proposed in "The Mystic Writing Pad" await a mate-

rial technology, in this case the writing pad itself, to metaphorize the temporality of the unconscious as writing.[2] To understand how the body is described in the moral and psychological discourses of the eighteenth century, this paper looks back from Freud's invention of the unconscious, and its release from the classical tropes, to that moment when, in the classicist milieu of late seventeenth- and early eighteenth-century England, John Locke's introspective empirical philosophy invents the subject of consciousness in the optical metaphor of the reflective "I." With the broad dissemination of Locke's theory of the conscious self, the conventions by which the self can be written also change: controlled by the trope of the mind's eye, this interior and expressive subjectivity necessarily reorients the moral principles of biography toward the internal distances of self-reflection, distances that establish both the rights and responsibilities of self-determination and the conventions of psychological depth. But if eighteenth-century philosophy and biography give us the outlines of the modern self possessed of an inner life transparent to the biographer's scrutiny, what becomes of the body of this pellucid consciousness? Using as a pivotal example Johnson's *Life of Swift*, this paper argues that the task of biography as it evolves in the eighteenth century is to hold the subject, who is after all only a virtual image, within a moral code that is extrapolated from the law of optical perspective and that suffers from marginal aberrations caused by the body. Johnson's *Life of Swift*, infamous for its hostile narrative of Swift's life and writing and for its peculiar account of Swift's decline, reveals the moral biographer struggling to put a powerfully distorting body into perspective.

Johnson's account of Swift's life is remarkable for the decisive role that it gives a mundane optical apparatus in the etiology of Swift's infamous final madness.[3] Swift, writes Johnson,

having . . . excluded conversation, and desisted from study, . . . had neither business nor amusement; for having, by some ridiculous resolution or mad vow, determined never to wear spectacles, he could make little use of books in his later years; his ideas, therefore, being neither renovated by discourse, nor increased by reading, wore gradually away, and left his mind vacant to the vexations of the hour, till at last his anger was heightened into madness.[4]

The detail of Swift's "ridiculous resolution . . . never to wear spectacles" is not original to Johnson, who preserves it from two of his source biographies, Patrick Delany's *Observations upon Lord Orrey's Remarks on the Life and Writings of Dr. Jonathan Swift* and John Hawkesworth's "Account of the Life of the Reverend Jonathan Swift."[5] These early biographies are doubly revealing: generally, as registers of the encounter between "Swift" and biographical writing in the eighteenth century and, more pointedly, as depositories of the material out of which we can see Johnson select and construct his "Swift." Both Delany and Hawkesworth make a pronounced effort to explain the sources of Swift's madness. Hawkesworth, for example, argues that Swift's avarice resulted in his social isolation, which resulted in his brooding on fixed ideas, which resulted in his madness. In both of the early biographies, the anecdote of the spectacles is qualitatively distinct from these explanations, less a serious part of the progress of Swift's illness than a nod to the forces of passion and irrationality that are so powerfully represented both in Swift's writing and in his fate. Swift's "resolution" is inexplicable; his adherence to it is "obstinate." But the story of the spectacles only apparently stands apart from the causal imperative that is so clearly at work in Delany's and Hawkesworth's biographies: the detail functions in their narratives as the unaccountable event that secures the causal sequence of the biographer's account, and so we may say that it is included not despite but because of its affront to causality. Its inclusion ensures that whimsical and arbitrary rebellion against narrative order, rebellion such as that implied by Swift's resolution against reading glasses, can be framed and controlled by the biographer's selection of material. What will become clearer in Johnson's *Life of Swift* is apparent even in the rather primitive biographies by Delany and Hawkesworth: that the story of Swift resolving never to wear spectacles is the biographer's prophylactic against the possibility that his biography is arbitrary, that it is not a life history, but a "ridiculous resolution" to be read.

In Delany and Hawkesworth, and more emphatically in Johnson, the task of accounting for Swift's final years becomes a proving ground for biographical writing, something like the biographer's licensing exam. This seems to be because Swift's madness presents itself as both wholly inexplicable and wholly predetermined, both random and necessary. The early biographies do not fail to find premonitions of Swift's end, either in his funding of St. Patrick's Hospital, for example, or in his reported conversations. Orrey goes so far as to claim that "Swift . . . certainly foresaw his fate."[6] The exact nature of the determination that results in Swift's madness differs widely and is ascribed, variously, to Providence, to Swift's flawed physiology or depraved imagination, and even to a perverse self-will. This last possibility, that Swift's madness was somehow consciously self-induced, substitutes an image of ultimate self-destruction for the less dramatic cultural and generic necessities evident in the explanations of Swift's madness, deflecting attention from the fact that these accounts of Swift's sensory deprivation follow the dominant eighteenth-century psychologies of sense perception and personal identity so completely that Swift becomes an exemplary case history. Orrey even takes the occasion of his narrating Swift's final days to review contemporary theories of lunacy. In the struggle visible in these biographies, between Swift's disturbing madness and the clichés used to organize and explain it, we can see biography facing its own necessary contradiction, personifying as "Swift" the dangerous oscillation between ephemeral singularity and persistent significance that the biographer must master for his work to be, as Johnson would have it be, "useful."

Unlike his predecessors in Swiftian biography, Johnson disassociates himself from Swift and his life story, refusing the role of an interested contemporary for that of impartial narrator and judge. In withdrawing from the opinionated disputes about Swift that characterize his sources (Orrey, Delany, Hawkesworth), Johnson uses the distance of his persona both to disguise the biographer's investment in the outcome of his narrative and to fix Swift within the biography as its object and spectacle. As mentioned before, Johnson preserves the detail of the repudiated spectacles in the story of Swift's life, and uses it, more skillfully than his predecessors, to gain the benefits of narrative and moral closure. With its discovery of an intention, of Swift's having "determined never to wear spectacles," Johnson's account of Swift's decline awards responsibility to Swift for his own madness. The logic of Johnson's narrative implies that Swift refused to wear spectacles and so he became one. Other biographers, both before and after Johnson, explicitly cite the usefulness of Swift's fate for moralizing. Orrey, characteristically hyperbolical, writes of Swift's peaceful death:

A man in full possession of his reason, would have wished for such a kind of dissolution, but Swift was totally insensible of happiness or pain: he had not even the power or expression of a child, appearing, for some years before his death, reserved only as an example to mortify human pride, and to reverse that fine description of human nature, which is given us by Shakespeare in an inimitable manner: "*What a piece of work is man! how noble in reason! how infinite in faculty! in form and moving, how express and admirable! in action, how like an angel! in apprehension, how like a god! the beauty of the world, the paragon of animals.*" Thus poets paint; but how vain and perishable is the picture? The smallest thunderbolt from heaven blasts it in a moment, and every tint is so effectually obliterated, that scarce the outlines of the figure remain. (Orrey, *Remarks*, pp. 265–66)[7]

Giving the visual control wholly to the biographer and reader, Orrey's text makes painfully clear the connection between visual and moral advantage. Swift "appear[s] . . . only as an example" and is kept alive or "reserved" just long enough for his body to serve as an illustration. Orrey's description of Swift already contains some of the complexities that I will discuss in Johnson's *Swift*, in particular its use of the ambivalent image of Swift's silent body to illustrate the failure of "vain and perishable" poetic figures. But it is more significant for my analysis at this point not only that Orrey describes Swift as a moral spectacle but also that it is Delany and Hawkesworth, not Orrey, who include the detail of Swift's "resolution" against spectacles; it is Johnson who brings these two together, linking the repudiated spectacles with the depiction of Swift's body as a moral spectacle.

In Johnson's *Swift*, this conjunction obviates any suspicion that the biographer may be the one making a spectacle of Swift, by encouraging the implication that Swift has made a spectacle of himself. This discovery of intention in his subject, of his "determination" against spectacles, exonerates the biographer from the charge of petty motives, giving a distance to his observations that classes them as moral judgments and elevates the biographer above the status of interested party or hack. The contradictory nature of Swift's determination, Johnson's admission that it is both willful and frivolous, that the "vow" was already "mad," compels rather than overrides the narrative's insistence that Swift somehow chose and so deserved his madness.

This awarding of responsibility is also, of course, the discovery of fault. The detail of the refused spectacles names an error that, as it is named, looms up out of this narrative with the protective power of a talisman. The detail's idiosyncrasy increases both because its source remains unclear and because the cause that it finds for Swift's disease is comically inadequate to its effect: an opinionated old man inexplicably refuses to wear spectacles and as a consequence goes mad. One broad "symptomatic" reading of this detail would suggest that it protects Johnson, whose anxieties were part of the public domain even in his own century, from the prospect of madness and senility. Although this account, which rests largely on generalizations from Johnson's identification with Swift, seems plausible, it leaves unexplained the particular place of the spectacles in Johnson's narrative, and the way in which they carry the claim that Johnson was unable to write judiciously about Swift.[8]

What is peculiar about this passage is not just that something as horrible as madness results from a slight and arbitrary decision. The grim ironies of Johnson's *vanitas* theme are complicated by the odd rhetorical behavior of the spectacles themselves, which produce a moment of apparently blind self-reflection in Johnson's text. This introversion occurs because there are actually two spectacles here: the eyeglasses that Swift was too proud or too foolish to wear and the spectacle that Johnson makes of Swift. This second, moralized spectacle emerges as the silenced, homonymic effect of the first. As Johnson recounts it, Swift's "ridiculous resolution or mad vow . . . never to wear spectacles" has the effect of transforming Swift himself into a complete spectacle, for Johnson leaves us with an image of the Dean passive before our view, "at last sunk into perfect silence." Reduced to this "silence," Swift is exposed to us, degraded and vulnerable, as a body. This, of course, is much like the effect that Johnson creates in "The Vanity of Human Wishes," when he writes that "Swift expires a driv'ler and a show."⁹

By using the refused eyeglasses to reduce Swift to a physical spectacle, this passage "hears" the unvoiced pun on spectacle that organizes the retributive logic of Johnson's description. This pun, once heard, is then focused on the other silent figure in the scene, Swift's body, which makes visible the effects of Johnson's rhetorical turn. The importance of this turn is not simply that it shows the biographer's subject blinded and silenced "to point a moral." The logic of causality is intricate and circular: when Johnson claims that Swift's refusal to wear spectacles causes his silence and madness, those same glasses bring a silenced pun on spectacle into our view, enabling us to see that, in this depiction of Swift, biography is reflecting blindly, through the synaesthesia of a pun, on its own use of spectacles. It is facetious but nonetheless true that Swift is not the only one in this text who needs spectacles. As this analysis makes clear, Johnson's *Swift* uses the detail of Swift's "resolution" to burden Swift's silent body with the theme of *vanitas*. But the proximity into which Johnson brings the spectacles that would "never" be worn and the moral spectacle of Swift's body also works to suggest that Swift and biography, because they are both spectacles, are somehow alike.

In turning the logic of causality back onto biography, Swift's body may be said to lay a counterclaim on the genre that silences it. Such reasoning returns us to the idea that the spectacles are prophylactic and that Swift, in the silence of his body, threatens biography with a figure of itself. This identity is also apparent in Johnson's descriptions of the nature of Swift's attention. Swift, he writes as part of his explanation of the Dean's peculiar habits and his inclination to exaggerations, "thought trifles a necessary part of life" and was often "busy with minute occurrences" (pp. 464, 465).

He lived "with that vigilance of minute attention which his works discover" (p. 468). These are characteristics he shares with biographical
writing, which, according to Johnson in *Rambler* 60, should "display the
minute details of daily life" (p. 183).[10] But the symmetry of this identification is not, as has often been suggested in analyses of Johnson's psychological involvement with Swift, the fear of madness. The threat that Johnson
averts by including Swift's "mad vow . . . never to wear spectacles" in his
text is not exactly lunacy or incompetence. The sense of horror evoked in
Johnson's account may be generalized as the fear of madness, but its
particular dimension is the image of Swift transformed into a mute mark,
of Swift "sunk" into the "perfect silence" of a sepulchral body. This is an
image not of madness but of untimely death: the mind and body fail to die
together and the body persists as an embarrassment, to become the text of
a lesson.[11] Biography, of course, does not suffer untimely death, but it is
the genre most sensitive to the question of timing:

> If a life be delayed till interest and envy are at an end, we may hope for impartiality,
> but must expect little intelligence; for the incidents which give excellence to biog-
> raphy are of a volatile and evanescent kind, such as soon escape the memory, and
> are rarely transmitted by tradition. We know how few can portray a living ac-
> quaintance except by his most prominent and observable particularities, and the
> grosser features of his mind; and it may be easily imagined how much of this little
> knowledge may be lost in imparting it, and how soon a succession of copies will
> lose all resemblance of the original.[12]

What Johnson's *Rambler* essay on biography reveals, and his *Life of Swift*
dramatizes, is that biography cannot find the perfect moment in which to
write its subject. Its incidents, being "volatile and evanescent," "soon escape the memory," leaving biography in an amnesia peculiarly like Swift's.
In Johnson's *Swift*, the rhetorical turn on spectacles transforms the spectacle of Swift's body, preserved as an image of untimely death, into a figure
for the biographer's inability to write a timely life: instead of perfect timing, there is "perfect silence." In this reading of Johnson's antagonism to
Swift, it is Johnson's professional fears, not his private ones, that motivate
the antipathy: in *The Life of Swift*, the biographer's violence admits that
there is no time, "never," in which the biography can be written.[13] With
biography's "resemblance of the original" either distorted by passion or
sacrificed to impartiality, the biographer of the *Life of Swift* deploys the
illusions of spectacle, setting the distance, measure, and uniformity of a
perspective narrative against the "never" of an impossible temporality.

In biography as perspective narrative, the ephemeral subject is frozen in
an unchanging and homogenous space and the narrator encourages the

reader to look "through" that space, as through a window or a pair of spectacles.[14] Through its complex structure of syntactic parallels and antitheses, Johnson's text visualizes Swift's body as the condition without which its own demand for a regular, proportionate "space" in which to see and evaluate could not be maintained.[15] Johnson evokes the necessary illusion of a transparent textual space by placing Swift's body, absolute in its "perfect silence," at the vanishing point of his narrative portrait, where it stands directly opposite the point of sight from which he observes and narrates. Where Johnson and his subject, "Swift," appear to be antipathetic personalities, we find that they are opposed across the visual space in which Johnson can know Swift. Johnson's visual control over the empirical space in which he sees Swift is evident in the epistemological claims of sentences like "He was always careful of his money" and "It is apparent, that he must have had the habit of noting whatever he observed"; Johnson even claims, with unequivocal authority, that "the last face that he knew was that of Mrs. Whiteway."[16] That Johnson equates observation and knowledge so emphatically in *Swift* indicates that Swift's life and his writing are too "volatile and evanescent" to serve Johnson's paradoxes. It also indicates that the climactic story of Swift's imbecility, relying as it does on truisms of eighteenth-century psychology and the aesthetic theory it supported, threatens biography with the possibility of its failure as a genre. In the long string of illnesses and attitudes that, we are told, gradually close the avenues of his perception, Johnson's "Swift" closes down the fiction of transparency on which Johnson's biography relies. Perhaps Johnson's *Swift* is not a window onto the man but an inadvertent allegory of biography as "Swift": a mistimed confusion of excessive rage and dumb impartiality, a body without perception, left on display. In the grand parallelisms with which the biographer displays Swift's fate as tragically inevitable and apt, we can see Johnson create a visual perspective designed to protect his text's ideally transparent surface from its own distorting temporality.

If the bizarre anecdote of Swift's obstinate "resolution . . . never to wear spectacles" seems to be a slim thread on which to hang this argument, consider that, whether or not it was true, the story records the popular perception that Swift had refused to say "I see." In this refusal, Swift renounces not just eyeglasses but a concept of the subject. The way that Johnson displays Swift's body, and the suffering through which that body bears the effects of Swift's refusal, suggests that the entire episode can be seen as precisely directed to affirm and preserve the optical metaphor for consciousness by scapegoating Swift's challenge to it, his "ridiculous resolution" against it. The moral closure of Johnson's text turns on a suppressed pun (spectacles-spectacle) which recalls that the biographical subject is not real but is constituted in a visual metaphor. Within the metaphor, the concept of optical distance creates and rationalizes the differentiations of subject and object, inside and outside, literal and figurative, that make psychological biography possible. Not only does the metaphor "I see" structure moral judgment as the distance of vision and the uniformity of measure, but it enables a perspective point of view to function as a form of judgment.

It is, without a doubt, ironic that the subjection of Swift's body to this spectacle enables us as readers to voice the dangerous pun that holds this visual space together. Where the detail of the repudiated spectacles would establish biography's prerogative by displaying Swift as both guilty and aberrant, the suppressed homonym spectacles-spectacle, with its under-handed allusion to an acquaintance between optical instrumentation and biographical comprehension, begins to reverse that relationship, register-ing both biography's investment in perspective glasses and Swift's as yet only partly explained power to destabilize the genre. Once we have heard the pun, we can see that Johnson's "Swift" goes mad in exactly the way that he does because he refuses to focus his look through the optical metaphor, which is all that sustains the illusion of the text's transparency and the fiction that the biographer controls the time of its writing.

The spectacle of Swift's body as a figure for biography's inevitable mis-timing not only leads back to the theory of consciousness promulgated in Locke's *Essay Concerning Human Understanding*, where the optical met-aphor for consciousness is most explicitly stated, but also highlights those moments in Locke's text when the body resists the optical metaphor and impedes the theoretical time of self-reflection. Like the perspective picture, Locke's philosophy imposes an ideal measure and clarity on the human subject.[17] For example, in prefacing the *Essay Concerning Human Under-standing*, he proposes that he will "take a Survey of our own Understand-ings" so that he can leave "the Extent of our Knowledge . . . discovered, and the horizon found, which sets the boundaries between the enlightened and dark Parts of Things."[18] In setting himself the task of discovering the absolute horizon of human knowledge, Locke explicitly restricts the un-derstanding to a finite space in which the single point of view that is the introspecting self can measure the distances of time and space and the rela-tions among ideas.[19] Of course, his most extended description of the un-derstanding is as a perspective box:

I pretend not to teach, but to enquire; and therefore cannot but confess here again, That external and internal Sensation, are the only passages that I can find, of Knowledge, to the Understanding. These alone, as far as I can discover, are the Windows by which light is let into this *dark Room*. For, methinks, the *Understanding* is not much unlike a Closet wholly shut from light, with only some little openings left, to let in external visible Resemblances, or *Ideas* of things without; would the Pictures coming into such a dark Room but stay there, and lie so orderly as to be found upon occasion, it would very much resemble the Understanding of a Man, in reference to all Objects of sight, and the *Ideas* of them. (*Essay*, II, xi, 17)

Locke's reliance on perspective images becomes particularly important to biography when he extends his claim for measurable and consistent proportions beyond the founding orders of things and ideas to include the complex abstractions of the moral sphere.[20]

The *Idea* of a supreme Being, infinite in Power, Goodness, and Wisdom, whose Workmanship we are, and on whom we depend; and the *Idea* of our selves, as understanding, rational Beings, being such as are clear in us, would, I suppose, if duly considered, and pursued, afford such Foundations of our Duty and Rules of Action, as might place *Morality amongst the Sciences capable of Demonstration*: wherein I doubt not, but from self-evident Propositions, by necessary Consequences, as incontestable as those in Mathematicks, the measures of right and wrong might be made out, to any one that will apply himself with the same Indifferency and Attention to the one, as he does to the other of these Sciences. (*Essay*, IV, iii, 18)

Although Locke characteristically avoids intricate technical language in this passage, his belief that "the measures of right and wrong might be made out" is set between the indifferent point of sight that is the "I" and the twin vanishing points of a mathematical deity and the self-reflective consciousness. His optimistic belief that, given these instruments, we can demonstrate the proportions of moral science is merely inverted in Johnson's melancholy discovery that "there is such an uniformity in the state of man" that "the greatest distance" between men emphasizes their submission to the same measure, to "the same causes still terminating their influences in the same effects" (*Rambler* 60, pp. 182–83).

But this uniformity, which would produce both moral science and biography, depends on the single exception that Locke imposes on the metaphor of the understanding as a perspective box: unlike the pictures cast in that dark "Closet," those coming into the understanding "stay there, and lie so orderly as to be found upon occasion." It is the implied presence of all of these mental pictures, persisting undamaged in their original condition, that creates the possibility that, in introspection, consciousness can comprehend itself in each of its present moments. But in his chapter entitled "Retention," Locke gives us a very different account of the condition of memory, one in which its structure is vulnerable to time and its contents are ephemeral:

The Memory in some Men, 'tis true, is very tenacious, even to a Miracle: But yet there seems to be a constant decay of all our Ideas, even of those which are struck deepest, and in Minds the most retentive; so that if they be not sometimes renewed by repeated Exercise of the Senses, or Reflection on those kind of Objects, which at first occasioned them, the Print wears out, and at last there remains nothing to be seen. Thus the Ideas, as well as Children, of our Youth, often die before us: And our Minds represent to us those Tombs, to which we are approaching; where though the Brass and Marble remain, yet the Inscriptions are effaced by time, and the Imagery moulders away. (Essay, II, x, 5)

The failure of memory described in this passage is an effect of sensory deprivation: as it turns out, the pictures coming into the understanding do not "stay" but wear out and decay unless they are "renewed." Locke's lesson here is that the self requires some upkeep: its coherence and continuity depend on the reiteration of those sensations and reflections that have shaped it thus far, that is, to its present moment. Consciousness arises from the perception of sense impressions and either maintains itself by remembering them or is maintained by receiving new instances of familiar sensations. These revived impressions become necessary because the marks of their originals, stockpiled in an imperfect memory system, are always fading away. Elsewhere in the Essay, Locke figures the final effect of memory's slow fade and age's dulling of the senses as total undifferentiation:

Take one, in whom decrepid old Age has blotted out the Memory of his past Knowledge, and clearly wiped out the Ideas his Mind was formerly stored with; and has, by destroying his Sight, Hearing, and Smell quite, and his Taste to a great degree, stopp'd up almost all the Passages for new ones to enter; or, if there be some of the Inlets yet half open, the Impressions made are scarce perceived, or not at all retained. How far such an one (notwithstanding all that is boasted of innate Principles) is in his Knowledge, and intellectual Faculties, above the Condition of a Cockle, or an Oyster, I leave to be considered. (Essay, II, ix, 14)

It is odd that Locke even pretends to offer us the choice of "a Cockle, or an Oyster," though the move works to emphasize that the examples, like the apparent choice, are featureless. His point, of course, is that without sensation and reflection there is no consciousness and no self, only a body.

Locke's rhetoric implies that the shape of such an ersatz body would be irrelevant. This implication is exaggerated by the graphic lumpishness of Locke's examples, in which the visible differences are overwhelmingly subordinated to the lack of physical distinctions shared by cockles and oysters. In the context of Locke's analysis of memory, this apparent choice means that if the perspective box failed, matter would lose its differentiation into distinct, articulated bodies.

The possibility of disarticulation troubles Locke's figures for memory in the passage quoted above as well. The figure that Locke uses there for the loss of memory is of early, untimely death, of a disordered life cycle in which "the Ideas, as well as Children, of our Youth, often die before us." Here, Locke relies on the central image of a disruption of the natural orders of life and death, children dying before their parents, to figure a failure of memory. The pathos of these dead children convinces us, as we read further, that we are seeing their graves, but in fact Locke goes on to imagine untimely death more intimately — as it is experienced by the understanding in the present moment of its introspection, when "our Minds represent to us those Tombs, to which we are approaching; where though the Brass and Marble remain, yet the Inscriptions are effaced by time, and the Imagery moulders away." This activity of self-reflection creates an image of a conscious graveyard, and so works not only as a figure of untimely death but more specifically as a figure of premature burial: consciousness is made to persist in order to perceive itself encrypted and forgotten. This vision of erasure becomes a possibility as soon as Locke introduces a temporal dimension to the ideally instant comprehension of the mind's eye. Time changes the present, pictorial clarity of self-reflection to the text of memory, where ideas are no longer pictures, they are "Print." Locke's figures for retention show how the necessity for including time and writing as components of identity changes the metaphor of the perspective box. Turning to renew the text of memory, consciousness now finds its "self" disarticulated — reflected in the unreflective surface of the tomb, marked by a stone without inscriptions or images.

Locke's introspective and elegiac account of forgetting finds a counterpart in Johnson's description of the isolation and evacuation of Swift's mind and of Swift's lapse into the uniformity of "perfect silence." The tomb with its effaced "Inscriptions" and rotted "Imagery" stands in Locke's description of memory just where the perfectly silent Swift does in Johnson's *Life of Swift*: as a dumb marker at the site of an untimely death. Consciousness sees itself as we see Swift, reduced to undifferentiated matter — an inarticulate body, as good as a blank gravestone. Swift's journey into perfect silence finds a double in the ghostly reflections among Locke's words that bring vocabulary and syntax spinning down into a perfect and silencing identity. The claim, for example, that "there remains nothing to be seen" once memory is lost is followed by an image of remains. And the statement "our Minds represent to us those Tombs, to which we are approaching" is a collapsing zeugma, where the verb begins to define two objects, and two meanings, but instead ends by identifying subject and object. Our minds represent Tombs because they are tombs, which isn't to say that they don't look like them. And this last moribund representation by and of our minds occurs because objects were not frequently enough represented, or presented again, to the senses. In each of these examples — in the shapelessness of the cockle and the oyster, in the persistence of Swift's silent remains, and in the mistimed tomb of amnesia — an inert and undifferentiated body appears as the distortion produced by time and writing in the optic "I." Time is not "lasting" but "perishing distance" (*Essay*, II, xv, 12), and it distorts clarity and measure with its dissolution. The text of memory reveals that it is impossible to time the writing even of one's own life, much less to write from memory of another.

But what is it about "Swift" that makes him the case against which Johnson's *Life of Swift* must prove that biographical writing can survive the flaws in Locke's optical figures for consciousness? We have seen that, in telling the story of Swift's spectacles, Johnson's text would control the trope of reflection, containing its potential collapse into undifferentiation within an example of biography's power to differentiate and govern through its mastery of the visual field. We can now posit that it is because the text of memory, not the reflecting look, is the paradigmatic form of life writing that Johnson as a biographer must leave Swift "motionless, heedless, and speechless" (p. 466). Swift is disarticulated because "the incidents which give excellence to biography are of a volatile and evanescent kind, such as soon escape the memory" (*Rambler* 60, p. 184). Johnson uses the spectacle of Swift's inert and silent body, that perfect blank, to prevent the figures of his own text from enacting, as explicitly as Locke's does, the collapse of the articulated self that follows from the failure of the optical metaphor for consciousness to accommodate time. Swift's timing is all off, a feature that marks not only his death but his writing as well.

Despite the narrative and epistemological control that Johnson as a biographer gains from his account of Swift's last days, the detail of the repudiated spectacles rebounds against him, a kind of Swiftian revenge. By revealing the link between Swift's fate in *Swift* and the biography's need for an optically organized space, the suppressed homonym spectacles-spectacle becomes a material distortion in Johnson's text, a physical event in the body of the text that disrupts its singular focus on Swift's disempowered and moralized body. This distortion occurs where the perspective biography relies on the concept of consciousness as a look into the mirror, because unless it mirrors its readers, biography can have no usefulness. Swift's spectacles remind us that the mirror forgets time — that is why bodies and not selves appear in mirrors. Conversely, it is the mirror's amnesia that allows us to imagine self-reflection as a timeless event, and allows us to forget the problem of memory's intrusion into the perfect present of vision. Like the converging labyrinth of representation in Locke's passage on lost memories, the homonym spectacles-spectacle denies that conscious reflection is simply an image in the mirror. And it denies as well that the axiomatic self-reflection practiced in biography's contemplation of others can be imagined as the reciprocated contemplation of the image in the mirror. Such configurations follow from the optical metaphor, and the unity they ascribe to the viewing or thinking subject is an effect of that retrospective identification of eye and image. But, properly speaking, reflection is the work of the mirror. We can see this in Locke's comparison of unretained thought to a looking glass:

To think often, and never to retain it so much as one moment, is a very useless sort of thinking; and the Soul in such a state of thinking, does very little, if at all, excell that of a Looking-glass, which constantly receives variety of Images, or *Ideas*, but retains none; they disappear and vanish, and there remain no footsteps of them; the Looking-glass is never the better for such *Ideas*, nor the Soul for such Thoughts. (*Essay*, II, i, 15)

Here the etymology of the word "Ideas" struggles to sustain the homology images-ideas-thoughts that would but cannot separate the looking from the glass. Half personified, this looking glass looks. It is in the partiality of this personification — through which we suddenly see the glass work — that the temporal dimension of self-reflection emerges. With the look of the looking glass, the characteristics of cognitive processes become again the attributes of the mirror. The fleeting reflections in the looking glass are its "Ideas." Thinking that is not retained "does very little, if at all, excell [the thinking] of a Looking-glass." As the mirror works, the figure of thought falls back through the etymology of the idea into the literal image, taking the tenor of the soul with it down into the apparent depths of the mirror. In those apparent depths it becomes clear that consciousness is nothing but the personification of the looking glass, the lingering effect of a trope, the "nothing" that remains to be seen when memory is gone. Where biographical writing accepts the metaphoric identity of vision and thought, it also loosens that identity into a simile which organizes reflection as a self contemplating itself *as* in a mirror. The affront of Swift's writing is to return reflection to the mirror, where it has no self or other and where it exists as the work of the mirror within the mirror.

What does it mean to say that the writing of Swift is the work of the mirror? Within the look of the looking glass, consciousness does not exist as an image of itself. It arises from perception as a virtual image that is focused somewhere between the dialectic surfaces of sensation and reflection. This image is not, strictly speaking, a representation of consciousness. As a virtual image it allows consciousness to be inferred from the fact of representation. In other words, representation is the virtual image of consciousness. I want to stress equally but differently the two words virtual and image. Representation may be said to be the *virtual* image of consciousness because it is the perceptible effect of something otherwise ineffable, and it may be said to be the virtual *image* because, though it is focused, it occupies an only apparent location. It is within the relation of this virtual image to the real images of perceived objects from which it is indistinguishable that the aspect of premature burial appears in the optical metaphor. Locke argues against understanding consciousness as a particular content, suggesting instead that it is a characteristic activity, that "the perception of Ideas [is] . . . to the Soul, what motion is to the Body, not its Essence, but one of its Operations" (II, i, 10). This operation is nothing more than the work of the mirror, and the thoughts and ideas that represent it are nothing but the afterlives of perceptual activity. Thus representation, as the virtual image of consciousness, brings the activity that is consciousness into cognitive focus only by imaging it in its silent afterlife, as "Ideas." The work of the mirror reveals consciousness, figured as self-reflection, to be itself an afterlife; it reveals the need for representation, or the text of memory, to be the stone marking the site of a premature burial.

In his article "Johnson and the Meaning of Life," Lawrence Lipking tells us that "Johnson's fear of death is more properly fear of the afterlife, in our terms, and death neither gives life its meaning nor takes it away."[21] Where Swift's writing works as a mirror, it provokes that fear in Johnson, and it works that way by refusing to imagine that perspective distance endows the self with any special coherence and by refusing to ignore the necessary connection between self-reflection and untimely death. In this, Swift's writing explicitly rejects the distance that endows a text with its "own" consistent point of view, a distance from which we traditionally infer an authorial consciousness. The multiplicity of speakers in Swift, the mercurial personae that have thwarted so many readings of his works, are aspects of this refusal. It is as if the "Swift" that Johnson immobilizes in an unperceiving body possesses in his writing the adjustable organs that Locke imagines the angels may use in order to know all things:

Whether one great advantage some of them [angels] have over us, may not lie in this, that they can so frame, and shape to themselves Organs of Sensation or Perception, as to suit them to their present Design, and the Circumstances of the Object they would consider. For how much would that Man exceed all others in Knowledge, who had but the Faculty so to alter the Structure of his Eyes, that one Sense, as to make it capable of all the several degrees of Vision, which the assistance of Glasses (casually at first light on) has taught us to conceive? What wonders would he discover, who could so fit his Eye to all sorts of Objects, as to see, when he pleased, the Figure and Motion of the minute Particles in the Blood, and other juices of Animals, as distinctly, as he does, at other times, the shape and motion of the Animals themselves. But to us in our present State, unalterable Organs, so contrived, as to discover the Figure and Motion of the minute parts of Bodies, whereon depend those sensible Qualities, we now observe in them, would, perhaps be of no advantage. (*Essay*, II, xxiii, 13)

Eyes capable of the adjustments that Locke describes here almost cease to be eyes by giving up, as they do, that distance from the object of view that he associates with the ideals of objective and indifferent knowledge. Adjustable eyes are the organs of infinity: they perceive without the bounded horizon that defines perspective space and human self-reflection. Such sensory relativism remains, for Locke, a heavenly possession and privilege. Swift himself imagines the adaptation of the visual organ to its object as the aging lover's anodyne in "Stella's Birthday":

> 'Tis true, but let it not be known,
> My eyes are somewhat dimmish grown;
> For nature, always in the right,
> To your decays adapts my sight,
> And wrinkles undistinguished pass,
> For I'm ashamed to use a glass;
> And till I see them with these eyes,
> Whoever says you have them lies.[22]

In *The Life of Swift*, however, Johnson describes a scene in which the eye's adaptation is transformed into an exquisite and pointed physical suffering: "Next year (1742) he had an inflammation in his left eye, which swelled it to the size of an egg, with boils in other parts; he was kept long waking with the pain, and was not easily restrained by five attendants from tearing out his eye" (p. 466).[23] It is hard now to understand Johnson's narrative of this event, in which Swift's eye is physically enlarged and deformed, as anything other than the "just" result of Swift's refusal to conform to the measure and proportion of the optical metaphor. He refused to wear his spectacles and to abide by the conventions of perspective distance that control the optical metaphor for consciousness; without that governance, his eye swelled to suit itself to "the Circumstances of the Object [it] would consider." In what Johnson describes as the "inflammation" of Swift's eye, Swift's visual organ begins to break down the distance between the interior, thinking subject and the objects of its view.

Locke relegates the confusion inherent in the possibility of adjustable eyes to another world and so retains the optical distance of perspective in his analysis of consciousness and identity. He holds the ideas that constitute human self-knowledge distinct by recovering the mind's perspective from the momentary and merely nominal anamorphoses induced by names:

Another default, which makes our *Ideas* confused, is, when though the particulars that make up any *Idea*, are in number enough; yet though they are so *jumbled together*, that it is not easily discernable, whether it more belongs to the Name that is given it, than to any other. There is nothing properer to make us conceive this Confusion, than a sort of Pictures usually shewn, as surprizing Pieces of Art, wherein the Colours, as they are laid by the Pencil on the Table it self, mark out very odd and unusual Figures, and have no discernable order in their Position. This Draught, thus made up of parts, wherein no Symmetry nor Order appears, is, in it self, no more a confused Thing, than the Picture of a cloudy Sky; wherein though there be as little order of Colours, or Figures to be Found, yet no body thinks it a confused Picture. What is it then, that makes it be thought confused, since want of Symmetry does not? As it is plain it does not: for another Draught made, barely in imitation of this, could not be called confused. I answer, That which makes it be thought confused, is the applying it to some Name, to which it does no more discernibly belong, than to some other. *v.g.* When it is said to be the Picture of a Man, or *Cesar*, then any one with reason counts it confused: because it is not discernible, in that state, to belong more to the name Man, or *Cesar*, than to the name Baboon, or *Pompey*: which are supposed to stand for different *Ideas*, from those signified by Man, or *Cesar*. But when a cylindrical Mirrour, placed right, hath reduced those irregular Lines on the Table, into their due order and proportion, then the Confusion ceases, and the Eye presently sees, that it is a Man, or *Cesar*; *i.e.* that it belongs to those Names; and that it is sufficiently distinguishable from a Baboon or *Pompey*; *i.e.* from the *Ideas* signified by those Names. (*Essay*, II, xxix, 8)

Once again, the mirror has the power to differentiate: it will resolve the anamorphosis into either Caesar or Pompey, man or baboon.[24] The mirror articulates language and, with it, the body. This particular catoptric mirror not only restores the "due order and proportion" to the chaos of lines reflected in it, but also adds a convincing three-dimensionality to the metaphor of self-reflection, reorganizing the scattered subject around the cylinder's center. Locke's use of a catoptric mirror to retrieve identity (Caesar or Pompey) from the highly artificial distortions of an anamorphosis back into our perspective view brings me, finally, to an excerpt from Swift's *Tale of a Tub*, in which the dominance of the eye is perplexed by a sequence of visual puns:

For, it is the Opinion of Choice Virtuosi, that the Brain is only a Crowd of little Animals, but with Teeth and Claws extremely sharp, and therefore, cling together in the Contexture we behold, like the Picture of Hobbes' Leviathan, or like Bees in perpendicular swarm upon a Tree, or like a Carrion corrupted into Vermin, still preserving the Shape and Figure of the Mother Animal.[25]

Whereas we have seen perspective biography rely on the illusion of a transparent text and the space of optical distance, Swift shows us another version of "the Contexture we behold." Here the picture of optical identity undergoes not a perspectival anamorphosis but a transformation into the temporal body. A parody of empiricism's pretensions, Swift's picture of the "Brain" multiplies visual identities in a violent dismemberment of the ideal distance of self-reflection and the mind's eye, breaking its fictional equation of self and sight into a "Crowd of little Animals." "Like" and "or," the rhetorical equivalents of the mirror, do not establish but dissolve distinctions, allowing the surface of the text to erupt in visual identities. We can now read Swift's final image, of "a Carrion corrupted into Vermin, still preserving the Shape and Figure of the Mother Animal," as the antithesis of the spectacular space in which Johnson places Swift's body: in Swift's text, body is a palimpsest in which we see the past, present, and future in congress. Whereas Johnson's *Swift* would preserve biography as a genre by substituting the spectacle of Swift's untimely death for its own mistiming, this body is not even buried: it is merely transformed. Given Johnson's commitment to his genre, perhaps it is not so surprising that he should say of Swift's *Tale of a Tub* that "there is in it such a . . . swarm of thoughts" (Boswell, *Life of Johnson*, p. 595). In the visual space of Johnson's biographies, thoughts do not swarm, they see.

Part 2

Technologies of Seeing

The charm'd eye

PETER DE BOLLA

$\mathcal{T}$his is an essay in the historical recovery of the activity of looking. It attempts to ground an analysis of looking in both an archival and a theoretical account of the metaphorics of the eye. This metaphorics is deeply embedded in eighteenth-century visuality and its attendant grammar of looking, but it has also been brought out of the archival record by a contemporary theoretical perspective on how the subject is inserted in the look. In the space of this brief essay it will only be possible to hint at this contemporary perspective, which is elaborated in greater detail in the larger work of which this is a part.[1]

The charm'd eye is one figure among a large number which constitute an eighteenth-century metaphorics of the eye. Other figures in which the eye is "thrown" or "carried," or in which it is filled up, sated, or alternatively hungry or restless give a preliminary sense of what I hope might be conveyed by this term. It is important to stress here that this metaphorics is embedded in eighteenth-century models of vision and visuality and is, in a sense, one of the ways in which these models figure the facts of vision. Indeed, the "truth" of the visual realm is primarily understood via reference to such a metaphorics. In noting this I shall insist upon the distance between an Enlightenment model of the visual realm, or visuality, and later models developed in the nineteenth and twentieth centuries, with the major focus of difference lying in the degree to which visuality is held to be constructed primarily upon the terrain of the body (nineteenth-century anatomies of vision) or alternatively upon the social and cultural (Enlightenment mappings of visuality). Although each and every age constructs its own metaphorics of the eye and corresponding "truth" of vision, the extent to which this metaphorics is openly held to ground the facts of vision differs. In the following I shall endeavor to make the case that for the eighteenth century the facts of sight can only be known through the metaphorics of the eye, which is to say that the "truth" of vision is precisely worked out in visuality, in the social and cultural domains, not in the anatomic. On account of this, visuality is the ground upon which vision is mapped, not vice versa.[2]

Introduction

If looking, which shall be defined below, is a culturally determined activity, how might we begin to recover specifically *historical* instances of it? Clearly we will need to delimit the field of our inquiry, since looking entails a vast array of different practices and occurs in a variety of contexts. The specific task, then, will be to describe and analyze the activity of looking in and at the landscape garden at a very precise moment in the larger history of this activity, that is, in the second half of the eighteenth century in England. The selection of this particular moment is far from arbitrary, for it is precisely the point at which a range of competing discourses begin to create considerable friction in their singular and combined attempts to define not only how and in what manner the landscape shall be represented but also, and perhaps more fundamentally, how it might represent particular interests, be they slanted by considerations of class, profession, or gender.[3] In this way both the land, and how it might be used, and the landscape, and how it might look, become terms around which considerable energy and friction are generated.

However, in moving swiftly to the central argument of this essay we shall pass over a number of important observations about the relationships between land and landscape at this period, all of which bear insistently upon the political and economic environment framing contemporary representations. Consequently my single-mindedness of purpose in the discussion of the landscape garden and the activities of looking at and in it runs the risk of avoiding or erasing extremely important economic and political motivations governing the transformation of land into landscape. We do well to remember here that the eighteenth-century garden was created by carving out of the land territory which had been used previously in different ways — let us say, for productive purposes — and also that economic considerations about land *use* were certainly heeded in the construction of landscape parks. Be this as it may, it is nevertheless the case that histories of the garden from Walpole to the present day have tended to forget this fact in deference to "purely" aesthetic considerations about the internal history of design.[4] For the purposes of the present argument it will be enough to call to mind that the garden we shall look at was termed a *ferme ornée*, and this will serve to highlight that we are silently passing over these practical considerations governing land use which are coincident with our productive needs for the land. That garden, William Shenstone's Leasowes, was created between 1743 and 1763, and the bulk of the material I shall investigate is taken from textual accounts of visits to the garden. I stress the textual here because the ways in which an experience of looking can be understood in relation to textual forms will be commented upon below. However, before we enter this garden a few general comments about the context for these visits is required.

The middle decades of the eighteenth century in England witnessed a considerable increase in domestic tourism.[5] The people engaged in this pursuit were substantially drawn from the professional classes, and indeed a profession grew up around the specific activity of documenting the landscape — many of the accounts of country estates that survive in published form were written by agriculturalists and local historians or topographers. There is an immediate distinction to make, then, between on the one hand a leisure-time pursuit and on the other a nascent professional activity which has as its object the gathering of specific knowledge. The latter, often referred to as a "tour," might describe, for example, the landscape of a particular county and document not only the grand houses and gardens contained within it but also the farming and husbandry techniques employed by local men and women who worked the land.[6] A further distinction is required here, since our central preoccupation in what follows shall be the examination of how viewers were instructed in the activity of looking at the landscape — something which might pertain to both leisure-time tourists and local topographers — evidence for which is primarily taken from textual forms. In the case of topographers or local historians such ways of looking are distorted and complicated by concerns adjacent to those governing the appreciation of the visual domain in and for itself, which is to say that looking in these latter cases is colored by other interests.[7] The following account is, therefore, partial, since it omits discussion of those "tours" which were undertaken for primarily documentary purposes, and it privileges accounts of the eye in its modes of looking over economic, social, or political points of view equally textualized in such accounts.

A second strand of the context for viewing is generated by the development of what we now term the landscape arts, which, from around the second decade of the century, began to take on the form of a coherent set of strictures and aesthetic principles concerned with how the landscape should look. These principles governed not only the creation of the English garden, in all its various styles — landscape, park, *ferme ornée* — but also the experience of uncultivated countryside (evidenced most clearly in the picturesque movement).[8] The feature of this coherent set of strictures I wish to foreground is the almost universal claim made by writers on the landscape arts that the landscape garden represents the unique contribution of English culture to the arts. In this way eighteenth-century histories of the English garden, most notably those by Horace Walpole and Thomas Whately, make specifically nationalistic arguments on behalf of the garden. At the time of their construction, then, parklands and landscape gardens were to be understood as expressions of Englishness.

Perhaps the most common form for this proclamation of national identity was the construction of oppositional national styles. There was little consistency to this ploy, so that a particular garden style might at one time be termed French, at another Dutch. This informs us less about changing attitudes to the Dutch or the French in eighteenth-century England than it signals the highly motivated form of eighteenth-century garden historiography and its presentist concerns. Walpole's history, for example, quite deliberately constructs a narrative about the English garden which is manifestly politicized around both the look of the garden and the access given to potential lookers within the landscape. Such ideologies informing the present of writing are everywhere in his "History of Modern Taste in Gardening": they range from his famous proclamation of Kent as the inventor of the English garden, a story fully embedded in almost all subsequent histories, to his explicit statement that the growth of landscaping was linked with political stability and perfection. In Walpole's words: "The English Taste in Gardening is thus the growth of the English Constitution, & must perish with it."[9]

By the 1760s, then, England was developing a highly nationalistic historiography of the landscape garden, which was itself changing in form. This change in how the landscape looked has been described by John Dixon Hunt as the movement from an emblematic to an expressionistic garden, terms which he takes from Whately's *Observations on Modern Gardening* (1770).[10]

Furthermore, the cultural environment in which these changes took place was also complexly informed by two specific activities: the first, noted above, was domestic tourism, and the second, the public viewing and display of art, both of which expanded very considerably indeed from mid-century on.[11] Consequently we should see the development of the landscape garden within this complex cultural milieu, not only in order to understand in more supple ways the overly nationalistic framework in which the history of the garden was told, but also to register the interconnections between how the landscape looked and how it was supposed to appear and to have appeared. In other words this cultural form, the English landscape garden, was necessarily implicated within modes of looking which were changing in response to as well as in advance of the object — the English garden — of sight. Hence these modes of looking were both productive of how the landscape looked and responsive to its changing styles. Thus, if we take John Dixon Hunt's argument at face value and assume that the *design* of gardens changed from emblematic to expressionistic forms, then it must follow that visitors and patrons alike also underwent a shift in how they appreciated these different forms, that is, how they looked.[12]

So what were these modes of looking? If we continue with the terms taken from Whately and elaborated upon by Hunt, we can begin to sketch the differences between an emblematic and an expressionistic viewing experience. Early eighteenth-century gardens in emblematic form require a mode of looking that strives to decode the messages played out in three-dimensional space.[13] Such gardens must be read in a highly systematic way — Stowe and Stourhead are the finest exemplars — whereas the later eighteenth-century garden in an expressionistic form has a far looser structure, almost abandoning a precise or systematic semiosis in favor of a set of associative triggers designed to prompt a sentimental or emotive response.[14] Thus, behind these two distinct designs are two differing assumptions about how to look. The first uses the eyes only in order to corroborate what the mind already knows; the second requires the evidence of the eye in order to stimulate a feeling or emotion.

If we make this distinction in modes of looking more precise, we can say that the first kind of garden, the Stowe type, requires what I shall term the studious gaze; furthermore it demands that the looker be educated in a semiprivate semantic and semiotic system, so that he or she might pick up specific references to a highly temporary (in the sense of it being relevant only to the lifetime of the framers of the allegorical system) set of coded meanings. A good example here is the playful Temple of British Worthies at Stowe, which requires that the viewer know not only who the various depicted people are but also their connections to a very specific political environment. You simply don't get the joke if you are ignorant of the personalities involved in the high politics of the period.[15] This kind of sealed, semiprivate universe of discourse is not unique to the landscape garden; it is a pervasive feature of Augustan modes in the arts. My point here is that in the emblematic garden one can only look from a highly specified vantage point, and the price of entry into that restricted culture of looking is, by any standards, exclusive. Such exclusivity depends upon the continuing educational and social elitism which trains the eye to rest on the object of attention, peering studiously until it gives up its meanings. It is a gaze founded in knowledge, a knowing eye that teases out allusions and delights in the play of wit. This first kind of looking is based in textuality, in a cultural education founded on classical literature, and the visual experience resulting from it is one in which various texts are, as it were, given body before one's eyes.

The second kind of garden, the expressionistic, requires a sentimental look in which the eye moves in and around the three-dimensional space, registering incident and contrast, generating expectation, and delighting in surprise. This garden typically contains aural as well as visual stimulation, both of which serve to animate the viewer into a sequential experience of distinct sensations.[16] Here visual experience has little to do with gleaning what is meant and all to do with the emotive response of the looker: the viewer's body is the text within which the garden is made visible. In the sentimental look the body is where the meanings are, whereas in the studious gaze the text is embodied in the visual domain of the garden.

We will take the Leasowes to represent this second kind of garden, which, as I hope to demonstrate below, not only requires another form of looking but also explicitly sets out to educate the eye through the viewing experience.[17] Consequently the sentimental look, in its contentment with surfaces which hurry the looker from one visual stimulus to another, leads the eye through the landscape, throwing the eye here and holding it up there in an educative progress. One need only look to see here, and all that looking requires is an eye prepared to be charm'd.

The differences between these modes of looking become most sharply focused if we think of alternative objects held up to view. Painting, for example, will be more likely to generate the studious gaze (and perhaps require it) than the sentimental look, but here again different painterly genres might make differing demands. Perhaps the most striking contrast between the modes is the seductions of fantasy created by the sentimental look, in which fantasy becomes the terrain upon which looking is played out. In this sense the screen onto which the eye projects its image in the look is fantasy itself.

Thus, if we think of the garden experience, the studious gaze operative in the emblematic garden requires intellection at a fairly high level as the viewer searches for the code needed to break in upon the semiosis of its buildings, grottoes, and statues, whereas the encouragement of the viewer's own response in the expressionistic garden prompts reveries and fantasy. These differences in modes of looking can also be seen in terms of the public and private, where Stowe represents a particular kind of public cultural form and the contemplative garden of the Leasowes a private one.[18] The final section of this essay will dwell upon the particular inflections of this shift from the public to the private in relation to the aesthetics of a specifically male fantasy experience generated in and by the landscape of seclusion.[19]

To summarize this introductory section: if a change in modes of looking is indeed consonant with the alterations in the style of the English landscape garden, then we are able to construct an interactive analysis of a historical cultural form. Looking, the activity we are here taking as a cultural form, is both a response to the changing object, the cultural product that is the landscape garden, and at the same time a formative power contributing to the changes in design of "real" landscapes. The one feeds into and upon the other in ways which in the third section of this essay will produce an account of the fantasy, termed the sentimental look. That this fantasy is equally one of the determining features of the project to historically recover the activity of looking, or any other cultural form, is the larger point that I hope the reader might take from here.

Directions from Shenstone: How to Look in the Leasowes

Now I shall take one garden, William Shenstone's Leasowes, and examine the ways in which contemporary eighteenth-century visitors to the garden went about the business of looking in and at it.[20] In 1747 the poet William Shenstone took over control of a modest family farm of 300 acres near Hales-Owen in Shropshire, and he spent the rest of his life creating one of the most important gardens in eighteenth-century England.[21] The interest of this garden for the current argument stems from the fact that Shenstone's efforts at landscaping lie on the cusp between the emblematic style and the expressionistic. It is partly happenstance that this should be so, since had Shenstone been considerably more wealthy than he was, it is at least possible that he would have created a far more classically allusive and monumental garden than he did. This speculation aside, the Leasowes of mid-century combined elements of the emblematic in the form of classical inscriptions, urns, and statues with the looser expressionistic and sentimental form which emerged after mid-century. The garden conformed to the "circuit" principle, ordering a set of views and experiences as one moved in and through the garden, but it lacked a specific allegorical meaning as can be found, for example, at Stourhead.[22]

The garden was one of the most visited in the country, but after Shenstone's death in 1763 it changed hands very frequently — as many as ten times in as many years, according to Goldsmith — and was altered considerably.[23] Today the post-Shenstone house serves as a clubhouse for a golf course, which has incorporated part of the garden into its fairways and greens.

Shenstone left us "Unconnected Thoughts on Gardening," which will provide a convenient means of entry into the garden he created. There are strands in "Thoughts" which clearly look back toward early eighteenth-century taste in the layout of grounds, such as the insistence on "variety," which can be found in Shaftesbury as well as Addison. For Shenstone variety, along with novelty, can be carried too far: "Variety however, in some instances, may be carried to such excess as to lose its whole effect. I have observed ceilings so crammed with stucco-ornaments; that, although of the most different kinds, they have produced an uniformity" (p. 127). The terms operative here — variety, novelty, uniformity — became a commonplace of early eighteenth-century aesthetic debate and were finally given canonical form in Burke's *Philosophical Enquiry* (1757). Shenstone, however, begins to depart from the mainstream of debate in his investigations of the metaphorics of the eye. We learn, for example, that "objects should indeed be less calculated to strike the immediate eye, than the judgment" (p. 126), or that the "eye requires a sort of balance" in experiencing variety (p. 129). The purpose of these investigations is to ascertain reasons for an increasing dissatisfaction with an older, more formal style of garden layout. Shenstone writes:

It is not easy to account for the fondness of former times for strait-lined avenues to their houses; strait-lined walks through their woods; and, in short, every kind of strait-line; where the foot is to travel over, what the eye has done before. . . . To stand still and survey such avenues, may afford some slender satisfaction, through the change derived from perspective; but to move on continually and find no change of scene in the least attendant on our change of place, must give actual pain to a person of taste. (p. 130)

Governing these precepts is a central preoccupation with the well-being of the eye, which "must be easy, before it can be pleased" (p. 133). It is this concern with a bodily response to the visual field which places Shenstone with later sentimental theorists of visuality. In point of fact Shenstone was not alone in developing this more responsive theory, and it is instructive to briefly consider another set of comments on landscape gardening which were certainly known to him.

Sir John Dalrymple composed his "Essay on Landscape Gardening" during the 1750s, and Robert Dodsley attempted to obtain it for Shenstone in December 1759. By March 1760, Shenstone had certainly received a copy of this work, so its observations were known to the author of "Unconnected Thoughts."[24] Dalrymple outlines a theory of the sentiments that are aroused by different visual experiences. In relation to the laying out of gardens he writes that "there seem in nature to be four different dispositions of grounds, distinct from each other, and which create distinct and separate sentiments" (p. 147). It is these distinct sentiments which give rise to a set of varying responses to the landscape. The "first situation," Dalrymple writes, "is that of a highland country, consisting of great and steep mountains, rocks, lakes, impetuous rivers &c." This kind of countryside arouses "in the breast of the beholder" a sentiment which everyone feels. That sentiment is "grandeur." Dalrymple continues in this manner, outlining a further three "dispositions" of grounds, all of which raise distinct sentiments in the viewer. This very programmatic form of response is somewhat softened in Shenstone's thoughts on the garden, but it is nevertheless very clearly the case that in constructing his own garden he attempted to create a landscape that prompted fantasy and feeling responses and that required the spectator to see with the inner eye as much as the outer.[25]

If we now examine how that landscape was experienced by Shenstone's contemporary and friend Robert Dodsley, we can enlarge the above comments on the metaphorics of the eye.[26] The account appended to Shenstone's posthumously published *Works* was to form the basis of a number of subsequent accounts of the garden, all of which plundered Dodsley's text selectively.

One of the most renowned aspects of this garden, and one Dodsley commented upon, was the sense of being in a "natural" landscape: the hand of art was fully concealed.[27] The term "natural" is always problematic, since it conveys both the sense of derived from the natural world and the sense of something being proper, as it should be in and of itself. Of course this latter sense is continually open to revision as different interests compete over the precise definition of how something should be. As far as Dodsley was concerned, however, Shenstone had respected the hand of nature: "Far from violating its natural beauties, Mr Shenstone's only study was to give them their full effect."[28] This is an illusion created by much "thought and labour," but one which is fundamental to the entire experience of the garden. Here, one *feels* oneself in a landscape unadorned or contaminated by human artifice, and that feeling allows one to experience the well-being of the eye.

This well-being results from a continual attention on the part of the designer to the eye's needs and desires. So we learn that at one point "the back ground of this scene is very beautiful, and exhibits a picture of villages and varied ground, finely held up to the eye" (p. 338), whereas a little further on we are led "by a pleasing serpentine walk" to a narrow glade where we find a common bench "which affords a retiring place secluded from every eye, and a short respite, during which the eye reposes on a fine amphitheatre of wood and thicket" (p. 339). It is important to remark the various needs of the eye here—that it be both active and at rest, both seeing and unseen—since these form the basis upon which a grammar of looking will be constructed in the wider cultural domain of visuality. Thus, some moments of the garden visit may encourage being seen while engaged in the activity of looking, and others will require seclusion and the refusal of the catoptric look.

Continuing the circuit of the garden we come to another view of the Priory, a fake ruinated structure, which is "more advantageous, and at a better distance, to which the eye is led down a green slope, through a scenery of tall oaks, in a most agreeable manner" (p. 344). The eye is then conducted to a narrow opening and on toward a path which "winds on betwixt two small benches, each of which exhibits a pleasing landskip, which cannot escape the eye of a connoisseur" (p. 349). The eye continues to "travel" and to be "drawn" to various objects in the visual field until the spectator reaches the cascade. At this point the "eye rambles to the left, where one of the most beautiful cascades imaginable is seen by way of incident, through a kind of vista, or glade, falling down a precipice over-arched with trees, and strikes us with surprise" (p. 365). In all these descriptions the viewer is educated into the visual experience via the movement and motion of the eye; and what tells the eye how to move is the visual field itself, that is, Shenstone's creation of the garden. What we have been following, then, is an educative progress which instructs the visitor to the garden in the grammar of visuality.

At this point in the tour the spectator has reached the most splendid artifice, the cascade, which Dodsley remarks upon in the following rather breathless manner:

It is impossible to express the pleasure which one feels on this occasion, for though surprise alone is not excellence, it may serve to quicken the effect of what is beautiful. I believe none ever beheld this grove, without a thorough sense of satisfaction; and were one to chuse any one particular spot of this perfectly Arcadian farm, it should, perhaps, be this. (p. 365)

This is the culmination of a fantasy experience in which one's feelings or sentiments overrun ratiocination. Here the imagination is stimulated into excessive activity and the spectator feels transported to another world.[29] It is noteworthy that these fantasy elements of Dodsley's insertion into visuality were excised from the reprinted versions of his description.

The first of these reprints, though not signaled as such, appeared in 1767 in *The English Connoisseur*, the collection of descriptions of "palaces and seats of the nobility and principal gentry of England" put together by Thomas Martyn. A careful comparison of the reprinted version with Dodsley's original yields a very clear logic to the principles governing excision. Martyn, and we assume tourists of his persuasion, seems to have been embarrassed by or at least uncomfortable with the notion of printing those sections of Dodsley's description which move closest to the fantasy experience outlined above.

Thus, for example, the first omission gives a good indication of the type of cuts made throughout. After the first poem "Here in a cool grot," appearing in both texts, Dodsley writes: "These sentiments correspond as well as possible with the ideas we form of the abode of fairies; and appearing deep in this romantic vally, serve to keep alive such enthusiastic images while this sort of scene continues" (p. 336). Four pages later Dodsley writes: "The eye is presented with a fairy vision, consisting of an irregular and romantic fall of water, very unusual, one hundred and fifty yards in continuity, and a very striking scene it affords" (p. 341). Again this has been excised by Martyn in conformity with the earlier cut. What this seems to indicate is a movement away from the "romantic" associations of a fairyland summoned up by Dodsley which determine to some extent his visual responses to the landscape.[30] I shall suggest some reasons for this in the third part of the essay where I discuss masculinity as it arises in the experience of looking.

Dodsley's text was reprinted a second time, again unattributed, in *A New Display of the Beauties of England* in 1787. The text here has undoubtedly been taken from Martyn's *English Connoisseur*, since it follows all the cuts made there. The central difference of this later version is the addition of English translations for the Latin inscriptions. The market for this book was clearly not the same as that for Shenstone's *Works*; this alerts us to the changing composition of the social background of tourists as the century moved into its last decades.[31]

We should pause to remark one further curiosity in these reprints of Dodsley's description. If we take as reliable evidence Goldsmith's "The History of a Poet's Garden" (1773), the Leasowes had undergone considerable change since the poet's death in 1763. Goldsmith writes:

I was led into this train of thinking upon lately visiting the beautiful gardens of the late Mr Shenstone, who was himself a Poet, and possessed of that warm imagination which made him ever foremost in the pursuit of flying happiness. Could he but have forseen the end of all his schemes, for whom he was improving, and what changes his designs were to undergo, he would have scarcely amused his innocent life with what, for several years, employed him in a most harmless manner, and abridged his scanty fortune. As the progress of this Improvement is a true picture of sublunary vicissitude, I could not help calling up my imagination, which, while I walked pensively along, suggested the following Reverie.[32]

This creates an even stranger scenario in which the 1787 reprinting of Dodsley's description could not have possibly corresponded with the garden as it then looked. The textual account, therefore, not only prescribes how to look at the garden, it actually functions as the "real" of looking, standing in the place of the evidence of the eyes.[33] Shenstone's instructions here become rather more than guides to how to look — they stand in the place of the visual itself. Where before one consulted the text in order to direct the look, in this later instance the text has become the eyes of the beholder. This deformation requires comment, since it suggests a counter-reading of the educative purpose of the garden. If Shenstone's text came to function as the law of sight, as that which determined what should be seen, then the metaphorics of the eye is overruled. In other words Shenstone's purpose was to educate the viewer in and through the activity of looking; here in the later situation it appears that one looks through the veil of the text, and this text begins to operate as the letter of the law.

If the foregoing gives some preliminary indications as to how the designer of this garden wished to instruct the eye of the viewer, we can test these against a lengthy account of a visit to the garden in 1777 by Joseph Heely. The turn to an archival source prompts a brief caveat. We should take care to note, for example, that the descriptions we shall examine do not constitute a "true" record of how visitors looked in the garden. Eighteenth-century visitors "looked" in highly determined ways, and, perhaps even more important, they framed their descriptions of what they saw according to the available generic models for accounts, whether touristic or agricultural/topographical. This observation, of course, merely reinforces what we have already staked as the terrain of this essay, namely, the cultural formation of the activity of looking. That the text under discussion "codes" the "real" of looking is, therefore, not an obstruction but on the contrary a significant aid to our inquiry.

Masculinity, Fantasy: The Sentimental Look

Heely published his account in *Letters on the Beauties of Hagley, Envil and the Leasowes*, 2 vols. (London, 1777), and in turning to the first of these letters we immediately come across a contrast between the country and the city. Although this binary pairing might be taken as conventional — it is of course a motif found in classical literature and continues to be productively used today — it is nevertheless an exceptionally fraught pairing in mid-eighteenth-century England.[34] Quite aside from the political ramifications of this contrast, what is equally noteworthy is that Heely makes the comparison in terms which have specific resonances of gender distinction. Heely has already informed us that gardening "fills the mind with every flattering sensation" and "charms the eye" (1: 5), which immediately places his description within the orbit of seduction. What is going to be confused in his account, however, is the operation of this seductive pleasure across the divide of gender. Put simply, it will be difficult to ascertain the precise structure of gender ascription in Heely's landscape. Hence what we might take to be our own rather crude imposition of a masculine gaze which goes to a female nature for its seductive pleasures will not yield much in terms of analytic precision. Although such commonplaces of contemporary figurings of the gaze may well stand in back of the following description, they only form a part of the complex distributions of gender-slanted terms. Here is Heely making the contrast between the pleasures of the country and the city:

The mind when surrounded by the pageantry of courts, the noise and bustle of cities, and the idle dissipations of a vicious, misguided multitude, is bewildered and confined; sinks into a contemptible effeminacy; is lost to every manly reflection; and dead to the tender feelings both of humanity and friendship: but in the calm undisturbed hours of retirement it is free, and open to every great and generous reflection worthy its dignity. (1: 6–7)

The semantic horizon of implication and nuance around the use of gender indicators in this extract is clearly highly ordered, sophisticated, and extremely complex. It would be a mistake to imagine that Heely is, in some sense, crossing his wires or utilizing a density of vocabulary items unconsciously, and equally absurd to imagine that the rather complex inflections of gender filiation are the invention of Joseph Heely. What seems to be happening is the investigation of a simple binary opposition in gender ascription in order to allow for a slightly more various deployment of gender indicators in the description of masculinity.

This can be seen in the rather unusual combination of terms we would ordinarily expect to lean toward one side or other of the gender divide. In these likely contradictory juxtapositions, terms begin to take on more carefully nuanced possibilities for mixed gender. Thus in the extract some terms, such as "effeminacy" or "manly," appear to give clear indications as to their gender filiation while others are more problematic. What of "pageantry," for example, or "noise and bustle"? Are we to take these as being troped masculine or feminine? In general, given the history of our language and its figurative ascription of gender labels, we would expect these things to lean toward masculinity, but Heely's process of thought is all in the opposite direction: an emasculation of the mind by these qualities found in the city takes place. Again, "tender feelings" and "friendship" are commonly troped feminine, yet here also Heely, at least superficially, reverses these oppositions in his claim that they are coincident with manly reflection.

What is, I hope, clear from this is that masculine typologies are being explored and somewhat extended to allow for more "feminine" versions of maleness. Thus the masculine is stretched into an effeminacy caused by an overplus of masculinity — the noise and bustle of the city — and into a softer, more caring "feminine" reflection or retirement. There is, therefore, a flexibility of gender typing, which, we should nevertheless underline as forcefully as possible, acts asymmetrically here in regard to men and women. This is to say that the category of masculinity is not opposed by a simple antagonistic "femininity" but is, rather, one point along a continuous arc which distributes gender categorization. The man, then, has the potential for being, let us say, stereotypically masculine — hard, powerful, aggressive, etc. — or, at another, more distant remove, feminized in the caring, feeling modes of reflection, friendship, and retirement. What this leaves out, and hence the asymmetry, is a corresponding distribution of gender ascription for women.[35]

This extension of the category of masculinity is complexly interwoven with the figurings of the country/city distinction. The city, which for this period would certainly be most obviously associated with masculine tropings, is distinguished by Heely from the softer and more welcoming shades of rural retirement. It is, however, the city in the extract which turns what we must take to be a previously hardened masculine mind into a "contemptible effeminacy." Making effeminate marks the negative extension of the masculine, whereas the tender feeling represents its positive mixed mode. Both, however, point to a conceptualization of the masculine that at the least allows for the possibility of a polyvalent gender. The extent to which this possibility is realized must, for the moment, remain an open question, as must the conscious revisionary force of Heely's invocation of what was, for the eighteenth century, a commonplace, namely, the "effeminacy" of modern society.[36] This is to signal that more than gender, so to speak, is at stake in the fall from unadulterated masculinity.

For present purposes it will be enough to examine the ways in which this expanded conception of masculinity, including both "effeminacy" and the "tender feelings . . . of humanity and friendship," works its way through a number of the prescriptions surrounding the activity of looking at and in the landscape. These prescriptions are in part the response to the threat of seduction which emerges in the garden, most obviously incarnated in the figure of Venus. The full force of this is not directed at the possible licentious activity of sexual arousal but, on the contrary, at being seduced out of or away from prestigious modes of masculinity. It is not the heterosexual that is at stake in civic humanism; rather, it is the homosocial.

This becomes clear when we examine one of the most prominent of these prescriptive indicators, that which makes the requirement that one be alone in the garden. This has already been signaled in the extract above where Heely suggests that one reason for going into the countryside is to get away from the noise of society, the noise of others.[37] Some eighteenth-century gardens, such as the one we are examining, were constructed with this expressly in mind. This having been said, there is a very important distinction to be made between the *desire* to be alone in the landscape and the possibility of actually being in a garden on one's own. It is highly unlikely, for example, that a visit to Shenstone's rural retreat would have taken place in complete solitude. Heely in point of fact visited the garden after Shenstone's death, but even during the poet's lifetime a visit to the Leasowes during the fine-weather months must have been closer to a contemporary bank-holiday visit to an English Heritage country estate than to a solitary walk among shades of retirement.[38]

What needs to be taken account of here is that by the time Heely makes his tour the ideological resonances to depopulated landscape are stacked up high; we might recall that this was the period in which Gray's *Elegy* began to speak for a particular constituency with specific political objectives vis-à-vis the countryside.[39] When Heely expounds upon the pleasures of rural experience he is, then, making an *ideological* commitment and, at the same time, he is constructing a fantasy encounter with the landscape. This, no more or less than Gray, pays scant heed to the "real" of the landscape itself.

Thus, Heely's account of his visit to the three gardens does, to some degree, give us indications of his own individual responses in the activity of looking, but we shall pass over these in order to highlight the extent to which Heely is buying into a more generalized set of ideological assumptions which determine the positionality of his look. This can most easily be achieved through an examination of the ways in which Heely both evokes and contributes to a communal class construction of a fantasy projection. This fantasy, in which the man of taste removes himself from the "real" world in order to gain an authentic experience of another "reality" (this one filtered through various perceptions and protocols governing the activity of looking), becomes a very explicit part of the visit to the Leasowes discussed below.

This communal class fantasy projection has a detailed history during the period. It can be imaged through the invocation of a Claude Lorrain canvas or a wilder, more terrifying Salvator Rosa picture, both of which represent to differing degrees official English cultural modes of "seeing" the landscape; that is, seeing it as if it were a representation on a canvas which conforms to an extremely specific Western high-art tradition (it also requires that one be able to recognize that tradition).[40] Heely, as I shall argue below, is ambivalent in regard to this particular framing, as another possibility exists for him, the production of a framework in which the garden of retirement educates the viewer into a slightly different fantasy projection. This alternative posits as its desired end-point the sense or feeling of authenticity, which ultimately is a sense of being authentic, but that authenticity is purchased at a price, namely, the fall away from an elitism which had hitherto determined modes of looking. In Heely's case there are considerable tensions at work which are resolved in the promotion of the ideal fantasy figure of the poet-gardener himself: William Shenstone, who is the eidetic afterimage of a culture now past projected into the potentially republican present of the look.

When viewed through this lens the entire project of the English landscape garden becomes counter-naturalistic; the point, indeed, is to construct ideologically committed visions of the natural, and to legislate and control the look of things in order that they might be understood as providing prompts for our own self-reflection.[41] In this manner the fantasized projection the viewer overlays upon objects in the world is returned, thereby generating the self-satisfaction of self-reflection, the recognition of authentic being. What this amounts to is the declaration that the viewer is a citizen in the republic of visuality, that I am someone. Consequently the politics of this fantasy projection distributes both the means of access to the garden-as-fantasy and the powers which determine the simulacrum of the natural. Hence the viewing experience represents a site of struggle over which people are allowed into the garden, and, once in, who or what they might see or be seen by.

What I am suggesting here is that the group ethics of an elite Augustan culture are being broken down. One no longer sees with the educated eyes of a classically informed elite, and, correspondingly, the activity of looking itself no longer testifies to one's belonging to that elite. What begins to replace it is an aesthetics of individualism in which the sentimental look is sufficient to indicate one's being part of a republic of visuality: one looks as the eye is directed by the landscape, and in doing so one says, "Look. I am looking." It may well be the case that this more educative and potentially democratizing form of looking is still only a possibility for Heely, who also recognizes the pleasures and advantages of the former elite fantasy projection. It is for this reason that the hesitations in his account are instructive.

Thus, the political inflections of Heely's description all point toward the desires of an upwardly mobile bourgeoisie wishing to distinguish itself from the larger morass of its lower-class compatriots. But as I have suggested, although this is the general direction, it is not the only effect of his description, which also points the other way, toward the opening up of the viewing experience in which the eye trains the observer how to look and what to see.

If we look closely at the kinds of fantasy invoked by Heely, the ramifications of this argument will become apparent. The following, for example, is Heely's description of Lord Lyttleton's seat, Hagley Park:

This elegant scene pertains to a garden, equally with the preceding; and though totally its opposite in every respect, you will be convinced that its intention is to fill the mind with the most romantic ideas; and you cannot help fancying yourself, as you recline upon a screen, under a bush of laurels, near the old oak, to be within those happy regions of the rural deities, which the classic muse so sweetly sings. (1: 160–61)

A deep romantic chasm to one viewer may be a thing devoutly to be wished for, but to another it might have a whole host of negatively troped political resonances. Similarly, the classical muse and all she represents and invokes might not sit happily with the freedom of the fancy to create its own romance. In the above passage Heely is certainly summoning up an Augustan group fantasy, the projection of oneself into a classical, arcadian bower of bliss. In this respect he is signaling his belonging to the elitist cultural form in which the viewer's gaze is fully educated by and within that culture. However, his invocation of this form of looking in 1777 needs comment in light of the revisions to Dodsley's description discussed above. We can recall that later printings of Dodsley's text systematically removed the resonances of a fantasy fairy land, precisely those indicators of one's insertion within an elitist cultural form of looking.

Here, then, we need to decide whether Heely is turning back toward those resonances consciously as a kind of resistance or unconsciously in his co-option into an elitist ruling ideology. Is Heely promulgating a civic humanist tradition through his recidivist leanings, or, on the contrary, is this bourgeois viewer entering into some contest with that elitist hegemony?

It is difficult to decide this question — indeed, it is *always* problematic because the adoption or imitation of elitist cultural forms by the non-elite is necessarily caught in a double bind. Imitation of the manners of one's betters can be viewed as either a succumbing to the elite's coercive force or as a parodic resistance to that force. Nevertheless, we might begin to sense the ways in which the question could be decided if we press further Heely's desire to be alone in the garden.

This is given its most forceful expression in his description of one of the cascades at Shenstone's Leasowes:

I believe every spectator who visits this inimitable cascade, quits it with the utmost regret: — for my own part, had I not been disturbed by one of those noisy, ridiculous parties, who come to view they know not what, I cannot tell when I should have been disposed to leave it. (2: 119–20)

Here it is the presence of the other which disturbs the self-absorbed subject from itself. Heely suggests that he could have been indefinitely suspended gazing at this scene, gazing into the depths and self-satisfaction of his self-definition. But what serves to jolt him out of this reverie is exactly the presence of those whose eyes are uneducated, who are there to remind him of how he is socially and culturally better than they. Heely craves a singular experience, filtering out the noise of others, so that an environment might be created in which a more authentic sense of being could become manifest. But, in order to reach such an authentic sense of being, the viewer needs to gain some kind of perspective on himself; that is, a perspective on his own positionality here in the now of vision. This, for elite culture, is interwoven with an experience of modernity. The manner in which this homosocial elite culture figures to itself its modernity is indirect, but it is that very indirection which serves to maintain the restrictive nature of this experience. Essentially an imaginary classical idyll is invoked in order to gain a differential view on the contemporary, that is, to see the modern in its correct perspective.

This classical idyll is nothing more than an imaginary recollection of a past time, imaginary in relation to the activity of recollection and the "real" of that classical past. So it comes to pass that modernity is best experienced when one takes leave of it through the invocation of an imaginary classical idyll, and this acts as the screen upon which precisely a fantasized construction of the present, of the modern, might now be projected.

This is the mechanism by which a self-regarding and self-satisfied elite culture obtains, creates, and polices reflective images of itself. It is the Augustan version of a heritage experience in which a viewer in the middle decades of the eighteenth century images to himself his person as endowed with and participating in those modes of conduct and being that are culturally fantasized as pertaining in a past ideal, that of ancient Rome. In claiming this fantasy as its heritage (for this time; its humanist ideals never existed except as a culturally disseminated fantasy), elite culture not only underlines its difference from popular cultural forms — one needs a very particular kind of education in order to register the references to classical art and society — but also colonizes the past in its own imaginary image. The heritage experience, then as now, is all about the coercion of the present, about the induction of the viewer into a cultural form that is only ever an ideologically motivated fantasy. It is not merely that our own contemporary experience of visiting eighteenth-century estates conforms to this heritage experience but that these houses and gardens were constructed in the service of such a group fantasy production, of an elitist, false class-consciousness.

Yet Heely wants the argument both ways, since the implied rejection of his social inferiors in the landscape experience is to be weighed against the educative progress through the garden which precisely opens up access for each and every visitor with eyes to see.[42] As Heely informs us:

Each [Hagley, Envil, and the Leasowes] may be called a school for taste — together, an accomplished one — where you are taught, whatever be the genius of your grounds, how the pencil should be guided — where the cascade should gush — where the tower, the obelisk, the temple, or the grot, best become their situation — it will teach you where woods, groves, and lawns should intermingle to grace each other — where water should be secluded, and where visible — where light and shade have the best, and most agreeable effect, and where the solemn and the gloomy more happily contrast the sprightly and the gay. (2: 231–32)

This ambiguity around the educative against the elitist purpose of the landscape experience cannot be easily settled, since the cultural construction of looking is prey to pressure from both sides of this contest. During the 1760s and 1770s there are continuous debates on the means of access to the visual domain, debates which earlier centered on the foundation of a Royal Academy, but which develop into the larger territory of visual culture *tout court*.[43] This can be seen in the competing arenas in which high art was exhibited; these included the extraordinarily popular Vauxhall Gardens, which essentially created a visual environment that was overwhelmingly pictorial as well as social, and the enclosed gallery space of the Royal Academy which attempted to restrict access to its exhibitions.[44] But these two examples only barely convey the complexity of this visual culture, one aspect of which was the exchange of self-portraits between individuals. This, it should be emphasized, was a practice current throughout a sizable range of eighteenth-century social stratifications.[45]

Thus, on the one hand the common people were excluded from the exhibition of paintings, for example, through the simple expedient of charging admission; on the other, modes of representation such as portraiture were increasingly available for non-elite sections of society. The point here is that once one is allowed into representation it becomes possible to adapt, learn, and imitate so that one might become educated into another representation. If, as seems likely, Heely's account bears witness to these pressures, his turn to the fantasy projection can also be read as a liberating move: the upwardly mobile bourgeois putting on airs and graces above his station.

Here we must return to the activity of looking itself, which is, as I have argued, to be understood as a specific cultural form and which is far from disinterested. The gender and class affiliation that, I have suggested, results from this activity is a complex weave of competing interests. Thus, when Heely writes that at Hagley "it is impossible for any one that has feelings, to sit, and look on the graceful combination before him, without rapture" (1: 152), the visual experience is one which *of itself* educates the eye: all one needs is "feeling."[46]

This requirement, which is importantly distinct from the necessity of elite education for instruction in the ways and means of looking, is a common property of the individual. Of course the "man of feeling" is a specific type within mid-eighteenth-century culture; he is precisely some-one who "emotes" and is not afraid to demonstrate his emotive responses. He is also, and this point will be discussed in conclusion, less "manly."

It is clear from Heely's account of his visit to the three gardens that he assumes a correct view of the landscape can only be one which is identical to the view taken by the designer. There are a number of things to say about this. First, the metaphoric arrestation of the eye in which we occupy precisely one spot in the landscape is required in order for the look to function correctly: our movement through time and space as we walk through the garden is continually arrested as we take up a fixed position. This viewing activity is of course more likely to be aligned with the gaze than the glance, but it is a gaze that moves on and through a physical enclosure.

Second, standing in the place of the designer is our signal to enter into the sympathetic registers of feeling: we look with a sentimental eye. And here, at this place, standing in Shenstone's own shoes, we note the full force of the educative and democratic purpose of the look. It is precisely in the creation of the man of genius who looks for us, with whom we look, that the later viewer is enabled to have things both ways: the insertion of the self within past time and the invocation and projection of the past into the present of looking. Heely writes:

One cannot help feeling for a man of genius, who has the will, and who actually does, with much study, labour, and expence, make his domain so exceedingly beautiful, as to fill every eye that looks upon it with wonder and delight; and at the same time, who is so amiably disposed, as to be highly gratified in seeing the un-distinguished, as well as others, indiscriminately walk, and enjoy it with the ut-most freedom. (2: 186)

This is the ideal fantasy figure who receives his pleasure from seeing others seeing, and who represents *for us* our self-reflection.

In occupying this place, we clearly take on the attributes of Shenstone, who is at least superficially male, but he represents a mixed male type: he is famous for not wearing a wig and for living without female company. He represents, then, another possibility for masculinity, and Heely's ac-count falls fully within the revisionary project of the fantasy experience described above. In this way the activity of looking takes on resonances within elite homosocial culture that impinge upon the division between heterosocial and homosocial cultural forms. Who one is, or aspires to be, will depend upon one's access to or entry within the republic of visuality, and at least one of the ways in which such entrance is gained is through the invocation of a fantasy heritage experience whereby one's masculinity is given these slightly different contours.

It is men, then, who look in Heely's garden, and men who create these scenes of rural retirement. But it is in the service of a "softening" of masculinity that the entire cultural complex operates. The man who visits the Leasowes does not go in order to impose his informed and classically trained eye on the "real," hoping thereby to "see" a Claude Lorrain image; he goes, on the contrary, in order to feel a sense of himself. And that self is precisely at home in the feminized contours of a "feeling" landscape. As Heely writes about the garden: "For my own part I confess I felt its influence, and could not sit without indulging a thousand agreeable ideas — every thing around me seemed calculated to infuse the tenderest, warmest wishes — concealment — delicious shade — spreading trees — a calm, transparent stream" (2: 173–74). This "new man" is certainly familiar with the older, sublime forms of transport in which the self is swiftly taken out of itself. This, a derivation from the Burkean aesthetic, has its most proximate analogues in the ecstatic experience of religious revelation. In the softening environment of the sentimental look, the man experiences another kind of difference in which masculinity itself undergoes transformation. This allows a less monolithic sense of the masculine to emerge in the effeminate activity of looking at and in the landscape. Heely describes it thus:

— when he casts his eyes on those variegated shrubby crossings, and slants of lawn above — on the green rising knole at the extremity of view, covered sometimes with the browsing deer, and crowned with a rotundo, in perfect character, and in perfect beauty! while round him the melody of the thrush, the blackbird, and other different warblers, give their wild, and cheerful notes, to make it still more delightful! — He stands in rapture — he gazes — contemplates — and with reluctance, leaves the elysian bower! (1: 135–36)

The sequence of sensations or "feelings" is noteworthy here: the shapes and contours of the land are to some degree sexualized, as is the ecstatic moment of rapture, but the terms which follow the end point of rapture — gazing and contemplation — significantly distinguish two kinds of looking. The penetrative "male" gaze is followed by a more indirect, "softer," inner contemplation. The experience is one in which the male viewer first feels his sense of power, which is then softened into an effeminate and more reflective mode of looking, of being.

For Heely the end result of the entire encounter is the turn away from society, to a fantasized environment in which the male viewer comes into a more varied experience of his masculinity. Heely states:

One cannot leave this sweet habitation of the sylvan deities, without extreme regret: the mind imbibes such a pleasing serenity in the contemplation it affords, that one is ready to wish to remain fixed within its happy bounds, never to mingle again in the follies of a busy and licentious world. (1: 155)

If we now overlay the class and social implications of Heely's descriptive registers, it becomes clear that his desire is for another kind of class, neither fully public nor private, in which the experience of masculinity allows a softening of the rigid divide between gender oppositions. It must be underlined that this is a collective fantasy, but it is precisely the work of group fantasies to define and shape a cultural form; that form here, the activity of looking, gives definition to the subject even as it reflects a homosocial elite image back within a fantasy historical surface that tells us of the modern. Heely, whether he likes it or not, had been charm'd by his eye to see what that homosocial elite wants him to see, a caring, considerate, feeling man, not made effeminate through his sentimental look but empowered by it to recognize more fully his own self-reflection.

Overloaded Portraits: The Excesses of Character and Countenance

DEIDRE LYNCH

> Not that always where the language is intricate the thought is sub-
> tle, or the image always great where the line is bulky; the equality
> of words to things is very often neglected, and trivial sentiments
> and vulgar ideas disappoint the attention to which they are recom-
> mended by sonorous epithets and swelling figures.
>
> — Samuel Johnson, Preface to *The Works of William Shakespeare*

> Just heaven! How does the *Poco piu* and the *Poco meno* of the
> Italian artists; — the insensible MORE or LESS, determine the precise
> line of beauty in the sentence, as well as in the statue! How do the
> slight touches of the chisel, the pencil, the pen, the fiddlestick, *et
> caetera*, — give the true swell, which gives the true pleasure!
>
> — Laurence Sterne, *Tristram Shandy*

Somatic and Semiotic Economies: The Insensible MORE or LESS

*T*ristram Shandy was indulging in wishful thinking when he made
truth and beauty hinge on ultrafine adjudications between the *"Poco piu"*
and the *"Poco meno."* No matter how strenuously neoclassical critics advocated the ideals of economy and "the equality of words to things,"
"swelling figures" regularly defied their attempts at symbol management.
Tristram pronounces confidently on "true" swells and pleasures. But,
along with many contemporaries, he never stops *at*, but repeatedly exceeds or falls short of, the proper quantity of added or finishing touches.

Mid-eighteenth-century discussions of the painting, dramatizing, and
writing of personhood were persistently troubled by the problem of set-

tling on the proper quantity of "strokes of character" (a term that recurs throughout *Tristram Shandy* and throughout many master-texts of English aesthetics). For neoclassical critics, the identity of the "character," and by extension the integrity of the individual art-form, were based upon the difference between enough and too much, the difference between a gestalt in which the component parts (or strokes) were properly related to the whole and one in which the whole was less than the sum of its parts. To examine the ambivalence with which the creators of character worried the question of the "insensible more or less" at the same time that they overloaded their portraits is to identify the transformations of neoclassicism's basic premises about the relations of individual identity to the visible body and to written language: it is to identify points of contact between new forms of material culture and new ways of envisaging the self. Examining this ambivalence also exposes the dynamics of eighteenth-century cultural politics. It exposes the exclusions and the appropriations that made relations between kinds of art, and between legitimate and popular modes, *political* relations.

Every reader knows that undersized noses and other preternaturally truncated body-parts abound in Tristram Shandy's autobiography. These are so numerous that we often forget that the Shandys are as vexed by swelling as by detumescence. Walter Shandy fears, for instance, that the body politic will soon "totter through its own weight," unbalanced by the expansion of the nation's moneyed interest — a "head [that grows] . . . too big for the body."[1] Tristram's concern with bodily surplus becomes apparent when he regales us with a romance by one Slawkenbergius. This mock-homage to the romance is as destabilizing for the conventions organizing the writing of personal identity, as the merchants' expansionist designs are for Walter's statecraft. In "Slawkenbergius's Tale," an oversized nose, property of a mysterious man who wanders in and out of Strasbourg, mystifies the academic community. Scholars despair of deciding whether gravity will in the end cause this man to fall off from his nose or this nose to fall off from the man (p. 261).

Physiognomic inflation gives Sterne a pretext to comment, not on fiscal arrangements, but on the ranking of artistic genres and their respective ways of presenting persons. Taking a part in the century's cultural politics, "Slawkenbergius's Tale" doubles as a sideswipe at the recognition scene — the conventional scene where hidden truths about identity come to light, to reunite long-lost friend with friend. Increasingly in the eighteenth century, the surplus materiality of the means by which those scenes of *anagnorisis* were generated came to embarrass writers on literature and theater. Critics began then to sanction only the recognition scene that arose from action, and to look with disfavor on the recognition arising from a bodily sign or material token, from a scar, for instance, or a curious ring. Putting together a new axiology of aesthetic value, they were eager to consign telltale rings, scars, and distinguishing features to the debased category of popular entertainment.[2] At *the* climactic moment in Slawken-bergius's tale, a visitor to Strasbourg hears through rumor about the big-nosed stranger, falls on his knees, looks up to heaven, and declares, " 'Tis Diego!"; he then rushes to the reunion (p. 268). Parodying the cheap thrills of hackneyed tales, Sterne anticipates and completes the critical argument with overvisible tokens of recognition and material-minded modes of knowing character. The enlarged nose attached to the now-discovered Diego, or to which the now-discovered Diego is appended, is the very image of the inartistic excessiveness that improvers of the drama came to discern in that model of recognition in which personal identity — "character" — might be established through a sighting.

Eighteenth-century writers, dramaturges, and artists thought a lot about the overloaded face — the face overdistinguished, as Diego's is, by a surplus of identifying marks. The debate on dramatic "recognitions" is just one of many instances in which questions about artistic kind and *quality* — about the identity of genres and the difference between legitimate and illegitimate modes — ended up centering on questions of *quantity*. It is just one instance, as well, in which the effort to regulate generic identity hinged on writing off the meanings hitherto inscribed in the appearing body.

As Walter Shandy's use of the metaphor of the body politic indicates, the human figure had once served men and women as a means of naturalizing their representations and conferring on them a visible definition and stability.[3] But as the arts in the eighteenth century posed new questions about the proper quantity of strokes of character (and came to articulate tenets that had previously gone without saying), they ended up displaying the human figure as a mere figure. They reclassed physiognomic signs as semantically supernumerary.

Thinking about the economy and diseconomy of *countenances* allowed for a reworking of extant decorums for fleshing out *characters*, for figuring strokes of the pen into life. Indeed, over the course of the eighteenth century the term "character" effectively reversed its meaning. Around the time "characters" emerged as a primary designation for the imaginary personages of fiction, the pictorialist episteme that associated "characters" with exoteric, visible information, like that conveyed by a wart or a ring, ceased to convince. Character was reconstructed through new definitions of "realistic" characterization. And if, on the one hand, the real meanings of character were now constructed in opposition to the perceived excesses of the appearing body and the graphic characters of the page (the supplementary materiality or body of written language), on the other hand, recognition of and even appreciation for excess came to be involved in the proper apprehension of character. Thus the novelistic character who wins our praise is customarily the one who is dissociated from (who has ceased, literally, to be circumscribed by) an environing textual medium: the one who has, as we say, taken on a life of his own.

The eighteenth-century experiments with the overloading of countenances that I trace in this essay proceeded from two, sometimes scarcely distinguishable impulses. In the transitional period with which I am concerned, the cultural commentator could use the overloaded face as a deterrent example: a warning signal marking the point at which culturally legitimate modes of representing personhood shaded into illegitimate modes, and marking the point at which the seemliness of the body, the propriety of meaning, and the artistic hierarchy came into jeopardy. But one can detect another motive impelling the period's discussions of semiotic economy and diseconomy. A pattern of disfiguration becomes visible in these discussions in which the added touches that are meant to particularize representations and to assist a more accurate and nuanced imitation of Nature come to mar as much as they mend identities. These added touches deform identities into what they are not. This means, then, that examples of the excesses of character and countenance could serve ends other than that of preserving the status quo in the system of representation and the cultural field. Surreptitiously, these grotesques could also provide eighteenth-century people with a means of thinking of character differently and with a means of acknowledging and distinguishing new art-forms — the new ways of displaying character that the public found in printshops and on the stage as well as in the narrative fictions we now call novels (which I will consider only briefly here).

I turn in what follows to three illustrations of this ambivalence in the period's symbol management. First, I examine the fortunes of the face in John Locke's *Essay Concerning Human Understanding* (1690) and in the Theophrastan character collections that answered Locke's call for an "empiricist" way of seeing. I move in the second half of this essay to the visual arts and the drama. In the middle decades of the century, English artists and aestheticians responded to a new craze for caricatures by trying to distinguish irrefragably between permissible and excessive attention to physiognomic particulars. Theater critics pondered the actor David Garrick's innovative ways of "looking a character" by trying to draw a line between "Nature" and "Grimace." Before turning to the controversies about added strokes and overloaded faces, I begin with the concepts of writing and of embodiment that neoclassicism mobilized to regulate the economy of character.

Bodies of Writing and Copy Machines

Neoclassicism inherited from the seventeenth century the conviction that it was best to *image* the linguistic grounds of human knowledge and an eagerness to apprehend the processes of signification in terms of analogies with that simultaneously social, natural, and symbolic entity, the human body. According to the prevailing understanding of linguistic behavior, discourse was embodied. Discourse was at ease with its immersion in a print culture in which language necessarily assumes visible, corporeal form. At the same time the body was discursive, a telltale transcript of the identity it housed. In the economy of inscription that went by the name of the Book of Nature, human bodies and the cultural texts that humans produced were assimilated to each other *and* assimilated to the animal, vegetable, and mineral works of Creation — to natural forms, which themselves were said to possess "signatures" indexing their affinities.[4]

Within this semiotic system a special significative cachet was ascribed to the human face and its representations. For the first part of the eighteenth century, the face was understood less as a natural fact and more as a prototypical sign, an exemplary sort of reading matter. This is the stake of the debates in which cultural commentators wrangled over the economy of portraiture. Not just the face's legibility, but its status as a figure for the legible was on the line when commentators disputed the degree to which the physical manifestations of identity should be particularized in order to secure a resemblance between a portrait and its subject, and when they disputed the conditions under which individual, obdurately "characteristic" bodies — like Diego's — could or should be represented at all. The human face was supposed to function as a rigid designator: as a distinct sign belonging to the same distinct person in all possible worlds. ("Every face must be a certain man's," Shaftesbury wrote in *Second Characters* in 1712.)[5] Besides existing as the somatic correlate of a proper name, the individual face was also, contrariwise, supposed to refer to Human Nature in general. A face indexed character: a social norm, a determinate place on the ethical map where every person had a proper place and where distinction was contained within limits.[6] Recognizing a face, or putting a name to a face, was thus an allegory for what eighteenth-century philosophy of mind valued as the most basic cognitive operation, that of discriminating and weighing samenesses and differences.

The rationale for the face's special status can be discerned if, consulting the entries under "character" in the *Oxford English Dictionary*, we note that "the face or features [or] . . . personal appearance" defines one sense of "character" and also note that references to technologies of writing and, particularly, typography and engraving explicate many of the other meanings of the word. The face derives its significative centrality from a semantic complex in which the ethical, the physiognomic, the typographic, and even the numismatic merge. It is not only the case that faces can be read and that they are intimately, iconically related to the personal meanings they articulate. "Countenance," as a cognate to "character," is directly related to a word that denoted the material supports of meaning in a literate culture and that also, in its broadest sense, bespoke the differential structure of signification itself. A "character" is a printer's piece of type, but, according to widely circulated eighteenth-century definitions, "character" is also "that which distinguishes one object from another," or that by which a thing "separates itself from others of its kind."[7]

In his description of cognition in the *Essay Concerning Human Understanding*, simultaneously the eighteenth century's most important description of the production of personality, John Locke exploits these multiple connotations of "character": they come in handy as he portrays human consciousness as a documentary genre, founded on observation and transcription. For Locke, cognition is the process whereby experience imprints the mind, inscribing ideas upon what was initially "white Paper, void of all Characters, without any Ideas."[8] The imprinting of a surface and the acquisition of "characters" produce "character," or personality, where before there was a blank. This account of character formation develops an earlier homiletic commonplace that had aligned the traits composing the moral character with the marks identifying the denomination of a coin, as well as with the marks identifying persons and rendering one face distinct from another. Preachers had long made the piece of metal, transformed into legal tender by the inscriptions it bears, a symbol for the person, whose lineaments or "characters" of virtue and vice set his soul apart from its originary state of innocence, vacancy, or sheer lumpishness. According to this commonplace, such lineaments or characters corresponded in turn to the lines, birthmarks, and features discovering themselves upon the face. The face, in its turn, could be seen either as the original issue of God's

Mint or as a transcript documenting the wear and tear to which currency was liable in the marketplace of experience.[9]

It is worth noting how ill suited these physiognomic, typographic, and numismatic analogies and this insistence that the surface is the site of signification are to our thinking about character's meanings. The importance of the countenance for this semiotics shows up by contrast the impossibility of claiming any distinctiveness or priority for what we think of as the primary signification of character. Our faith in the deep-seated singularity of the "personality" makes us uncomfortable with how closely identity is associated here with the conspicuous graphic or corporeal signs that make it public knowledge. (The linking of character and money also makes us uneasy.) Furthermore, the sense of character we prioritize as literary historians — the usage in which "character" denotes an imaginary person portrayed in a work of art — is a mere postscript to this material-minded insistence on en-visaging character.

The *Oxford English Dictionary* identifies Henry Fielding as the originator of that usage, and scholars who plot the novel's rise and its mastering of the truths of individuality would like to see Fielding's "new species of writing" as an antetype for nineteenth-century realism. But however forward-looking he might have been, Fielding happily complied with the arrangements en-visaging character. The conventions for representing and individualizing to which he conformed lent themselves to a semiotic understanding of the person, and not to a mimetic theory, not to the notion that what literature does for a reader is convey an illusion of a credible second self.[10] It is worth noting that while Fielding meditates on "divisions in authors" in *Joseph Andrews* (1742) and touts his practice of signposting readers' journey through the book, he not only compares chapter titles to "inscriptions over the Gates of Inns," he also uses this same trope to model how readers become informed about characters.[11] The group of characters whom Joseph, the reader's surrogate, encounters on his journey includes a publican, Tim. Tim's inn is known by the "Lion on the Sign-Post," and the physiognomy by which Tim is recognized matches the inn's sign: "in Countenance," the narrator says, Tim "doth . . . greatly resemble that magnanimous Beast" (p. 44).

In the seventeenth century Samuel Butler had also talked up the similitudes linking the body of the person to the discourse denominating him. His collection of Theophrastan characters is populated by bodies that live for the page. Butler's characters strain to make themselves recognizable. His "Busy Man" "frequents all public Places, and like a Pillar in the *old Exchange* is hung with all Men's business both public and private." His

"Hypocrite" takes a printer's composing stick for his model of being and "sets his Words and Actions like a Printer's Letters, [so that] he that will understand him must read him backwards."[12] Both Busy Man and Hypocrite *embody* the media that exhibit them and that transmute them into reading matter.

With their labeled bodies, these early modern characters are typical products of a discursive context that insisted on the affinities between verbal designations for persons—epithets and proper names—and the bodies that gave identity visible form. The first principle of much aesthetic discussion in the period was that visual imitation and verbal documentation should look (and read) alike; that people's conceptions were at once representations and resemblances of things. Tellingly, for eighteenth-century speakers "person" was a word for someone's physical appearance and a word for someone. "Trait" signified a minimum unit of the stuff of character, an identifying mark or characterological "seme"; and it was cognate with words like "stroke" or "line"—words for the graphic elements composing the gestalt of a whole character. Thus to draw or write a character was, optimally, the same activity. It was in both cases a question of transcribing (recopying) documentation that was already in place, of matching stroke with trait in an equal exchange.

Thinking about discursive production in these terms—as a transcription that under ideal conditions maintained the "equality of words to things," or of sign to sign—gave eighteenth-century people a way to view the print products of their age as a group. (And for us, thinking in these terms suggests another reason for not privileging fiction's narrative representations of identity and for not isolating "personality" from the other, semiotic senses of "character.") In this typographical climate the term "characteristic writing" provided aesthetic debate with a locution that covered, indiscriminately, the iconic and narrative, the visual and verbal.[13] "Characteristic writing" designated the so-called character sketches that inventoried character traits; novels' representations of their heroes and heroines; the caricatures of "celebrated Ladies, Generals, Players" and effigies of "Truly humorous . . . droll characters" that were displayed in printshop windows.[14] These many modes of characteristic writing were grouped together as instantiations of a copy theory of knowledge. All exemplified that model of knowing that Locke illustrated when he referred to the characters of experience.

The copy theory of knowledge postulated a mimetic relation between ideas and the external objects of sensation ideas imaged. Traditionally, the communication and acquisition of information had consisted in the production of a resemblance, of that sort of likeness that subsists, in Plato's account of cognition, for instance, between the stamp and the surface that bears its imprint. Technological change replaced stamped wax tablets, which gave Plato his framework for apprehending cognition, with the printing presses that organized the thinking of a Samuel Butler as well as a John Locke.[15] That transition also laid the groundwork for a shift in the understanding of mimesis and of the economy of character. The transition to print raised the questions about quantity — "how much" and "how many strokes" — that could compromise the legibility of face and character.

Once *copies* are *prints,* an unprecedented attention to detail is demanded of the perceiving subject who adjudicates between the claim that an original and its imitation are similar and the claim that they differ. The wax tablets Plato invoked in the *Theaetetus* to speak of the mimetic relations between ideas and their objects might be of various consistencies. They might register impressions differently, with relative blurriness or clarity. By contrast, the Enlightenment metaphor that reinflects the copy theory of knowledge permits a newly intense emphasis on uniform reproduction: faithful imitation is conceptualized in narrower terms than before, and in terms not so much of resemblance but of high fidelity, or virtual equivalence. The metaphorics of the printing press make it possible to understand the replica or representation as an instantiation of (in every sense of the word) a type.

Empiricism and Excess

In the line of thinking opened up by the new, print-based understanding of the activities of knowing and copying, the character and the countenance are located — ideally — at the interface of what is particular and what is general. In this typographical context the individual specimen of character should refer to an overarching standard of uniformity. A seventeenth-century imitator of Theophrastus, Samuel Person, maintains that the character has not only the "*Signatura rerum*" but also *Personarum* stamped upon it." He argues, that is, that the meanings saturating a character are at once generic *and* individual. A similar confidence in representation's capacity to induce the particular into the general and to make the imprint refer to the type informs another seventeenth-century definition of "the character," as "some person" or, equally, "some sort of person."[16]

Despite the ease, however, with which these character writers move from individuals to classes, the enhancement of communications technologies in the early modern period does not just draw writers to this harmonizing vision of types and imprints and general principles that comprehend particulars. It also begins to generate other disturbing visions, which had important effects for the deregulating of characteristic writing's regulating decorums of representation. As a result of that enhancement, the replica is scrutinized with a new thoroughness, because it is now necessary to check the particulars in which the replica manages or fails to be strictly faithful to the original. For a start, then, print technology pushes to the forefront questions about the specular structure of figuration — the balance maintained between seeing and reading — in the eighteenth-century episteme. Raising this question of "the insensible more or less," the new attention to the particular puts pressure on the conceptual paradigm that sets the limit beyond which a replica becomes an imitation and beyond which sameness becomes similarity. (The portrait caricature can be considered a by-product of that attention to the particular: the invention of that form of characteristic writing presupposes "the theoretical discovery of the difference between likeness and equivalence" that entry into the Gutenberg galaxy makes possible.)[17] Second, an incipient effect of the boom market in printed words and images was the development of that cultural politics Julie Stone Peters describes as "anti-print romanticism": the project of reinforcing the social hierarchies and the divisions between artistic kinds that had been destabilized by the swollen masses of print products, the first truly mass-produced commodities of commercial capitalism.[18] Ironically, then, one outgrowth of the new ease of copying is an anticommercial, antimodernist position (thoroughly elaborated by the late eighteenth century) that disdains "mere" copies, holding that meaning is vulgarized by the modern traffic in signs, that real truth lies beyond the compass of names and pictures. "Anti-print romanticism" imperils the organizing power ascribed to the metalanguage of character, sign, and copy. After the late eighteenth-century stratification of the culture market, the period's rearrangement of genres, and its rethinking of characterizing, some characters could be dismissed as *mere* types.

Locke's *Essay Concerning Human Understanding* expounds at length the implications of casting the processes of copying, or representation, as metaphors for explaining acts of knowledge and communication. At moments in the *Essay* ideas are compared to pictures; words are the marks of ideas; Nature "stamps" its workmanship with "characters" or marks of distinction; experience, as we have seen, imprints the mind as if it were a page. And meaning hinges in the *Essay* on a logic of synecdoche and a logic of reproduction: meaning hinges, that is, on the correspondences linking the particular to the general and the copy to the original. For Locke defiance of the forces of semantic oblivion depends on the way in which the data of sensation or the data of reflection (i.e., "such Combinations of simple Ideas as are not looked upon to be characteristical Marks of any real Beings") correspond to the word that "ties them fast together" (*Essay*, II, xxii, 1; III, v, 10).

The empiricism for which Locke is remembered involves correcting for semantic fraud and negligence by disengaging singularities from projectors' and Schoolmen's notions of species and essences. Locke aims to emancipate particularity from the thrall of conceptual categories and systems of names. Throughout the *Essay*, he directs readers' gaze to things heterogeneous and seemingly one of a kind, things occluded by the generalities of others' language. Locke was a member of the British Board of Trade, with a special interest in the expanding empire. The exotic flora and fauna — cassiowaries, parrots, and pineapples, for instance — that were introduced into a commercializing England under the aegis of his sort of enterprise are held up throughout his *Essay* as specimens of a diversity that is ill served by the crudity of current modes of utterance (e.g., *Essay*, II, xxv, 8; II, xxvii, 8; II, i, 6). As Chandra Mukerji remarks, "Material novelties . . . were so varied and so new to European travelers and traders that they created a crisis of meaning only solved by new attention to the material world, i.e., by envisioning ways to explain and use it."[19] The cassiowary (no ordinary "bird") and the pineapple (no ordinary "apple") provide Locke with examples of how much, if the human mind were sufficiently attentive to the nuance and the nonpareil, there would be talk about. By striving to connect the abstractness of language to the singularity of these new things, Locke aims to render language accountable to the complexity of phenomenal experience. This means, obviously, that redirecting the mind back to general concepts, back to the labor of sorting and assembling a "bundle" of things (*Essay*, III, iii, 20), is perforce a tricky matter. The crux for the *Essay* is that this rerouting from the particular back to the general is requisite if cognition is to be a social event.

Throughout the *Essay* the problems Locke builds into the empiricist project of copying Nature — problems in selecting the particular accidents and differenda that will be "pared away" to form general concepts, in regulating the relation of those parts to wholes, in balancing abstraction with particularization — are played out, luridly, on the body's surfaces. The abstraction that Locke subjects to piecemeal particularization is more than once the gestalt of the human face. The semiotic convention he denaturalizes is the expressive connection thought to obtain between this surface and the invisible interior (the character, in our sense) it images.

Locke's philosophic interests in copying and in the semantics of the *alter idem* — the dissimilarity that can be detached from seeming synonymy — lead him to consider human reproduction as an instance of semiosis. For Locke, birth involves, above all, the perpetuation of a family resemblance and the transmission of the human form. Especially attentive to aberrant products of human reproduction, Locke turns repeatedly to the example of a "changeling." This infant's congenital deformities, which are in some manifestations bodily and in others mental, signal a disturbance in the sequential copying and recopying of the human body or mind.[20] The changeling makes his most spectacular appearance in the *Essay* when Locke reviews arguments about how the knowledge that is registered in humanity's names for things has no relevance to things' "real Frame[s] and secret Constitutions." To put us in a position where we may judge of the fictions of identity that are registered by names, Locke initiates a step-by-step mutilation and inflation of his changeling's face:

The well-shaped Changeling is a Man, has a rational Soul, though it appears not; this is past doubt, say you. Make the Ears a little longer, and more pointed . . . and then you begin to boggle; Make the Face yet narrower, flatter, and longer, and then you are at a stand; Add still more and more of the likeness of a Brute to it, and let the Head be perfectly that of some other Animal, then presently 'tis a *Monster* . . . it hath no rational soul, and must be destroy'd. Where now (I ask) shall be the just measure; which the utmost Bounds of that Shape that carries with it a rational Soul? (IV, iv, 16)

Two problems in the knowledge of identity are dramatized here. First, at each stage in the passage it is increasingly the case that the face, as a sign by which a changeling gets recognized, is dissociated from what it signifies: it is displaced from any substantial ground. Locke demonstrates how, regardless, the fate of the changeling continues to hang, as he puts it elsewhere, on the "sort of Frontispiece" he is joined up to (III, xi, 20). Locke raises, that is, the problem of judging the book by its cover, of appraising character by face value. Second, Locke unfixes the system of differences underwriting our notion of what is proper to humans. The general names "brute" and "man" and even the terms "changeling" or "monster" that mediate between "brute" and "man" one by one prove inadequate to the task of labeling the welter of states of being that have come to occupy the interstices among the names. Locke produces objects that beggar description. The proliferation of nameless faces (of various ear-lengths and degrees of flatness) highlights the difficulties that the knowledge-seeking subject of empiricism must take on in adjudicating between identity and difference or, to put it otherwise, in determining the point at which the resemblance of the human image that is blazoned on the well-shaped changeling's body no longer resembles. The questions bringing us to "a stand" as we witness the alteration of the well-shaped changeling's looks are At what stage in this process is the human no longer the human? Does the body possess one feature or stroke of character that is crucial to the preservation of human image, and, if so, which is it? These correspond to the questions that surreptitiously trouble Locke's program for more attentive vision and more nuanced utterance: At what stage in the particularization of a thing does it become something other? When do differences and peculiarities count as part of the thing's intrinsic meaning, and when do they count as mere accessories to its significance? The predicament of each changeling is like that of the bookseller Locke mentions "who had in his Ware-House Volumes, that lay there unbound, and without Titles; which he could therefore make known to others, only by shewing the loose Sheets" (III, x, 27). Saddled with *their* frontispieces, the changelings cannot identify themselves any more effectively.

Given the cachet the human face possesses in early modern thinking about language's relation to its objects, the stretching of the original changeling's ears and lengthening of its visage appear acts of semantic vandalism. Locke puts an intolerable pressure on the culture's arrangements for figuring forth meaning: if the multiple changeling-faces communicate anything at all, it is testimony to the monstrously generative powers of language released from its bond with things, of representation unmoored from physical grounds.

Worse still, Locke's writing adds to rather than subtracts from the lineaments of the well-shaped changeling. Progressively distending, and overloading, the face, it produces what Renaissance teratology, the science of congenital deformities, classified as a "monstre par excès," and not a "monstre par défaut." Locke's empiricist way of seeing is *productive*. It disengages differences from seeming similarities, and fills the perceptual field with more things that the knowledge-seeking subject may single out.[21] Yet the *Essay* seems to register ambivalence about this diversified, replete world, however, insofar as the question of "the just measure" that Locke poses at the end of the changeling passage — the problem of the line between the "*Poco piu*" and "*Poco meno*" — haunts the *Essay*. As the *Essay* progresses, its imagery comes increasingly to connect propriety of language to bodily size and personal identity. Locke asserts, for instance, that the ideas he communicates in the *Essay* are "fitted to Men of my own size" ("Epistle to the Reader"); he wishes that men would back their words with ideas and so realize how "small [a] pittance of Reason . . . is mixed with those huffing Opinions they are swell'd with" (III, v, 16).

It is for this reason ironic that Locke makes his case for economy in symbol management in the context of a book that, he himself avows, "grew insensibly to the bulk that it now appears in": "new discoveries" led him on and on ("Epistle to the Reader"). This covert predilection for over-production also manifests itself in the changeling passage: Locke seems never to finish adding finishing touches to the face. Seemingly despite himself, Locke points away from conceptions of embodied words and discursive bodies and points toward notions of the body and the sign as surplus to significance.

The character writers who were Locke's contemporaries worked according to the same logic of more-is-better that informs the *Essay*'s overloading of the face. Their imitations of Theophrastus were books whose contents grew, in a "Lockean" manner, ever more motley from edition to revised and expanded edition. In striving to encompass an increasingly quirky assortment of social particulars, the character collections produced by Samuel Butler and others stymied the cataloging capacity that had been established for their genre by Theophrastus' typologies of ethical types. They did the same with the imaginative order that had been set out in Renaissance literature of the estates — catalogs of the character and defects of each social estate, from the clergy to the peasantry. This sort of setting for character exerted pressure, as well, on the classifications of the temperaments suggested by humor theory. In Butler's character book, the "Humorist" is one character among almost two hundred.

The book of characters makes it apparent that the social and ethical divisions set out in preceding representational schemes — divisions regulating the relation of the individual to the totality, and asserting the permanence and unity of character beneath contradiction and transitory appearances — have the potential to be subdivided *ad infinitum*. The character writers of the mid-seventeenth century and the mid-eighteenth century (when there was a minor revival of the Theophrastan collection) operate in an environment where notions of the social *type* and of a character portrait bearing a "signatura rerum" are far from self-explanatory. Evidence of diversity is increasingly available and even marketable for these writers who inhabit an age marked by, for instance, an accelerated differentiation of society by occupation.[22] The character writers proceed accordingly by begging the question of how many characters it might take to anthologize and to sum up Human Nature. The composition of each portrait within the book of characters raises the specter of analogous subversions — a Butler or a La Bruyère proceeds by begging the question of how many traits, or characteristics, must be set down for a character portrait to be complete.

As these writers all but acknowledged, their characteristic writings had to win a place in an increasingly diversified culture-market, where distinction and not typicality was a selling point. Commodity fetishism was fueled by the fiction that the commodity was a nonpareil: character writers knew theirs was the age of the novelty item. (Such is the status of the pineapple in Locke's *Essay*.) The practitioners of characteristic writing pursued the singularity that could not be contained within the extant system of names and categories; they pursued a more comprehensive account of a diverse and diversifying Human Nature. And while they cast their nets more widely and augmented their materials, they called into question the ongoing identity of their project and of the "character" they purported to write up. Theirs was an exercise as much in marring as in mending identity.

The Added Touch and the Finishing Touch: Hogarth and the Royal Academy

Not surprisingly, by the mid-eighteenth century commentators were prone to call for a zero-growth policy to be applied to the economy of character. With one eye on contemporary character-books, Joseph Warton in 1753 lamented La Bruyère's propensity for "over-charging" his characters: to Warton the individual portraits seemed overloaded with "many ridiculous features that cannot exist together in one subject."[23] Henry Gally in his *Critical Essay on Characteristic-Writings* was similarly worried about the economy of character. He urged authors not to dwell too long on a single idea but rather to pass on to another as soon "as the masterly stroke is given" (p. 39). (He neglected, however, to set out a method for discriminating a master stroke from any other sort.) Gally declared the characters published in seventeenth-century England to be "far-fetched" (p. 89) and asserted, with a dig at La Bruyère, that anything French "convert[ed] Men into Monsters" and "turn[ed] Nature into Grimace" (p. 74).

Locke's exercise in overloading the changeling's physiognomy was being repeated in still other forums. In the 1730s habitués of the London art-scene also began to complain that someone was converting Nature into Grimace. In that decade, the fashion for portrait-caricatures was intro-

Overloaded Portraits 127

duced into Britain by gentlemen returning from the Grand Tour. Between 1736 and 1742, Arthur Pond, dogsbody to the English aristocracy and their cicerone on the Continent, published a series of engraved copies of Italian drawings. His folio reproduced grotesque heads designed by Leonardo da Vinci, by Annibale and Agostino Carracci, who had jointly invented the practice of personal caricature in the sixteenth century, and by Pier Leone Ghezzi, who specialized in satiric portraits of tourists visiting eighteenth-century Rome. Arthur Pond also expedited the printing of the likenesses that his aristocratic patrons executed of one another after he had tutored them in caricature drawing. He thus paved the way for printsellers, beginning in the 1750s, to print, distribute, and show "due Honour to" the pictorial inventions of "ladies and gentlemen"; in starting England's caricature craze, Pond enabled printsellers to profit from the vanity of well-to-do amateurs.[24]

Eighteenth-century commentaries on this new import divide their attention between two of its features — features that, from our perspective, caricature appears to have shared with the expanded and diversified book of characters. According to this commentary, caricature couples the act of willfully carrying representation to excess — of swelling figures and being prodigal in one's handling of the signs of humanity — with the tendering of a truth claim, the claim that the drawing improves on extant modes of imitating Nature and conveys characters' truths more truly. Where the producers of caricature differ from the writers of Theophrastan characters is in their audacity: caricaturists *flaunt* the ways in which the identity of the person has come to hinge, in their chosen form, on the production of a surplus. The term "caricature" derives from the Italian *caricare*, to load: as the French synonym, *portrait chargé*, indicates, a caricature is a loaded portrait (i.e., *rittrati carichi*), a portrait with extras. A 1773 complaint against the caricature-drawing Marquess of Townshend maintains that the loaded portrait aims "With wretched pencil to debase / Heaven's favourite work, the human face, / To magnify and hold to shame / Each little blemish of our frame."[25] Caricaturists concern themselves with the metamorphosis that ensues when the part is released from the whole. The caricaturist's magnification of a blemish reverses priorities. One looks at a caricature and one finds oneself (as did the scholars of Slawkenbergius's tale) gazing not so much at a nose appended to a face, but at a supernumerary face that has attached itself to a nose.

This, critics pointed out, was a crime against representational decorum. The particularization of physical appearance — the emphasis on how bodies differed rather than on what they had in common — that caricature traded on diverted beholders from truths of general application. It conducted them toward the libelous pleasures of "particular reflections" on private persons. The artist Henry Fuseli used revealing terms to plead the cause of the type: even if, according to Fuseli, "comic painting" did not "degenerate into caricature, the chronicle of scandal," it would still become "unintelligible in time."[26] Comic painting and caricature annoy Fuseli because, that is, they portend a state of oblivion in which the concrete particulars of images would not be matched with verbal messages set out in captions, in which nondescripts would proliferate, and in which the system of differences underpinning intelligibility and identity would be pulled asunder.

However, the eighteenth-century public happily disregarded such strictures on the relative values accruing to the particular and the general. And the enthusiasm with which this public consumed and produced caricature prints contributed to a new phase of style wars in the art world. High art set about defining itself in contradistinction to popular or amateur art by identifying itself with an ideal of "pictorial abstemiousness," and identifying others with excess.[27] It was a short step from a concern with the semantics of character (with the legibility of the human form) to a concern with the political economy of artistic kinds.

Thus members of the Royal Academy of Art insisted vehemently in the last four decades of the century that "real" art depended on the artist's getting above (in Joshua Reynolds' words) "singular forms, local customs, [and] particularities."[28] In the Academy's map of the cultural field the caricature's allotted place was alongside waxworks and so-called Flemish pictures — with the works of "copyists," who engaged in a mercenary and "mechanical trade" rather than a "liberal art" (4, p. 57), who excelled in "minute finishing of the features" (14, p. 259), and who, "unwilling that any part of [their] industry should be lost upon the spectator, [took] as much pains to discover, as the greater artist does to conceal, the marks of [their] subordinate assiduity" (4, p. 59). To avoid the excesses that disrupted the economy of character, and to secure their claims to high cultural status, some Academicians were seemingly all but ready to forgo character (and so difference) altogether. Thus James Barry explained to his pupils that "character" related to beauty as a "distortion" of "the central form of the species" related to that form. In Barry's tripartite division of the field of figural representation, "character" differs from "deformity," only in being constituted by a lesser degree of distortion, in having fewer qualities superadded to it, and in continuing to intersect with a name.[29]

Even the national physiognomy could seem a risky object of representa-tion to the Royal Academicians. As cast from Nature's die, the English face could appear too particularized and marked up to be a proper, read-able figure. The countenances that Apelles and Zeuxis had at their dis-posal provided those ancients with a means to intuit humanity's central form from particular somatic circumstances. By contrast, the face of the modern English model was liable to look busy. It displayed "numerous little hollows [and] . . . too many conspicuous dimples." The English face looked as if it were not complete and as if it had not quite integrated its surfeit of parts.[30]

Yet the fact remained that, their surpluses of marks notwithstanding, modern English faces represented so much money in the bank for English cultural producers. They represented so many shillings per stroke or per mark "of the painter's . . . assiduity." The Academy's professors made aesthetic value a function of the painter's transcendence of the particu-lars that make it possible to recognize an individual person. Nonetheless, commercial realities dictated that portraits depicting real, individual sit-ters composed the largest percentage of works submitted to Academy exhibitions.[31]

This sort of association of faces with money, an association based not on the legibility that linked faces and coin faces but on the fact that both were tokens of pecuniary gain, organizes William Hogarth's campaign against caricature drawing and for character. A cultural politics with a highly ambivalent relation to the popular market generally and to the popularity of the overloaded face specifically organizes Hogarth's *Anal-ysis of Beauty* (1753) and his engravings *Characters and Caricaturas* (1743) and *The Bench* (1758). The campaigning Hogarth undertakes in this treatise and these engravings is of a piece with Hogarth's jingoistic touting of modern English art and his frustration with the dearth of com-missions that would enable him to work in the grand style of history painting. The text and images replay, that is, the equivocations that char-acterized Hogarth's dealings with the connoisseurs ("picture-jobbers") who dismissed portraiture as the expression of a mere mechanical abil-ity to seize a likeness. Hogarth attempted to ward off the connoisseurs' charge that he was in the art business for the money, and at the same time he took the unprecedented step of advertising his print series in the papers. He sought to reconcile the universal moral applicability ascribed to the ideal, decorporealized forms of history painting with the attractiveness but meaninglessness of the empirical particular. He negotiated between, on the one hand, deference toward traditional hierarchies of the sort that

ranked artistic kinds and that ranked members of English society, and, on
the other hand, social aspirations, which were at that particular historical
moment best realized by accepting commissions for portraits.[32]

In his "Autobiographical Notes" Hogarth complained that, after the
success of his progresses or "comic history paintings," "the whole nest of
Phizmongers were upon my back every one of whome has his friends and
all were taught to run em down [and to call] my women . . . harlot and my
men charicatures" (*Analysis*, p. 218). His explanation of the genesis of
Characters and Caricaturas states that the engraving was executed to distinguish the meanings of two words — character and caricature — which
were too often confused, even though (as Hogarth later wrote in the
inscription to *The Bench*) "there are hardly any two things more essentially different."

Hogarth wanted to ensure that all recognition he received was for in-
venting *characters*. Caricatures provoked identity crises for Hogarth.
They disarranged the ideological matrix where bodily seemliness, the distinction of art forms, and the distinction of persons intersected. For a
start, the adepts of caricature drawing, who consciously aimed to do a bad
job of imitation while nonetheless seizing the "air" of their subjects, embodied a threat to the professional identity that an artist like Hogarth
pieced together in his academic training. Like "picture-jobbers," caricaturists threatened Hogarth's place in the market. Furthermore, caricature
added to its association with the frankly mercenary print-market, an association with genteel amateurism (after all, even women were invited by the
printsellers to try their hand at caricatures) or even courtly *sprezzatura*.
The genre gives place of privilege to the likeness that proves the artist to be
above taking pains over what s/he is doing. Nonetheless, the grounds of
Hogarth's opposition to caricatures are not nearly as clear-cut as they
would be if in his mind the genre's only transgressions were its enshrine-
ment of venality and feckless draftsmanship. The problem was that, on
the contrary, "character" resisted Hogarth's attempt to establish it as the
antithesis of caricature, and so as one pole in a tidy binary opposition.
Questions about quantity undermined Hogarth's attempt to assert differences of quality.

"Character's" unruliness in the face of Hogarth's efforts to make it
make sense has ramifications that extend through the whole range of mid-
eighteenth-century efforts to regulate the economy of character. When, in
Joseph Andrews, Fielding seeks to legitimate his characteristic writing and
to define his project by showing what it is not, he evokes the preference
people of taste give to Hogarth over the caricaturist who "paint[s] a Man

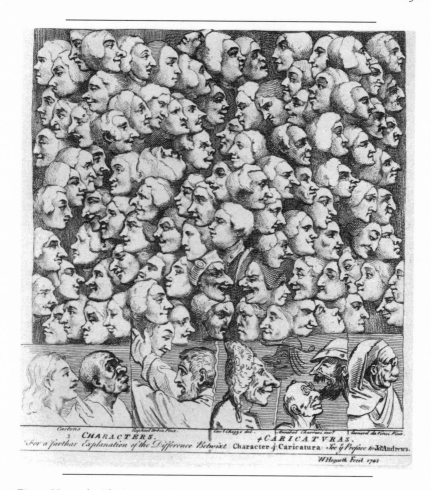

Fig. 1. Hogarth, *Characters and Caricaturas* (1743). The engraving is supposed to present us with a graphic illustration of the difference between "character" and "caricature," but the plentiful physiognomic detail overwhelms that ostensibly simple and self-explanatory opposition. (Photograph courtesy Department of Special Collections, University of Chicago Library)

with a Nose, or any other Feature of a preposterous Size," and who exhibits "Monsters, not Men" (pp. 5–6). Hogarth's *Characters and Caricaturas* (Fig. 1) — which returns Fielding's favor and directs public attention to *Joseph Andrews* — aims to polarize the grotesque overstatement and what Fielding called "the exactest copying of Nature." Yet the engraving seems instead to be about the *fine line* differentiating the mimetic structure of character from the mimetic structure of caricature. Only a fine line separates the marks that individualize the countenance from the marks that exaggerate it. The bottom fifth of Hogarth's engraving is divided vertically into two parts, one dedicated to "Character" and the other to "Caricatura." In the left half, Hogarth has installed copies of profiles from Raphael's cartoons — images that represented in 1743 the quintessence of history painting. The matching space in the engraving (the lower right side) is occupied by heads that duplicate those of the persons who flaunted their oddity in Pond's anthology of Italian caricatures. Above this strip of heads one sees a jumble of at least a hundred heads more. Each profile, Hogarth seems to say, belongs to a *character*, and characters not caricatures are what we can expect to see again in his *Marriage A-la-mode*. (*Characters and Caricaturas* served originally as the subscription ticket for that 1745 series.) Not one profile, Hogarth seems to boast, is exaggerated.

The odd effect of Hogarth's engraving derives from these extra hundred heads. They invite us to probe the limits of resemblance and identity. The beholder is obliged to try to specify the characteristic particulars in which the countenances differ. This is no easy task — it is obvious that Hogarth set out, in delineating these hundred-odd characters, to keep to a minimum the different kinds of strokes he would have to deploy. (The visages are dissimilar, but not overly so; with one possible exception, all are male; seen in profile; beardless; etc.) The quantity of physiognomic detail overwhelms the contrast that ostensibly gives the engraving its meaning. In fact, this overloaded image suggests the qualities of "minuteness and particularity [that] are," according to Walwyn's *Essay on Comedy*, "necessarily assumed of caricature."[33] The proliferation within Hogarth's image of copies that copy copies (copies of Pond's copies of the Italian masters) shows how English print culture allows excess — the overaccumulation of images — to threaten cognition.

Furthermore, the longer one looks at the engraving, the more it seems that Hogarth's subject is literally the fine line between character and caricature. Hogarth puts into play the opposition he means to exemplify. The line that divides the heroic Raphael heads from Ghezzi's, Annibale Carracci's, and da Vinci's quizzical phizzes is continued, subtly, into the area of the engraving consigned to characters, by a line formed initially by the ornamental braid or epaulette on the shoulder of one character, and then extended partway up. Hogarth has not drawn a dividing line through the plate from top to bottom, but such a line is suggested. At the lower center of the image, the profiles from the right side meet nose to nose with the profiles from the left side: playing the games of recognition that caricature seems to require, we can see in this group the face of Hogarth himself, nose to nose with the face of Henry Fielding.[34] And when we look closely at the two "characters" who are positioned immediately below Hogarth and Fielding and immediately above the Italianate heads, it appears that these unfortunates have managed to flatten their noses against that fine line between character and caricature. The dividing line between good and bad characterizing itself becomes the cause of physiognomic distortion.

In the catalog published by Sayer and Bennett's print warehouse in the year 1775, an advertisement for *Characters and Caricaturas* described Hogarth's manifesto as demonstrating "Character to be a small deviation from general Proportions, and [showing that] Caricatura is only that deviation exaggerated." The ad rewrites Hogarth's attempt to polarize the two modes of characterizing and two kinds of art. It opposes them, precariously, in terms of a quantitative rather than a qualitative difference. At the same time, the catalog's reinterpretation makes Hogarth's aesthetics commensurable with the categories of Academic neoclassicism. Sayer and Bennett reveal how the Royal Academicians also situated their ideal forms, precariously, on the slippery slope leading to excess; how James Barry's "beauty," for instance, was only uncertainly and ambiguously distinguished from "character" as well as from "deformity."

Joshua Reynolds proposed in his third discourse that the artist might, without impropriety, conceive of the human "species" as being divided into a certain number of "characters" or "classes," each possessing its own central form, as exemplified for the class of strong men by, for instance, the Farnese Hercules, or for the class of active men by the Borghese Warrior (3, pp. 46–48). This scheme maintains the doctrine of the central form while introducing character into painting (a necessary introduction if, as a history painter, the artist is to communicate a story). Its flaw, however, is that it makes no logical provision for limiting how far beauty might be subdivided.[35] The painter's options appear to be confined either to painting the classically beautiful body, which is to say nobody's body at all, or filling the canvas with a riot of characters. To permit even a single division of the central form is to initiate a drift that leads inexorably beyond types and forms, and from orderly deviation to deformity.

As if in illustration of this slipperiness, in his second attempt to diagram the nature of character, Hogarth found that he could no longer get by with only the two categories, "character" and "caricature." In *The Bench* (Fig. 2), Hogarth added a third category, that of the "outré," or the exaggerated: the heads exemplifying the new category are the same heads that in

Fig. 2. Hogarth, *The Bench* (begun 1758; left unfinished upon Hogarth's death in 1764). Hogarth's return to the topic of character's difference from caricature doubles as an indictment of the English judiciary, who are more apt to doze — or to partake of the latest fashion and draw caricatures — than they are to serve justice. Note Hogarth's last-minute emendations of the part of the caption explaining the "outré." (Photograph courtesy Department of Special Collections, University of Chicago Library)

the 1743 engraving represented caricatures. In this revision, however, "caricature" denotes, in contradistinction to the outré, the sort of minimalist squib that, for example, seizes the look of "a certain Italian Singer" by means of "a Streight perpendicular Stroke with a Dot over it."

Such a definition of caricature was, some commented, "by no means to the purpose"; there was no reason why an image of a straight line and a dot should have prompted Hogarth to worry about misrecognitions of his characters.[36] Indeed, further on in the inscription appended to *The Bench*, Hogarth betrays himself and all but admits that it is not abbreviation but excess that jeopardizes the identity of character. As an afterthought Hogarth has edited the part of the inscription that explicates the outré — and that cites as examples "a Giant," who may be considered "a common Man *Outré*," and "a Nose or a Leg, made bigger than it ought to be." He has added to the passage, as a finishing touch, the words "or a Dwarf" and "or less," attempting through these emendations to make it clear that the category also comprehends those deviations from the form of character which involve deficiency rather than surplus. The fact that Hogarth evidently forgot that hyperbole extends in two directions — that it means augmenting *or* diminishing to excess — indicates the ambivalence in his attitude toward caricature's techniques of overcharging and its manipulations of physical dimension, an ambivalence he has covered up here by using his odd definition of "caricaturas" as a decoy. His mistake reminds us of the attractions of the added touch, even as Hogarth repudiates them: what jeopardizes the decorums of the characteristic face is, in the first instance, a condition of too much rather than too little.

Hogarth did discover a way to sample the dangerous attractions of the added touch. In the two series of figures that accompany his chapter "The Face" in the *Analysis of Beauty*, the human visage becomes malleable. In the first series, Hogarth sets up a cartoon strip illustrating the degrees of deviation that lead from the masculine visage whose lineaments satisfy the most demanding taste, to a figure "totally divested of all lines of elegance, like a barber's block" (*Analysis*, p. 136). In the second, he puts a female face into his cartoon strip, and demonstrates that the variety and number of lines on that face are augmented as a woman passes from infancy to maturity, and as she is progressively marked, in conformity to Locke's documentary paradigm, by experience.

The conditions of the face that are polarized in Hogarth's propagandizing *The Bench* and *Characters and Caricaturas* are recast by his drawings in the *Analysis*. The face possessing character and the caricatured face are in the *Analysis* rendered as points on a continuum. Caricature becomes a contingent stage into which character passes, and vice versa. Caricature, far from being the antithesis of character, may be read as its extension. The conflict between these notions of character and the conflict between these notions of the function of the added stroke indicate a significant pattern of disavowal. Here the finishing touch, the increase in detail that enables the image to realize its claim to truth value, is reconceived as, past a certain limit, something else — a something that disrupts rather than extends. As "comic history painting" realizes its generic identity, character breeds a monster — a caricature — and then disavows this constituent part of itself.

Tellingly, when he outlined his *Rules for Drawing Caricatures* (1788), Francis Grose conjured up a picture of semiotic and physiognomic infla-tion that very much resembled Hogarth's. (When it was published, Grose's manual was bound with the *Analysis of Beauty*: the proximity of Grose's caricatures to his characters must have caused Hogarth to roll in his grave). Grose writes:

The sculptors of ancient Greece seem to have diligently observed the forms and proportions constituting the European ideas of beauty; and upon them to have formed their statues. These measures are to be met with in many drawing-books; a slight deviation from them, by the predominancy of any feature, constitutes what is called *Character*, and serves to discriminate the owner thereof, and to fix the idea of identity. This deviation or peculiarity, aggravated, forms *Caricatura*.

Logically there is no reason for the accumulation of differentiae that Grose plots to halt once the image has prompted the beholder to zero in on an individual's identifying features and to recognize and to label that person. Accordingly Grose advises caricaturists to be wary of "over-charg[ing]" the "peculiarities of their subjects." With too many strokes of the pen, they will produce "the hideous instead of [the] ridiculous and instead of laughter excite horror."[37] Grose's attempt to arrest the snowball effect that ensues from the added stroke, from the introduction of a notion of difference into the canons of representation, is clearly hopeless.

Garrick's Face

If the complaints of the critics as they wrote about his face are any indication, David Garrick's acting also exemplified the dangers of extra strokes. Neoclassical theories of acting shared with prevailing concep-tions of the graphic inscription of character the notion that mimesis pro-ceeded through the assembly of discrete strokes.[38] The stage was not so much a place where the guides to characterization that the playwright had written into the script were fleshed out, as it was a place where the passions were put through their paces, delineated by the players in isolated actions and declamations for which the soliloquy and the set speech provided pretexts.[39] While demonstrating that "anger, fear, pity, adoration . . . and almost every other passion ha[d] a look, attitude, and tone of voice, peculiar to itself," the players confirmed that the motions of the Human Mind were externally manifested, and in uniform, predictable, and so readable ways.[40] Commentators on David Garrick's immensely successful career lauded him for delineating in his performances as finely tuned a taxonomy of these human passions as had ever been seen — an achievement he supposedly secured via his introduction of what Joseph Warton praised as his "little touches of nature."[41] Commentators who were less impressed saw in those added touches not naturalism but a surplus threatening sense. The emblem for that unruliness was Garrick's face, which — like the countenance that manifests the extreme stage of the caricaturist's process of overcharging — exhibited too many lines and too many of the marks that make a character.

Samuel Johnson called Charles Burney's attention to the traces of "wear and tear" discernible on their friend's visage; he also said to Hester Thrale, "David, Madam, looks much older than he is, because his face has had double the business of any other man's."[42] Johnson was taking sides in a full-fledged debate over Garrick's face. That debate constituted a forum, like the controversies about portraits and caricatures, for renegotiating what was involved in achieving a faithful resemblance, and for renegotiating the relation of personal truths to the visible body and to systems of shared meaning.

The player's face was supposed to serve as a screen on which the operations of a natural semantic system might be viewed with special distinctness. That face was a *model* simulating Nature's production of "marks and impressions on the body [in general]." Through this visual "imitation of the passions," the player provided spectacular evidence of how the passions, working by means that were consonant with the copy theory of knowledge, "stamped" the muscles of the face.[43] This mid-eighteenth-century account of the purpose of playing prescribed, at least in theory, an indifference toward the particularity of the player's looks. Particularities were to be assimilated to the general categories that the player made visible. The spectator was supposed to look at the sentiment that was written across the player's body.

It was the famous "ductility" of his facial lineaments — the way their particularity was their patent lack of determinate character — that made Garrick's fortune. As rival thespian Samuel Foote admitted, Garrick's features were admirably configured for "what is called the looking of a Character."[44] Thus in one scene Garrick's countenance was observed to evince consecutively, and in five seconds, the distinct signs of: wild delight, temperate pleasure, tranquility, surprise, blank astonishment, sorrow, "the air of one overwhelmed," fright, horror, despair, and then back to the point from which he began — all with spectacular transitions between each passion.[45] For some, this was Nature; for others, "grimace."

Garrick's accumulations of kinesthetic details could be viewed as too much: as déclassé transgressions of the boundaries dividing kinds of art and dividing patrician from popular culture. Commentators could accordingly point to his overloaded face precisely in order to adjust or to fortify those boundaries. In an era when the culture of the crowd had in the eyes of the self-appointed civil classes come to represent a delirium of overembodiment, the physicality of Garrick's performances looked like trumpery meant to "draw in" the "Groundlings" (Foote, *Treatise on the Passions*, p. 18).[46] Theophilus Cibber bemoaned at length Garrick's "overfondness for extravagant attitudes, frequent affected starts, convulsive twitchings, jerkings of the body, sprawling of the fingers, slapping the breast and pockets — a set of mechanical motions in constant use, the caricatures of gesture suggested by pert vivacity; his pantomimical manner of acting every word in a sentence," and so on, and so on. The bits of stage business with which Garrick supplemented his lines exceeded what his detractors called, troping the language of commercial ethics, "the fair business of character."[47]

For those detractors, Garrick's strokes of character were somatic static — overvisible frivolity that interfered with the information a character should display. Expressing his part "more by the grimaces of his face, than the proper modulation of his voice," Garrick effaced textual meaning.[48] And with this gestural overlay, overloading even the nonverbal moments of the playtext, Garrick threatened the legibility of the theatrical body.

One can detect in criticisms of his busy-ness traces of the Royal Academy's aesthetic canons, which underscored the baseness of particularized representations by associating them with a putatively female enthusiasm for "baby-sizes, toys, miniatures" and trinkets.[49] According to this axiology Garrick's use of accessories was particularly vexing — it was low, *and* it was effeminate. Foote reacted to Garrick's Lear by complaining about unmanly sniveling and demanding that the player get a painter to "draw an enraged Monarch, and see whether he will make any use of the Handkerchief" (*Treatise on the Passions*, pp. 17–18). The added touch of nature Garrick brought to his Hamlet was still another accessory: the specially commissioned wig he put on for the ghost scene. Using a mechanical device that he hid in his costume, Garrick could activate the hairs on the wig and so satisfy to a tee aestheticians' formulas for the appropriate expression of Fright. As aspiring tragedians and history painters maintained (with risible solemnity), Fright causes "the Hair of the Head [to stand] on end."[50]

What was troubling about these added touches was compounded, in a coup de grâce, by Garrick's genre-bending association with the pantomimic harlequinades that were the toast of the so-called impolite elements of the town. These harlequinades owed some of their popularity in the mid-eighteenth century to the immense sums producers such as John Rich invested in special effects. Those apparently took in kinetic and nonverbal thrills of the sort described in a *London Chronicle* of 1772, which reports on a performance where the contents of a kitchen — pots, pans, chairs — began to dance while the crockery began to smash itself. In a criticism of the unnatural frenzy he perceived in Garrick's naturalistic style, Horace Walpole wrote sardonically of the "exhibitions of the animal or inanimate part of creation, which are furnished by the worthy philosophers Rich and Garrick."[51] In support of this coupling of Garrick's and Rich's names, it was rumored that Garrick's acting debut was not, in fact, in the role of tragic Richard III but as "Harlequin student."

Harlequin regularly invaded England's high art in just this way: testing the dividing lines that composed the cultural hierarchy, transforming and deforming his body, and so assaulting the categories and figures with which eighteenth-century culture made sense. To escape from Pantaloon, Harlequin would adopt the guise of an ostrich or would arrange for his own and others' decapitation. Harlequin's deliquescent body dealt an insult to culture's basic theorems of identity: in Garrick's own play *Harlequin's Invasion* (1759), Harlequin's arm is lost and then reappears, skipping about the stage to taunt him.

Perhaps the ductility and changeability evinced by Garrick's demonic double gave the theatergoer a way to entertain notions about character's multivalence that were rather more difficult to extract from the patent theaters' ways of imitating Nature. By extension, the debate over Garrick's added strokes may have made it possible to suspect or even to wish that the languages of the body might communicate on their own, without the consent of the person in the body, and without conforming to the unwritten contract of decorum that constructed character as reading matter. Peter de Bolla has noted how the eloquence of the face became a point

at issue in the handbooks of the late eighteenth-century elocution movement. The problem for the theorists of the art of speaking seems to be that
the face, though the body part that is most meaningful, is also the part that
the performer arranging for the public textualization of his or her body is
least able to see. As the body part that concentrates the signs of self-
distinction, the face is in one sense of the term proper ("Every face must be
a certain man's," as Shaftesbury said), but it is also the part of the body
that is conceptually least like property. Thus John Wesley warns his reader
in *Directions Concerning Pronunciation and Gesture* (1770) that " 'tis the
face which gives the greatest life to action: of this therefore you must take
the greatest care, that nothing may appear disagreeable in it, since 'tis continually in the view of all but yourself."[52] De Bolla comments: "This is the
central problem posed by the face: it may give a different impression from
that conveyed by what one says or intends to say." The discursive analytic
of the texts on elocution moves, de Bolla claims, toward naming the place
where this excessive writing originates; it moves toward describing or
prescribing the text of the unconscious. Thinking about the surplus significance of the face leads to a reinvention of subjectivity as "an excess . . . in
relation to the body" and in relation to the body's representations.[53]

Like the pictorial effects wrought by caricatures, the theatrical effects
wrought by Garrick's face aroused controversy because they occasioned a
reconsideration of character's status as figure. They reworked the notions
of character as an instantiation of a type, as a body of writing, and an
object of sight. The symbolic confusion the popular theater and the caricature introduced into systems of character was for this reason attractive to
the very texts that denounced it: the denunciation could enable a covert
rethinking of character.

For this reason perhaps, references to the Garrick stage and also to the
printshop figure prominently in those characteristic writings of the mid-
century that we now class as novels: the habit of intertextual reference
assisted the generic consolidation of the novel, the processes by which the
genre asserted its distinctiveness. In his fiction Tobias Smollett reiterated
the terms in which the critics decried the excesses of Garrick's face. Roderick Random, for example, finds out the inside story of "Mr. Marmozet's"
social success: the player is admitted into genteel company only because of
"his talent of mimicking Punch and his wife Joan." Peregrine Pickle concurs with a Frenchman's judgment of Garrick's " 'grimaces' ": " 'his whole
art is no other than a succession of frantic vociferation, such as I have
heard in . . . Bedlam.' "[54] The novelist could *use* Garrick's overloading of
the theater's iconography of character — the fact that the player's refine-

ments of drama's gestural language seemed not only to produce richer representations but also to construct a character whose body, monstrously, defied or exceeded writing up. Garrick's overloading supplied the novelist with an alibi for the way he wavered between different options for construing the interrelations of characters, bodies, and writing. Furthermore, Smollett found in Garrick's surplus touches of nature, and in Hogarth's excesses too, an alibi for the problems of readability and closure that he brought upon himself in his efforts to elaborate a social knowledge that would adequately inventory all the characters composing a vastly diversified society.[55] The problem of the added stroke is, after all, built into that baggy monster the novel — which is, Smollett maintained in his Dedication to *Ferdinand Count Fathom* (1753), "a large diffused picture, comprehending the characters of life."[56]

While setting out on intertextual excursions that lead it to the theaters and printshops, while holding itself apart from others' "Flemish painting," and while maligning the semaphore of the dramaturgical body, the Smollett text disavows its own proclivity for going too far. Allusions to Rich's loathsome metamorphoses of "the human Shape" in his harlequinades perform a similar function for Fielding (*Joseph Andrews*, p. 32); so do the sneers at caricatures and the praise of Hogarth's characters.

While Smollett, Fielding, and Hogarth in his own peculiar way elaborated a demonology around popular players and venal caricaturists, each attempted to ascribe to his own work a distinction, a special capacity for mimesis that set that kind of work apart. Tracking their exercises in disfiguration and the scare tactics they deployed to ward off disfigurement brings to light the ambivalences and paradoxes accompanying their disruption of the economy of characteristic writing. New genres like the novel and like comic history painting were assembled as practitioners of characteristic writing looked askance at the overloaded faces produced by others. At the same time these debaters on faces, and would-be founders and improvers of genres, were aware that the differences of quality they asserted were undermined by the differences of quantity they allowed.

The Ends of Disfiguration: Characters Who Cannot Be Figured Out

The "stroke of character" eventually meant something new. Whereas character had been manifested previously by a patterned aggregation of discrete signs, aesthetic treatises of the late eighteenth century initiated Romantic hermeneutics' privileging of the multivalent fragment. The treatises find, as aesthetician Isaac D'Israeli asserts, the happily chosen single stroke of character to be more meaningful "than an elaborate delineation, as a glance of lightning will sometimes discover what has escaped us in full light." In a similar turn against the cultural attitude that had played up the *mise en page* of communication and had seen the character as the sum total of its traits, Archibald Alison in his *Essays on the Nature and Principles of Taste* argues that the artwork must be founded on "simplicity," meaning by this an emotional unity achieved by easy transitions among parts. In 1790 Alison decries the work that is mere "assemblage," and so makes it less possible to think of a character as a creature of letters. It would be wrong, however, to see Alison and D'Israeli's insistence on the individuality, or indivisibility, of the meaning of the character as a move that puts an end to characters' excesses or their illegibility. At this historical moment, the novel secures its hegemony within the cultural field, because, as we customarily claim, it reinvents character and becomes psychological: yet the psychological complexity the novel represents does not make mental states transparent, but institutes, rather, a contradictory relation between personal truths and the forms that make them publicly apprehensible, between actual and stipulated mental states. Instead of expressing a singular interiority, the novel-form locates subjectivity in the lack of fit between multiple accounts of the self. Victimized by her problems in managing her image, her character *mis*represented by her situation, her reputation, or her countenance, the blushing heroine who comes to preside over the novel-form offers another version of the overloaded portrait.[57]

As a last sign of the flux in the understanding of character — of the cultural contests and shifts that usher in a new, psychological novel and that Alison and D'Israeli formalize in their reconsiderations of the character trait — one might consider the marketing blitz that in the mid-eighteenth century surrounded the puzzling, extravagant persons of so-called remarkable characters or real characters. The hot commodities of the print market were portraits and texts devoted to beings preternaturally endowed with a surplus of characteristics, beings who were nondescript in the eighteenth-century sense of that term. At the end of the seventeenth century the "real character" had (as in John Wilkins's *Essay Towards a Real Character and a Philosophical Language*) been associated with projects for universally legible languages. Usage in the mid-eighteenth century, the heyday of the English eccentric, indicates, by contrast, that the phrase "real character" had at that point taken on the sense we give it now — the sense the *OED* glosses as "odd, extraordinary, or eccentric person," and the sense we have in mind when we talk not about someone "having" but about someone, like Sterne's Tristram Shandy, for instance, "being" a character.

In 1770 the correspondents' pages of *The Town and Country Magazine* sponsored a hunt for "Oddities": Thomas Chatterton contributed a description of the bizarre habits distinguishing a "proper candidate" of his acquaintance. The tabloid tastes catered to by the craze for real characters had their provenance in, above all, the transformations of the metropolitan marketplace. The late eighteenth-century collector who compiled a scrapbook titled "Remarkable Characters, Exhibitions and Fireworks" included among his mementos a number of mid-century broadsheet accounts of two eccentrics named Pinchbeck. The Pinchbecks, father and son, flaunted these eccentricities as a means of drawing custom to a shop where they sold things that we would now call novelty items or gizmos: clockwork models; the patent alarm for stopping sedan coaches; "the royal mourning buckle, button, and snuff box." The Pinchbecks' place of pride in the scrapbook speaks volumes about the affinities between the overloading of characters and the diversification of economic production that occurred as England made the transition to commercial capitalism.[58]

The history of overloaded countenances (the history of how "character" has exceeded its meaning) must, then, take into account the print- and book-market craze for the "queer card," the "original" (a character without precedent), and the "rum fellow" (so called, because books too arcane to find a readership in Britain were shipped to the West Indies and traded for rum). A particularly interesting label for the odd character came into use in mid-century when a Dublin theater manager, having laid a wager that he could in a single day introduce a word of no meaning into the language, chalked these four mystic letters, Q — U — I — Z, on all the blank walls in town.[59] The "quiz" who puzzled the dupes of this eighteenth-century Dubliner *is* a body of writing, but only just.

A character in this style cannot be figured out. By mid-century, by the time its "realness" had come to depend upon its indecipherability, "character" had begun to signify its own opposite.[60]

Cosmetic Poetics: Coloring Faces in the Eighteenth Century

TASSIE GWILLIAM

*T*he long history of attacks on the immorality of cosmetics, fueled by the association of makeup with feminine duplicity, has as its shadow history the use of cosmetics as the source for metaphors and analogies in visual and verbal art. Rhetoric as a form of "painting" and painting as a form of makeup enrich and complicate the representation of cosmetics. Fear of the moral duplicity of women imbues suspicions of rhetorical art, even though the glories and pitfalls of artistic representation are reflected in the composition of women's faces.[1] Cosmetic poetics is a special case of the eighteenth-century problematic of the dichotomies of surface and depths, mind and body, particularly as applied to women. Cosmetics on women's faces exemplify the pervasive anxiety about female surfaces, but because cosmetics have such a volatile, transferrable presence, they also become available as the site for other anxieties, other concerns.

In this essay I want to examine two eccentric eighteenth-century works that display central cultural anxieties — about race, femininity, and representation — through cosmetics. The first is a combination "Oriental tale" and cosmetic recipe book, *Abdeker: Or the Art of Preserving Beauty*, purporting to have been "Translated from an Arabic Manuscript," but in fact written by Antoine Le Camus, regent of the Faculté de Médecine in Paris, and translated from French into English in 1754.[2] The second work is an (unproduced) play by the actor and playwright Samuel Jackson Pratt, writing under the name Courtney Melmoth: *The New Cosmetic, or the Triumph of Beauty, A Comedy* (1790).[3] Using the customary association of cosmetics and women as the point of departure, I will explore the ways the two works, particularly through their deployment of exotic and unexpected contexts, offer alternative angles on cosmetic poetics.

Abdeker and *The New Cosmetic* install cosmetics in discourses other than misogyny.[4] *Abdeker* belongs in part to the emerging consumer society of the eighteenth century; some of its oddness diminishes if it is seen in the context of the commercialization of fashion rather than simply as a disrupted oriental tale.[5] *The New Cosmetic* delineates a remarkable if not unprecedented intersection between questions about race and women's use of makeup. In both texts, cosmetics are used ostensibly in service of women, although that apparently beneficial effect is complicated by the presence of other concerns. Both works take place in alien or exotic settings that absorb or deflect some of the energy that might otherwise be employed in accusations of feminine duplicity. Both texts also feature forms of oppression that define "coloring faces" and cosmetics as significant outside the confines of female vanity, though both ultimately return to an acceptance of feminine self-indulgence. In *Abdeker* cosmetics at one point mark resistance to tyranny and surveillance; in *The New Cosmetic* the recipe for rendering the skin white threatens briefly to undermine the system of racial difference. Without substantially altering the discourse on female coloring and painting itself, these texts alter the ground against which cosmetics are seen. By presenting the stabilization of a woman's complexion as a hedge against unjust sexual surveillance, *Abdeker* justifies feminine disguise, removing the woman from the prying eyes of patriarchal authority and returning her to a world of private and personal sexuality; however, in this transfer, she becomes subject to a domestic, "romantic" authority. By placing the desire of a European woman to whiten her sun-darkened skin in the context of black slavery, *The New Cosmetic* disturbs both the discourse of race and the discourse of sexuality. Color — the "white" and "red" — becomes charged with new significance in these exotic contexts.

That cosmetics violate nature's distinctions is one of the main arguments in the standard critique of their use; for example, an article in *The Gentleman's Magazine* of 1736 frowns on the ability of paint to obscure differences between "real" and "sophisticate" beauty:

In *France*, the Center and School of the Arts of Living, the Women are almost equally beautiful, and 'tis difficult to make a Distinction, tho' at never so little Distance. Those who are indebted to Nature for a fair Skin find themselves obliged to lay on Red. Those to whom Nature has not been so liberal, make no Difficulty of daubing their Skin all over; and if White is not sufficient, they add Blue, and streak their Veins with it. So that nothing is left for real Beauty to distinguish itself to Advantage from what is sophisticate. The Art of Daubing is not yet fashionable among us: but if our fine Ladies be not well upon their Guard, I fear they will soon be bubbled out of their natural Advantages. . . . So that Art, which was design'd to be the Servant and Assistant of Nature, takes at present, the Reins of Government in her Hands, and insolently drags Nature as a chain'd Captive at the Wheels of her Triumphant Chariot.[6]

This scenario of wicked female and imperialist triumph poses as a defense of the value of female beauty. It aligns itself with natural beauty and against those women who could, through French subterfuge, con their viewers. A female reader whose beauty is less than perfect, however, might not take the lesson from this warning that the author intends.

The use of cosmetics to erase differences between women or to counteract the effects of age produces some of the fiercest moral condemnations and the sharpest mockery. In most cases this mockery proclaims that paint is wholly inefficacious; that is, writers like François Bruys triumphantly skewer the glaring failure of makeup to mask age and ugliness in women:

How wilt thou fret proud CHLOE, when the shocking Reflection of thy wrinkled visage shall fright thee from thy Looking-Glass, and the hideous Ruins of thy former Beauties shall make thee fancy thyself a ghastly Sprite.

THEN, to be sure, wilt thou endeavour to conceal the Ravages of age, and with all the deceitful Powers of Cosmetics, smooth and plump up the Wrinkles of thy Brow. The natural *Lillies* and *Roses* of thy Bosom being withered, thou wilt be for laying on artificial colours: But all to no Purpose; for, maugre all the Art and Paint in the World, the Deformities of Old Age will show themselves.[7]

"Paint" is thus reassuringly transparent and easy to dismiss — and the woman who seeks to recapture what she has lost earns contempt for the self-delusive nature of her quest.

Abdeker, in contrast, holds out the lure — familiar from cosmetics advertisements in our own time — that paint will transform, actually remaking and rejuvenating the face. It speaks to a female reader able to believe the unbelievable, and willing to be soothed by seductive, magical metamorphoses. For example, the book extols the virtues of "the *Tea of the Sultaness*," which can be made at home by mixing "a Spoonful of Spirituous Vulnerary Water" with "two Spoonfuls of River Water": "It preserves the Complexion so fresh and fair, that a Woman of Seventy after using it will look as if she was not above Thirty-five." In the East, the plant from which the tea is made is protected — but not very successfully:

It grows at the Foot of a Mountain near *Mecca*; and the Grand Signior sets such a Value upon it, that it is Death for a Man to go within a certain Distance of the place where it is cultivated. The Sultanesses make great Use of it, and so do several Women in *Constantinople*, who buy it very dear from those that venture to steal it. (p. 80)

The paradoxical claim that the fabulous and unique can be reproduced in the humdrum world of the home is familiar from advertising and from the columns of popular magazines. The equally extravagant claims of efficacy — seventy to look thirty-five — can be seen either as feeding the delusions of easily fooled women, or as utopian fantasies about the reversibility of time, to be dreamt of but not performed.

The sultaness' tea, like the recipe *Abdeker* offers for restoring virginal constriction to female genitals made flaccid by too much intercourse, is labeled as a supplementary or covert aspect of the text. The Introduction proclaims the book's usefulness to the "Fair Sex" and promises a painlessly educational reading experience:

Abdeker was a Physician; he was in Love with the most beautiful Lady in the World; he let her into all the Mysteries of Beauty, and after so engaging a Manner, that by reading his Book you will be instructed in all the Secrets of his Art, though you will be at the same time persuaded that you have read nothing but the History of his Amours. (p. vi)

The recipes may constitute the selling point of the book, but the story of the love between Abdeker, court physician, and Fatima, the sultan's favorite, is presented as the aesthetically respectable aspect of this heterogeneous text. However, the cosmetics recipes and the disquisitions on "painting" often disrupt and overwhelm the erotic narrative, becoming foreground rather than backdrop, despite the editor's proud assertions that *Abdeker* is seamless narrative.

Abdeker appears to celebrate and encourage a woman's ability to resist penetration, and to demonstrate ways of keeping her feelings private under an oppressive system of surveillance. Although that system of surveillance is touted as "Oriental" — particular to the sultan's court — its resemblance to the ordinary situation of European women gives it additional resonance for the reader; that is, the sense that women are always being looked at and judged does not exist only in the exotic setting. This mapping of domestic concerns onto the fantasied, highly colored East has a function parallel to the somewhat uneasy coexistence of narrative and advice: the East, with its fabulous extremes of subjection, recasts the family and class problems of Europeans in an absolutist and defamiliarized form, rather as the erotic narrative glamorizes and justifies the process of self-construction through cosmetic art.

In a paradigmatic moment in *Abdeker*, cosmetics appear as a kind of mask behind which the free play of erotic possibility and expressiveness can take place. Fatima is temporarily free of the sultan's visits because he has been distracted from love by military concerns. Instead, "she enjoyed peaceably the Visits and Conversation of her Lover." But these visits spell danger because her emotions are written too clearly on her face, a problem she herself registers: "His Presence was so dear to her, that whenever he enter'd her Apartment, her Heart leap'd with Joy. This Satisfaction she perceived might easily be discern'd by her Countenance, as it was soon succeeded by a Blush" (p. 146).

The blush is, of course, the prized sign of female sensibility and modesty, a sign over which much ink was spilled. According to Dr. John Gregory, author of a conduct book purportedly addressed to his daughters, "When a girl ceases to blush, she has lost the most powerful charm of beauty."[8] Roy Porter pinpoints cosmetic blushes as a major source of "male ambivalence about make-up" in the eighteenth century:

The test of the modest woman lay in her capacity to blush. She who couldn't blush was a woman without shame. But the woman who wore rouge . . . wore an artificial blush, which (men feared) all too readily camouflaged lost innocence, that inability to blush, hid the bare-faced cheek of the shameless woman.[9]

The anxiety about the absent blush — a readable sign of lost modesty, lost shame — is transferred to the anxiety about the unvarying, artificial blush. The neat binary opposition between blush and lack of blush is converted to the more ominous problem of laminated versus unlaminated surfaces — more ominous because to engage the difficult question of female surfaces and depths is to enter a minefield. The artificial blush is ordinarily read as a threat to the system of signs; it undermines and makes unreadable supposedly "natural" distinctions, particularly distinctions between modest and immodest women.

The fear that a stabilization of color could mask fundamental distinctions reappears in another form in eighteenth-century thought: in the belief that black skin, like makeup, stymied interpretation of the face. Thomas Jefferson, in *Notes on the State of Virginia* (1781–82), using terms that replicate the discourse on the artificial blush, asks:

And is this difference of no importance? Is it not the foundation of a greater or less share of beauty in the two races? Are not the fine mixtures of red and white, the expressions of every passion by greater or less suffusions of colour in the one preferable to that eternal monotony, which reigns in the countenances, that immoveable veil of black which covers all the emotions of the other race?[10]

This almost uncanny displacement of rhetoric from one register of color to the other suggests the chameleon nature of cosmetic discourse, its volatile availability for expressions of deep anxiety about the disguises of the Other. The desire to see the face as a transparent guide to the emotions rather than having to interpret conflicting or problematical evidence is a feature of eighteenth-century semiotics as applied both to race and to gender.

In *Abdeker*, as we will see, the artificial blush becomes a positive defense against illegitimate penetration. Fatima's emotion-tinged blushes render her vulnerable to interpretation by those who wish to pry into her secrets, not to satisfy their own desires, but to report on her to their imperial superior:

The Eunuchs, who, to please their Master, interpret all the Proceedings of his Favourites, and endeavour to dive into their most hidden thoughts, might well guess the Cause of such Changes; and they might account it a great Piece of Merit to reveal it to the Sultan, who would most severely punish the Offender for an Action that shew'd such a Contempt of his Love and was an outragious Insult upon his Imperial Power. (p. 146)

Through the "Oriental" context, what could otherwise be construed as the sordid scenario of a jealous husband using servants to watch over an erring wife is transmuted and exalted into a whole system of political and sexual surveillance; and evading such authority turns from the indulgence of transgressive desires into a bold rejection of despotism. The systematic pervasiveness of patriarchal power is turned to absolutism, and Abdeker and Fatima become, not adulterers, but rebels.

ABDEKER foresaw the Danger, and resolved to shut up all the Avenues that might lead to it. To this End he proposed to give *Fatima* a different Countenance from what she had naturally. As an ingenious Painter he form'd artificial Features, that might serve as a Covering or a Sheath to the natural Colours that shone upon the Face of the Sultaness. Formerly he invented a kind of Paint that could hide from the most penetrating Eyes the tawny Colour of the young *Zinzima*. Calling to mind this Success, he thought he might also give *Fatima*'s Face a fix'd Colour, instead of that Paleness and Redness which alternately succeeded each other, when she was agitated by the Motion that necessarily accompanied her Passions. He therefore chose Vermilion to give a lively Colour to the Roses which began to grow pale upon so beautiful a Skin. It was under this apparent Veil he imagined that the Passions might have their Play without being perceived by the *Argusses* who endeavour to read and interpret what the Heart imprints upon the Face. (pp. 146–47)

Although this stabilization of color is given a status different from that of the pernicious artificial blush, that difference is, again, more in the context

than in the paint itself. The artificial blush here repels the assaults of
perception — by the eunuchs on behalf of the hypermasculine sultan — and
maintains the privacy of the lovers. The "apparent Veil" that Abdeker
constructs, however, takes on a peculiar, almost nonphysiological meaning; in what sense can the "Passions . . . have their Play" behind the veil of
color applied to Fatima's face? The *"Argusses"* cannot see the passions,
but neither can anyone else. Although Fatima ought to be the locus of
affect in this scenario — her ability to feel without revealing initially appears to be central — in fact Abdeker's privacy and safety receive greater
stress. Abdeker, as artist-lover, clearly holds a privileged position with
respect to Fatima's veiled passions, but the visual component of that position is at once emphasized and occluded. Abdeker takes possession of the
process of interpretation by wielding the tools of his art, but he does so
essentially by making interpretation impossible — except for himself:

Your Face perhaps may decide the Matter against us: We must hide the Sentiments
that would undoubtedly cause our Ruin. The Eyes of your Keepers read and
interpret the Motions which Love excites in your Countenance with Darts of
Fire; therefore let us cover that faithful Interpreter of your Thoughts and Sentiments. (pp. 147–48)

Cosmetics assume a critical role in this politicized context, and the erotic
triangle (wife-husband-lover) is obscured and covered over by the harem
setting. The presence of eunuchs as spies and the multiple wives glamorize
that banal triangle, in part by reconstituting it as politically significant.
Cosmetic disguise takes on a new vitality through this deflection or reorientation; disguise assumed against oppressive penetration is validated
in a larger sphere, but the displacement of disguise into the exotic world of
the harem seems also in danger of collapsing into a way of dressing up
cosmetic indulgence and adultery.

The violent implications in the patriarchal politics of painting emerge
most strikingly when the sultan wields his power over life and death to
illustrate his connoisseurship:

[The Sultan] gave no less Proof of his Cruelty by the Method he took to let *Belino*
understand that he had great Knowledge and Capacity in the Art of imitating
Nature by Colours. This famous Painter employ'd all his Skill in drawing a Picture
which represented the Beheading of St. *John* the Baptist. . . . *Mahomet* examined it
with Pleasure, and discover'd great Beauties therein. But to shew that he did not
judge like a blind Admirer, and that his Criticism proceeded from Skill and Reason, he blamed the Painter for not having studied the Effect which Nature is wont
to produce upon the like Occasion in the Sufferer's Flesh . . . he resolved by a most

evident Demonstration to convince the ingenious Painter of his Ignorance. He accordingly sent for a Slave, and cut off the poor Wretch's Head with a Stroke of a Sabre, giving by this means to the Artist a Model that was capable of solving the Difficulty. (p. 149)

This act sensationalizes pictorial representation; the sultan produces a model after the likeness has been made, undermining the independence of the representation, which becomes a pale precursor of the decapitated slave, a far more riveting object than any painting. As Fatima's face is remade by cosmetics, detached from the promptings of her body, so is this slave's head turned into an object for interpretation and literally severed from his body. The artist becomes, willy-nilly, complicit in murder; representing decapitation leads to an actual decapitation by a logic that reverses and renders frightening the benign if spooky feats of *trompe l'oeil*.

Mahomet's power to kill to reproduce a painting — and to reproach an artist — reorients in a scandalous fashion some of the motivating concerns of *Abdeker*. The slave's death in the service of the sultan's capricious interpretive eye also has implications for the dangers Abdeker and Fatima court by using paint to hide from that eye. Too, the fixity of the picture of John the Baptist's head has subterranean links with the fixity of the artificial "veil" or sheath that conceals Fatima's face; each is a masklike portrait, equivocally detachable, with an ambiguous relation to something living — or at least something newly killed. The picture of John the Baptist's beheading is obviously not the precise equivalent of Fatima's retreat behind her mask of paint, but the two show a similar process of arrest and removal as well as the detachment of head from body. The idea that painting has an affinity with corpses further recalls, in the cosmetic context, the attacks on women's attempts to revivify outworn flesh through makeup, attempts reviled as futile efforts to repeal age and death: "Now get you to my lady's chamber, and tell her, let her paint an inch thick, to this favor she must come. Make her laugh at that," as Hamlet says to Yorick's skull.

Abdeker's response to Fatima includes a double perception of her as art object and as beloved, and the intersection of the two makes her status as living human being increasingly problematical. Abdeker calls her "so excellent a Mirrour of Beauty, that one cannot look at you without reflecting upon a charming Face and Shape, and without desiring to preserve them when present, as to recover them when absent" (p. 62). The troubling interest in "preservation," a form of arrest, is further complicated by the idea of "recovery"; Fatima exists less and less as a person, and more and more as a painting — not just a painted woman, but a painting. In fact, she responds to Abdeker's application of the cosmetic mask by confusing herself with her portrait:

[Abdeker] pull'd out a small Box that contain'd Vermilion; he took a Pencil, dipp'd it therein, and dexterously painted the Cheeks of the Sultaness. *Fatima* consulting her Looking-glass, I do not know myself, cried she: Heavens! What a Prodigy! My Cheeks are as red as *Tyrian* Purple, and as radiant as a Flame. . . . I remember it was thus that *Belino*, by the Emperor's Order, drew my Picture upon a Piece of Linen. His Portrait was so true and lively, that I believed he had communicated Part of my Existence to his Cloth, or that by his Magic Art he had enliven'd another *Fatima*. Pardon me this Crime: you know that the Maxims of the *Alcoran* forbid the *Mussulmans* to make a Representation of living Things. (p. 148)

Alien contexts — the explicit link forged between cosmetics and portraiture and the assertion that Belino's portrait dangerously violates the anti-representational taboo of Islam — remake and energize the purely conventional nature of Fatima's praise for the portrait and her delighted sense that she herself has been transformed. The decapitated slave as authorizing presence for the portrait of John the Baptist also produces a resonating frisson. However, Fatima's willing participation in her metamorphosis does not entirely obscure the fact that she is essentially in the process of being removed from the picture and replaced by a series of representations and cosmetic supplements; the representations, it is implied, serve the purposes of those around her as well as she could, and the cosmetic supplements clearly emerge as the actual point of the text. Thus preserved and recovered through various arts, Fatima the woman may no longer be necessary. Because of the flatness of representation in *Abdeker* itself, because of the book's generic indeterminacy, and because of its absorption in and celebration of the power of surfaces, the question of Fatima's subjectivity seems moot.

In *Abdeker* painting the face removes the woman thus painted from the sphere of public interpretation and makes her the subject of purely private knowledge; this exotic, oriental text returns the heroine to a domestic, heterosexual haven. The painted woman is thus drained of threat and secured for the social order.

Abdeker focuses on cosmetics as an accretion of surfaces and as a kind of mask applied to the face; the makeup that Fatima wears smooths out variations in color and conceals her emotions from those who would probe her. In contrast, *The New Cosmetic* reveals the meaning of "color" and the body through a "cosmetic" that violently excoriates the flesh. The "cosmetic" in this play is equivocally related to paint; although its primary use is for whitening the skin, it seems more an agent of removal than of addition. The recipe promises that "the skin will come *off* in a mask," and the descriptions of its effects are linked to flagellation as much as to painting (p. 37).

The New Cosmetic, despite its apparent eccentricity as a dramatic work, clearly capitalizes on contemporary interest in the colonial sugarcane plantations of the West Indies. The late eighteenth-century ferment over slavery, and over political liberation in general, here metamorphoses into the material for a farcical romantic comedy, one in which, however, the early action takes place to the offstage sound of slaves being whipped.[11] This unstable text links the traditional topos of a woman's vanity-inspired pursuit of cosmetic improvement with forays into the realms of slavery, race, colonialism, and sexual transgression.

The play begins with the arrival on an island in the West Indies of Lovemore, a gentleman seeking out the woman he courted back home in England. Lovemore quickly learns from the local men, however, that his Louisa is not what she once was: her complexion and hence her beauty have been destroyed by the harsh sun and climate.[12] The men discuss Louisa's simultaneous loss of looks and lovers in terms that underline the perception that a darkening of skin color can be construed as a change of race: "I loved the girl once, when she was white, but never thought of her once after she became a Mulatto," says Greville, one of the locals.[13] He adds, with a certain sadistic satisfaction, that her devaluation has taught Louisa a lesson: "It has broke her of her coquetry; she is in as bad a condition as a peacock stript of its plumes" (p. 30). Becoming the wrong color removes her privilege as a European woman and opens her to the abuse of her former admirers; she becomes undesirable, or at any rate an inappropriate object for "love." But her loss of desirability is also tied to the sexual availability of slave women — who are, significantly, wholly absent in their own persons in the play. It seems that Louisa as devalued woman has to stand in for this other disruptive category of women whose sexuality constitutes their primary reason for being, at least in the literary economy that encloses them here. Lovemore, for example, later responds to Louisa's transformation by saying that he "must take consolation with a black wench at last" (p. 51). The sense that the "black wench" — ambiguously Louisa herself or some nameless, faceless slave — is an almost inevitable sexual recourse for the white male colonist makes Louisa's need to reclaim her racial difference all the more urgent. As "blackamore," "Mulatto," or "black wench," Louisa becomes the site for the community's anxiety about sex and race, despite the fact that, as discolored white woman, she lacks sexual attraction and racial privilege. Her *difference* from those women with whom she is identified — her unplaceability as either sexual or marital commodity — makes her valueless. Because she cannot conclusively be categorized as "white" or "black," she cannot be married or raped. What appears to be Louisa's status as a woman in fact depends on race; only whiteness can return her to her "feminine" privileges and desirability, and keep her from being paradoxically perceived as entirely defined as a sexual body.

Regaining those privileges, which no longer seem natural components of femininity because they can be lost through a change in color, emerges as an arduous but imperative task. Louisa's envious cousin, Hannah Bananah, dangles before her a recipe that will avert a life of spinsterhood by turning her white again: "I could put you in a way now cousin, if I chose it, to make a blackamore white" (p. 33), Hannah says of her "cashoo oil" treatment, giving a proverbial phrase of absolute impossibility literal force, but producing additional overtones from the presence of actual, not metaphoric, "blackamores." But in the West Indies, "washing a blackamoor white" did not always describe an impossibility; it was used to denote incestuous "transformation" of the race of one's offspring, as Thomas Morris, in the notes to *Quashy, or, The Coal-Black Maid* (1797), reveals: "The amorous intercourse of masters with black Slaves is too well known to need explanation; the poor creatures dare not resist: and the horrid practice of *washing a blackamoor white* has by some old wretches been gloried in; that is, intriguing with the mother, daughter, granddaughter, &c. till the black color disappear."[14] The association of anathematized forms of sexuality — incest and miscegenation — reinforces the taboo against racial transformation, but also renders it more exciting to the imagination.

The process of changing Louisa's race will be painful; Louisa will be "well burnt for it," but she will then be "like a new tried piece of gold, finer for going thro' the fire" (p. 37). The invocation of gold underlines Louisa's loss of value on the marriage market as well as her need for vigorous measures to restore her status as a commodity.

But on this island the recipe reverberates outside the familiar purviews of feminine vanity and female commodification; problems of sex, race, and gender combine and recombine through the agency of the "new cosmetic." Hannah's description of the cashew oil cosmetic is overheard by the eager Greville, whose description in the dramatis personae as a "petit Maitre" signals his vulnerability to "feminine" faults such as vanity and an obsession with appearance. Greville decides to try the recipe for whitening on one of the slaves before he tries it on himself: if Quacou can endure the pain of the experiment, then Greville will restore his own complexion. Quacou, of course, has his own reasons for being vitally interested in color; he wants to know if the recipe will "make a negroe man white, Massah." "Whiteness" means something quite different for the slave Quacou than it does for Greville. To lure the slave into enduring the suffering entailed by the cosmetic, Greville tells Quacou that the recipe "is kept a profound secret from all the blacks, lest they should become as white as ourselves, and so no longer continue in subjection to us" (p. 39), suggesting that slavery is an artificial construct dependent on racial difference, which in turn depends wholly on color.[15] Furthermore, according to Greville, one form of stripping or unmasking may lead, metonymically, to another: "Set them about skinning their faces, and in a little time they will shake off the yoke and fetters of servitude" (ibid.). But Greville also holds out to Quacou the supposedly overwhelming temptation of intercourse across racial lines, along with the magical liberation from slavery, thus returning the focus to the intersection of race and sexuality: he asserts that using the cosmetic will make Quacou "so lovely, that the very white women will be glad to adopt him as a husband" (ibid.). Not only black women but white women too become available for exchange among men, even across the (dissolving) line of racial difference — and even though one of the men is already himself a slave, the quintessence of commodity. Underlining the sexual component of the racial transformation he offers, Greville neatly links his own banal wish for sexual "conquests" to Quacou's hope for actual liberation: "Faith the experiment will do well, if as it gives the black fellow the opportunity of shaking off his chains, it should enable me to lead fresh captives [i.e., women] in mine" (pp. 39–40).

Both the "naturalness" of black slavery and the "naturalness" of femininity are put into question by the "new cosmetic." Louisa's desire to regain her white skin signifies her desire to regain both racial and sexual privilege, but the notion that an artificial aid can procure that change has at least the potential to disturb the binary racial opposition of "black" and "white." Further, offering the possibility that removing a black skin to reveal a white skin beneath can liberate a slave does potentially uproot racial difference by turning it into a matter of exchangeable surfaces, rather than of deep anatomical structure. If racial difference is a detachable mask, its significance seems far more trivial and inconsequential.[16] The desirability and naturalness of whiteness of course remain paramount, but, just as women's cosmetics threaten to obscure the difference between kinds of women, this cosmetic may obscure and redefine racial difference.

The play also employs the cosmetic to interrogate the slave system's need to brutalize the body, as well as to create startling if covert inversions of power over the body. The story is told of a planter who tried to raise the slaves "above their brutal state," but who found that as their intellects improved "their corporeal faculties relaxed," making them useless as slaves — so the attempt was abandoned without hesitation and whipping reinstated. These tortured bodies recur insistently throughout the play. Quacou lures Greville into self-torture by pretending that the hot oil treatment does not hurt. When Greville, in agony, asks Quacou how he could bear it, Quacou taunts him with slavery's dependence on physical punishment: "How can a negroe feel pain; we never feel when you beat us?" The myth of the impervious black body returns to wreak vengeance on the white man. Through the agency of the cosmetic, and without ostensibly rebelling, Quacou succeeds in turning the world upside down, and having Greville, the white man, "whip" himself — chemically. Even protests against slavery's torture of the body partake of the cosmetic's effect. Lovemore, for instance, complaining that "slavery is a damned thing," says that he "was near slinging an overseer t'other day into a cauldron of hot liquor for flogging a slave beyond his deserts" (p. 55). The island seems obsessed by whipping and full of excoriated flesh, both black and white.

Quacou's willingness to endure pain in pursuit of liberty is explicitly linked to Louisa's willingness to endure pain to retrieve her feminine status, although the depiction of the cosmetic in terms of whipping and beating is replaced in her rhetoric by other forms of torment characteristic of the islands. Louisa reports that "I actually felt as if my face was the prey of scorpions and centipedes or of mosquitos. . . . Indeed it was the most comical, and at the same time the most painful sensation I ever felt" (pp. 47–48). The insistence on the amusement in this pain, like the topsy-turvy farcical suffering of Greville, seeks to keep the play within the bounds of comedy, despite its depictions of physical violence and injustice. By returning to the "feminine" uses of the cosmetic as the primary subject, Pratt tries to control tone and genre; the need to marry seems a much less explosive topic for comedy than slavery's violence.

The drama's denouement, however, refuses to let go of the interconnectedness of race, representation, and sexuality. Louisa's transformation is insistently tied to the context of slavery's violation of the body as well as to other forms of racial mixing under colonialism. In an apartment of waxwork statues, Louisa, newly white, enters and stands on a pedestal.

Among the other statues is a waxwork of the slave whom Louisa's father, Mr. Winstone (despite his reputation for relative kindness), had lashed to death. This slave has haunted his master's conscience so much that he has erected this memorial to appease the ghost. Lovemore, who does not know yet that Louisa has turned white again or that she is present in the waxwork gallery, portentously links the fates of the dead slave and the devalued Louisa, and figures the daughter's racial metamorphosis as the price paid for the father's cruelty: "Heaven I see has revenged the old man's severity, and for a slave killed has returned a daughter burned; for a black lost, a mulatto gained" (p. 60). This incongruous yoking forms part of the play's pervasive, if unstable, association between women's shifting surfaces and racial transformation. Louisa's putative status as "mulatto" — between black and white — magically alters the supposedly unalterable, but also has a more realistic context in the usual method by which mulattoes were produced — the rape of slaves by their masters. The figure of the mulatto, for whom Louisa stands, is a politically and erotically charged presence in these surroundings. Janet Schaw, in writing of her visit to Antigua in the 1770s, has an extraordinary outburst about "the crouds of Mullatoes" she sees there. Although their existence signals the "crime" of the white male colonists, she transfers the blame — and her visceral distaste — for that crime onto "the young black wenches" who "lay themselves out for white lovers. . . . This prevents their marrying with their natural mates, and hence a spurious and degenerate breed, neither so fit for the field, nor indeed any work, as the true bred Negro."[17] The basis of the magical change from black to white in cross-racial sexual abuse is alluded to directly in *The New Cosmetic* when one of the onlookers in the waxwork scene remarks, with transparent innuendo: "For my part I expect to see all the other figures start into life. They are all black, white, and yellow the natural children of old Winstone" (p. 65). The actual "natural children" on the island, illegitimate offspring of masters and slaves and themselves born into slavery, mark the real form of racial transformation that would be taking place. The "new cosmetic" only displaces that reality.

In a parallel instance of magical transformation, the play also revives the Ovidian tradition of metamorphoses that turn women into art objects and art objects into women. Lovemore responds with admiration and desire to the "statue" of Louisa, commenting on its fleshly verisimilitude, and linking himself to Pygmalion — despite the fact that he, unlike Abdeker, is not the artist: "Would you be so obliging as to permit me to touch this wax, for upon my soul the artificial vermillion of the lips looks so much like real, balmy, benign true blood, that I am almost tempted to kiss them. If I gaze longer, like the statuarist of old I shall forget myself, and fall in love with a piece of wax" (p. 61). But when he moves to embrace the statue, it reacts; Louisa jumps off the pedestal "and falls back into the attitude of a fencer, with her fan in her right hand," according to the stage directions (ibid.). Despite Louisa's pugnacious response, however, the former lovers are ultimately reunited, with Lovemore's apology for rejecting Louisa in her blackened state standing as a characteristically illogical and capricious solution to the play's difficulties: "If I had any idea you could have been so metamorphosed, I vow and protest I would have taken more pains to have deserved your love" (p. 63).

The neat comic resolution for the two lovers does not, however, reach to include the rest of the cast — nor does it succeed in containing the more peculiar aspects of the investigation of sex and race in *The New Cosmetic*. The cosmetic turns out not to be universally efficacious; from the height of its possible service as a magical transformer of race, it dwindles to being nothing more than a mundane whitening agent with limited utility, probably no more painful or dangerous than other cosmetics in common use.[18] In fact, it succeeds only on the lucky Louisa, who is after all a rather recent import to the island, as well as the (basically white) heroine of the play. No racial transformation actually takes place, unless the fact that both Quacou and Greville look as if they have leprosy and are said to resemble Harlequins indicates a leveling of racial difference, and Hannah Bananah has put off using the cashew oil until too late, according to Louisa: "Poor girl, she has been trying, but all to very little purpose: the sun burn and yellow jaundice together has sunk so very deep into her face, that nothing under the surgeon's knife could ever possibly eradicate them thence" (p. 76). Ever more radical, useless mutilations of the body thus appear on the horizon; the cosmetic has changed little.

Both *Abdeker* and *The New Cosmetic*, in widely disparate ways, place the conventions of the discourse on women and cosmetics in an exotic context in order to render intelligible — and, ultimately, to domesticate and defuse — questions of sexuality and representation. In both texts, however, the exotic backdrops infiltrate and complicate the enclosed worlds of feminine vanity they seem intended merely to support and glamorize. The masculine control of representation that appears in the sultan's decapitation of the slave in *Abdeker* — a highly "Oriental" scene of despotic power — in fact mirrors Abdeker's normative creation of the carmined mask that Fatima assumes. The lurid scene of murder uncovers an aspect of the conventional use of cosmetic transformation that otherwise could remain obscure: that is, both the sultan and Abdeker take over ownership of the body and emotions of the subjected person through their interventions in the process of representation. In *The New Cosmetic*, the siting of feminine cosmetic vanity in the minefield of race and slavery reveals more about the explosive interreactions of sexuality and race than the play seems able to digest or absorb.

By displaying their incongruities quite openly — *Abdeker* marks its generic heterogeneity with interpolated recipes; *The New Cosmetic* deliberately represents the horrors of slavery through farce — the two works allow the reader to view clearly the process of construction that often remains hidden in more consciously coherent works. The crucial interpretive status for the culture of a woman's face is marked in black and white — or red and white — in these two eccentric texts.

Part 3

The Limits of the Body

The Powers of Horror and the Magic of Euphemism in Lessing's 'Laokoon' and 'How the Ancients Represented Death'

DOROTHEA VON MÜCKE

*T*he title of this essay clashes with the widely accepted view of Lessing's aesthetics. In terms of an affective register we generally associate Lessing with pity/*Mitleid* and recall the deliberate exclusion of *phobos*, fear or horror, from his poetics of the bourgeois tragedy. And if we think of his semiotic and aesthetic theory we will remember already from his early treatise on the fable the condemnation of gratuitous poetic ornamentation.[1] Surely I do not want to question the adequacy of characterizing Lessing's poetics in these terms. However, I would like to direct my attention to some seemingly marginal aspects of Lessing's theory of representation. Except for Carol Jacobs's analysis of Lessing's critical performance, the last chapters of the *Laokoon* about ugliness and disgust have received little attention.[2] Whereas Carol Jacobs has focused on the pivotal position of these passages for an understanding of Lessing's self-reflective deployment of figural language in order to argue that these passages undermine presumably stable structures of authority, origin, and history, I shall analyze some of the same passages in order to examine how they invoke the human body. I will show how these at first sight marginal or excessively digressive passages are indeed absolutely central to Lessing's theory of representation. Lessing's semiotic and aesthetic theory is intricately linked to an attempt at organizing the threatening or disruptive aspects of corporeality.

First I shall analyze the role of the human body in Lessing's *Laokoon*. Then I shall focus on *How the Ancients Represented Death* (*Wie die Alten den Tod gebildet*) in order to examine how he transforms the image of death in such a manner that it supports a rational subject position without having recourse to the scare tactics of Christianity or the denial of sentience within the sublime. I shall show how Lessing situates the adherence to an order of law — be it the Law of Beauty, the rules of rational discourse, or the conventions of euphemism — within the order of sentience and even pleasure.

Lessing begins the *Laokoon* with a polemic against Winckelmann's celebration of Greek sculpture.[3] He quotes Winckelmann's idealizing description of the Laocoon sculpture: "He [i.e., Laocoon] does not scream like Virgil's hero, the opening of his mouth would not admit a scream: it is rather an anxious and oppressive sigh. . . . Laocoon suffers . . . his misery touches our soul; but we wish to bear the misery like the great man."[4] Lessing objects to Winckelmann that screaming as an expression of pain is merely human, and this aspect of human nature finds ample documentation also among Greek artists. If the Laocoon of the Greek sculpture does not scream like Virgil's Laocoon, we cannot argue that this proves the Greeks' superiority over the Romans. It is merely due to the fact that he is hewn in stone. If he were screaming, the position of his mouth would be frozen in time, and this gaping mouth would be utterly ugly.

This brings Lessing immediately to the central issue of his essay: the boundaries between painting and poetry. Painting deploys visual signs in a spatial order; poetry deploys audible signs in a temporal order. Therefore the natural contents of visual representations are the depiction of bodies in space. For poetic representation the appropriate subjects are the depiction of actions in time. Considering the practice of contemporary portraits and Dutch still-lifes, Lessing admits that it is culturally variable whether or not artists have been restricted by what made their representations beautiful, that is, by the Law of Beauty. However, this initial move suggests already that beauty itself is not the result of observing some arbitrary norm or convention but, like ugliness, a gut-level response to the proper or improper use of the medium. In other words, beauty belongs to a fundamental order of human sentience, which Lessing affirms. The Law of Beauty, as a prescription of specific content selections, seems to belong to the order of societal norms. Yet, as based on the observance of media-specific limitations, it is grounded in a natural, affective order.

Lessing's main argument concerns a reexamination of the Horatian *ut pictura poesis*. For him all the visual arts are subsumed under the rubric of painting, whether he is dealing with sculpture or with painting proper. Less concerned with actual visual perception than with the visual impression modeled on the perspectival illusion of a tableau, he is talking about the vision produced by the imagination, our mental faculty that produces images. It is the free use of the imagination by which a work of art has to be measured. The wise sculptor of the Laocoon chose what Lessing terms a "pregnant moment," the moment just before the climax, which allows the imagination to flesh out what had been going on before the scene represented and what would come afterward. In brief, the aim of all art is the illusionary effect of a transparent representation, the "presence to mind" of an existentially absent object.[5]

The boundaries between the art of painting and poetry must then lie in the different ways by which they realize this common goal. For painting the case seems to be clear: it can and should only represent visible bodies in space such that they evoke the immediate presence to mind of the intended scene. What makes the signs of painting natural is that the mode of reception resembles the actual mode of perception of the existentially absent object. And this mode of perception and reception is the instantaneous and simultaneous apprehension of an organized whole, of bodies arranged in a spatial order. Verbal language can of course also represent a visual scene, though not in this immediate manner. Since it is subject to the successive articulation of individual sounds, the totalizing impact of the entire scene is merely the outcome of piecing back together what has been fragmented into individual parts in the verbal description of the scene. How, then, can poetry naturalize the arbitrary signs of language? It can do so if it refrains from description but instead sticks to its proper medium by focusing on the representation of actions, which are perceived as unfolding in time. Narration can make us visualize a whole scene as if we were looking at a movie.

But why should the instantaneous apprehension of a whole, the illusionary presence to mind of an existentially absent object, be the source of aesthetic pleasure and the defining feature of the beautiful? How are we to understand the nature of aesthetic pleasure? How does Lessing establish the norm of what is beautiful and what is ugly? We have already seen that his theory of aesthetic representation is grounded in the semiotic ideal of transparency, of a mode of signification which ideally veils the arbitrary nature of signifiers. Yet, with regard to the fine arts, as long as they stay away from allegorical representations, this issue would be of no concern: a screaming Laocoon hewn in stone, mouth open, would not call for a major decoding effort. This was not the problem that led the artist to abstain from representing him this way. Rather, it was the consideration that the open mouth would have drawn attention to the materiality of the medium, the lifeless, hard nature of the marble as mere stone. And this would have prevented our imagination from fully realizing the entire scene in which the legendary Laocoon was involved.

Could we conclude from this that the ugly has something to do with the sensuous, weighty stuff of matter? Furthermore, that it is some aspect of materiality which aesthetic signification is supposed to bracket? For if aesthetic representation is to result in bringing before our mental eyes an existentially absent object, this form of quasi seeing must not be turned back into a real physical sensation. This means, then, that aesthetic pleasure is qualitatively different from any actual physical enjoyment, that it has somehow to do with our ability to distance ourselves from the actual physical sensations originating in our bodies.

Indeed, this seems to be the issue for Lessing's discussion of the pleasures we experience through representations, when he argues together with Mendelssohn that many affects that would be exclusively unpleasant if evoked by actually existent objects (objects of fear, sadness, horror, and pity), are not at all unpleasant to us if they are evoked by representations. Now, this requires a modification or specification of the previously elaborated model of aesthetic illusion: if I previously emphasized the fact that aesthetic representation should evoke the presence to mind of an existentially absent object — now, the emphasis is on the fact that we must by no means confuse this ideational object with a real object. Although we should see the signified as if it were given to our eyes, we must also know that it is merely the imaginary product of an *as if*.

Does this mean that aesthetic pleasure is to be understood as the self-reflective pleasure of the imagination, the enjoyment of our ability to distance ourselves from the material involvement in the world and the physical limitations of our bodies? This is certainly suggested if we consider what Lessing defines as the utter opposite of and obstacle to aesthetic pleasure, when he argues that there is one unpleasant affect that does not become pleasurable by virtue of its illusionary nature. This affect is disgust. Disgust resists the transformative power of aesthetic illusion because this affect is utterly indifferent to whether its object is given in its concrete existence or whether it is merely given at the level of representation. "According to the law of the imagination, the repulsive sensation of disgust comes from the mere representation in the soul, the object might be taken for real or not. There is no point in foregrounding the artificiality of the imitation in order to soften the injured sentiment. The unpleasure resulted not on condition that the evil was real, but it originated from the mere representation of it, and as such it is really there. This is why the sensations of disgust are always nature, never imitation" (p. 154). Our physical response, the sensation of disgust, remains the same unpleasant urge to vomit. In other words, disgust asserts the here and now of our bodily existence and our limited control over our bodily reactions. Like the aesthetic illusion of the beautiful it can make an object of representation real to us, in the sense of *wirklich*. However, disgust is opposed to aesthetic illusion in the sense that it cancels the boundaries between representations and the real: it confronts us with a real that cannot be ideationally apprehended but exists in its undifferentiated, unsemioticized crude materiality.

Lessing's discussion of disgust situates the aesthetic ideal of transparency in relation to the human body. Already the introduction of disgust as the limit of the aesthetic indicates that aesthetic pleasure and the beautiful are related to a particular screening out of our own concrete bodily existence. The examples Lessing uses in this discussion will allow us to gain a fuller understanding of this mechanism.

With regard to the representation of a beautiful body, Lessing discusses at length the example of Helen. Although Homer never gives us a description of this most beautiful of all women, we nevertheless are convinced of her beauty. He narrates how the elders of Troy when she appears at the wall express their desire for her. What could convey a stronger impact on our imagination than this scene in which old wise men for a moment forget their dignity in order to gaze at Helen. Not the description of a vision but the words of the elders produce the desire and make us imaginatively visualize Helen's beauty. Yet, the painter Zeuxis, the only one whom Lessing deems comparable to the poet Homer, chose an altogether different route in order to show Helen's beauty: "As the wise poet chose to show us beauty only in its effect, knowing he would not be able to show it in its components, the equally wise painter showed nothing but its components and deemed it indecent were his art to have recourse to any other aids. His painting consisted exclusively of the figure of Helen in all her nudity" (p. 142).

Why does Lessing have to evoke the issue of decency? Why does he call the poet wise who manages to portray Helen's beauty indirectly through the representation of the elders' self-oblivious expression of desire, whereas he applauds the painter's direct and exclusive representation of the nude female body? Apparently the painterly representation would become indecent if instead of merely representing Helen, the object of desire, it had also represented the elders as desiring her. Count Caylus, who had recommended the Homeric scene as one that should be painted, made exactly this faux pas and Lessing rebukes him: "A greedy glance makes the most venerable face ridiculous and an old man who betrays youthful desires is even a disgusting object" (p. 143). The representation of Helen's effect on the elders in the painting would lend a visible body to the verbal expression of desire, it would draw attention to sexual desire as an uncontrolled physical affect. It would remind us as beholders of our own potential loss of body control.

Lessing further chastises Caylus for his suggestion that Helen in this painterly scene as in the Homeric scene should be veiled. For if in the painting the object of desire is not even visible but has to be imagined under the veil, the nature of the imaginary projection that is at the bottom of this illusion of beauty becomes painfully obvious, Helen a figment of the old men's sexual imagination. What fuels Lessing's anger against Caylus's suggested painting is the fact that this artifact could be viewed as mapping and foregrounding aesthetic illusion as a conventional mechanism of a "fort-da machine" that can work as an extension and cover-up for our mortal, imperfect bodies only as long as the mechanism of this machine remains invisible. Aesthetic illusion produces the visual presence of a classical beautiful body, and it makes the mortal, sexualized body of the beholder disappear from sight.

Whereas the previous example bearing on the representation of beauty in painting and poetry focused on the technique of the presencing (the "da") of the classical body, the following examples deal with ugliness and the eclipse (the "fort") of the mortal body. At first it seems that poetry cannot even try to represent ugliness of forms, since it cannot represent bodies in space. Yet Homer represents the ugly body of Thersites. By breaking up the overall picture in the descriptive enumeration of the individual body parts, the effect of the whole is reduced. But this is exactly what makes ugliness of forms a permissible ingredient in poetic representation as opposed to painting. Once its effect has been softened it can be mixed with other sentiments and therefore ultimately work in the service of the pleasant affects.

Another example Lessing uses in order to illustrate how disgust becomes a necessary ingredient of the ridiculous is a passage from the English weekly *The Connoisseur* describing a wedding ceremony of the Hottentots. He quotes the passage not in the main text but only in a footnote. The main text retells and analyzes the passage in the following manner. He isolates three elements: (1) the description of a vision, (2) the affective response to that vision, and (3) the language and style of description. First he asks the reader to think of a flattened nose, flaccid breasts hanging down to the navel, a body smeared in its entirety with lard and soot, etc. Then he asks the reader to imagine all of this as an object of a fiery, respectful, and tender love; should the reader hear this expressed in the noble language of seriousness and admiration, certainly he or she would not be able to abstain from laughter (p. 160). Lessing's segmentation of the *Connoisseur* passage emphasizes the power of verbal expression to reduce and to alter the affect evoked by a visual impression.

By rendering the *Connoisseur* passage this way, Lessing suggests that our imagination first of all conjures up the absent object of description, by which we would be naturally repulsed. Yet, since we are dealing with the successive enumeration of descriptive details, the object of disgust remains sufficiently vague not to remind us of our own bodies. At the same time it is just enough present to emphasize its inherent incompatibility with the affect of fiery love and admiration evoked by the rhetorically elevated style of description. Is the laughter an expression of relief over the fact that the language of heroic poetry remains impervious to the disgusting materiality of a concrete body? The result of an assured difference between *res* and *verba*, the content and the expression level of the representation, the signified and the signifier?

It seems noteworthy that the actual passage from *The Connoisseur* focuses on the mock-heroic description of the Hottentot woman in the context of the preparations and the process of a marriage ceremony. *The Connoisseur* achieves the comical effect through its particular focalization: the vision of the woman is rendered through the perspective of the bridegroom, and the verbal expression of the vision is rendered in the rhetorical conventions of a connoisseur of classical poetry. Here, the irony seems to be fueled by the "ethnographer's" inability to read the ritual. It provokes a clash between, on the one hand, familiar and civilized, and, on the other hand, opaque and barbaric conventions. This performance-oriented aesthetics of *The Connoisseur* grounds its pleasure in an assurance of group identity. It seems to run exactly counter to Lessing's representational aesthetics that wants to anchor aesthetic pleasure in a universal human response rather than in a social rite.

However, Lessing introduces the example with the remark, "It is well known how dirty the Hottentots are, how many things they deem beautiful, delicate and holy that evoke in us disgust and repulsion" (p. 160). This statement seems to do the same as the *Connoisseur* passage: to pit our cultivated taste against their barbarism. But this is not quite so: it defines their being dirty not as negligence or ignorance of hygiene but as a fundamental confusion or perversion, their ability to desire that which affects us with repulsion. On the one hand, Lessing asserts a natural order based on the opposition of those things that evoke repulsion and those that evoke desire, admiration, and love. On the other hand, he says that this fundamental opposition can be changed.

It seems to me that with the Hottentot example Lessing has marked that point where an easy nature/culture opposition breaks down, where the boundaries of the symbolic order, the grid that stabilizes meaning, becomes loosened up, only to be secured again and even expanded in a ritual of defilement and abjection. We should remember that when Lessing introduced the definition of disgust he argued that disgust provokes our repulsion by virtue of the mere idea of it, regardless of whether this idea corresponds to an actually present physical object or whether the idea is part of a mere illusion. Yet, when he argues that the disgusting can be permitted as a component of the ridiculous in verbal representations, this involuntary physical reaction seems to have been brought under control, reduced from an overpowering effect to a mere affective stimulant in a homeopathic dosage. In a way, Lessing's invitation to enjoy the Hottentot passage proposes to do something very similar to what makes the Hottentots so dirty: take something dirty and disgusting and turn it into an experience of pleasure.[6]

That this is indeed the direction of Lessing's argument is confirmed by the discussion of disgust and horror that immediately follows. He argues that the poet cannot represent famine unless he invokes the disgusting. In other words: in certain situations we need the disgusting, we have to be dirty, to confound the boundaries between the desirable and the repulsive, in order to expand the limits of representation.

Why would Lessing claim that above all things it is hunger that resists representation? The focus on hunger seems to be motivated by the challenge hunger poses to the aesthetics of illusion and the construction of a classical body that operates as the phantasmatic counterpart for the ideational object of aesthetic pleasure. For hunger, one might argue, is that feeling which asserts the physiological neediness of the body in its crudest form. It resists representation because, if there were to be an object of hunger, there would no longer be the dire feeling of hunger but already a lesser evil, a particular desire for this or that nourishment. Apparently hunger is the feeling that can no longer differentiate between what would be appropriate and what would be inappropriate for its satisfaction; hunger is omnivorous and radically cancels the boundaries of bodily integrity, such that it does not shun self-mutilation and cannibalism — in brief, it is a feeling that would negate any cultural order. And yet, although there is hunger as the utter indifference to cultural differentiation, as the experience of the real, crude, mortal human body, this challenge to representation can nevertheless be met. Even in the narratives of ordinary life we can express extreme famine by depicting all the disgusting things we would willingly consume to satisfy our stomach. From there we would be able to infer the overpowering feeling of hunger in view of which even disgust can be overcome: "Even in common life we express extreme famine through nothing else but the narration of all the unnourishing, unhealthy and particularly disgusting things we would need to satisfy the stomach. Since the imitation cannot evoke in us anything of the feeling of hunger itself, it has recourse to another unpleasant feeling which in the case of dire famine we take for a lesser evil. The imagination seeks to evoke in us this feeling in order to let us conclude from the unpleasure of the latter how strong that unpleasure would have to be that leads us gladly to ignore the present unpleasure" (pp. 162–63). Hunger's indifference to any cultural order is represented, domesticated, integrated into the realm of narrative representation through exactly that procedure of defilement that constituted the ridiculous in the Hottentot passage: we evoke the feeling of hunger by representing as desirable all those things that would otherwise be considered utterly repulsive. However, here, instead of reacting with laughter, we are asked to objectify and understand, to interpret, to read this "unnatural" reversal of the order of the desirable and the objectionable. A gut-level response of repulsion is transformed into an interpretive activity. We are asked to take an imaginative leap, to differentiate degrees of unpleasure, to quantify the repulsive impulse, to frame it as something that can under extreme conditions be overcome as a result of an even more forceful bodily sensation of unpleasure.

With this last example Lessing has led the comparison between the visual and the verbal arts to a surprising conclusion: initially poetry seemed to be restricted through its inability to convey the simultaneous visual impression of bodies in space and thus painting seemed to assert its superiority by offering to us the full view of the beautiful body. However, if we take into account that this beautiful, classical body of the illusionary representation has to be constructed as a shield for our own imperfect mortal bodies, in the case of painting the mortal body of the beholder will always remain apart from and opposed to the classical beautiful body. Ultimately, poetry is the victor by virtue of its very limitations. For, as Lessing has demonstrated in his discussion of ugliness and disgust, only in poetry can the uncontrollable bodily reactions and affects be actually transformed and allied with, or sublimated into, the representation itself. In other words: only poetry can dematerialize the body and redefine physical attraction and repulsion within a differentiated illusionary representation.

From here I would like to turn to Lessing's antiquarian pamphlet *How the Ancients Represented Death* (*Wie die Alten den Tod gebildet*) from

1769. This text appears to be a mere defense against an attack by Klotz, who doubted Lessing's remark in the *Laokoon* that the ancients did not represent death as a skeleton. However, much more is at stake. In his preface Lessing reminds his readers of the Enlightenment project and admonishes them not to be disgusted by a pamphlet.[7] Furthermore, he remarks that squeamishness vis-à-vis pamphlets is quite often in the case of writers a cover-up for "self-love" and "arrogance," for the polemical tone of a pamphlet is "dangerous to the surreptitious name" (p. 190). Even if a dispute does not establish any stable truth, it nevertheless always serves the cause of truth by encouraging critical examination.[8]

At first sight it might seem a bit out of proportion that a scholarly pamphlet about the interpretation of some ancient tombstones should propose itself as a test case for the reader's ability to participate in the project of enlightenment. Yet, if we consider the systematic claims involved in this essay this appeal makes more sense. Analyzing how the ancients *could* have represented death, Lessing provides, as in his *Laokoon*, an account of the correct reading of pictorial and literary representation. And as in the earlier text, this text also places the semiotic account of the medial difference in relationship to the human body. Only this particular attention to the human body allows him to turn what might have been a merely antiquarian point into the following provocative conclusion: "However, it is certain that that religion that first revealed to man that even natural death was the fruit and the payment for sin had to increase the terrors of death infinitely. There have been sages who thought life was a punishment; however, without the aid of revelation it could not have occurred to any rationally thinking human being to take death for a punishment" (p. 245). The Christian notion of death, that even natural death is a punishment for sin, inscribes human fallibility into the human condition. All human attempts at rational and ethical behavior are ultimately doomed to fail. This fatalist strain of Christianity must rouse the ire of an enlightened thinker, and Lessing sets out to offer an alternative to this image of death. His argument about the ancients' representation of death is to liberate us from an irrational, unnatural terror created by Christian ideology or divine revelation. However, he cannot simply put forth an alternative notion of death in order to displace the Christian one, for the power that the frightening and false image of death exerts on us is deeply intertwined with our relationship to language and representation.

He begins with the defense of his proposition that the ancients represented death not as a skeleton but as the twin brother of sleep. This similarity between death and sleep had been suggested in Homer's description of Sarpedon's death.[9] Lessing concedes that the personification of death as the sensuous representation of an abstract idea is an arbitrary sign and that in principle death could have been represented in other ways. However, once this similarity to sleep had been established subsequent attempts at representing death had to adhere to this convention.[10]

From here Lessing proceeds to analyze concrete examples of ancient tombstones. At first Lessing seems to remain merely at the level of an empirical, iconographic investigation. The inverted torch signifying extinguished life, the butterfly signifying the departing soul, or the horn, urn, or crown may but need not necessarily be associated with the twin brothers. The only sign that links them and establishes their fundamental similarity is the one of the crossed legs. It is by that sign that we can unmistakably recognize death in its similarity to sleep.

By isolating and dwelling on the crossed legs as the unmistakable mark of death and sleep, Lessing shows that what appeared initially as a mere iconographic convention (the linkage of death with sleep) becomes now situated at the level of a quasi-universally accessible bodily reality. Lessing's analysis installs the crossed legs as an easily legible body posture signifying a general state of repose. This body posture does not obey any willed, accidental, or conventional gestures, nor does it reveal the body as subject to physiological needs, external or internal stimuli, pleasure or pain. Rather, it shows a body perfectly contented and at peace with itself, self-sufficient and self-oblivious, a body beyond need, desire, and language. Although Lessing does not attempt to argue for a natural necessity by which death had to be signified in this manner, he nevertheless situates this allegory of death on the axis of narcissistic desire: Would we not all wish that death were nothing but this sleeping body?

Once he has launched the ancients' representation of death on this trajectory of a narcissistic desire for the reduction of all tension to a minimum or zero degree, he turns to the second issue on his agenda, to the proof that for the ancients a skeleton could never have represented death. Not even for the depiction of a horrible death would they have chosen a skeleton: "The paintings of death are frequent among the poets, and not rarely very terrible. It is the pale, pallid, livid death; he roams around on black wings, he carries a sword; he shows his hungry teeth; he tears open his greedy jaws; he has bloody nails by which he marks his victims; his figure is so large and terrible that it overshadows an entire battlefield, and runs away with entire cities. But where is there the slightest suspicion of a skeleton?" (pp. 227–28). Indeed, death appears here with all the horrible, disgusting attributes we encountered in the *Laokoon* argument about repulsion and ugliness as those attributes that came to remind us of the mortal body's vulnerability.

How can Lessing admit that ancient poetry depicted death in this violent, horrifying, repulsive, and overwhelming image and at the same time propose that fundamentally the ancients adhered to an image of a beautiful, calm death as the twin brother of sleep in pictorial representations?

The poetic paintings are of an infinitely wider scope than the paintings of art: in particular, if art wants to personify an abstract notion it can merely express what is general and essential to that notion. It has to refrain from all accidentals which would be exceptions to what is general, which would contradict its essence; for such accidental characteristics of a thing would render the thing itself unrecognizable, and art is primarily concerned with recognizability. The poet, however, who elevates his personified abstract notion into the class of acting beings, can, so to speak, allow this notion to act against itself. He can introduce it in all the modifications given to him by any singular case, and we still would not in the slightest lose sight of its proper nature. If art wants to signify to us the personified notion of death: how can it do so but through that which is attributed to death in all possible cases? And what is it other than the state of calm and anesthesia? The more accidentalities art wanted to express that in a singular case removed the idea of calm and anesthesia, the more its picture had to become necessarily unrecognizable.... The poet need not fear this. For his language has already elevated abstract notions into independent beings; and the word in question never ceases to evoke the idea in question, even if he associates with it all kinds of accidentalities contradicting it. He can depict death as painful, terrible and cruel as he wants. Nevertheless, we do not forget that it is merely death and that this horrible gestalt is not an essential one but merely one due to the particular circumstances. (p. 229)

In this passage Lessing combines an argument about the nature of abstraction with his fundamental consideration of the media-specific differences between painting and poetry in order to arrive at a conclusion about the essence of death. His argument draws its force from the way in which he introduces the distinction between two types of death: first, death as it is accessible to empirical observation as the sight of a body subject to pain, sickness, violence, and decay, the death of individual human beings; second, death as an abstract concept which is not accessible to our immediate, sensate knowledge but which can be arrived at through conceptual labor. Lessing approaches the question of what are the essential features of death by turning it into a question of sign production: How can a painter represent an allegory of death through a particular form of expression without the risk that the expression material will introduce content units that would destabilize the content substance?

Let us recall here that Lessing in this pamphlet as opposed to the *Lao-*

koon sets a task for painting that is not genuine to this art form. Since painting is limited to the representation of bodies in space and since painting deploys natural signs, allegorical signs in painting require an additional effort in sign production: the painter must represent the body of death in such a manner that it does not entail any features that would confuse it with a representation of a particular, individual, mortal body, a body in motion, subject to sensations and affects. In order to do so the painting depicts a body that is furthest removed from and diametrically opposed to a particular living human body: a body in the state of anesthesia and calm, a sleeping body then becomes, according to Lessing, the only way death as the universalized allegory of the end of the human body can be figured.

By assigning the task to the painter of striving for a special kind of semiosis, of establishing discrete, self-identical content units which can only be achieved by overcoming the concreteness of his expression material, Lessing relegates the issue of uncontrollable chance, of *Zufälligkeit*, to the realm of matter and sense perception. The multiple visual features of painting have to undergo a process of reduction and formalization so that they risk no longer the potential interference with the content substance. Accidentality, chance, in this argument is introduced as the potential of undifferentiation, semiotic destabilization, the risk of unrecognizability, misreading, and semiotic opacity. Yet, openness and vulnerability to accidents is of course also one of the most prominent features of inhabiting a mortal body.[11] The fabrication of death as a stable, recognizable sign then becomes an exercise in banishing or freeing us from our corporeal situatedness. Semiosis is characterized as the process by which we can filter out and control the randomness of matter.

The poet's range of content selection is so much wider because he is not, like the painter, involved in the production of arbitrary signs but has always already at his disposal a full repertoire of discrete expression tokens. Since his expression material (sound) is, according to Lessing, fundamentally immaterial he may even draw on such content material (*Stoff*) as the pain, violence, or horrors of dying and not risk a semantic undifferentiation between the abstract concept of death automatically evoked by the word and the unessential particulars of an individual experience of dying. Lessing writes, the poet "can depict death as painful, terrible and cruel as he wants. Nevertheless, we do not forget that it is merely death and that this horrible gestalt is not an essential one but merely one due to the particular circumstances." This statement attributes to language the powerful apotropaic function of holding the mortality of the body at bay.

Unlike our impoverished language that encourages the confusion between the abstract concept of death and the death of an individual, the
language of the ancients supported this distinction. They had two words:
thanatos or *mors* for a natural death, the extinction of life in the general
sense, and *kēr* or *lethum* (according to Lessing) for the fate bringing death
in a cruel, violent, and painful way to an individual. And as the ancients
personified thanatos as the twin brother of sleep, they also personified *kēr*,
the horrible death bringing fate: "She appeared as a woman with horrible
teeth and crooked nails like a rapacious animal" (p. 232).

Why does Lessing have no problems with the ancient personification of
kēr but adamantly argues that by no means would they or could they have
equally used a skeleton for this allegory? Lessing's suggestion that the
skeleton is an insufficiently motivated sign since the body does not reach
this state until long after death seems fairly weak. In fact, it seems to me
that Lessing rejects the skeleton as an image for a cruel, violent death for
exactly the opposite reason, because the skeleton indiscriminately associates dying and decay with any body by situating the accident of death or
mortality *within* the body rather than attributing it to an external fate
that can attack the body. And it is this understanding of *lethum* or *kēr* that
Lessing wants to rule out when he rejects Joseph Spence's conjecture that
the ancients might have meant by *lethum* "the general seed or source of
mortality" (p. 230). Similarly, it seems like a minor issue when Lessing
corrects Klotz's translation of *kēr* as *mors fatalis* to *fatum mortiferum*. Yet
it is precisely in this substitution of the "inescapable fate" (*mors fatalis*)
by the "death-bringing fate" (*fatum mortiferum*) that Lessing's argument
culminates.

Death in general should not be seen as something inherent in our human
condition as sentient, embodied creatures. We should, rather, see death as
an external accident that might happen under unfortunate circumstances.
By no means should we conceive of our mortality as a constant condemnation to death. For in this case we would not be able to forget our body, and
our corporeality would then take over.[12] But why should language make a
difference in our attitude toward death? In order to address this question
Lessing considers the Greek practice of euphemism:

Finally I want to call to mind the euphemism of the ancients; their delicacy in
substituting for those words which immediately evoke a disgusting, sad, horrible
idea less conspicuous words. If they, according to this euphemism, refrain from
saying straightaway "he died" and say instead "he has lived, he has been, he is gone
to the majority," and similar phrases; if one of the reasons for this delicacy was the
avoidance of anything ominous, then there is no doubt that the artists also tuned

down their language to this milder tone. They too will not have represented death in an image which for everybody unavoidably includes all the disgusting notions of putrefaction and decomposition; not in the image of the ugly skeleton: for also in their compositions the unsuspected sight of such an image could have become as ominous as the unsuspected hearing of the proper word. They too would have rather chosen an image for it which leads us to its signified over a graceful detour. And which image could serve this purpose better than the one whose symbolic expression language itself likes so much in order to signify death, the image of sleep?

Euphemism that exchanges words for more gentle ones does not banish those words from language for good, it does not cancel their use in general; rather, it reserves these repulsive and therefore often avoided words for even more horrible occasions than the less offensive ones; for instance, it says of that person who died a quiet death, that he does not live any longer, of the one who was murdered under the most terrible tortures, that he died. In the same manner art will also not entirely banish those images by which it can allude to death but which it does not want to use because they are so horrible. Rather, it will save those images for those occasions on which they will in turn be the more pleasing or even the only ones that can be used. (p. 233)

Note that Lessing sketches two related strategies prescribed by the Greek practice of euphemism. On the one hand, euphemism requires the linguistic detour around the ominous word, the substitution of a weaker expression token for the proper word. On the other hand, the initial substitution affects the entire system of signifiers. Euphemism is not just the exclusion of certain representations or signs from the semiotic repertoire. The exclusionary principle primarily defines the Law of Beauty in painting where it entails the prohibition that one may not introduce corporeal, ugly components that would cancel the aesthetic illusion and reduce the representation to the mere material, accidental realm as opposed to the mental, ideational sphere. The euphemistic taboo introduces an economy of rarification and thereby one of carefully differentiated indices of intensity. The signifier, once barred from its immediate relation to the signified, is thereby established in its value as relative to other signifiers.

Although euphemism cannot cancel the reality of death and mortality, it can prevent the sudden confrontation, the accidental, unprotected encounter with death as the real, as decomposition and undifferentiation. Opposed to the proper word that immediately calls up the idea, euphemistic circumlocutions foreground the distinction between signifier and signified. Subjects of euphemistic discourse are part of a polite coding activity which protects them from direct contact with the object of the discourse. According to Lessing's model it seems that this rhetorical strategy becomes necessary when the topic or object of discourse would threaten to destabilize the subjectivity of the beholder or listener. As I have remarked above, what distinguishes the skeleton from other horrible representations of death is the fact that it also refers to the invisible reality of each human body. As signifier of death in general, the skeleton would threaten to collapse its signified with the referent "my body." As an object of disgust, as a graphic reminder of mortality inherent in the human body, the skeleton provokes the involuntary physiological reaction destabilizing the subject's body boundaries. For it not only evokes a mental image but also fuses this image with a physiological response which suspends the subject's freedom of adjudicating the referential dimension of the signified. In brief, the skeleton as a representation of death insists on the presence of our physiological condition and thereby threatens to undermine exactly that forgetting of our corporeality which constitutes the prerequisite for our functioning as rational, speaking subjects. That it is this ability to forget the body in which Lessing's semiotic is anchored is even suggested in his misspelling of *letum* as *lethum*, thus associating the Latin word with the Greek Lethe, the river of oblivion.

At this point it is possible to summarize in a more general fashion the role the human body plays in Lessing's aesthetic and semiotic theory. Certainly Lessing's notion of the body might be seen within the long trajectory extending from the Renaissance to today, a tradition that juxtaposes a classical, beautiful, healthy body on a pedestal and a grotesque, ugly body of a corporeal intensity and excessivity that challenges individuation as well as normativization.[13] Yet, if these are two extremes among possible body images of the last four or five centuries of Western civilization, it will be immediately clear that, though we can find in Lessing a certain version of the classical body, its opposite, the ugly or grotesque body, is associated neither with carnivalesque collectivity nor with a joyful affirmation of bodily excess. Remember how his rendition of the Hottentot passage that came closest to the carnivalesque played down both the ritual and the collective engagement. For Lessing, the body in question is always the body of an individualized human subject.

What, then, are the two body poles within which he situates his aesthetic and semiotic theory? There is a classical body, though — and this will have to be specified — this classical body is not a given entity from which he would want to deduce idealizing rules and specifications; rather, this classical body is a transitory, imaginary stand-in within the sphere of aesthetic illusion. There is a version of the ugly body, associated with the concrete, physiological body of any mortal subject. It is considered a fundamental threat to intellectual engagement, the order of civilization, and autonomy. If one were to employ a Lacanian language, the ugly body would be situated within the realm of the Real, of that which resists representation. In this sense it is associated with uncontrollability and chance occurrences, with undifferentiation and crude materiality, pure stuff, not even an object with definite contours.

And yet, this ugly body is nevertheless not entirely separated from the imaginary and the symbolic realm. It must also be understood as a liminal phenomenon that, whenever it comes into contact with the semiotic, affects the status of signs and the range of the symbolic. We have seen how as a basic physiological condition it can intrude upon the rational subject and articulate itself in the affect of disgust. The urge to vomit can certainly be understood as a fundamental loss of body control. Yet, Lessing also explored this affect in terms of its provocation of semiotic undifferentiation: an ugly body evokes disgust, first, for instance, in the case of the widely opened mouth of a screaming Laocoon, where the iconographic representation of the mouth becomes a mere stain (*Fleck*); or, second, at a more general level, when Lessing argues that as soon as disgust is involved we can no longer differentiate between an ideational construct at the level of representation and an objective, external reality. As this liminal phenomenon, the ugly body is the anchorage point and hinge for Lessing's semiotics and aesthetics. Whereas the ugly body acts as threatening, destabilizing other for the imaginary order of pictorial representation, within verbal representation the contourless physiological real can be transformed through the network of arbitrary signs. The fragmentary body can become part of a verbal representation, without destabilizing the position of the subject of speech. And even the affect of disgust must be understood not only as the loss of body control but also as a powerful defense mechanism of the boundaries between the interior and the exterior of the body. In terms of hunger Lessing argued that what appeared to be unrepresentable could nevertheless be represented with the aid of disgust. By way of evoking, differentiating, and quantifying this energy of abjection, we are able to posit an even less representable affect. However, this control over the mortal body of the real through the order of the symbolic as a network of differentiated signifiers would not be possible without the mediation of the aesthetic, the heuristic construction of a beautiful body within the imaginary. Within the realm of painting we can attend to the presence of a classical, full, unblemished body that screens out the corporeality of the beholder by having its presence replace his or her lack.

Yet, ultimately it seems to be the image of death as twin brother of sleep that elevates the human subject above his mortal condition and wards off the threat of mortality. This particular allegory of death as sleep braids together the imaginary and the symbolic in exemplary fashion: on the one hand, it is a purely arbitrary sign, the result of a coding convention initiated by Homer. As in euphemism one signifier replaces and stands for another signifier. And through its emphasis on the conventionality of the code, it wards off the ominous signified. But the allegory of death is not exactly the same as the rhetorical strategy of euphemism, since the sign that stands in for death, the twin brother of sleep, provides the beholder with a quasi-natural sign that need not be deciphered but suggests the presence of a contented body. In this sense the ancient representation of death in its very semiotic structure provides the culminating conclusion to Lessing's aesthetics. The *ut pictura poesis* has come full circle: the painterly medium follows the example of poetry in its renaturalization of an arbitrary sign and perfect oblivion or screening out of corporeal materiality. And this aesthetization of death might constitute the beginning of a tradition that would find its most powerful and rich elaboration and complication in Freud, who also defines pleasure as the absence of pain, as the reduction of all tension to a minimum, as the end of the body's corporeality.

Morphisms of the Phantasmatic Body:
Goethe's 'The Sorrows of Young Werther'

DAVID E. WELLBERY

*T*here is nothing self-evident about the idea of approaching a literary text in terms of its fashioning of the phantasmatic body, but in the case of *The Sorrows of Young Werther*[1] much speaks for the fruitfulness of such a line of questioning. Considered generically, *Werther* marks a powerful innovation vis-à-vis its major predecessors. The epistolary novel as exemplified by Richardson's *Clarissa* or Rousseau's *Julie ou La Nouvelle Héloïse*, despite occasional effusive passages, maintained a high degree of dramatic objectivity by virtue of the fact that the letters concatenated to produce the narrative are written by several correspondents and exchanged among the actors within the narrated story. This means not only that the letters themselves play a role in the unfolding of the narrative intrigue (who knows what, and when, is always important) but also that the perspective of any one character is counterbalanced by the perspectives of the other letter writers. In *Werther*, however, letter writing is the privilege solely of the eponymous protagonist, and his addressee is a figure (Wilhelm) effectively absent from the narrated story. Thus, whereas the earlier novels placed the reader in the position of an observer of the story's events, Goethe's novel affords no spectatorial vantage. *Werther*, in other words, asks the reader not to behold from the outside a drama of tangled motivations and stratagems, but, rather, to listen to (I shall justify this auditory verb subsequently) and imaginatively reenact the movements of a particular subjectivity. *Werther* is the first European novel in which subjectivity per se — the per se of subjectivity — attains aesthetic concretization. My claim is that this novelistic project involves, as one of its central components, the literary rendering of incarnate self-reference and that this occurs through the linguistic projection of the phantasmatic body.

A second reason for reading *Werther* with regard to its rendering of the phantasmatic body has to do with the fact that the experience of this imaginary corporeality reactivates aspects of the ontogenesis of bodily experience during early childhood.[2] It has become a commonplace in the historical literature to locate the emergence of childhood — conceived as a separate sphere of experience, a kind of emotional cocoon — in the latter third of the eighteenth century. The structural implosion of the family onto the nuclear triad of father-mother-child, the ascendance of the mother to the role of first educator and in general the maternal monopolization of care, the consequent emotional-erotic charging of primary socialization, and, disciplinarily speaking, the pedagogical magnification and discursivization of childhood as a domain of inquiry and manipulation from Rousseau forward: all these interlocked historical developments contribute to a reorientation of the literary imagination toward the deepest strata of personal history.[3] Thus, it is no accident that Goethe's protagonist identifies so insistently with children, borrowing from them the orientation of his desire. He reads Homer as if listening to a "cradlesong" and spoils his "heart" as if it were a "sick child" (p. 7; p. 10). Werther's subjectivity, in short, is imbued with the affective dynamics of the passage through childhood, and his particular pathology derives from the conflicts the process of becoming an adult subject has left, virulently unresolved, within him.

The phantasmatic body does not have a fixed form; on the contrary, it is caught up in a process of transformation that continuously alters its dimensions and shape, its pulsations and rhythms. Metamorphosis, then, is the medium of access to the phantasmatic body, and, more specifically: metamorphosis experienced as the movement of desire or anxiety. Description and analysis, therefore, must cleave to the changing forms through which this metamorphosis passes. I call these recurrent patterns of transformation morphisms and in what follows I shall trace out what I take to be the predominant morphism inflected in Werther's nearly monologic letters. In the second phase of the analysis I shall argue that the insistence of this morphism in the novel bears a strong internal connection to the type of reading the novel elicits.

The Morphism of the Absolute Body

Werther's eleventh letter (June 16, 1771), that letter which installs his 'love' for Charlotte within the narrative structure, recounts a ball in the countryside. The ball begins with a minuet, a dance characterized by strict orchestration of movement and ritualized exchange, but then passes over to a waltz, a differently structured dance which only two of the couples seem to have fully mastered. Among those fluent in the new language of dance are Werther and Charlotte: "Never had I danced more lightly. I felt myself more than human, holding this loveliest of creatures in my arms, flying with her like the wind, till I lost sight of everything else; and— Wilhelm, I vowed at that moment that a girl whom I loved, or for whom I felt the slightest attachment, should never waltz with another, even if it should be my end! You understand what I mean" (p. 17; p. 25). Historians interested in the cultural shaping of corporeal expression and behavior have found evidence in the cited passage of a historical transition. The ball sequence in *Werther* registers a large-scale shift in the social organization of bodily movement that affected the entire cultural semiotics of corporeality.[4] The waltz (or German dance, as it was sometimes called) was an innovation of the late eighteenth century. In contradistinction to the aristocratic minuet, a group dance of pose, constellation, rank ordering, prescribed movements, and theatrical display, the waltz accorded independence to the dancing dyad, involved whirling, improvised movement, and highlighted the self-enclosure of the couple's intimacy. Within the waltz the bourgeois values of individual autonomy and expressivity and of the familial privatization of the couple, it is claimed, found an appropriate corporeal expression. The emergence of this new corporeal code, it should be noted, did not occur without inciting moral outrage. As late as 1771, the intimacy and turbulence of the dance could still be perceived as scandalous.[5] No doubt this pronounced sexual connotation of the waltz (as prelude to and simulation of intercourse) prompts the jealous vow that interrupts Werther's memory of the scene.[6]

The feature of this historical mutation that interests me here is that the waltz, as it enters the fiction, becomes the site and occasion of a specific morphism of the phantasmatic body. Waltzing with Charlotte, Werther experiences a transformation of his own corporeality: the heaviness of the body falls away ("light"); the dancing couple attains equivalence to a meteorological or cosmic movement, flying "like the wind" ("wie Wetter");[7] finally, the surrounding field of objects that would relativize the body—the field, let us say, of corporeal alterity—disappears.[8] The transformative aspect of this complex is indicated by the fact that Werther claims to become, within the waltz, "more than human" ("kein Mensch mehr," literally: "no longer a human being"). The significance of this statement only becomes clear when one recalls that the concept of human being ("Menschheit" or "Menschsein") in the novel is inextricably tied to the concept of limit ("Grenze") and therewith to the concepts of finitude, relativity, determination through difference. Waltzing with Charlotte, then, Werther senses something like a transcendence of human corporeal limitation, a possibility of corporeal movement that would be centered within itself and would course, without resistance, through a boundless space. The dancing couple becomes a transfinite body, isolated because unrelated to any alterity, and yet within this isolation total unto itself. I call this transformational type the morphism of the absolute body.

The reading I have adumbrated deviates from the sociohistorical account. According to the latter, the transition involved in the passage from minuet to waltz is to be interpreted in terms of abstract values inhering in large-scale social structures: hierarchical stratification and its attendant forms of ritualized greeting and exchange are replaced by individual autonomy; public and ostensive definition of identity passes over into a privatized, familial definition. Thus, both dances are viewed as *ways of representing* categories that ultimately derive from a theoretical discourse of macro-structural sociological description. To be sure, this representational model has a certain validity as regards the minuet and its placement within aristocratic society, the hierarchical order of which constituted a highly articulated code that could be (and was) mapped onto a variety of visibly accessible practices.[9] But the waltz is not a mechanism of representation in this sense. Rather, it is a socially circumscribed occasion for the production of the morphism of the absolute body, a social space within which the self-referential experience of an asociality becomes possible. Thus, the historical shift I register in the quoted passage from *Werther* does not substitute one represented content for another; it abandons this mode of semiosis altogether. Instead of organizing bodies within a dual system of signifying elements and their correlated signifieds, the waltz, or at least its fictional version, generates a phantasmatic corporeality that extinguishes representation.

I alluded above to the fact that the waltz, especially at the time of its historical emergence, bears sexual connotations that elicited moral censorship. The specific deployment of these connotations in *Werther* allows us to begin to measure the novel's historical innovation as regards the organization of sexuality. In Sophie La Roche's *Miss Sternheim* (see note 5), what the enraged Seymour perceives in the waltz is something like the prince's actual sexual possession of the heroine. This act (which, of course, is not accomplished in La Roche's novel) would be a symbolic 'triumph' inscribed on Miss Sternheim's corporeality and fulfilling thereby the agenda of a 'rake' and 'voluptuary'. Opposed to this code of 'rakish seduction' centered on a scenario of 'violation,' the novel also operates with a code of 'sentimental love' in which sexuality is subordinated to friendship and shared norms of virtue. In *Werther*, however, neither of these opposed codifications of sexuality remains in force. The 'rakish' variant completely disappears and the 'sentimental' variant is decisively transformed insofar as it is no longer grounded in an intersubjectively available criterion of the good. To be sure, the figure of Charlotte embodies, for Werther as well as the reader, certain socially defined standards of virtuous behavior, but this is not the motivation of his desire. As the waltz scene reveals, Werther 'falls in love' with Charlotte because, dancing with her, he experiences the particular morphism he does. This morphism is the scenario that organizes his libidinal investment, a scenario different in every respect from the 'violation' dreamt of by La Roche's prince. Werther's desire is quite simply to become what the waltz holds out for him as an imaginary possibility: the absolute body.

One way of formulating the historical innovation sketched out in the previous paragraph is to say that the sexual component in *Werther* undergoes a process of universalization. Sexuality here is not limited to the coital act, but, rather, suffuses a range of experiences which, at least on the surface, have nothing to do with the relations between the sexes. Thus, a sort of pansexualism[10] makes itself felt in the novel, perhaps nowhere more forcefully than in Werther's famous letter of May 10, 1771:

When the lovely valley teems with mist around me, and the high sun strikes the impenetrable foliage of the trees, and but a few rays steal into the inner sanctuary, I lie in the tall grass by the trickling stream and notice a thousand manifold things; when I hear the humming of the little world among the stalks, and am near the countless indescribable forms of the worms and insects, then I feel the presence of the Almighty Who created us in His own image, and the breath of that universal love which sustains us as we float in an eternity of bliss [das Wehen des Allie-benden, der uns in ewiger Wonne schwebend trägt und erhält]; and then, my friend, when the world grows dim before my eyes and earth and sky seem to repose in my soul like the form of a beloved — then I often think with longing, Oh, if only I could express it, could breathe onto paper all that lives so full and warm within me, that it might become the mirror of my soul, as my soul is the mirror of the infinite God! (p. 6, slightly modified; p. 9)

Reinhart Meyer-Kalkus has discussed this passage as an exemplification of the Lacanian mirror stage, arguing that it displays Werther's capture by his own specular image and consequent alienation within the imaginary.[11] Although this reading has the distinct merit of replacing the vague evocation of Werther's feeling for nature typical of much commentary on the passage with a clearly stated, and powerful, structural hypothesis, it seems to me to go wrong in significant respects. The mirror stage, according to Lacan, inaugurates a structure in which the infant, not yet in command of the internal diversity and turbulence of its body, relates to an image (the specular image offered by the mirror) with which it identifies. The jubilatory response of the infant derives from the anticipation of a corporeal integrity that it does not possess. Within the medium of vision, the circumscribed and unitary corporeal image, to which Lacan attributes a formative capacity, fixates the ego, a process that introduces, at the very root of this subjective structure, alienation and misrecognition. Of course, the cited passage from *Werther* does employ at one point the word "Gestalt" (rendered as 'form' in the translation), with which Lacan designates the formative image, and it likewise calls on the figure of the mirror. The drift of the text, however, moves in a very different direction than that prescribed in Lacan's account, and we can mark this difference, I think, by saying that whereas Lacan describes the fixation and stabilization of the ego within the domain of representation, Goethe's text is oriented toward a corporeal morphism — the absolute body — that comes into being as the dissolution of this domain.

I note, first of all, that the scene is bathed in mist and that the sun, a precondition of clear vision, is carefully held outside the enclosing sanctuary (a 'valley' and, within this earthly fold, a tree-shaded hollow). Indeed, the function of the sun here is not to illuminate but, rather, to 'penetrate'; that is, to pierce, with its warmth, Werther's supine body. Nor is it a singular figure, a formed and formative image, that catches his attention, but a proliferation of a 'thousand manifold' things. The semantics of the text, then, multiplies forms to the point of indiscernibility (the auditory 'humming' of the English version translates a visual "Wimmeln", or 'blurring', in the original). Quite in contrast to the Lacanian description of the mirror stage, the passage moves toward a 'dimming' ("dämmern") of perception, toward a blending of distinct contours, and toward a mode of reception ('feeling', "fühlen") that does not externalize itself as a visible, free-standing shape. To state the matter as simply as possible, Werther does not see himself as an object, as Lacan claims the ego does. And for this reason he cannot, as the conclusion of the passage states, objectify his phantasmatic corporeality in a visual representation.

What is the morphism of the absolute body if not a visible, contoured form? In the variant under discussion it appears as a structure I should like to call infinite crossing. Two worlds intersect at the point marked by Werther's subjective position: that of the infinitely small and manifold and that of the infinitely large. Werther's body, then, is felt as being without limitation, as a point of passage where one infinity crosses over into and becomes another. The absolute body is not an object defined by other definite objects; rather, it relates only to the infinitudes whose crossing and equivalence it is. Parallel to this, the passage also deploys a structure I want to call the total embrace: the world 'reposes' within Werther 'like the form of a beloved' while at the same time the 'universal love' ("der Allie-bende") permeating everything holds ("trägt und erhält") him in a state of 'floating' ("schweben"). The absolute body is an embrace in which container and contained are identical.[12] These two structures — infinite cross-ing and total embrace — demonstrate that the mirror functions here not as an operator of visual objectification (as in Lacan's theory) but as a figure of paradoxicalization installing within the text a scenario that can never be seen.[13]

To delineate the function of this paradoxicalization, I want to press the reading of the passage under discussion a bit further. I suggested earlier that it exemplifies a characteristic expansion within the novel of the scope of sexuality, a tendency of the text toward a certain pansexualism. This term takes on special pertinence when one notes that it translates the name Werther accords his *pantheistic* deity ("der Alliebende," literally: 'the all-loving one') and that pantheism, in its Spinozist formulation, provides the paradigm of an absolute amorous relation. In particular, the Spinozist notion of *amor dei intellectualis,* in which the mind participates in divinity by loving God as God loves himself, seems to anticipate the structure of the infinite embrace adumbrated above. The love Spinoza attempts to think shares with Werther's the predicates of joy, eternity, and repose. In addition, the connection to the *Ethics* lends Werther's experience a hereti-cal connotation that fits well with his views, expressed elsewhere in the novel, on religious orthodoxy. But in the context of the present argument the comparison is urgently relevant insofar as Spinoza's *amor dei intel-lectualis* names a type of love that transcends corporeal limitation. In *Werther,* this amorous transcendence assumes fictional salience as the morphism of the absolute body.[14]

My argument is not that the Spinozist conception of an intellectual love of God is the meaning the letter of May 10 transmits, merely that that con-ception resonates within the text, that it provides the text with a schema of non-objectival love. The figuration of the absolute body, however, sets other semantic resources into play that deviate from the philosophical-religious register and introduce within the text a decidedly non-Spinozist inflection. I mentioned earlier the double enclosure that situates the scenario: the valley and, within this, the shady pocket formed by the trees. A reading of this enfolding figure as 'feminine' seems beyond dispute, and this all the more so when we consider the verbs employed to designate Werther's "floating" through eternal bliss. "Tragen" — 'to carry' — is the verb of pregnancy (a mother-to-be 'carries' her unborn child), and "erhalten" can designate the act of giving vital sustenance. The absolute body — unhindered by alterity, floating in a quasi-liquid medium that bears and nourishes it — is the autoerotic unity of mother and child.

Thus far my reading has been moving backward, from the dance scene to the letter of May 10. Continuing in this direction, I want to call attention to a passage of considerable compositional prominence. After dealing in its opening two paragraphs with matters left over from the past, Werther's first letter of the novel (May 4) turns to his new circumstances. The world in which the novelistic plot will unfold, the very scene of Werther's unhappy destiny, is introduced with this remark:

For the rest, I am very well off here. Solitude in this terrestrial paradise is a wonderful balm to my emotions, and the early spring warms with all its fullness my often-shivering heart. Every tree, every bush is a bouquet of flowers; and one might wish himself transformed into a cockchafer, to float about [herumzuschweben] in this ocean of fragrance, and find in it all the food [Nahrung] one needs. (p. 6; p. 8)

This is Werther's first enunciation of desire, and it is a kind of program for what is to follow. The hovering movement of the insect anticipates both the freedom of the dance ("herumzufliegen") and the sense of floating ("schweben") in the medium of universal love. From "balm" to "ocean," the scene is bathed in liquidity, dissolving the alterity of contoured objects into a flow that bears, soothes, even feeds (as in the maternal variant) the transformed subject. Thus, at the point where the morphism of the absolute body is first installed within the text, it appears as an exquisite oral gratification: a suffusion and nourishment that sustain the entire body in an autoerotic lubrification. All the subsequent scenes of transformation — the expansion to cosmic freedom within the dance, the pantheistic embrace — adhere to the structure of this wish.

The cited passage allows me to develop more explicitly than has thus far been the case what I mean by the morphism of the absolute body. The 'transformation' (explicitly named as such in the English translations, verbally enacted — "man möchte . . . werden" — in the German original) of the body into its phantasmatic counterpart is in fact a double operation. On the one hand, a domain of corporeal experience that I shall designate with the term "oral gratification" (liquid intake, satiation, quiescence) is hyperbolically metaphorized in the figure of the 'floating insect.' On the other hand, the enunciating subject projects itself into the position of the insect, a projection that could be called optative self-metaphorization. The morphism of the absolute body, then, is the fusion, the cooperation, of these two metaphorical processes:

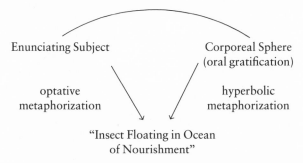

Enunciating Subject   Corporeal Sphere
                                       (oral gratification)

        optative   hyperbolic
     metaphorization   metaphorization

              "Insect Floating in Ocean
                   of Nourishment"

I want to stress that metaphorization, as employed here, does not imply substitution. In other words, I am not arguing that the figure of the 'floating insect' is merely a stand-in for what the text really means (for example, the infantile experience of liquid intake), or that that same figure simply externalizes an emotion that exists, apart from its optative projection, within the subject. On the contrary, the sheer organic facts that inhere within the field I have designated as oral gratification undergo a process of infinitization and totalization (for example, liquidity becomes an 'ocean') that decisively alters their relativized character and engenders a substantially new (psychic) reality in which the organic sphere persists *as trace*. Likewise, what might be thought of as the emotional tenor of the passage comes into being only through the optative projection that casts Werther's body into the 'ocean of fragrance.' The wish does not seek to recapitulate a previously experienced fulfillment; rather, it brings forth the scenario of that fulfillment, which, therefore, has a (psychic) reality only as a functional component of the wish itself. In both of its operations, then, metaphorization is *originary*, irreducible to a literal meaning that would be its organic-corporeal or subjective truth. Indeed, a kind of zero point, at which my subjectivity or my body would appear to me without such metaphorization, without such ec-static displacement beyond itself, is unthinkable. There is no *incarnate subjectivity* (the loop of the diagram is meant to indicate this unity of the two poles) without such epiphoric transference.

I have repeatedly urged that the morphism of the absolute body is

sexual in character, a scenario of desire, and that this sexuality is essentially autoerotic. The process delineated in the previous paragraph enables
me to specify this claim. Sexuality, I want to say, is the domain of experience that opens up through the metaphorization of the organic functions
(in this case, oral gratification), through the displacement of the corporeal
onto a metaphorical plane. Sexuality, as this novel conceives it, is the
originary becoming-metaphor of incarnate subjectivity.[15] The autoerotic
character of the morphism can be explicated in two ways. First, it too
results from metaphorization: that is to say, through metaphorization the
corporeal functions are turned toward the subject, become something that
exists for-the-subject, a scenario into which the subject — again originar-
ily — projects itself. (In this sense, sexuality *tout court* is autoerotic.) Second, Werther's self-displacement into the morphism of the absolute body
is autoerotic in the (restricted) sense that that particular scenario involves
no other subjects, no other bodies, indeed, as I have often pointed out, no
alterity in general. One of the truly remarkable features of Goethe's novel
is that, rather than restrict sexuality to the genital farce, it discloses a
sexuality that inheres in the very process of self-metaphorization. For this
reason, to speak of the novel's pansexualism seems to me even technically
correct.

The scenario organizing Werther's desire is the morphism of the absolute body, and one of the variants of this dream of nourishing lubrification
is the unity of mother and unborn child. Hence Werther's passionate attachment to Charlotte, who lives according to the promise to raise her
siblings as if they were her own:

"Be a mother to them," she [Charlotte's dying mother] said to me [Charlotte]. I
gave her my hand. "You are promising much, my child," she said — "a mother's
love and a mother's eye! I have often felt, by your tears of gratitude, that you know
what that means; show it to your brothers and sisters. And be as obedient and
faithful to your father as a wife; you will be his comfort." (p. 41; p. 59)

Tears, which flow so often in this novel, are grateful testimony to the
Mother's infinite gift, and this because they correspond, in their liquidity,
to that gift (of life, of love, of nourishment).[16] Before she presents herself
as image, as contoured figure, the Mother is this liquid donation. Werther's first vision of Charlotte confirms this: she stands surrounded by the
children, who, with the outstretched arms of their demand, reach for the
bread — the nourishment, the bread of life — she distributes to them. Viewing this "scene" ("Schauspiel"), Werther finds his attention drawn to the
"pink ribbons" affixed to her dress "at the arms and breast" (p. 15; p. 21).

These ribbons, which are so proximate to the source of the Mother's liquid gift of nourishment (and in the first sketch of the novel, which calls them "flesh-colored," even mimic the color of that source), become a fetish for Werther, the single token of his love he takes to his grave.[17] And the letter (June 16) that begins with this scenario of the gift of nourishment into which Werther projects himself, installing his 'love' for Charlotte 'at first sight', ends by metaphorically fulfilling the promise of the liquid-maternal donation that the metonymic ribbons seemed to offer him: "I remembered at once that magnificent ode which was in her thoughts, and *sank down into* the flood of feelings that she poured over me with this watchword. It was more than I could bear, I bent over her hand and kissed it in a stream of the most blissful tears" (p. 19, substantially altered; p. 27). With this baptism, Werther is as if born anew in the sign of the Mother's liquid gift, and he repays this gift, as Charlotte had already repaid it, with the liquid testimony of his gratitude.[18]

To verify this thesis regarding the essentially oral character of Werther's love for Charlotte, I introduce one further piece of evidence. Late in the novel, as Werther's agony approaches its apex, Charlotte acquires a canary as a gift for the children, who, of course, have been the mediators of Werther's desire from the first scene of nourishment. Moreover, she refers to this canary as "a new friend," endowing it thereby with the title Werther himself enjoys within the family. Thus, the canary is introduced into the text in such a way that a double path of identification — via the children and via the term "friend" — is opened up for Werther. The bird, a creature of the 'air', of 'flight' and therefore of 'unhindered movement', becomes a figure for Werther's desire:

A canary flew from the mirror and settled on her shoulder. "Here's a new friend," she said and coaxed him to perch on her hand; "he's a present for the children. What a dear he is! Look at him! When I feed him, he flutters with his wings and pecks so nicely. He can kiss me too — look!"

She held the bird to her mouth and he pressed lovingly [lieblich] into her sweet lips as if he could feel the bliss he enjoyed.

"He shall kiss you too," she added, and held the bird toward me. His little beak moved from her mouth to mine, and the touch of his peck was like a breath, a foretaste of love-filled pleasure.

"His kiss," I said, "is not without desire [Begierde]; he wants food [Nahrung], and turns away unsatisfied [unbefriedigt] from this empty caress [leeren Lieb-kosung]."

"He eats out of my mouth too," she continued. She reached him a few morsels with her lips, from which the joys of innocent sympathetic love smiled in delight [Wonne]. (p. 56, slightly altered; p. 80)

What is most instructive about this passage in the context of my argument is the way in which Werther at once elicits and suppresses a phallic interpretation of the bird. He sees the 'loving' ("lieblich") penetration of the lips, he reduces the bird synecdochically to the phallic 'little beak', but disqualifies the kiss ("Liebkosung") as "empty." He refuses, then, a genital-coital interpretation of the figure and insists on another, for him more powerful 'desire' ("Begierde"): the desire for the oral intake of 'food' ("Nahrung"). For him, the 'kiss' is not acceptable as a prelude to the genital act, but is, in its orality, itself the scenario he longs for. What Werther desires, in short, is a kind of oral-oral linkage with the Mother that would suffuse his body-become-bird (much as it had become floating insect in the first letter) with satiation. The metaphorization that has fixed Werther's sexuality is incompatible with the parcellation of the body in intercourse. He does not want to possess Charlotte in the focused functionalization of genital sex; he wants to drink her.

To drink her as she, the liquid Mother, drinks herself:

She turned to her piano for relief and in a sweet, soft voice breathed sounds in harmonious accompaniment of her playing. Never have I seen her lips more attractive [reizender]; it was as if they thirstingly [lechzend] opened that they might drink into themselves [in sich schlürfen] those sweet tones that quelled up [hervorquollen] from the instrument, the secret echo of which returned out of her pure mouth. (p. 62, substantially altered; p. 87)

Music is a liquidity flowing from the instrument that itself vibrates with the emotional undulations of Charlotte's — of the Mother's — interior body.[19] The introduction of voice, and, more specifically, of voice in its presemantic form as 'sound', into the oral complex I am tracing out here will prove important in a subsequent phase of my argument. At this point, I merely want to accentuate the structure of a *closed circulation of liquidity* the passage instantiates, as well as the fact that the corporeal site through which this circulation passes, becoming thereby a kind of 'eager drinking' ("schlürfen"), is the oral orifice. Thus, it is no accident — rather, a systematic consequence of Werther's incarnate metaphorization — that Charlotte's singing lips become, as the letter closes, "lips on which the spirits of heaven *float*" ("Lippen, auf denen die Geister des Himmels *schweben*") (p. 62, substantially altered; p. 87, my emphasis). That is to say, the lips, as the point of insertion into the maternal economy of pure liquid circulation and nourishment, become the site where the morphism of the absolute body is realized.[20]

The same verb of eager drinking ("schlürfen") characterizing oral intake within the economy of maternal-liquid circulation is employed in a letter that precedes the just-cited passage by three days: "She does not see, she does not feel that she is preparing a poison that will destroy us both; and with full voluptuousness [Wollust] I drink deeply of the draught [schlürfe den Becher aus] that she gives me to my ruin" (p. 61, slightly altered; p. 87). I mentioned earlier in connection with the ribbon at Charlotte's breast (see note 17) that Werther takes in his destiny orally, consuming not merely his love but also his death through the mouth. The morphism of the absolute body which determines Werther's desire seems to be inherently *ambivalent*, and the passage just quoted illustrates this ambivalence as a reversal of valence from the 'nourishing' aspect of 'drinking' to a 'poisonous' variant.[21] Werther's self-metaphorization as absolute body suspended within the liquidity of life and love becomes a self-metaphorization as absolute body suffused with poison, a projection which, however negatively charged, is nevertheless sexually invested (see "Wollust").

Documenting this reversal of valence is, as I shall soon show, easy enough. More difficult is the task of theoretically accounting for it. My effort in this direction takes its departure from a passage in Lacan's early text *Les Complexes familiaux*, a rather surprising reference, perhaps, in view of what I said earlier about the inadequacy of the Lacanian concept of the mirror stage as a model for reading *Werther*. But this inadequacy is precisely the point here, since, in the passage in question, Lacan attends to a level of psychic organization that, as I argued above with regard to the letter of May 10, is inaccessible to representation. "Thus, this stage being anterior to the advent of the form of the object, it does not seem that its contents could represent themselves in consciousness." The organizing figure of this stage (a figure which does not, and cannot, appear as a visible form) is the "maternal imago," or the "imago of the nourishing relation." Before the play of mirrors, before the constitution of a representational world, there is the Mother, and this imago, so named because it organizes a psychic complex and not because it appears as an object, is characterized by what Lacan calls a *primordial ambivalence*. The "basis of this ambivalence," Lacan speculates, is the "sensations of sucking and prehension." The being that absorbs is itself absorbed; the being that is suspended in the comfort of an embrace is likewise strangulated by that embrace. Focusing especially on the aspect of feeding, Lacan goes so far as to name this ambivalence a "cannibalisme fusionnel": the eater eaten, the eager drinker gulped.[22] My claim is that this same ambivalence is expressed within the novel in the reversal we are following from a "schlürfen" ('eager drinking') of the life that emerges as liquid from the maternal body to a "schlürfen" of 'poison' likewise 'given' to Werther by the Mother. The morphism of the absolute body — the self-metaphorization that organizes Werther's sexuality — is intrinsically unstable, oscillating between the embrace of life and the violent annihilation of corporeal limitation in the embrace of death.

This oscillation is thematized in Werther's letter of August 18, which begins with the question: "Must it always be so — that the source of our happiness becomes the fountain of our misery?" (p. 36; p. 51). An interesting question, bearing, as it does, on the source of liquidity. And to illustrate how extreme this reversal from happiness to misery can be, Werther recalls the pantheistic experiences described in the letter of May 10 and analyzed above as a variant of the absolute body that evokes the nurturing unity of pregnant woman and her unborn child. The linguistic rendering of this memory draws on figures of 'infinite flight,' 'liquidity,' and 'drinking' that are utterly familiar to us: "Ah, how often then did the flight of a crane, soaring above my head, inspire me with the desire to be transported to the shores of the immeasurable ocean, there to drink the pleasures of life from the foaming goblet of the Infinite, and to realize, if but for a moment within the confined powers of my soul, the bliss of that Creator Who accomplishes all things in Himself, and through Himself!" (p. 36; p. 51). Now, however, such bliss is inaccessible to Werther and nature presents itself in a scenario of monstrosity:

It is as if a curtain had been drawn from before my eyes, and, instead of prospects of eternal life, the abyss of an ever-open grave yawned before me. Can we say of anything that it is when all passes away — when time, with the speed of a storm, carries all things onward — and our transitory existence, hurried along by the torrent, is swallowed up by the waves or dashed against the rocks? There is not a moment that doesn't consume [verzehrte] you and yours — not a moment in which you don't yourself destroy something. . . . My heart is wasted by the thought of that destructive power [verzehrende Kraft] which lies latent in every part of universal Nature. Nature has formed nothing that does not destroy itself, and everything near it. And so, surrounded by earth and air and all the active forces, I stagger on in sheer anxiety. I see nothing but an all-consuming, all-devouring monster [ein ewig verschlingendes, ewig wiederkäuendes Ungeheuer]. (p. 37; pp. 52–53)

The earlier dream of "drinking the pleasures of life" (in German: "jene schwellende Lebenswonne zu trinken," a formulation that suggests the 'swelling' breast as the source of 'vital bliss') persists within the second, horrific vision insofar as both phantasms occupy the semantic register of 'infinite oral intake.' The valence of this hyperbolic orality, however, has undergone an exact reversal. Now the liquidity itself (the torrent), as the translation felicitously puts it, "swallows" everything. The oral cavity becomes a "yawning," bottomless grave: an "abyss" or "Abgrund." Second by second the world is eaten up ("verzehrt"), so that all that Werther can see is the infinitely consuming, infinitely chewing monstrosity of the omnivorous world-mouth. "Ewig verschlingend": the same verb of oral consumption that marks Werther's ingestion of his love through the metonymy of the ribbon, the verb that ties him to the maternal breast (see note 17), here names the other pole of the primordial ambivalence — a universal cannibalism.

Some two weeks prior to his suicide, Werther's vision of the all-consuming "Abgrund" of nature becomes a reality: a flood, induced by unseasonable thawing, has engulfed the "beloved valley" ("liebes Tal," p. 69; p. 98) that was the privileged site of his experience of the absolute body. The nourishing maternal hollow fed, as the letter of May 10 had specified, by a "trickling stream" (p. 6; p. 9) has become "a single storming sea" (p. 69; p. 99). Despite this reversal, however, Werther still longs to be absorbed by the infinite embrace of liquidity: "Oh, with open arms I stood at the edge of the abyss [Abgrund] and breathed: down! down! and lost myself in the bliss [verlor mich in der Wonne] of storming down my agony and suffering, of surging them away like the waves!" (p. 70, substantially altered; p. 99). But one last step remains to be taken, one last oral ecstasy must be achieved: Werther must kiss Charlotte, must touch the lips of the Mother with his own. This occurs during his last visit to Charlotte on the eve of his suicide. The kiss is nothing other than the enactment of the scenario that from the beginning had organized his desire, the drinking-in of the maternal liquidity: "The sacred fire that flowed [strömte] from your lips still burns on mine and new, warm bliss [Wonne] is in my heart" (p. 82, substantially altered; p. 117). And a few lines later: "I tasted [geschmeckt] it in all its heavenly bliss, this sin, and sucked [gesaugt] force and the balm of life [Lebensbalsam] into my heart." By the law of ambivalence that governs Werther's oral desire, this infantile 'sucking' consumption of 'life's balm' — the same balm in which the insect of the novel's first letter floats and finds nourishment — becomes the imbibing of his death. The pistols Werther borrows for his suicide come to him from Charlotte's hands: "They passed through your hands — you wiped the dust from them. I kiss them a thousand times" (p. 84; p. 121). And thus the instrument of his death becomes the chalice from which the maternal donation flows: "You see, Charlotte, I do not shudder to take the cold and fatal cup from which I shall drink the frenzy of death. Your hand gave it to me, and I do not tremble" (p. 86; p. 123). It only remains for Werther to tie together the destiny of his desire by taking the pink ribbon with him to his grave: "Wie ich das alles verschlang!" According to the editor's report, "The bullet had entered the forehead over the right eye; his brains were protruding" (p. 87; p. 124). But that description applies only to the real. By the logic of his own self-metaphorization, Werther took the pistol in his mouth.

The Interior Body of Reading

In his discussion of *Werther* in *On Naive and Sentimental Poetry* (1795), Schiller astutely depicts the novel's hero as "a dangerous extreme of the sentimental character" ("dieses gefährliche Extrem des sentimentalischen Charakters"). This extremity derives from an irreconcilable polarization: on the one hand, Werther "strives for a substanceless infinite" ("nach einem wesenlosen Unendlichen zu ringen"); on the other hand, he comes to experience even "his own existence as a confining limit" ("in seinem eigenen Dasein nur eine Schranke sieht"). Such extreme polarization, Schiller implies, quite naturally leads to Werther's suicide as an effort to "tear down" this limit and thereby to reach what he holds to be "true reality" ("zur wahren Realität durchzudringen").[23] This observation, I believe, can be translated into the terms of the argument developed across the foregoing pages. What Schiller calls a "substanceless infinite" — for Werther the sole and true "reality" — corresponds to what I have designated (less moralistically than Schiller) as the morphism of the absolute body; what Schiller refers to as Werther's "striving" is the movement of his hyperbolic metaphorical self-projection, enacted, finally, in his suicide. Schiller's observation, however, calls attention to a feature of the novel that I have ignored up to this point: that the morphism of the absolute body does not, as it were, saturate the novel, that it stands in opposition to a contrary phantasm of the body, to a morphism that, rather than freeing up corporeality to the experience of an unhindered movement, collapses the body onto itself in a sensation of constriction and constraint. Schiller writes that Werther "sees in his own existence . . . a confining limit," that his being-there ("Da-sein") itself is a kind of wall or enclosure that separates him from the infinite, with which he seeks to merge. Again translating the terminology of Schiller's gloss, we can say that Werther phantasmatically projects his experience of corporeal particularity — his experience of his body as separate, defined by its alterity to other bodies — as a kind of imprisonment. The counterexperience to the morphism of the absolute body is a phantasm of entrapment and enclosure in which the very 'thereness' of existence becomes an immobilizing prison wall, the skin of corporeal particularity a straitjacket. I call this the *morphism of the incarcerated body.*

It would be possible to trace the ramifications of this morphism throughout the novel, starting, for example, from Werther's reflections on human existence in the letter of May 22, which culminate in the sentence: "And then, however confined [eingeschränkt] he [man, der Mensch] may be, he still preserves in his heart the sweet feeling of liberty, and knows that he can quit this prison [Kerker] whenever he likes" (p. 10; p. 14). The metaphor of the prison along with related projections of confinement recurs often, reaching its apex perhaps in the vision of the torrent that has swept over Wallheim and into which Werther would like to plunge: "Won't this imprisoned soul [dem Eingekerkerten] someday be released for such bliss?" (p. 70; p. 99). By a peculiar reversal of values that inheres in the logic of his self-projections, Werther conceives of the very positivity of his existence as a deprivation and a captivity, as a negative condition that isolates him from absorption into the fluid and unconstrained unity of the absolute body. The body as thrown into the here and now of its being-there, the body as this particular body, limited and material, is the source of a kind of claustrophobic torment, and the fundamental impulse governing Werther's every action is the impulse to get out. Hence the darkly suggestive first sentence of the novel: "How glad I am to have got away!" (p. 5; p. 7).

For reasons of space, I must leave to others the investigation of the morphism of the incarcerated body in order to take up here a different line of questioning.[24] My query still bears on the pole of Werther's characterological "extremity" explored in the previous section, the morphism of the absolute body, but approaches this aspect of the novel from a different perspective. The question I want to raise is this: if the morphism of the absolute body is the *predominant* (which is also to say, not the only) imaginative projection of corporeality in the novel, then what consequences does this have for the process of reading? How does the reader find access to this morphism? This question touches on what might be termed the immanent aesthetics of the novel. I claimed above — for example, in the discussion of the standard sociohistorical interpretation of the dance and of the inadequacy of the Lacanian concept of the mirror stage as applied to Werther's absorption into the encompassing maternal oneness of nature — that the morphism of the absolute body comes into being as the dissolution of representation, that the absolute body is precisely the body without contours or limits, that it has its source in the pre-representational experience of oral satiation. If this is the case, however, then it is clear that readerly access to this morphism cannot be achieved on the level of figuration, be it the local figuration of specific images or the overriding figuration of narrative construction. Stated more radically, if the morphism of the absolute body indeed determines what the Russian formalists called the *dominant* of the text, then its effects must be sought out on a level that is pre- or at least asemantic, and the process of reading this text must be conceived in such a way as to include, along with the various dimensions of the novelistic figuration, an asemantic level of apprehension. But what might this level be? How does such apprehension work?

We can begin to answer this question by returning to the letter of June 16. As the group of young people is on the way to the dance, a conversation unfolds in which Charlotte expresses her views first on novels and then on dancing. Werther describes his attentive listening to her speech as follows:

How I gazed into her rich dark eyes as she spoke; how my own eyes hung on her warm lips and fresh, glowing cheeks, how I *sank down into* the wonderful sense of what she said — so much so, that I often did not hear her actual words! In short, when we arrived at the dance, I alighted from the carriage as if in a dream and was so lost in the dimming world around me that I scarcely heard the music which came from the brightly lit ballroom. (p. 16, slightly altered; pp. 23–24)

The same letter culminates, of course, in the scene at the window where Charlotte utters the name of "Klopstock," linking their joint act of witnessing the receding storm to the reading experience each has had, separately, of that poet's "magnificent ode": "I remembered at once that magnificent ode which was in her thoughts, and *sank down into* the flood of feelings that she poured over me with this watchword. It was more than I could bear. I bent over her hand and kissed it in a stream of the most blissful tears" (p. 19, substantially altered; p. 27). The juxtaposition of these passages tells us something about Werther's mode of reading: in both, the same verb of 'sinking' (versinken), of liquid absorption, defines his apprehension of language. Exactly that experience to which Werther found access in his reading of Klopstock's ode, in other words, is opened up for him as he listens to Charlotte's speech. And this listening, although it submerges the protagonist into what is called the "wonderful sense" of what she says, could hardly be thought of as semantically oriented. Werther does not even distinguish the words pronounced. His audition receives a sense (Sinn) that is not carried by the additive sequence of individually partitioned words, but rather flows beneath it, an asemantic sense that unleashes and sustains the liquid flow of emotion evoked in him. Werther, as reader or listener, does not interpret or conceptualize. Rather, he experiences a kind of inner dissolution of the lexical-semantic code that becomes for him a point of access to the morphism of the absolute body.

The claim I want to make here is that the account of reading as an asemantic listening these passages sketch out applies to the kind of reading the novel itself elicits; that the novel takes effect when the intellectual labor of constructing semantic relations withdraws from the foreground of the reader's attention, yielding to an *apprehension of the interior body as suffused with a flowing, liquid emotionality*. And I want to claim further that the semiotic mechanism through which this apprehension is conveyed is *the voice*. But this voice is not an oral utterance sent out into the real world of spatial distances; it is not oratorical. Rather, it is an interior and remembered voice, a kind of vocal phantasm experienced within the reader's body as a soothing liquefaction. If Werther, riding in the carriage, does not distinguish Charlotte's words but nevertheless "sinks down into the . . . sense" of what she says, it is because this "sense," far from being a semantic structure, is *her voice itself* as the oral-aural conduit to the interior body.

To bring this set of claims into sharper focus, I find it useful to consider a passage I alluded to at the outset, Werther's first reference to Homer in his letter of May 13:

You ask if you should send me books. My dear friend, for the love of God, keep them away from me! I no longer want to be guided, animated. My feelings are so stormy by themselves! I need a cradlesong to lull me and this I find abundantly in my Homer. How often must I still the burning fever of my blood, for you have never seen anything so unsteady, so restless, as my heart. But need I confess this to you, my dear friend, who have so often witnessed my sudden transitions from sorrow to joy, and from sweet melancholy to violent passion? I treat my heart like a sick child, and gratify its every fancy. Do not repeat this; there are people who would misunderstand it. (p. 7; p. 10)

Note here that Homer's epics do not fall within the class of what Werther calls "books," that they do not belong to a literary culture. Such books take their effect in what might be termed a traditional rhetorical dimension, either "guiding" (that is, instructing) or "animating" (that is, promoting pathos). Werther rejects both dimensions of rhetorical efficacy, much as throughout the novel he repudiates accumulated bookishness. But Homer, although Werther unquestionably reads his works, elicits

from him another sort of response, lulling him into an emotional quiescence, and the reason the Homeric text does this is that it works like a
"cradlesong." Homer affords access, in other words, to an experience of
language that precedes reading, precedes even the ability to construct semantic relations; to an experience of language as the voice of the Mother,
as a tonal flow that soothes the "sick child" Werther's heart is. There is a
line that runs from this passage to those on Charlotte's singing at the
piano, in which, as I remarked above, her voice and mouth (note that in
the carriage Werther focuses on her "warm lips") become the point of
insertion into the maternal economy of the absolute body. The Homeric
epics are not, for Werther, heroic narratives; they are the Mother's lulling
lullaby.

Werther's localization of Homer in the sphere of what I want to call
primordial orality is not an isolated or idiosyncratic gesture, but rather is
continuous with literary currents in the 1770s. To make this point, I call
attention to a passage on Homer from Herder's introduction to his edition
of *Volkslieder* (1778–79):

He did not sit down on velvet in order to write a heroic poem in twice twenty-four
songs according to Aristotle's rule or, if the muse so wished, outside the rule, but
rather sang what he had heard, represented what he had seen and vitally seized
hold of: his rhapsodies did not remain in bookshops and on our rags of paper, but
rather in the ear and in the heart of living singers and hearers, out of which they
were much later collected and finally, buried beneath glosses and prejudices, came
to us. Homer's verse, as encompassing as the blue heaven and communicating itself
in such myriad ways to everything that dwells beneath it, is not the hexameter of
schools and art, but rather the meter of the Greeks that lay ready in their pure and
subtle ear, in their resounding language, and waited, as it were, like a formable clay
for the figures of gods and heroes. Infinite and untiring it flows in gentle cascades,
in repeating epithets and cadences, such as the ear of the people loved. These
features, the agony of all translators and epic poets, are the soul of its harmony, the
soft cushion of rest, that at every line's end closes our eye and puts our head to
sleep so that it might awaken to new vision with every new line and not tire of the
long way.[25]

Herder is a great, that is, historically decisive, critic not because of the
accuracy of his observations and judgments but because he formulated a
new imaginary of language and literature. Thus, to read this (utterly typical) passage in a strictly referential way ("Here Herder contrasts the oral
culture of Homer with the modern culture of writing"), even if such a
reading bears an ideology-critical accent ("Here Herder compensates for
the alienation of the emergent literary market by valorizing the oral culture of Homer"), is to fall short. The task, rather, is to reconstruct the

imaginary constellation, the mythical horizon, within which the values of orality and writing (for they are, like all mythic elements, not facts, but mutually defining signs) receive their respective definitions.

I start, then, with the observation that Homeric song, as Herder here construes its existence, has nothing at all to do with oral culture in the technical sense of the term. There is no mention, no perception, of the noisy give and take of preliterate cultural production, of its ritualistic features, of its problems of memory and storage, the necessary redundancies and the laborious construction of tradition. The voice of Homer is no real voice burdened by limitations of volume and projection, and his listeners are no real bodily assembly galvanized by corporeal proximity. Finally, there is no mention of the rigorous discipline (the mnemotechnics, the schooling of the voice, the training in set forms) characteristic of oral cultures; it is as if everything ushered forth from spontaneity. In short, orality here does not occupy a place in the world, is not a technology of the word. Quite the contrary, Homer's voice and song go directly to the heart and ear of his auditors without ever passing through an exteriority, and these auditors themselves are the sheer internality of their attentive listening. To put the matter another way, Herder imagines the collectivity of oral culture as a collective individual that, in the inwardness of its audition, hears the originary song of its language.

Two operations, then, produce the value of primordial orality that Herder's text endows with such mythic dignity: a singularization of collectivity and an internalization of sound. The group becomes an individual subject attentive to the movements of its own inwardness. Both of these operations come together in the phrase "such as the ear of the people loved": the people as a single ear affectively bound to the gentle cascades of voice that resound within it. At this point, the imaginary character of Herder's concept of orality — the phantasmatic scene it evokes — profiles itself most clearly. We are dealing here with an intimate emotional tie, with the 'love' of an individual subject for the voice that vibrates within it, and in particular (as the cited passage goes on to say) for the 'soul' whose audibility, whose existence, that voice is. Any remaining doubts as to the private, individual, and inward nature of this primordial orality, this circuit of voice and ear, are dispelled by the transformation of the "soul of its harmony" into a "soft cushion" that soothes us (suddenly Herder is back in the contemporary world) into sleep. The rhapsode's performance before his assembled listeners has become, exactly as in *Werther*, a lullaby sung to a child. The "gentle" ("sanft"; one might also translate "tender") cadences the ear so 'loves' emanate from a maternal instance.

To substantiate this reading, I call attention to a further passage from Herder, this time from his *Treatise on the Origin of Language*:

The nursing infant that stammers its first words repeats with this stammering the feelings of its parents and swears with each early stammering through which tongue and soul form themselves to render these feelings eternal, as truly as it calls them his father- or mother-language. Throughout its life these first impressions of its childhood, these images from the soul and heart of its parents, will live and act within him: together with the word the entire feeling that early overflowed his soul will return: with the idea signified by the word all of the associated ideas that then lay before him in his morning-view into the realm of creation — they will return and act more powerfully than the pure and clear central idea itself.[26]

I select for emphasis three intertwined ideas of this passage. First, Herder clearly conceives of orality as the medium not merely of the tongue's training but of the formation of the soul. Subjectivity emerges within the audibility of the voice. This implies (second idea) that the voice is the carrier of what might be termed an ontogenetic semantics: into adulthood it maintains a link to the experience of language acquisition and to the familial network of feelings, symbolic positions, and perceptual colorings that characterized that experience. We might say that language for Herder takes on a personal-historical density, that it bears the sedimentations of childhood experience even into the phase in which such experience is forgotten; in short, that my language is so intimately connected with my childhood that it remembers more than I do. These two linked notions are important in understanding the "sense" that Werther, in the passage cited earlier, "sinks into" without differentiating Charlotte's words, and they are likewise a key to his reading of Homer as "cradlesong." The sort of reading alluded to in these passages actualizes the anamnestic potential of language as voice, recapitulates, as a resonance within the interior body, the formation of the soul in the movements of the voice, and allows the resonant traces of childhood impressions shaped within the familial network of affectively invested symbolic positions to become audible once again. These vocalic traces and not the "pure and clear central idea" of the words (that is, their lexical-semantic nucleus, their conceptuality) are what reverberate within the reader's interior body.

The third idea of the passage I want to emphasize does not receive explicit mention. It has to do with the overall point of Herder's remarks, their function within a larger context of argument. Herder wants to claim that the transition from nature to culture the nursing infant negotiates is itself a natural event, or, more precisely, that it obeys a natural economy. The economy in question (the economy that structures the entirety of

Herder's argument in the *Treatise*) is that of lack and supplement. As a sheerly natural being, the human infant is poorer and weaker than any of the animals. But this weakness is itself the condition of strength, for nature supplements the instinctual poverty of the human creature with the richness of education, development, culture, and community. And the instrument through which this process of natural supplementation occurs, of course, is language, the orality through which the child internalizes the "feelings of its parents" and therewith shapes its "tongue and soul."

I stress this point because it is crucial to understanding how the concept of primordial orality functions in Herder's theory and who the agency of this orality actually is. The transition from nature to culture is smooth and continuous, it is accomplished not by the violent imposition of an arbitrary law as in Rousseau but by what Herder calls the "economy of the nature of human kind." Here is another "look," as Herder says, at this economy:

The woman, in nature so much the weaker part, must she not accept the law from the experienced, providing, language-forming man? Yes, if it be called law what is merely the mild beneficence of instruction? The weak child, so literally called immature, must it not accept language, since it enjoys with it the milk of its mother, the spirit of its father? And must not this language be rendered eternal if anything is to be rendered eternal? Oh, the laws of nature are more powerful than all the conventions which cunning politics concocts and the wise philosopher claims to enumerate! The words of childhood — these our early playmates in the dawn of life! with which our entire soul formed itself —, when will we fail to recognize them, when will we forget them? Our mother language was simultaneously the first world we saw, the first sensations we felt, the first activity and happiness we enjoyed.[27]

The deficiencies of the natural creature do not run up against a heterogeneous law of culture which would press the infant into conformity; rather, they are compensated by a gentle benevolence, by a sort of loving care that the economy of nature guarantees. The man, as the stronger, language-shaping agency, conveys his 'law' (if 'law' be called this protective charity) to the woman, who in turn transmits it to the child. The child, then, is twice removed from the violence of the law, first by the father's love of the mother, and then by the mother's love for the child. And especially this latter love — the maternal donation through which the child receives its first language — can be stylized as 'natural.' The infant passing into culture drinks in the mother's voice like milk from her breast. The maternal voice nurses the child and provides therewith the natural supplement that transforms our creaturely poverty into cultural abundance. Pri-

mordial orality is the voice of the Mother, the medium of a natural cul-
turation. And the meaning carried in what I referred to above as the
ontogenetic semantics of language is the affective tonality of the vocal
cocoon that unites mother and child. This is why the poetry of Homer is a
lullaby whose tender cadences, according to Herder, we "love"; and this is
why Charlotte's singing at the piano is Werther's point of insertion into the
liquid-maternal economy.

This brief excursus through Herder's theory of language allows me to
formulate more explicitly the claims made above regarding the kind of
reading *Werther* elicits. Beneath the lexical-semantic differentiation of the
text there flows — much as for Herder the "gentle cascades" of Homer's
song flow within the loving ear of his listeners — a *melos* that is the very
medium, the existence, of the "soul." This is what I meant when I said at
the outset that *Werther* is the first European novel in which subjectivity
per se becomes audible. The voice (conceived, to be sure, not as oratorical,
not as emitted into the world, but as primordial orality) is the existence of
subjectivity: "This subjectivity for itself is, wholly abstractly, the pure
process of time which, in the concrete body, is as time realizing itself, as
vibration and tone."[28] The category of empathy has often been employed
to characterize the pragmatics of the novel, but this vague notion of emotional identification misses entirely the psychological, medial, and corporeal dynamics of reading that the text sets into motion. The reader of
the novel, I want to say, is drawn into a fantasy scene that is not a scene,
not a visual or representational objectification, and not an empathetic
actualization of the feelings of a fictional individual; this scene is, rather,
the hallucination of the oral-aural circulation of voice within the interior
body, the experience of the interior body as dissolved in primordial orality.

This voice, however, only becomes audible intermittently; it is interrupted, checked, fragmented, and suppressed by everything in the novel's
language that is not voice, by everything that derives from its *written* character. This point emerges in an especially revealing fashion in Werther's
first note addressed to Charlotte herself: "Yes, dear Charlotte! I will take
care of everything as you wish. Do make me more requests, the more the
better. I only ask one favor; use no more writing sand with the little notes
you send me. Today I quickly raised your letter to my lips, and it set my
teeth on edge" (p. 29; p. 41). Just as the granular residue of the writing
process blocks Werther's fantasy of orally consuming (kissing, drinking)
Charlotte's language, just as the sand desiccates the liquidity of ink, so too
in the novel generally do the mechanisms of writing block access to the
domain of primordial orality.

The interference of orality and writing produces an alternation of flow and disruption that lends the novel its characteristic rhythm. Surges of language emerge only to be halted and are halted only to be repeated again. This rhythmic pattern profiles itself globally in the novel's overriding material-semiotic structure as a concatenation of letters, fragments of letters, and self-addressed notes, with the force of interruption and fragmentation becoming ever more insistent as the novel bends toward its sorrowful end. But the same pattern emerges in local passages as well. A telling example occurs with the first mention of Charlotte's piano playing:

Sometimes when we are talking she lays her hand on mine and in the eagerness of conversation comes closer to me, and her divine breath touches my lips — I feel myself sinking away [versinken] as if struck by lightning. And yet, Wilhelm, with all this heavenly intimacy — if I should ever dare — you understand. No! my heart is not so depraved; it is weak, weak enough — but isn't that a kind of depravity?

She is sacred to me. All desire is silenced in her presence; I don't know what I feel when I'm near her. There is a melody which she plays on the piano with the touch of an angel — so simple is it, and yet so full of spirit! It's her favorite song, and when she strikes the first note all my worry and sorrow disappear in a moment. (p. 27, slightly altered; p. 39)

Both in terms of the events described and in terms of the internal rhythm of the description, the passage moves from the simulation of orality to a phase of staccato interruptions in order to return to an oral glide. And the trace left by these interruptions of the oral stream is a purely graphic marker of division, — the dash, a punctuation that Werther at one point claims not to like at all.[29] This emergence of the dash precisely at that moment when the oral phantasm edges toward fulfillment is by no means unique. The two other piano scenes in the novel (pp. 62/87; pp. 64/91) exhibit the identical rhythmic alternation, the identical fracture of orality by the severance of writing.[30]

The rhythm of oral flow and scriptural interruption that constitutes the phenomenology of reading in *Werther* corresponds, on the level of narrative, to the conflict of love and law. This is why the dash, in the piano passages just referred to and throughout the novel, takes effect as a force of censorship, impeding explicit acknowledgment of Werther's desire. Thus, it is no accident that Albert is a successful secretary at court, a profession one could characterize as writing in the name of the law, exactly that profession at which Werther — in part due to his supervisor's insistence on proper punctuation — did not succeed. This interweaving of the issues of orality and writing, love and law, takes on a special salience at that moment when Charlotte, acting in anticipation of her husband's proscription, tells Werther he must not visit her again before Christmas Eve, imposing thereby a rhythm of regulated intervals between their meetings: " 'We can't go on like this any longer!' He turned away from her, walking hastily up and down the room, muttering between his teeth, 'We can't go on like this any longer!' " (p. 72, slightly altered; p. 102). And when Charlotte, in the same scene, goes on to speak of his attachment to her in words Werther recognizes as Albert's, the text again notes: "He gritted his teeth and looked at her gloomily" (p. 72; p. 102). Just as the dental consonant interrupts and articulates the vocalic flow — introducing thereby phonemic articulation, the very possibility of language as a diacritical structure — Albert's word, the word of prohibition, sets Werther's teeth on edge, forces his mouth into a kind of dental rigidity. The passage, recalling Werther's earlier remark on Charlotte's use of "writing sand," illustrates the internal severance of orality by the law and by writing that constitutes the fundamental structural principle of the novel and its reading. Hence the peculiar quality of Werther's anxious fantasy of retribution for the transgression he dares not admit to: basking in the "heavenly expression" of Charlotte's "words," giving himself over to his dream of oral-aural union, he suddenly feels something "grab me like an assassin around the throat" (p. 38, slightly altered; p. 55).[31] The law is to love as writing is to voice: a regulated strangulation.

In the passages on Klopstock and Homer and in the carriage scene cited above, the novel installs the scenario of its own reading. The voice becomes audible beneath the level of lexical-semantic articulation. A similar paradigmatic status can be attributed to the following excerpt: "Yesterday, as I was leaving, she took my hand and said, 'Adieu, dear Werther.' Dear Werther! It was the first time she called me 'dear'; it penetrated my whole being. I have repeated it a hundred times since and last night, as I was going to bed and talked to myself about nothing in particular, I suddenly said, 'Good night, dear Werther!' and I could not help laughing at myself" (p. 61; p. 87). To love, as this passage defines it, is to love the voice that says "love" and in doing so suffuses even the body's skeletal rigidity ("ging mir durch Mark und Bein"). To love is so thoroughly to identify with the voice intoning the predicate of love ("dear"; "lieber") that that voice is held within the body, awaiting the inattentiveness of freely associating speech to return and, in my voice, address me once again. Werther's voice becomes the echo of Charlotte's and Charlotte's, in turn, the echo of a more primordial orality. For it is not a quotidian "adieu" that the returning voice addresses to Werther, but a "good night," as if whispered to a child going to sleep. The Homeric "cradlesong" in its most reduced and purest form: the voice of the Mother, the voice *as* Mother.

The chain of concepts I have developed here to characterize the relation between semiosis and corporeality specific to the novel — the morphism of the absolute body, the liquid maternal economy, primordial orality, the intermittent rhythm of voice and writing — requires one further notional link. As the natural supplement, the articulation of nature and culture, the voice occupies an ambiguous position. In the sentence I cited from Hegel, it is said that the voice is the existence of subjectivity as time. The time that characterizes the voice is at once the sheer presence of its audibility and its audible disappearance. The voice dies with every instant of its life; it is the pure expression of organic-corporeal vitality and at the same time of death. Thus Herder notes in his *Treatise* that suffering animals give expression to their death as voice: "the sound of death resounds [der Todeston tönet]."[32] And Hegel develops much the same idea: "In violent death every animal has a voice, expresses itself as negated self."[33] This has important consequences for the aesthetic structure of the novel. If, as I have argued, Goethe's novelistic project is to bring primordial orality to aesthetic concretization, to make that voice — intermittently — audible in its writing, then that novelistic project must also include the experience of voice as pure negativity, as the death of the body. And the reader's listening to that voice must be a kind of labor of mourning.

The ambiguity of the voice corresponds to that of the oral fantasy of the absolute body: simultaneously nourishment and poison, enclosure within the maternal-liquid economy and drowning, drinking, and being swallowed. Interestingly enough, the passage in which Werther imagines the world as an omnivorous monster, a kind of all- and self-consuming mouth, also includes the novel's most explicit thematization of time: "Can we say of anything that it is when all passes away — when time, with the speed of a storm, carries all things onward — and our transitory existence, hurried along by the torrent, is swallowed up by the waves or dashed against the rocks?" (p. 37; p. 52). Moreover, the ambiguous position of the voice as life/death determines the narrative structure of the novel's love story. If to love, as Werther loves Charlotte, is to identify with the voice, to wish to coincide with and dissolve in that voice, then it is likewise to identify with one's death. To love the voice is to love death as pure negativity. The eroticization of death so often noted by critics of the novel is a function of its set (Einstellung) toward language.

And what of the reader's work of mourning? Where does this listening to voice as death find its correlate in the novel? The answer, of course, is in the infinite lament of Ossian's songs. "Ossian has superseded Homer in my heart," Werther writes, about two-thirds through the novel (p. 58; p. 82), announcing the displacement of his identification with the epic "cradlesong" onto the dolorous litany of the bard. And at the close of the novel, when he reads from his translations of Ossian at Charlotte's request, the voice that rises from within him is that of death and absence. The insertion of these translations into the novel is often regarded as an aesthetic failing, an awkward halting of narrative pace, and when they are accorded a function, the passages are usually viewed merely as an index of Werther's unhappy state of mind. If my argument up to this point is correct, however, then the Ossian translations, in all their monotony, must be viewed as that moment when the novel achieves its most radical authenticity. The songs that Werther reads are nothing but an enclosure of voices within voices, each voice recalling and rehearsing the death of voice. Here the equivalence of voice and soul posited in Herder's language theory finds perfect expression; but the souls are not forms of vital animation, they are shades, audible traces of the dead. Goethe's translation of Macpherson's forgery thus opens up a kind of ghostly echo-chamber within the novel in which death, without locus or body, reverberates. And this echoic effect vibrates in the reader, disclosing the hetero-affection of one's own voice, its invasion by another. Listening to the *evocation* of the dead that echoes through Werther's translations, to this voice without origin that is voice in its purest form as negativity, Charlotte and Werther experience once again the flow of the liquid-maternal donation and the possibility of an erotic union that, as bodies, they will never know: "They felt their own misery [Elend] in the fate of the noble ones [Edlen] — felt it together, and their tears united [vereinigten sich]" (p. 80, substantially altered; p. 114). The "Edlen" — the dead — echo in the "Elend" that is the poverty, the abandonment, the disappropriation of vocalic time.

Werther, I have argued, identifies with the voice, both in his love and in his suicide, an identification that corresponds to his self-metaphorization as absolute body. But this correlation also applies to Goethe's singular aesthetic achievement in the novel. At the most fundamental level of the text, prior to its play of narrative and scenic representations, prior, I am tempted to say, to its fictionality, this text is a single — if interrupted — evocation. Voice (not fiction) is the movement of transport that dissolves the reader's organic body in the audition of subjectivity per se. Voice is the originary metaphor of the novel itself, the semiotic-corporeal *atopia* of the novelistic event.

Deconstruction of the Hermeneutical Body:
Kleist and the Discourse of Classical Aesthetics

HELMUT J. SCHNEIDER

$\mathcal{H}$einrich von Kleist's intricate little essay "Über das Marionetten-theater" (1810) was read for generations as a straightforward, if at times somewhat puzzling, exposition of the classical topic of grace in the context of the idealist philosophy of history. Only in the past one and a half decades or so has this understanding been severely challenged.[1] The text, one might say, finally opened up its enigma; in an emphatic sense it was *read* for the first time. Readers have since tried to come to grips with the countless inconsistencies, leaps, even blatant absurdities of its argument. How can, to mention the most obvious point, a marionette, or a trained fencing bear for that matter, serve as the unsurpassed model of grace and utopian bliss? If anything, the wooden puppet with its clattering limbs, suspended from numerous strings and controlled by an invisible pup-peteer ("Maschinist," as the text calls him), symbolizes the exact opposite of the redeeming values of beauty and freedom addressed in the aesthetic concept of graceful human body movements. It represented the extreme of mechanical reification and external dependence. Quite logically, the first-person narrator protests the extravagant claim of his dialogue partner, the dancer, as the latter makes a provocative case for the puppet even against his own art: "I said that, however skillfully he presented his paradoxical case, he would never make me believe that more grace could be contained in a mechanical puppet [Gliedermann: literally, jointed man] than in the structure of the human body."[2] To be sure, the narrator's defiant self-assertiveness falls apart only too quickly. At the end of the fictional di-alogue, he himself volunteers the conclusion from his opponent's argu-ment and receives gracious acknowledgment for it. Readers followed suit and subscribed to the idea of having "to eat again from the Tree of Knowl-

edge in order to fall back into the state of innocence." They interpreted
this idea along the lines of the paradoxical axiom of *Geschichtsphilosophie* which claimed that the same evil, civilization, which had deprived
mankind of its original paradise would also, through its completion, bring
the original state back in some distant future. After we lost our paradisiac
unity with ourselves through consciousness, we would recover it on a
higher level of self-conscious perfection. But there is nothing in Kleist's
text that suggests such a spiral development through time, which was
constitutive for the philosophical model. As far as the theme of paradise
lost and regained is concerned, it is illustrated here in spatial metaphors
suggesting repetition, but not overcoming; here, *re*lapsing into the *pre*lap-
sarian state simply means restaging the first Fall, as the paradoxical word-
ing indicates ("in den *Stand* der Unschuld zurückzu*fallen*": "falling" back
into — literally — the "stand," not standing back up from the Fall). Also,
the fact that the narrator draws his conclusion in a "slightly distracted"
state of mind ("ein wenig zerstreut") does not bode well for its logical
soundness. Is he not already in that fallen, or scattered, state of body, a
spatial sense that the root meaning of the word "zerstreut" suggests? If the
narrator gives in to the dancer's argument because he finally 'understands'
it, then this *resolution* of the "paradox" comes across as a *dissolution*, a
"fall."

"Zerstreuung" — dissolution, distraction, dispersion, fragmentation:
this is not only what the argument concerning the marionettes is about,
but what the text "On the Theater of the Marionettes" itself articulates in
its form. Under the all-too-successful influence of the idealist tradition,
which Kleist attacked and parodied, readers concentrated too deeply on
the philosophical content of Kleist's text and overlooked (overread) its
dispersed surface. By calling on us to eat again from the forbidden apple —
the object, as we know, of a physical seduction as well as a spiritual promise — the essay may have mocked this hermeneutical ingesting of its utter
senselessness all along. The philosophical understanding was only disturbed when attention was focused on the fictional and rhetorical qualities
of the dialogue. The new readings see in Kleist's text an early document of
our contemporary concerns with the shaky character of theoretical language and the tenuous distinction between philosophical and poetic discourse. "On the Theater of the Marionettes" has now become one of the
classic reference texts for the "deconstructive" turn in literary criticism.[3]

These recent readings, however, tend to neglect the traditional aesthetic
theme of grace, or they treat it in isolation from the poetic form. But the
essay's dominant topic is the human body and its representation, espe-

cially in language. The inextricable meshing of these two aspects, body and language, also places the essay firmly in its historical context. Kleist draws to the fore and places at center stage a body which exposes crucial characteristics of the classical body paradigm. He deconstructs what through his text turns out to be a hidden intersecting point of the discourses of aesthetics, hermeneutics, and *Geschichtsphilosophie* at the end of the eighteenth century and the beginning of the nineteenth. The theater metaphor needs to be taken literally here. The text's fictional form, that is, its scenic presentation, is not simply a medium to convey a theoretical argument; it is the self-presentation of the same body which is being spoken about. Only by staging what it says in the manner how it is said, does the text demonstrate, literally, *present*, its argument — if it then can still be called an argument (or, for that matter, the essay an essay). The dialogue on the marionettes embodies the argument in its action and as action and thus, quite properly, situates the discussion on the body in the body.

The classical concept of grace corresponded to the new unified and disciplined body image that emerged in the eighteenth century in response to the global process of rationalization. It relied on a complete internalization of the disciplining force of civilization and therefore set itself off not only against the premodern (popular) "grotesque" body, as Bakhtin has described it,[4] but also against the baroque theatrical body. In grace, civilizational discipline was naturalized. The graceful body anchored bourgeois autonomy and individuality on a level where it was not conscious of itself and was unmediated by any signification. As Schiller, the main philosophical authority on the topic, succinctly put it, grace was a "beauty not given by nature but produced by the human subject itself" which at the same time hid its man-made character: "Grace leaves to nature an appearance of freedom where she follows the commands of reason."[5]

The assumption is plausible that Kleist's provocative image of the graceful marionette was designed to counter this idealist notion of nature on the invisible leash, or the hidden strings, of her master, reason.[6] But ideological demasking is not the primary intent of his essay. Rather, Kleist aims at the covert *theatrical character* of the constellation that Schiller describes and that is inherent in any idealist elimination of difference in favor of ultimate unity. Grace was supposed to exclude all elements of show and representation, it was defined by its very un- and antitheatricality. But it was also conceived as an *object of aesthetic perception* for a beholder who recognized in or behind the natural appearance the "commands" of reason. In the graceful body, nature split herself; she performed the rational order of her opposite while appearing to follow only her own spontaneous law (the law of gravity, in the case of Kleist's puppets, which is exploited by the technical "antigravity" manipulations of the puppeteer). Reason delimited an area — a stage — where nature was allowed to be herself or, better, to play herself out, as long as she ultimately conformed with the preset rules. For the spectator, the graceful movements and gestures of the body coincided — miraculously, unwittingly, fortuitously — with his (her?) civilized expectations; in the spectacle of grace, he recognized his own internalized discipline as nature's spontaneous and gracious gift. The Schillerian grace is the staging of nature by a self-empowering human subject which yearns to reflect itself precisely in that which is beyond its control, controlling the very uncontrollable, manipulating the body's contingency.[7] "It is the legislator himself, the god in us," Schiller says, "who plays with his own image in the sensory world."[8]

The graceful embodiment of reason, then, as a deceitful masquerade? Kleist takes up the classical paradigm in order to deny any unity which we may project onto our body; and even more, in order to show how this unitary phantasma is destined to cover up a primordial split which we cannot escape. The dismantling of this phantasma cuts right to the heart of classical aesthetics and its idealist philosophical assumptions. The "Marionettentheater" essay — this is my thesis — turns the value hierarchy of the classical discourse upside down, or, more exactly, *inside out*. It questions the priority of the interior over the exterior, the spiritual over the corporeal, the meaningful over the accidental, the metaphor over the literal, the signified over the signifier, the soul or mind over the body. It does so by *presenting, in the suggested theatrical sense, the classical discourse "from the outside."* What this means, I want to illustrate first with the essay's scenic fiction, before proceeding to the crucial symbol of the marionette and then to the anecdotes of the beautiful youth and the bear.

How can we ever be at unity with our body and with ourselves; how can we even *speak* about our body without removing ourselves from it, turning it into an external, thinglike object? Do we not constantly, by physically presenting ourselves to others and to ourselves, put it on stage or display? The very concept of embodiment implies the split that the theory of grace sought to eliminate; embodiment in the sense of cultural production is a constant process of disembodiment, of projecting ourselves out of ourselves into a different kind of body — in other words, a way of acting.

As Kleist's text *enacts* the classical discourse on grace on its fictional stage, it rehearses the split of the body against itself and the other body through a series of dual constellations which are combative (agonistic), pedagogical, and theatrical at the same time. First there is the relationship between machinist and puppet; then the episode between the young man and his older mentor, who makes him repeat his graceful pose and thereby lose his innocence; and finally the two fencing matches between the dancer and the student and the dancer and the bear. These major scenes (there are more, many of them also physically demarcated as onstage or in an arena) are in turn embedded in a dialogue which resembles a verbal contest. As the two interlocutors speak about the body and its grace or non-grace, they also speak about and with their own bodies, and since they assert their argumentative stand vis-à-vis each other, their dialogue assumes a quasi-physical quality. We may call this rhetorical-dialogical language which aligns itself with the body a discourse of exteriority; it stands in sharp contrast with the discourse of spiritual interiority which was the hermeneutical heartbeat of classical aesthetics and *Geschichtsphilosophie*.

The narrative begins with a chance meeting of the two men in the city park, when the narrator accosts the popular first dancer of the local opera and expresses his surprise at having "found him several times" in a puppet theater in town. This is a place of vulgar amusement for the "rabble" (which, it should be noted, the narrator himself has obviously visited more than once), a place on the margins of official culture — or even beyond its limits, as the contemporary prohibition of puppet shows proves[9] — the frequenting of which clearly needs to be justified. Near the end of the text, the scene of the dancer's fencing anecdote is a Livonian country estate that he visited "during my journey to Russia" and where a trained fencing bear is about as much aesthetic culture as one would expect; the bear's "wooden stall" in the courtyard, incidentally, echoes the "clapboard shack" of the puppet theater "put together at the marketplace." In this context, it is no accident that the narrator links his anecdote of the youth who recognizes himself in a Greek statue — the paradigmatic art-form of elitist classicist culture — to a visit to the Louvre in Paris, the center of all cultural centers.

The puppet theater (and, by extension, the trained bear and the skill of fencing)[10] represents a marginal popular art-form which is more material, more technical, more superficial, more physical, altogether more external ("äusserlich," with its specific German connotations) than its high-art counterpart. There is something forbidden and hidden about it, so that the "first dancer" of the city opera feels exposed when his presence there is observed. Does he seek to protect his secret of mundane physicality with the oversophisticated, far-flung arguments which elevate it to the level of the high classical discourse of the time?[11]

The formal structure of the text offers a clue. It is neither straight narration nor dialogue, but a narration of dialogue in which perspectives from the inside and the outside intermingle. Thus, the dancer's explanations of the enigmatic puppets are only partly given in his own voice; the other part is rendered in indirect speech, often (but not always) in the subjunctive (something that is lost in the English translation). The mediation through the narrated dialogue is stressed even more by the narrator's hermeneutical gaze at Herr C., whose physiognomy, gestures, and fashion of speaking become the object of his interpretation. The first example is the dancer's reaction to that opening question, or provocation, of what he was doing in that strange place. As rendered by the narrator, he "let it be noted in no uncertain terms [liess nicht undeutlich merken] that any dancer who wished to improve his art might learn all sorts of things from them." Similar comments, especially in the first half of the text,[12] help build, on the level of the narrated discourse, a tension between outside and inside or surface and depth that corresponds to an analogous opposition on the level of the discussed argument. As the dialogue goes along, the narrator takes the peculiar manner of the dancer's utterance ("Äusserung," literally: "externalization") as a hint to learn more about his views: "Since the remark, because of the way in which he brought it up, seemed to me more than a mere fancy, I sat down beside him in order to question him more closely about the grounds on which he would support so strange an assertion."[13]

Again, it is the rhetorical and gestural *appearance* of the dancer's speech which causes the narrator to draw closer and interrogate him about the reasons for or behind such a statement — a statement which seems to be more than something that just occurs to, literally falls on, oneself ("ein blosser Einfall") but which may be grounded in some internal reasoning. By surmising what is behind the rhetorical surface, the narrator in effect breaks his dialogue partner into halves and *opens up an internal space* in which the ensuing dialogue takes place. It is the estranged space of an "externalized interiority," the space in which the dancer both hides and reveals the secret of this other cultural place, the puppet theater.

The physical, bodily character of that secret will obstruct the transparency of perfect rational understanding. Contributing to the obstruction, or obscuration, of a transparent meaning is, here as elsewhere, the consistent play on the literal meanings of words, the outside, so to speak, of their inner, metaphorical meaning: "Äusserung" (making external, utterance), "vorbrachte" (bring forth or up, present), "Gründe" (grounds, reasons), "Behauptung" (claim, with the root "head"), "stützen" (support) — all of them can be read in their original spatial and corporeal sense. Even the word "vernehmen" (interrogate, question) may not be coincidental; for as much as one can expect juridical nomenclature from Kleist (in itself an external, violent hermeneutics), it would be out of place here if it were not for its literal, gestural connotation.[14]

For indeed, the dialogue is, on its most basic level, about taking oneself and the other apart, about projecting or bringing oneself forward and outward to the other ("vor-geben," "vor-bringen"), about trying to hold together in front of him, about standing erect and being firmly grounded ("Be-hauptung," "Gründe," "stützen") or falling ("Ein-fall"). When the narrator inquires more specifically about the mechanical functioning of the marionettes, he takes a threatening look behind the scene of our corporeal unity. Here is the dancer's answer explaining how the hidden puppeteer can move the individual limbs "without having myriad strings on his fingers":

that I should not imagine [mir vorstellen] that each limb was individually placed and pulled [gestellt und gezogen] by the machinist at the various moments of the dance.

Every movement, he said, had its center of gravity; it was enough to control this, within the figure; the limbs, which were nothing but pendulums, followed of themselves mechanically without any assistance.

Again, the identity of the root word "stellen" here connects the mental activity of self-reflective representation ("mir vorstellen") with the external manipulation of the mechanical puppet. The ambiguity of words like "vorstellen," "darstellen" (represent), "ziehen" (pull, draw), "folgen" (follow; cf. "Folgerungen ziehen," draw consequences, which appears two times), "hervorbringen" (bring forward, produce), "begreifen" (grasp, understand), either in their literal-physical or metaphorical-intellectual meaning, is as constitutive for the marionette as it is for the text as a whole.[15] The effect is a peculiar inversion: the puppet is not just the referential object of the discussion, it is *produced* by it. The analytical discourse, language itself, dissects the unity of the body, as the German word "zergliedern," "dissecting (into limbs)," and the identical root meaning of its Latin equivalent "articulation" suggest. The artifact of the "Gliedermann" (which also alludes to "Knochenmann," the skeleton of Death) is the body dismembered by descriptive, analytical speech.

But this same body which represents the threat of disintegration, also averts it by total external control. The puppeteer, according to Herr C., directs (governs, "regiert") it through the single center of gravity "inside" around which all limbs fall into place by themselves as "sheer pendulums." Any additional (cf. "Zutun") pulling is not only unnecessary but flatly impossible, "since the machinist simply, by means of the wire or string, has no other point in his power." As has often been noted, this runs against the conventional idea of the functioning of a marionette. In the dancer's account, the marionettes are denied the freedom of having their extremities disrupt the body's enclosing contour, whereas their human counterparts are under the constant temptation to show themselves off in contrived and stretched poses. But the contradiction that the puppet represents simultaneously the threat of fragmentation and the ideal of unity is resolved if we take it as the projection of the protagonists' bodily engagement in their dialogue. They also, as they dance around each other and strike various rejecting or seductive poses, put their body at stake. If the text is the arena where the two men constitute themselves as body, constitute their body through their relationship which is theatrical, rhetorical, and physical at the same time, the marionette is the allegory of their effort.

In man, according to Herr C., the physical center (the point of gravity) is in persistent discord with the psychological center, the source of expression. The effect of this is affectation, "Ziererei": "For affectation, as you know, appears when the soul (*vis motrix*) finds itself in any other point than in the center of gravity of the movement."

In "Ziererei," the human body becomes foreign to itself and freezes into an empty ornament ("Zier"). The affected appearance displaces the "soul," the center and source of interiority which the parenthetical Latin reference specifies with a plain physiological term as the "moving force." What is this displaced inside other than desire? "Sich zieren" in German has a distinct undertone of erotic teasing, and there seems to be an erotic element to the derisive tone of voice in which the dancer rebuffs his non-accepting partner's challenge about the "advantage" the dancing puppets have over humans. I must quote the original:

Und der *Vor*teil, den diese Puppe *vor* lebendigen Tänzern *vor*aus haben würde?
Der *Vor*teil? Zu*vör*derst ein negativer, mein *vor*trefflicher Freund, nämlich dieser, dass sie sich niemals *zierte* [My emphases, except for the last]

And the advantage of such a puppet over living dancers?
The advantage? First of all, my good friend, a negative one: namely that it would be incapable of *affectation*.

The mocking repetition of the prefix "vor-" ("pre-") throws back to the narrator, or "puts before" him, his own false pretension. (I will not speculate about the literal meaning of the word "Vor-teil," "advantage," "fore-part"). The signifier mimics the exterior side of language, which on another level is represented by the rhetorical decor, the traditional "ornatus" or "Zier" of speech, which again corresponds to the body's self-ornamentation in the affected posture. The erotic character of what Herr C. condemns as "Ziererei" becomes more than apparent from the two dancing scenes which he uses as illustrations. Here, the body loses itself (its center) by reaching out and bending over to the other sex; yearning, chasing or being chased without fulfillment, this body is outside itself:

Simply take a look at Madame P——, he continued, when she plays Daphne, and, followed by Apollo, she looks around to see him. Her soul sits in the whirls of her buttocks; she bends as though she were going to break, like a naiad of Bernini's school. Take a look at the young dancer F——, when, as Paris, he stands among the three goddesses and hands the apple to Venus. His soul (it is a horror to see it!) sits in his elbow.[16]

The body that extends beyond itself and out of its center of gravity breaks apart. The living body of self-presentation and desire is confronted with fragmentation, castration. It is the price for seeing and being seen, the price for human dependence on this most far-reaching and most self-conscious of the senses. The theatrical scenes of seduction and attraction disturb the individual in his or her pastoral bliss of self-sufficiency; they are primal scenes which catapult man(kind) into the throes of history. The second scene, of course, represents the beauty contest that was at the root of the Trojan War, the fall of the ancient world. Quite appropriately, this classical allusion is followed by another to an even more prominent fall, with another apple as requisite: "Such blunders, he added, breaking off, are unavoidable, since we ate from the Tree of Knowledge. But Paradise is bolted shut and the cherub behind us. We must make the journey around the world and see whether it is not open somewhere in the back again."

Here, at the exact middle of the text, we have reached the interpretive bait which the narrator and the reader, eager to grasp the sense in all this, will gratefully take. But what if this philosophical hint were itself a "blunder" or "mis-take," a "Missgriff" or 'Missbegriff,' an out-of-place concept which its author just "adds" to the scenes in order to use them for the rhetorical seduction of his dialogue partner? Does not the dancer himself enact the fall of sense making, the breaking and offering of the fruit from the Tree of Knowledge about which he speaks? And is the seducer not likewise threatened by breaking apart, as he "breaks off" even while he reaches over to his opponent? The (rhetorical and gestural) figure of "adding while breaking off" or "breaking off while adding" ("fügte er abbrechend hinzu"), that is, adding sense to the graphic description of our fragmented physical appearance, mocks in a spatial (mechanical, external) manner the temporal-spiritual schema of the split and its redemption in the narrative of *Geschichtsphilosophie*. (The same spatialization applies to the notion of the "journey around the world" to the backdoor of paradise, where the Copernican globe becomes the stage for the performance of history. Later in the text, the perfection "in this field" of grace is said to be found in either "the marionette or the God," "and this," the dancer continues, "is the point where both ends of the circular world interlock" ["ineinander*griffen*," they grasp each other or lock hands, the counterpart to the "Missgriff"]. The "world" ties back into itself to shape a theatrical or a "circus" arena for the spectacle of grace.)

If we follow the dancer's later exhortation for a careful reading of Genesis I, 3, we will find two body gestures responsible for the original Fall of Mankind: the opening of the eye, instilling infinite and insatiable desire, and the extending of the hand to break the fruit. God seals paradise behind the expelled first couple with his command to Adam: "lest he put forth his hand, and take also of the tree of life, and eat, and live forever."[17] "Missgriffe," then, are not just ostentatious gestures which are aesthetically flawed, they are "Griffe," "grips" as such, which transcend the body's confines and cause its fall into disunity and inauthenticity. Only the puppets with their "dead, pure pendulums"—limbs as "they ought to be," Herr C. says—conform to God's (gravity's) law and are not threatened by his angel who guards the entrance to paradise "with the naked, brandishing sword" ("mit dem blossen, hauenden Schwert," in Luther's translation) as long as men extend their arms and hands.[18]

This body version of the Fall deconstructs nothing less than the human quality of expressivity, which resides in, and draws on, the difference between a (spiritual) inside and a (material) outside and which the philosopher and anthropologist Helmuth Plessner in our century has appropriately called man's "position of eccentricity" (or "eccentric positionality"). The marionette, to which we now return, negates this essential human condition after the Fall by driving the division of the expressive subject against itself to its technical, external extreme. The *discourse* on the marionette which both expresses and produces the eccentric desire of the interlocutors also ventures into fantasies about a new body which would not be plagued by lack, desire, difference.

This utopia of a non-body lies at the core of the description of the relationship between puppeteer and puppet. The difficult constellation translates the living into the artificial body; it formalizes (mechanizes) and ultimately abolishes the organic condition. The puppeteer or machinist was a common eighteenth-century image for God. As the dancer speaks and reflects with his partner about the controlling of the puppet, he projects himself into the godlike role of creating a new and more perfect body in which its maker would disappear. Although the product of a creative act, this would be a body void of expression, a body of a pure exteriority in which the soul as difference loses itself. It would be the reversal of God's creation of man: not breathing life into matter but emptying the body of its life and spirit, "Geist."

Herr C. makes conflicting statements about the "line" of the center of gravity which the puppeteer has to "delineate" or "describe" ("verzeichnen," "beschreiben") to make the puppets dance. On the one hand he presents it as a mechanical and "easy" task, expressible in simple geometrical formulas, only to assert on the other hand that it could not be done without "feeling" ("Empfindung") and that the relation between the arm's and the puppet's movements is of a more complex mathematical nature. This line, he says, is "the way of the soul of the dancer" — "and he doubted whether it could be found other than by the machinist displacing himself into the center of gravity of the marionette, in other words, *dancing.*"

The machinist who represents ("describes") the dance displaces ("versetzt") himself into the puppet with which he becomes ideally one, virtually dissolving himself. Whereas an actor's embodiment of a role — for instance, of the classical characters of Daphne and Paris — is marked by an inner tension, a difference which translates into the representation of desire (wanting to be somebody else), the puppeteer becomes the puppet and is absorbed by its mechanics. The arm and hand do not reach over to the role and the partner in a gesture of seductive representation, but they are reduced to their operating function. Contrary to the idealist and romanticist notion of aesthetic creation which Kleist reverses, there is no preexisting interiority which would unfold into a continuous outward expression; there is no soul before and without dancing. There is only a "soul of the dancer" whose "way" or "path" ("Weg"; cf. "bewegen," "to move") is "found" where a path can only be found — outside, in the realm of spatial extension. In an act of reverse empathy, the soul is constituted through exterior movements, as a function of the body and its physicality.

This externalization of the creative process comes consequently into its own with the project of the automaton whose movements are "brought forth . . . by means of a crank." Here, soul or "Geist" is reduced to nil, in a total reification of the constructive mind that would invent it and that now only envisions its invention. But it is also at this fantastical climax of the human body's abolition — or, to say the same thing differently, of the technological self-replacement of the subject — that the strictly utopian character of the project is expressed. There will always be *some* difference. This at least seems to be addressed with the notion of "play": "In the meantime he believed that even this last fraction of spirit of which he had spoken could be eliminated from the marionettes, that their dance could be played across [hinübergespielt] entirely into the realm of mechanical forces, and could be brought forth [hervorgebracht], just as I had imagined, by means of a crank."

The "fraction" of spirit is the "fracture" between the spirit and the body which can never be completely eliminated as long as there is life and difference. Even the technical art which turns its back on the classical notion of a humanized nature can only "play across" this fracture; its place is literally the "in between," "inzwischen." The playful crossing over, then, of life, spirit, interiority into the realm of artifice is Kleist's answer to life's eccentric — and ungraceful — *reaching* out and over into the incalculable detours of desire.[19] It is the answer to Schiller's ideal of grace as reconciliation of reason and nature. The puppeteer becoming the puppet, removing ("entfernen") his body into the perfect automaton, reduces Schiller's aesthetic project, which had human production (freedom, art) appear as nature, to a technical task. *Dehumanization* is Kleist's answer to the classical projection of artistic creativity into a humanized nature which was to be more and other than human but was at the same time stripped of its otherness and exteriority. Conceiving of art in nonrepresentational constructivist terms, Kleist contributed to a paradigm shift which led eventually to aesthetic modernism.[20]

The two stories which together form roughly the second half of the text appear as narrative confirmations of the essay's anti-classicist argument. This is especially true of the first one. The story of the young man who tries in vain to recapture the unique moment of graceful self-recognition and who virtually disintegrates in front of the mirror ("one charm after the other fell from him," "verliess ihn"), this story of the sudden demise of the beautiful body carries with it a powerful intuitive conviction. The youth's fall is the step beyond himself, the (physical) transgression of stepping out of the water (the origin) and "placing [setzte] his foot on a stool," the ex-centric movement that subsequently falls into the exteriority of the mirror, bringing about a recognition of self as the embodiment of somebody else, the "famous" statue. Did the petrification not occur at the very moment when the liquidity of life froze into the drying posture, evoking the "numerous copies" ("Abgüsse," casts) of the Greek original to be "found in most German collections," of which the young man now becomes just another? Like the two dancers embodying classical roles, the youth incorporates himself into the aesthetic discourse of his time. He also appeals to the partner, his older mentor, and he likewise reaches over to the other in his desire to be seen by him and to gain acknowledgment of his self-recognition.

It is language which definitively throws the youth out of himself. The older man — the narrator himself — to whom he mentions his "discovery" doubts this claim for pedagogical reasons (he says) and makes him repeat the pose, "in order to show it [the posture of the statue] to me [um es mir zu zeigen]." By forcing the young man to "bring forth [produce] the same movement again," he brings him literally "out of his position [stand]" ("ausserstande, dieselbe Bewegung wieder hervorzubringen").[21] Language (denial), combined with the look of the other,[22] completes the scenario of cultural disciplining which started with the eccentric gesture and the classical reminiscence (in itself evocative of repetition and reproduction) and which finally casts an "iron net" over the "free play of his gestures."[23]

Initially, the anecdote reads as a straightforward tale of alienation from primal purity, the story of *Geschichtsphilosophie*. There is only a slight hook to this reading, namely, the little thorn in the foot of the statue with which the young man identifies and which taints its unity with a primordial wound (recalling the biblical curse that the snake will "sting man in the heel").[24] Just as the represented character of the "thorn-puller" (Kleist calls the statue by its well-known German name, Dornauszieher) is trying to heal this split (remove the "splinter," "Splitter"), so the statue's classical wholeness itself appears as an imaginary healing. Is not the youth similarly stung by the "mere," literally, the "bare remark," the exposing look of his mentor against which he defends himself by attempting to escape into the artwork's gracious enclosure?[25] This reading is confirmed if we look at the function which this truly mythical story fulfills in the rhetorical action of the dialogue. Together with its counterpart, the bear anecdote, it stages the myth of *Geschichtsphilosophie* itself as a creation and performance of body.

The narrator's story is the answer to the dancer's provocative suggestion that his partner is not worth talking to because he does not seem to have "read attentively" the story of the Fall in the book of Genesis. In an

obvious effort to refute this rude mistrust of his intellectual background —
or, rather, his ability to *read* the role of the body in the story — and to
cover up his exposed deficiency, the narrator tailors his anecdote into an
example of the biblical paradigm, into another Fall.

I said that I knew only too well what disorders in the natural grace of the human
being consciousness brings about. A young man of my acquaintance had, through
a mere observation, lost his innocence right before my eyes, and had never afterwards found the paradise of that innocence again, despite all imaginable effort.
But what conclusion, I added, could be drawn from this?

Again an addition ("setzte ich hinzu") of sense to a mere occurrence
or "incident" ("Vorfall," immediately following this passage) — a word
which echoes the "Einfall" (idea, fancy) from the beginning. Similarly we
could say here that at stake is "more than a mere incident or accident,"
because it is "brought up" as proof for something (and to somebody) else.
Just as the youth *in* the anecdote attempted to reassert his threatened
integrity before his mentor, the narrator, this same narrator, who has
received the sting of the dancer's insult, tries *with* his anecdote to prove
himself to *his* mentor, the dancer. And just as the youth was forced, for the
sake of his (self-)recognition, into the cultural pattern of the classicist
statue, the narrator, in his wish to gain the recognition of his threatening
partner, hands himself over to — incorporates himself into — the anonymity of a prevailing cultural discourse.

That storytelling is an act of quasi-physical self-affirmation against a
perceived threat to one's identity or an exposure of one's frailty, becomes
fully clear if we consider the question of belief that guides the exchange of
the two narratives. At stake is not only the rhetorical issue that narratives
carry greater conviction than arguments. The more far-reaching issue is
that stories stand in for their authors, enhancing their physical presence
and replacing it at the same time — enhancing it through the replacement.
This paradox emerges when Herr C., after relating his bear anecdote with
which he reciprocated the narrator's story of the fallen youth, asks the
latter if he "believes this story" — a very appropriate question indeed,
given the content of this anecdote. The narrator responds in a strangely
emphatic manner: "Completely! I shouted with joyous applause. I would
believe it from any stranger it is so probable, all the more so from you."

Believing a story is a response to its internal plausibility ("probability,"
in the poetological terminology of the century), but also to the credibility
of the storyteller. But on which grounds does the listener give credence to
Herr C., whose arguments about the marionettes he has, for good reason,

resisted so far? It is only the stories which bring the two dialogue partners closer to each other, not by way of their argument or what they say, but by what they do as rhetorical gesture and performative act.[26] After the narrator has told his story, Herr C., for the first time, turns toward him "in a friendly manner." He offers him "on this occasion," as he says, "another story of which you will easily comprehend [begreifen, grasp] why it belongs here." Again, the spatial meaning is significant: the dialogue partners do not meet in a rational argument, but they come together in a common arena of competitive storytelling. When the narrator applauds his opponent's story, when he literally "falls" for it and "to his side" ("Beifall"), Herr C. has every reason for satisfied condescension: "Now my excellent friend . . . now you are in possession of everything necessary to understand [begreifen] me." Herr C. has maneuvered his partner into a position, a "seat" ("sind Sie im Be*sitz*") from which to "grasp him" and to "see" — him as body?

At one crucial point in the dialogue it emerges beyond doubt that the argument about the artificial replacement of the human body is embedded in a subtext where the interlocutors talk about their own replaceability. Herr C. boasts of his technological project, and his partner, perhaps embarrassed by the preposterous claim, but perhaps also feeling that *he* is substitutable, "casts [schlug] his eye silently to the ground."[27] The dancer follows up with the question of whether the narrator has "heard" about the artificial legs manufactured by English artisans ("Künstler"; also "artists"):

I said, no: I had never seen anything of the kind.

I am sorry, he replied; for if I told you that these unfortunates dance with them, I am almost afraid you would not believe me.

This is the context in which the issue of belief comes up for the first time. The opposition between seeing and hearing (telling) stresses the issue of reality confirmation, but also the difference between the visual perception of grace and the nature of language. As the narrator has temporarily lost both sight and speech, the dancer talks about the (absent) handicapped dancers and performs through language on the living body the violent act of mutilation and mechanical reconstruction. He develops a vision of better-engineered humans whose "range [Kreis] of movements" is "limited" but who perform within this narrow circle — as in a circus or on the stage, we might add — with unsurpassable grace, "stunning [literally: placing (setzen) into astonishment] every thinking mind." Eventually, the narrator will again become speechless: "I became more and more astonished and did not know what I should say to such strange assertions." It is at this point of utter bewilderment and loss of self that the narrator is given the chance to gather himself together again in the imaginary presence of his story. In other words, after his opponent has threatened to dismember him, he offers him (with the hint at the biblical Fall, in the middle of the dialogue) the chance for a cultural reconstruction. But the same imaginary unity — here, the narrative enclosure, which is underlined by the almost exaggerated circular structure of both stories — with which the ego wishes to protect itself from the threat of fragmentation, also shakes his sense of immediate physical presence. This at least is how I read the narrator's concluding hypertrophic affirmation of the story's historical truth: "There is still someone living who was a witness to this strange and unhappy incident and who could confirm it word for word as I told it."

Can the story not stand on its own? Does it need additional physical confirmation ("bestätigen," with the root of "standing"), although all an eyewitness could do is again only confirm or not confirm in his or her words the words of another? The story is given mythical dimensions (after all, it happened only "about three years ago") to heighten its power, but at the same time the temporal distance creates the need to tie it back into the immediacy of the physical speech situation, for which, however, it has to appeal to another, an absent Other ("there is still someone living"). There is no escape from this vicious circle of language and body which mocks the synthesis of classical aesthetics, be it the synthesis of the beautiful statue or the teleological narrative.

If the dialogue demonstrates how myth is formed in narrative interaction, Kleist's text itself can be regarded as a mythical narrative. Here is the place to remember that the text is not a dialogue proper, but a narrated dialogue, that is, a dialogue which has been worked into a unified narrative by a single narrator's voice. To be sure, since this narrator is the inferior partner in the dialogical contest, his story — the story of the argument with the dancer which he started and lost — can be seen as the attempt to heal his own wound. But the text does not close this wound any more than the statue of the Dornauszieher represents perfect classical wholeness. At the end, the "distracted" or "scattered" narrator appears himself as the marionette letting itself be pulled to unity by the puppeteer. In a parody of hermeneutical understanding, he has been made to say what the dancer wants him to say. Thus, the narrator narrates his own defeat, which is simultaneously the failure of meaningful narrative. When he cedes the final word to the other voice to legitimize his conclusion (the conclusion, as we remember, that by eating from the Tree again, we would

regain paradise), he replaces the rational outcome of a teleological argument with the arbitrary stamp of textual closure: "Indeed, he [the dancer]
answered; that is the last chapter of the history [Geschichte; also "story"]
of the world."

The internal self-destruction of the teleologically meaningful narrative
now appears to be mirrored in the bear anecdote with which the dancer
answers his partner's story. This is also the story of defeat and body disintegration, but unlike the narrator who had built himself up at the expense
of the youth, the dancer turns the defeat against himself, so as to indicate
to his partner that he sees through his trick. First, the overbearing young
student "who was playing the virtuoso" gets his deserved beating from the
more experienced man: "His rapier finally flew into the corner." There is
an obvious resemblance between Herr C.'s defeated fencing partner and
the narrator, whose provocation had initiated the intellectual match of the
dialogue. But the anecdote goes on only to show the winner being defeated
in turn. Now it is he who virtually dissolves ("the sweat dripped from
me") in front of the fencing beast, who parries all of his thrusts and does
not even react to the "seduction" of his "feints." "Now I was almost in the
same situation as the young Herr von G——," literally, "in the case" or
"fall" ("in dem Falle") of the young hothead; in other words, "now falling
myself." But unlike his two partners, the student and the narrator, Herr C.
faces and describes his fall: "everything in the world finds its own master."
There is no ultimate master-narrative, he seems to tell his antagonist, who
had just offered one.

Why does the bear win? Because he does not "fall" for the eccentric
feints or fictions of his seducing opponent, and also because he does not
"fall out" of his posture, i.e., does not lunge in attack ("ausfallen" is the
technical German term, repeated twice here). The defensive poise of the
bear grants prominent roles to both hand and eye: the right paw raised for
the strike ("schlagfertig erhoben"), the eyes fixed on the eyes of his opponent. The trained bear mimics the erect posture of the human species,
which in evolutionary history opened up the enormous potential of hand-
eye coordination. It is more than doubtful that the bear illustrates the
instinctual superiority of animal to man. After all, it is an animal "whom
the father was having raised." "Auf*erziehen*" is a strange word combining
the "pulling (of strings)," in its spatial sense of upward, with the pedagogical activity, "erziehen." Also, the bear is of course not free-standing but is
chained to a post, and therefore no more in the position to lunge and
thrust forward than the marionette was to affect poses. The bear, in other
words, copies or, rather, is *made* to copy the human erect posture without

its constitutive flaw, eccentricity. Like the marionette, he is an instrument of body representation released from any representational intent of its own, following only its innate law of self-preservation against the realm of human difference, the eccentric expressivity of "aus-fallen."

"Eye to eye, as though he could read my soul there": much has been done with this remarkable statement of the dancer. De Man calls the bear the "super-reader" and the hermeneutician who, by not falling for tropes of fencing and of language (and, we can add, counterfeit body poses), signals the end of reading, since there is nothing to uncover or to interpret anymore.[28] By making the outward/forward thrusts ineffective and even ridiculous, the bear reduces to nil the expressive and eccentric efforts of the dancer, who would be better off as the marionette with its limbs like pendulums. The bear, one could say, teaches the dancer the superiority of the marionette which renounces the difference of the representing body. In this perspective, Herr C.'s defeat and dissolution could even be seen as a felicitous fall, the fall from human eccentricity back into the state of a purely physical centeredness. To give the final paradox of the text ("in den *Stand* der Unschuld zurück*fallen*") yet another twist: we can only stand *by* falling, by collapsing our extremities into or around a center which is the opposite of the spiritual center of concentration (Sammlung). We should give in to the force of gravity instead of splitting ourselves.

Part 4

Unnatural Bodies

Goethe's 'Clavigo': The Body as an "Unorthographic" Sign

SUSAN GUSTAFSON

$\mathcal{A}$s his friend stands at the edge of a devastating mésalliance, Carlos informs Clavigo of the flood of marriage proposals Clavigo has received from the delicate little "paws" of innumerable ladies. These feminine writings reveal themselves most significantly to be "as unorthographic as only an original love letter from a girl can be."[1] The beautiful donnas, who write their beseeching letters to Clavigo, produce a "writing" or "style of writing" which is riddled with mis-spellings. The body of their text creates scarcely legible miscombinations of its signifiers. Curiously, it is precisely the unorthographic character of the women's writing, which despite its relative insignificance to Carlos's urgent warnings, foregrounds the obsession of Goethe's *Clavigo* with the question of mis-spellings and mis-writings.[2] Writing in the play is all about writing woman, writing the body, and "righting" the mis-writings or unrevealing bodies in an attempt to determine their meaning. Whether the writers in *Clavigo* are men or women, their attempts to write/right the body reveal the body as an unorthographic sign. By this I mean that the body is unspellable, i.e., unwritable, and as "written" in the play it does not function as ortho (correct, right) graphic (giving a clear or vivid picture). It is precisely the tension between the characters' attempts to treat the body as an orthographic sign and the inevitably unorthographic results of those attempts which I hope to illustrate in the following pages.

Clavigo reflects, in a unique manner, the significatory possibilities (i.e., possible roles for women and men and the division of signs) generally represented in the domestic tragedies of eighteenth-century Germany. The issue of writing or style and the control of written discourse by men as opposed to the visual, gestural silence of women becomes a central concern of the play. Although the dichotomy between the virtuous passive and aggressive monstrous women of the domestic tragedy is maintained within the gendered divisions of representation (i.e., men-discourse and women-gesture), these "boundaries" begin to dissolve in *Clavigo*. The general instability of representation in the play is most clearly marked by Clavigo's unstable position socially, that is, his relationship to Marie, and by the concerted efforts of the other characters in the play to "write" and "read" Marie's body. The linguistic crisis which ensues threatens to deny the representational divisions essential to the male protagonist's conceptions of virtue, woman, body, and language. As opposed to earlier bourgeois tragedies, *Clavigo* marks a radical shift in its explication of the body as the site of semiotic indifferentiation.

The shift in *Clavigo* to a morally conflicted male protagonist allows a notably different representation of a crisis in subjectivity, of a linguistic crisis, and a more explicit representation of the role of writing in the establishment of identities in the play. In this manner, Goethe's *Clavigo* diverges significantly from the focus of the domestic tragedy on the virtue of the middle-class woman and her potential seduction. Subsequently, the issue of Marie's virtue, the relationship of fathers to daughters, the reaffirmation of bourgeois values, and the condemnation of aristocratic caprice, though certainly all still present, tend to recede from view in the play.[3] In *Clavigo* the traditional juxtaposition in the domestic tragedy of virtue and vice, of monster and angel, is established through a process of "writing woman," of "writing" and "hearing" not the voice but the body of the woman. Moreover, the focus of *Clavigo* on writing and various miswritings reveals the impossibility of reducing woman to either monster or angel, and the precariousness of trust in the reliability of the body as visual sign (usually of the woman's virtue).

The real crux of Clavigo's crisis is his inability to come to terms with Marie as simultaneously "ideal woman" and "body/infirmity." Carlos and the other characters try to overcome the unorthographic character of the body as sign, by insisting on reductive readings. As Carlos asserts, there is nothing more pitiful in the world than an undecided person who hovers between two sentiments and desires to unite them both, "and doesn't understand that nothing can unite them except the doubt and uncertainty that torture him" (p. 17). The "solution" in the play is to choose one of those sentiments or one possible meaning for the body and to disregard any others. Following this reasoning, Clavigo can never decide that Marie or her body is simultaneously ideal/body/infirmity. He must limit his reading by opting for one of the many possible meanings of

Marie's body. As we shall see, the rigid categorical divisions mandated by the male characters in the play (and crucial to their own sense of subjective unity) involve a fantasy of feminine unity which is disrupted by the dichotomous character of Marie.

Although on one level the impulse of the characters in *Clavigo* is to "write" the body as an immutable visual sign (as orthographic), throughout the play the decipherment of the body by both men and women refutes the possibility of a stable, reliable reading. The instability of the body as visual sign surfaces precisely through the obsessive and questionable codings of the body in *Clavigo*. Because the men are the principal "writers" in the play, and Marie is the "principal body" read, the crisis in subjectivity manifests itself more substantially in the male characters. As Marie suggests to Sophie, the women are not the writers in the play but the written. They are nothing but "Vaudevilles" (p. 265). But that does not preclude the crises of the women in *Clavigo* — and certainly does not preclude Marie's linguistic crisis. Throughout the play and at various levels subjective instability is prefaced by the instability of the body as visual sign. The crisis in *Clavigo* is the indecipherability of the body.

The opening passages of *Clavigo* foreground the significance of writing in the play. Both Clavigo and his assistant Carlos are writers by profession. In the opening scene they are discussing the stylistic merits of the latest issue of *The Thinker*, a moral weekly which Clavigo writes and which is clearly directed to women:

CLAVIGO: (*Standing up from the desk.*) This paper will have a good effect; it will charm the women. Tell me, Carlos, don't you think that my weekly is now one of the best in Europe?
CARLOS: We Spanish have no other author who combines such strength of thought, so much blossoming imagination with such a splendid and light style.
CLAVIGO: I must yet become the creator of good taste among the people. They are very impressionable. I am renowned, I am trusted by my fellow citizens, and just between us, my knowledge and my sensibilities gain ground every day, and my style becomes truer and stronger. (p. 260)

Initially it is important to recall the fact that moral weeklies often sought to instruct women in the "useful" arts and sciences. Although cloaked in terms of intellectual equality and openness, the moral weekly was essentially a means to control discourse. As Martens suggests, the main focus of the moral weekly is those moral or philosophical works which "can have significant impact on the education [of the woman], on her moral behavior, her social relations, yes even on the sentiments of her heart."[4] Only subjects appropriate for women were discussed: Christian dogma, moral-

ity, graceful language, drawing, music, childcare, domestic responsibilities, geography, and history. Indeed, as Schreiber points out, the ultimate
purpose of these publications was to train women for their "subsequent
role in married life" so that they could become "sensible companions for
their husbands, able housekeepers, and skillful, loving mothers."[5] Above
all, the moral weekly served to define the "good woman" as the paragon of
virtue. Their goal was to "make" woman virtuous, "to make the Word
Wife the most agreable and delightful Name in Nature," to enhance the
"Honour and Improvement of the fair Sex."[6] Over time, Martens indicates, the moral weekly begins to focus on the virtue of woman and the
"understanding and knowledge of a woman become less valuable."[7]

Clavigo's role as the author of a moral weekly makes him not only the
author of "taste" in Spain but also the author of female virtue. The repetition of the possessive "my" — "my weekly," "my knowledge," "my sensibilities," and specifically "my style" (p. 260) — reveals Clavigo's desire to
determine a particular image of woman. The moral weekly establishes a
certain style, a style with woman as its subject. Clavigo, as stylist, attempts
to outline the "essence" or "presence" of the ideal woman. The function of
his style is not to merely describe but to inscribe or construct that "ideal."
To the extent that Clavigo's writing delimits the concept of woman, it veils
or denies the "truth" that "woman will not be pinned down."[8]

The myth of the essence of woman, Clavigo's style, is necessary for him
to attain a stable sense of self. In their opening dialogue, Carlos points out
to Clavigo that his style was much more effective when he was still in love
with Marie: "I liked your writing much better when you were still at
Marie's feet, when that dear happy creature still had influence on you"
(p. 260). Clavigo's style attained its height when Marie still constituted for
him the ideal woman. Clavigo's comments demonstrate that his rank,
name, and sense of self are derived from the success of his style: "Haven't I
done pretty well for a stranger who came here without rank, name, or
wealth? Here at a court where it is so hard to make an impression among
the pressing crowd. I am quite pleased when I consider the path I have
followed. Beloved by the first men of the realm! Honored for my knowledge! My rank! Archivist of the King!" (p. 261). Before Clavigo established his style, he was a nameless stranger. Marie isolates Clavigo's style
as the divisive mechanism of their separation: "When he was still Clavigo,
not yet archivist of the king, when he was a stranger, a newcomer in our
house, how dear he was, how kind" (p. 265). It is only since the development of his "own style" that Marie feels the distance between them.

Clavigo's image of the ideal woman hinges on the fantasy of the woman as supplement to his own subjectivity. She ought to double his sense of completed/unified self: "Heaven lies on the bosom of this dear girl as always. All of the renown which I attain, all of the greatness to which I rise, will fill me with twice as much joy, for the girl shares it with me, who makes me a 'doubled' man" (p. 280). Clavigo ultimately rejects Marie because she cannot be assimilated to his vision of the ideal woman — to his vision of his own "doubled self." Clavigo's "love" for Marie reigns between the borders of narcissism and idealization. It glorifies itself in the mirror of an idealized other. But as soon as Marie fails to participate in Clavigo's fantasy of unity, she becomes the abject. She explicitly denies the narcissistic unity Clavigo desires when she insists that the satisfaction of their relationship will be "half" if at all: "I tell you, I am only half happy to have him back again. I will hardly enjoy the happiness that awaits me in his arms — perhaps not at all" (p. 297). Marie explicitly rejects Clavigo's fantasy visions of the unity of woman and the possibility of unity with woman. She undermines his entire stylistic project, for, as we remember, his style ought to facilitate the unity he seeks: "I hope to contribute [through writing] in some measure to the improvement of taste and the dissemination of learning in my own nation. For that is the only way to bind nations together, to make friends of the most distant souls and maintain such a delightful union among them" (p. 268). The "untruth of truth" which Clavigo cannot envision is that his writing and Marie ultimately deny any possibility of either social or subjective unity.

Clavigo's inability to keep his promise to Marie, his crisis of subjectivity, results from his desire to sustain his vision of an ideal woman/style despite his increased suspicion of its impossibility. In spite of his forced confession to Beaumarchais that Marie has never given him occasion "to complain about her, or to think less of her" (p. 273), it is clear that Clavigo cannot come to terms with her physical appearance. The "unstable" character of Marie and Clavigo's recognition of her "contradictions" threaten the view of woman which is crucial to his own sense of identity — his sense of supplemented self.

While Clavigo's "style" constructs an ideal image of woman as supplement to male subjectivity, it ought also to seduce women. It ought to "bezaubern" (p. 260), that is to "bewitch," to "enchant," to "charm," to "fascinate," and above all to "captivate" the female reader.[9] As Martens points out, historically, style was a very important consideration for the writers of moral weeklies.[10] Because the subject matter of their weeklies was rather limited (i.e., virtue, etc.) style became the means to engage readers. In other words, the weekly undermines its moralistic content with a style which appeals directly to the sensuousness which it denies on the contextual level. For this reason, Clavigo's style is described in overtly seductive terms — it ought to seduce, to bewitch its female readers. Through the process of constructing a particular image of the woman and through its very seductiveness, the style of Clavigo's moral weekly ought both to determine the virtue of woman (or woman as virtue) and to render her accessible to male desire. This is precisely the effect of the moral weekly as described by Carlos: "I have known few men who have made such significant impressions on women as you have. Among all classes there are good children, who are busy with plans and hopes of catching you. Some have beauty to offer, some wealth, some rank, some wit, and some their family. You should see the compliments I receive because of you" (p. 288). According to Carlos, there are numerous "children" (women) of various classes and backgrounds scheming for Clavigo's favor. He inventories them in terms of their bodily attractiveness, their social standing (i.e., relatives), or their economic worth. Several of these have fallen into Carlos's hands because of the effect of Clavigo's moral weekly. Carlos continues by boasting about the number of love letters and affairs he has had due to the power of Clavigo's style.

The "truth" of woman in *Clavigo* is that she is understood solely in terms of her body: physical beauty, usefulness as a mother, and appropriateness as the accompanier of men. In his conversation with Carlos, Clavigo's desire to distance himself from Marie reveals itself through their descriptions of her physical infirmities. Marie is not "worthy of her male companion" because she is "a tripping, little, hollow-eyed Frenchwoman, whose every limb speaks of consumption" (p. 291). She has the "color of death" indicative of the "plague," which she would pass on to any progeny. Clavigo retracts his second proposal to Marie because she is "disfigured," "pale," and "emaciated" (ibid.). He finds it dangerous to draw Marie — "a sickness" (ibid.) — to himself. By shifting to a purely physical inventory of Marie, by reducing her to a string of abject nouns and adjectives, Clavigo is able to define her as "non-woman," i.e., as a sickness.[11] After their reunion Clavigo remarks: "I was shocked when I saw Marie again. . . . It was as if in the fullness of joy, the cold hand of death brushed across my neck" (ibid.). Marie's physical condition appalls Clavigo. He perceives simultaneously joy and death. The innate dichotomy between presence (joy) and absence (death) which Clavigo senses in Marie threatens his denial of absence and his denial of representational multiplicity. This unsettling experience of Marie is reduced by Clavigo to an inventory of negative physical impressions. He concludes finally that "it was all over, so stiff, so constrained." This type of reductive distancing is a protective measure against the disturbing prospect of "woman" or "non-woman" as an indeterminable quantity.[12]

Clavigo's stylistic project is evident. Marie as "written," as male construction, cannot be reconciled with the real, physical Marie. Because Clavigo senses the multiplicity of Marie, he rejects her as an ideal and reconstructs her linguistically as physical infirmity. In both "constructions" Marie is reduced to an absolute, fixed meaning. Clavigo tries to position Marie as body, as a transparent sign of infirmity/body, in order to protect his notion of a woman-ideal. Clavigo's literal equation of Marie with sickness separates her from the concept of woman — it transposes her to the realm of infirmity, to the status of non-woman. This transposition is crucial to Clavigo, for without it he would have to admit that Marie/woman cannot be reduced to either ideal or body or to ideal body or infirm body. He would have to accept her dichotomous multiplicity. Clavigo can only sustain his view of Marie from a distance: the closer he gets to her both physically and linguistically during the course of the play, the more impossible it becomes for him to retain his fixed vision of a woman-ideal.

As the site of clear, vivid representation, Marie's body is constantly being read by other characters — it is understood as a transparent representation of her feelings. Marie's general silence in the play and the reading of her body by Clavigo are foregrounded at their reunion:

CLAVIGO: Marie! Don't you still recognize my voice? Don't you still perceive the tone of my heart? Marie! Marie!
MARIE: O Clavigo!
CLAVIGO: (*Jumps up, clasps her hand, and covers it with ecstatic kisses.*) She forgives me, she loves me. *He embraces Guilbert, Buenco.* She still loves me! O Marie, my heart told me so! If I had thrown myself at your feet, not voiced my pain, only wept my repentance, you would have understood me without words, as I receive your forgiveness without words. No, the intimacy of our souls has not been destroyed, they perceive each other as before, when no sound, no gesture was necessary to communicate our innermost feelings. (p. 285)

Marie says nothing other than "O Clavigo!" which Clavigo interprets as a sign of total forgiveness. He reads her body and her silence, asserting his belief in a mystical, natural union of souls which transcends any verbal, visual, or written representation — their communication could even have been conducted "without words." He assumes, in essence, a type of fusion of intention which relays itself without any formal system of representation.

Marie's virtual muteness leaves little evidence of her true state of mind.

The context suggests, however, significant doubt about Clavigo's reading of Marie's body. In light of the fact that Guilbert has just informed Marie that if she does not agree to Clavigo's proposal, Clavigo will kill her brother, it is uncertain that Marie's silence indicates forgiveness. It may simply mark concern for her brother's welfare. Buenco voices additional doubt when he comments: "No, he [Clavigo] will not get my voice, even if Marie's heart itself were to speak for him" (p. 282). The continual interpretation of Marie's silent body highlights the instability of communication in the play—and underscores the ambiguity of her monosyllabic speech.

Although we never hear Marie say she still loves Clavigo, the characters assume it: Guilbert insists that "he [Clavigo] still has her heart." Marie does not confirm this observation—her only response is: "You are cruel" (p. 282). Is he cruel because he is right, or because he has misrepresented her feelings? When Beaumarchais asks if Marie has forgiven Clavigo, her response is: "Leave, leave me! I feel faint." Buenco must provide the answer: "It appears so" (p. 285). By the time Sophie returns to say that Marie forgives Clavigo and loves him, we must doubt her words as well. Even as Marie expires after being abandoned by Clavigo a second time, Sophie interprets her single word "Clavigo" as a sign of her love for him.

Throughout the play it becomes evident that Marie's language is couched in ambiguity—there is a curious disjuncture between her speech, her body, and the interpretations of those around her. Her comments lend themselves to multiple explanations. Marie is clearly associated with "unstable meaning." The reading of Marie, of her body in the absence of decipherable comments, leads the characters of the play to any number of assumptions. Their discourse is directed around Marie, past her, or in spite of her in order to construct her/woman as the site of orthographic representation. But there is no assurance here that the reading of Marie's body has been orthographic. Indeed, the tenuousness of Marie's comments specifically accentuates the lack of significatory certainty underlying the characters' interpretations of her body.

Although Clavigo mis-reads Marie's body, Sophie prepares Marie to "read his body." She asserts that Clavigo's appearance convinced her of his good faith (in this case, an obvious misreading): "There is something so bewitching in his appearance, in the tone of his voice. He is still the same old Clavigo" (p. 281). It is Clavigo's look, the supposed correspondence of his voice to "truth" that "bewitches" Sophie—convincing her of the one-to-one correspondence between signified and signifier—and leads her to believe he is still the "old Clavigo." She continues insisting to Marie: "The first sight of him will undoubtedly affect you strongly. . . . You will thank me for helping you to overcome this anxious uncertainty which is only a sign of your deepest love for him" (ibid.). Sophie tells Marie how to read/misread Clavigo's body and how to interpret/misinterpret her own feelings. As Sophie sees it, Marie will overcome her "anxious *uncertainty*" (my emphasis) by accepting her assessment of Clavigo's body. Although Marie's body is read in the play as "orthographic," Clavigo's body, as a clearly false signifier of his good faith (since he promptly abandons Marie at the next opportunity), questions once again the viability of an orthographic reading of *any* body. Within the linguistic logic of the play, Marie ought to be the site of clear, vivid, orthographic signification. She is not only body but a dangerous, infirm body. Marie's physical inferiority suggests in classical understanding a moral infirmity. The infirm body represents the infirm soul. Lessing, for example, reiterates the classical understanding of the body as reflective of the spiritual state in the *Laokoon*, when he asserts that a misshapen body and a beautiful soul are as impossible to mix as oil and vinegar. Durrani accepts this position in his analysis of *Clavigo* and avers that Marie's infirmity reveals her "Irrweg" (transgression), a psychological ailment similar to Ottilie's in *Elective Affinities* (p. 98). Marie's physical infirmities represent her psychological and moral infirmities. Durrani points to Marie's visions of revenge as proof of her disturbed emotional/ethical state, which may be the result of her "estrangement from life itself" (p. 99). I would suggest that Marie's physical reactions to Clavigo are hysterical. They symbolize her inability to come to terms with Clavigo's behavior and with the stringent restrictions placed on her, as a woman, by the other characters in the play. Moreover, it is precisely Marie's hysterical, physical reactions to Clavigo's disappearance which evoke another series of questionable readings of her body.

We first learn of Marie's sickness from Clavigo, who insists that it is his fault. He suggests that Marie is "wasting away" because he abandoned her. Later in the play he asserts that Marie fell into convulsions when he left her. Carlos rejects this hypothesis, insisting that Marie has consumption. References to Marie's illness and conflicting interpretations of its cause abound in *Clavigo* and justify a closer evaluation of their import. Her hysterical symptoms are the following: she falls into convulsions, she intermittently manifests joy and cries, she suffers from insomnia and shortness of breath (p. 272). Sophie describes the anxiety and morose fantasies with which Marie torments herself. Her heart attacks her with an uncontrollable pounding and she is constantly fainting. The sources of her hysterical symptoms are constantly thoughts of and encounters with Clavigo.

Readings of Marie's symptoms, readings of her body as symptom, evince both the precariousness of those readings and the interpreters' subjective investment in the implications of those readings. Sophie consistently reads Marie's symptoms as self-induced and as signs of Marie's love for and forgiveness of Clavigo. It could, however, also be assumed that it is not her love for Clavigo which plagues Marie, but her hatred of him.[13] Her first hysterical attack occurs after the announcement of Beaumarchais's intention to come to Spain and investigate her situation. His letter reveals his function as Marie's judge and avenger. Her initial response to his accusatory letter is shortness of breath and insomnia. To Sophie she exclaims: "I am trembling. He [Beaumarchais] will come. I am not trembling for me. . . ." (p. 264). Marie's fearful trembling manifests itself each time she envisions either her own or Beaumarchais's revenge against Clavigo. Each time Clavigo abandons her, Marie trembles. As he leaves her a second time, she appears to lie to Beaumarchais, suggesting they should wait to see what this second disappearance means. Beaumarchais reads her trembling body as a sign of her rage and consequently as justification for his revenge against Clavigo: "Your tongue lies. The paleness of your cheeks, the trembling of your body, everything speaks and shows that you cannot wait for that" (p. 298). As for Beaumarchais, Marie notes, "How he trembles" (p. 299). In this instance Beaumarchais reads Marie's trembling as he would read his own . . . her physical symptoms mirror the rage which he feels toward Clavigo. The ambiguous "that" for which Beaumarchais asserts Marie cannot wait, is, for him, clearly the revenge he reads or projects onto her body. But within the context of the play, the "that" for which Marie waits is never certain. Does she wait for Clavigo to return, for his love, for their marriage, for revenge, or for her own death? The play offers all of these readings of Beaumarchais's ambiguous "that."

Beaumarchais's insistence that Marie cannot wait for "that," coupled with conflicting readings of Marie's trembling body, foregrounds the ambiguity of the body as visual sign. Marie's comments about her own trembling body are just as opaque: "My entire body trembles. I was close to fainting, when I heard he would come. . . . I can never see him again" (p. 281). Marie offers no explanation for her trembling. It is not at all clear that her trembling and fainting evoke any particular discernible emotion. Her comments are as illegible and unorthographic as her body. It is anyone's guess why Marie cannot see Clavigo. Sophie consistently denies Marie's desire for revenge: "Don't consider this anxiety, this embarrassment which seems to consume your senses, the effect of hatred or aversion. Your heart speaks more for him than you think" (p. 281).[14] Sophie chooses to deny the possibility of Marie's hatred for Clavigo. Both Sophie and Buenco censure Marie for her vengeful outbursts. Sophie chooses to reinterpret them as signs of love. Buenco acts scandalized when he hears her shocking comments: "For God's sake, Mademoiselle" (p. 264).

Marie is in a state of turmoil, because, as she claims, "I don't know what I want" (p. 264). Ironically, her admission of her own confusion, of the inexplicability of her feelings, provides the most determinable reading of her trembling body. Precisely because her emotions cannot be reduced to one or the other, neither can her symptoms be read to spell out correctly, exactly what those emotions are. Although it is clear that Sophie reads only Marie's love in her trembling and Beaumarchais reads only her hatred, Marie admits only that she can "sometimes" hate Clavigo: "Hate! Yes, sometimes I can hate him!" (ibid.). Marie's "sometimes" is crucial, for it indicates both the ambiguity and the transitory, unstable character of her emotional state. It is this unorthographic nature of Marie's emotions which cannot be spelled out clearly by her symptoms or on her body.

When Marie's hysterical symptoms become too overwhelming, she often experiences an attack which results in a fainting spell. Even after Clavigo returns to her, she continues to suffer from "empty fears." Marie's fantasies of revenge seem to simultaneously draw and repulse her. It is the abject, her self as the abject, which beseeches and pulverizes Marie. She finds the impossible (her hatred of Clavigo) within, she finds that it constitutes her mixed-being. Marie's hysterical ailment is not directly caused by Clavigo's loss, nor is it representative of her (transgression), in the sense of immorality. Her transgression could be read as her hatred for a man who has mistreated her and her attempts to express that hatred in a society which denies such feelings to "the good-hearted French girl" — to the "ideal woman." The linguistic machinations of Clavigo, Sophie, and Buenco certainly all reveal their intent to deny any possibility of Marie's hatred for Clavigo. The ideal woman in *Clavigo* is the silent, faithful sufferer. Regardless of his actions, Clavigo will insist that Marie waits and dies for him. It is the "veiling" of Marie's hatred, the stylistic construction of "the good-hearted French girl," in which all of the characters participate. On the other hand, it is equally clear that Marie's "unreadable" body is also a transgression. Her body in no way provides a clear, vivid picture of her emotional state or her feelings for Clavigo. Both the ambiguity of her comments and the cryptic nature of her symptoms evoke the instability of representation in the play.

The juxtaposition of Marie and Beaumarchais as trembling bodies forces the revaluation of the body/symptom as orthographic sign. Can the same symptom manifest in the bodies of two such different persons be read as an index of the same meaning? Or could the same index represent different emotions on different bodies? Marie does not offer an interpretation of Beaumarchais's body; she merely notes that he is trembling. Her failure to interpret Beaumarchais's trembling underscores the tenuousness of symptomatic readings. Marie's remark concerning his trembling isolates the symptom, but leaves it "unread." In Beaumarchais's case the unread body remains both open to all possible readings and provides no reading at all.

Clavigo, Carlos, and Beaumarchais are all stylists — writers of moral weeklies, declarations, and letters. They are involved in a duel of pens, a crisis of subjectivity which ends in the violent deaths of Marie and Clavigo. Beaumarchais's first action in the play is to demand a written declaration from Clavigo, assuring his sister's innocence and establishing his blame. Clavigo responds initially: "I will not write this declaration." Beaumarchais: "Write the declaration demanded." After further stalemates Clavigo suddenly acquiesces: "I will write the declaration, I will write it as you dictate it." When the moment arrives he declares: "Leave the writing of the declaration to me." Beaumarchais counters: "No sir! Write it as I dictate it to you" (pp. 276–77). It is these forced words, Clavigo's forced confession, written in Beaumarchais's words which ought to establish Marie's innocence. The repetition by Beaumarchais that this declaration should not appear forced underscores the doubtfulness of the document itself and poses the question of its actual function.

Through their negotiations it becomes clear that Marie is simply the nodal point around which the two main male characters attempt to define their positions/identities. Marie is defined within this discourse battle only in terms of male identities. As Carlos suggests of Marie: "If Clavigo hadn't had an affair with her, no one would even know she exists" (p. 290). Likewise, Clavigo defines Marie in terms of her brother, Beaumarchais: "If I could have known that she had such a brother, she would never have been an insignificant stranger in my eyes" (p. 275). As Clavigo pleads for Marie's hand his attention is deflected from her to her brother: "What bliss awaits you in her arms! in the friendship of such a brother!" and "You inspire me, sir, with the greatest respect for you. . . . Give me your sister again . . . how happy I would be to receive from your hands a wife and the forgiveness of all my transgressions" (ibid.). This series of exchanges between Beaumarchais and Clavigo reveals Clavigo's attempts to position Marie in terms of his desired relationship to Beaumarchais.[15] The interpretation of Marie's body, and the positioning of her body by these male characters in the play, reveal her importance as orthographic body to their sense of a stable social and subjective identity.

Encountering Clavigo, Beaumarchais describes the intention of his visit. He comes armed with dagger and pen to establish the innocence of his sister: "I come armed with the best cause and all determination to expose a traitor . . . to draw his soul with bloody strokes on his face and the traitor — is you!" (p. 272). Beaumarchais wields his style/stylus/rapier in an attempt to preserve the image of his sister Marie as virtuous and to counter the unthinkable/terrifying possibility of her guilt and the antisocial behavior of Clavigo. Beaumarchais's act of writing ought to inscribe or represent Clavigo's soul, i.e., his moral infirmity, through the mutilation of his face. Clavigo's face, as opposed to Marie's, is not the site of orthographic representation. His face does not "naturally," "clearly" reveal his infirmities, his immorality. Beaumarchais must bring them to the surface through dis-figuration. Clavigo's "truth" can only be revealed through visual/written supplement. The mutilation of Clavigo's face is, however, paradoxical to the extent that his disfiguration, Beaumarchais's "writing" on his face, entails simultaneously a physical, visual re-presentation which is in effect a figuration. Without Beaumarchais's "writing," without the (dis)figuration of Clavigo's face, his body is unreadable. It is either a "blank page" and thus indecipherable, or it encourages a misreading through a miscombination of signifiers which Beaumarchais feels obligated to correct.

The "bloody strokes" of Beaumarchais's stylus and the disfiguration of Clavigo's face highlight the underlying connection between the violence of writing on the body and the struggle for identity. Beaumarchais's brutal inscription ought to establish Clavigo, once and for all, as impure, as the unconscionable criminal. The dichotomy formed between Marie (as pure) and Clavigo (as impure) reveals Beaumarchais's identificatory investment in Marie's purity. The opposition established between the pure and impure is "a coding of the differentiation of the speaking subject as such, a coding of his repulsion in relation to the other in order to autonomize himself. The pure/impure opposition represents . . . the striving for identity, a difference." In order to establish a sense of his own subjectivity, Beaumarchais must disfigure Clavigo, foreground his impurity, and reject him

as the abject, the "Not me. Not that" (or not she, not that).[16] Beaumarchais rejects Clavigo/the impure/the corporeal — the lover of his sister
(i.e., representative of their carnal sexuality) — to ensure his own subjectivity. His vision of revenge leaves us no doubt that his sense of subjectivity
attains its fulfillment through the physical annihilation of Clavigo:

> Ah! a grim, dreadful thirst for his blood possesses me. God in Heaven, I thank you
> for sending me relief in my burning, unbearable anguish! How I feel the thirsting
> revenge in my breast! how the glorious desire for his blood tears me out of self-
> destruction — tears me out of dull uncertainty — tears me beyond myself — re-
> venge! . . . I am panting and puffing on his trail — my teeth yearn for his flesh, my
> palate for the taste of his blood. Have I become a raving animal? My pulse is
> racing, desire for him makes my every nerve tremble. . . . If only I had him beyond
> the seas! I'd capture him alive, bind him to a stake, dismember him limb from limb.
> Then I'd roast his limbs before his eyes and eat them with gusto! I'd serve you
> women a portion as well! (p. 300)[17]

Beaumarchais's revenge "tears [him] out" of the dullness and uncertainty
which plagues him and which Clavigo is unable to overcome. He achieves
unity of purpose, a sense of complete subjectivity. By killing him, Beaumarchais expels the "impure" Clavigo and thereby establishes the boundaries of his own identity. But Beaumarchais's cannibalistic revenge yields
other unities as well. Before this moment Beaumarchais's precarious position in the symbolic order was underscored by the fact that he was the surrogate father for two absent fathers: Marie's biological father, who sent
her to Spain, and her Spanish guardian, who has died and left her without
financial resources. The "cherished fruit" of Beaumarchais's crime is the
"appropriation of paternal attributes"[18] and the reaffirmation of the patriarchal order. Finally, we recall that abjection is the fantasy of devouring;
that cannibalism signifies the desire to interiorize the abject: "A primal
fantasy (lust for swallowing the other) if ever there was one. That theme
unremittingly accompanies the tendency toward interiorizing and spir-
itualizing the abject. It acts as a pedestal for it; man is a spiritual, intel-
ligent, knowing, speaking being only to the extent that he is recognizant of
his abjection — from repulsion to murder — and interiorizes it as such, that
is symbolizes it."[19] Beaumarchais's vision of revenge is just such an interiorizing of the abject. It is a representation of self as abject — of the uncertainty of the borders between the inside/self and outside/other. His cannibalistic act symbolizes not only the expulsion of the abject body but also
the realization that the abject body can never really be completely banished. By ingesting Clavigo's dismembered body limb by limb, Beaumarchais demonstrates that the unreadable body is as much a part of his
identity as Clavigo's.

Beaumarchais's abjection of Clavigo is, nonetheless, the abjection of the illegible body. The simple disfiguration of his face does not suffice to "right" its unorthographic effect. Beaumarchais opts therefore to dismember and devour Clavigo's body, a gesture which, when completed, leaves nothing left to be read. Beaumarchais's cannibalistic act implies his conviction that the body which cannot be read, which cannot be read except ambiguously, must be destroyed, never to be read again.

In contrast to Beaumarchais and Clavigo, Marie is relegated to a marginal position outside the symbolic order (language and revenge). She is limited to a nonlinguistic realm. Marie cannot resolve her "instability" through revenge. Without her own access to "writing," she cannot be separated from the orthographic body. Nonetheless, like Beaumarchais, Marie also experiences a vision of inscriptional/stylistic revenge:

Oh recently, when we met him, the sight of him filled me with warm love! and as I returned home and recalled his behavior and the calm cold look he directed to me as he accompanied his brilliant lady—then I became a Spaniard at heart and reached for my dagger and took poison with me and disguised myself. . . . I followed him in my imagination. I saw him at the feet of his new love. I saw him as he lavished on her all the friendliness and meekness with which he poisoned me. I aim for the heart of the traitor—but suddenly the good-hearted French girl is back again, who knows no love potions, no daggers of revenge. (pp. 264–65)

Marie's vision of revenge is triggered by her reading of Clavigo's "Anblick," his appearance and his glance at her during their last encounter. Here Marie is momentarily "revealed" and "re-veiled." In her fury, she envisions herself as a type of "veiled" phallic mother, crossing into the symbolic order—that is, language and revenge—in order to "kill the master signifier."[20] She can only threaten Clavigo as master signifier when she is disguised as a Spanish woman. Her vision of revenge is that which cannot be seen. Marie covers her body, she disguises that which ought to signify. Her gesture of veiling makes the precariousness of the visual sign, of the body as visual sign, visible. Her action represents the failure of language, it reveals the gap/split between the signifiable and signifier, the splitting of subjectivity. Marie reveals the phallus, language, as a function of veiling, of deferred meaning, as deception.

Only by abandoning her "mother tongue" and resorting to a "foreign language," Spanish, can Marie carry out her vision of revenge. Spanish is Clavigo's language, the language of the symbolic order. Marie's "mother tongue" seems to be silence (or at best "monosyllabic ambiguity"), a silence she breaks by adopting Spanish discourse—the language of the men in the play. Her silence is the language of the "undifferentiated mother" before it is altered, before it is "pierced, stripped, signified, uncovered, castrated and carried away into the symbolic order."[21] Both French and Spanish represent male discourse: Beaumarchais's and Clavigo's. Their inaccessibility to Marie is underscored by the fact that they are the languages of her two absent fathers. She has no contact with or attachment to her absent fathers or the languages of their paternal order. Marie is marginalized in Spain because of her French nationality and language. Indeed, the main difficulty in forcing Clavigo to keep his promise to Marie centers on the fact that the French have no voice in the Spanish court.[22] The French language, on the other hand, is equally inaccessible to Marie — indeed, it is the good Frenchwoman, that is, the good woman as positioned in the French language, which disrupts her vision of revenge and draws her back into silence. Paradoxically, Marie must adopt the language of the symbolic order, of the dagger/stylus, in order to carry out her act of revenge. Ultimately, the "good-hearted French girl" gains the upper hand, and Marie's vision of revenge dissolves.[23]

Marie's step into the writing process involved ironically a type of re-veiling/revealing which leaves us little knowledge about her — only that it is clear that the writing by the male figures in the play entails an erasure of Marie's changeability or multiplicity. Marie veils herself so she can participate in the symbolic order which already veils her as either transparent ideal or infirm body. Her transitory vision of revenge foregrounds the failure to capture that which is woman, and it represents the process of writing itself, in which the trace of writing is followed by its erasure. The process of writing in *Clavigo*, and particularly of writing by or on the body, demonstrates the impulse to create stable, fixed meaning which is continually undone.

Marie's Spanish language is threatening because it represents her potential ability to enter the symbolic order. By ultimately reverting to a more primal language, silence, Marie reaffirms her position outside signification as silent orthographic body. But the reaffirmation of the symbolic order, the designation/castration/definition of woman as mute transparency is also clearly threatened by the possibility of woman as speaker — by the contradictions of woman. Marie is threatening because she cannot be reduced to a transparent ideal, nor can she be reduced to a concept of non-woman-monster/sickness. The scandal of Marie is that she is contradictory, she cannot be relegated to a purely extra-linguistic position. As opposed to Orsina and Emilia in Lessing's *Emilia Galotti* — in which Emilia plays the role of silent woman-virtue and Orsina the role of woman/philosopher (lover of words)/monster — in *Clavigo* the terrible secret is that Marie is both. The gap between paternal order and the daughter widens in

Clavigo to the extent that Marie represents the innately conjoined virtue and transgression of female subjectivity. This "truth" of Marie must be censored. Indeed, as Buenco reacts to Marie's vision with incredulous surprise, Marie comments: "All in my imagination, of course" (p. 264). Thus they relegate her vision to the realm of fantasy — meticulously divorcing it from any suggestion of reality.

As opposed to Lessing's plays in which the division between the language-wielding whores and the mute women of virtue is more clearly marked, in *Clavigo* the undecidability, the contradiction of woman manifests itself within one character. In *Clavigo* the marginal figure of the monstrous woman disappears. It is no longer necessary because the boundaries of representation begin to dissolve in Marie's character. This constitutes a radical shift in the structure and import of the domestic tragedy, because although Beaumarchais and Clavigo deny Marie's contradictory nature, it is evident in the dynamics of the play that the strict representational boundary established between two types of woman — pure, passive, virtuous, transparent body and wanton philosopher-speaker — cannot be maintained.

According to Sophie, Beaumarchais's vision of revenge against Clavigo kills Marie: "Take him away, he is killing his sister" and "You are dead, my sister, because of the rashness of your brother" (p. 301).[24] In terms of the structure of the play, Beaumarchais's vision of revenge displaces Marie's; her vision dissolves, his is actualized. But it seems that Beaumarchais's (s)word has both Marie and Clavigo as its object. The annihilation of Clavigo establishes Beaumarchais's own sense of subjectivity and also reestablishes Marie outside the symbolic order as the silent, transparent body. Marie's reentry into the myth of woman-ideal is only possible through her death. Death is the only way to ensure her purity and to deny her multiplicity once and for all. For this reason, Clavigo can "marry" Marie in death. He says to Beaumarchais as he is being stabbed to death: "I thank you, brother, you marry us" (p. 305).

Once again, Beaumarchais plays the discursive mediator between Clavigo and Marie. It is only through his murder of the two that they can be reunited. Clavigo accepts his death because it is at the hand of Beaumarchais.[25] Their united effort to establish Marie outside the symbolic order as ideal woman prevails. Here, as in *Miss Sara Sampson* and *Emilia Galotti*, the patriarchal bond is obtained over the dead body of a woman.[26] Through death Marie is established inconvertibly as orthographic body, and for Clavigo she no longer represents the threat of instability, of contradictions. Now Clavigo can say: "You are mine [Du bist die Meinige]"

(p. 306). In death Marie is "die Seinige" (his), the unity sought is found. Marie becomes "sein Stil" (his style).

In *Clavigo* the concentration on Clavigo's and Beaumarchais's unstable positions in the symbolic order reveals their desire to retain a vision of Marie as orthographic body. Structurally, *Clavigo* marginalizes the female protagonist in the domestic tragedy further still by concentrating on Clavigo as opposed to a virtuous woman. Paradoxically, it is this very marginalization, the concentration on Clavigo, that brings the issue of the positioning of women in the discourse of the play to the fore. In Lessing's plays the objective was to protect Emilia and Miss Sara from the fate of Orsina and Marwood, that is, to preclude their becoming monsters, but in *Clavigo* the obsession with establishing Marie as woman-truth results from the desire on the part of Clavigo and Beaumarchais to deny her instability, her undecidability. The censorship of Marie is necessary because she represents the inherently conjoined virtue and transgression of female subjectivity. She denies the representational divisions between genders which are so essential to the main male characters' conceptions of virtue, woman, body, and language.

The body in *Clavigo* remains unspellable, unwritable, and for the most part either misread or unread. Various characters in the play provide monolithic/monologic readings of the bodies of Beaumarchais, Clavigo, and Marie. The reductive readings of the characters, together with the instability of the body and its symptoms, evince the multiplicity of representation, the impossibility of clear, vivid representations of the body or sentiment. The indecipherability of the body underscores the impossibility of positioning woman as orthographic body. It is precisely the instability of the woman's body which precludes what Clavigo envisions as female supplement to male subjectivity. Despite the efforts of the characters in *Clavigo* to isolate the unity of Marie's body or the singular meaning of her symptoms, the multiple interpretations, incomplete readings, ambiguous comments, and reductive gender constructions demonstrate that the body can be nothing other than an unorthographic sign; it is everything but an orthographic sign of the sentiments of (the ideal) woman or the emotional confusion reigning within the infirm body.

Disfiguring the Victim's Body
in Sade's 'Justine'

THOMAS DIPIERO

*A*t the end of Choderlos de Laclos's *Les Liaisons dangereuses,* the scheming Madame de Merteuil is forced to flee the social circle on which she wreaked her havoc. Merteuil, whose desire for revenge leads to the death of one person, the seclusion into religion of two others, and the unjust accusation of rape of still another, is eventually spurned by all who knew her, and on the evening during which she is literally hissed out of polite society she comes down with a fever "that people thought was the effect of the violent situation in which she found herself."[1] It turns out, however, that the fever is not a psychosomatic manifestation of Merteuil's social ills; she has contracted smallpox, and the general opinion is that she would be better off were she to die from the disease. Nevertheless, she pulls through, but she does lose an eye. Her hideous countenance prompts a local muckracker to remark that "now her soul is written on her face" (p. 378).

There is, of course, a tremendous potential for bitter irony or poetic justice in Merteuil's loss of an eye. In the famous letter LXXXI, in which she proclaims to Valmont that "I can say that I am my creation" (p. 172), Madame de Merteuil traces the origins of her manipulative social supervision to her natural penchant for recognition, not pleasure. Affirming that even during her first sexual encounter "I desired not gratification, but knowledge," she claims that "I observed pain and pleasure in their precise manifestations, and saw in these different sensations nothing but facts to gather and to meditate upon" (p. 173). The loss of Merteuil's eye thus represents the enervation of her controlling gaze and the depletion of the social mastery she achieved through observation; in addition, the conspicuous and unsightly facial mark functions as a brand of ignominy that seems both to warn others of the marquise's savagery and to repay her her ruthlessness.

Les Liaisons dangereuses is a typical eighteenth-century French novel to the extent that its author claims to perform a public service in exposing the ruses that evil people employ to corrupt the innocent.[2] Typical also are its claims to referential veracity and its use of female characters whose problematic relationship to the predominant conception of virtue constitutes the work's central intrigue. Nor is the graphic and severe punishment meted out to Madame de Merteuil in the form of conspicuous physical affliction uncharacteristic of eighteenth-century novels. Yet, if the human body often serves in fiction as the medium in which is inscribed the visible moral result of the causal sequences recounted — if it functions, in other words, to represent graphically the putatively self-evident moral of the story — it also occasionally functions as the organ of textual or narrative strain itself. That is, the body becomes the site on which the differential elements constituting a work's signification play themselves out, and it becomes, in fact, the graphic medium itself.

I plan to turn to the Marquis de Sade's Justine ou les malheurs de la vertu in order to demonstrate that the principal tensions operating in eighteenth-century French fiction — tensions fundamental to the novel genre and to the concomitant phenomenon of literary realism — are rhetorically inscribed in the heroine's body. I will argue that eighteenth-century French fiction negotiates significant social antagonism, antagonism which focuses primarily on class and which subsumes into itself questions of gender, and that the female body becomes the site where this antagonism plays itself out. Justine, like many if not most eighteenth-century French novels, explicitly rehearses the contemporary debate on the nature of virtue and vice while implicitly subordinating that debate to one concerning the decorousness and utility of prose fiction. Consequently, the work blurs the distinction between a poetics concerned with such issues as verisimilitude and literary form and a politics engaged in determining the cultural representation and production of a gendered and classed individual.

As I will demonstrate, the heroine's remarkably problematic body serves as the medium in which Justine's concern with the poetics and politics of social identity is inscribed. Justine undergoes a bizarre and ceaseless series of unthinkable tortures and abuses; what is more remarkable than the ordeals she undergoes, however, is the fact that her body never retains a trace of the violence done to her. Like the mystic writing pad whose capacity for infinite but temporary inscription Freud exploited as a means of conceptualizing the Perception-Conscious system, Justine receives the marks of libertine activity, but almost as quickly allows all trace of them to deliquesce. Consequently, her body heralds the failure of difference and the attendant end of writing. The meaningless repetition of violence to which she is doomed, I will argue, contributes to the creation of a protective narrative shell whose nefarious realism cushions the work's critical investigation of novelistic practices, primarily its relationship to truth and its capacity for self-demystification. Justine occupies a paradoxical position as both the object of libertine violence and the narrating subject of that violence; because of the discursive nature of the transgression and the violence in *Justine*, continued repetition of fantastic scenes of abuse indicates the potential for the destruction of the subject and, I will argue, an accompanying desire for the end of meaning.

Prose fiction entertained a problematic relationship to high culture in the eighteenth century, primarily because religious, political, and aesthetic authorities worried that readers would misconstrue its outward transparency for social and ideological truth. Thus, it has been argued, in order to escape critical castigation and potential political persecution, novelists began claiming that their works were not fabrications, but the truth; new advances in literary realism rapidly followed.[3] As novelists claimed their works were true — or, more frequently, that they were found memoirs or bundles of genuine letters — they concomitantly tried to attenuate fiction's form as well as its political investments. They suggested, in other words, that the work could be seen as an adequation of the real world. *Justine* is no exception: its opening paragraph loftily aims for the attainment of such a state. The long inaugural sentence, pronounced by a third-person narrator who later yields to Justine, reads: "The masterpiece of philosophy would be to uncover the means Providence employs to arrive at the ends that it proposes for man, and to sketch out, accordingly, some plans of conduct that might inform this unfortunate bipedal individual how he must proceed along the thorny path of life, in order to foresee the bizarre whims of this destiny to whom we give twenty different names without yet having succeeded either in knowing it or in naming it."[4] The tale of physical abuse that follows focuses on what kind of meaning, including a sort of abject meaninglessness, can issue from the brutal violation of Thérèse, the name Justine takes for herself as she narrates her woeful tale.

In the history of French fiction, the end of meaning has traditionally been encoded as *vraisemblance*, or verisimilitude. I refer to *vraisemblance* as the end of meaning here because in general it summoned a foreclosure of interpretation. It fostered the illusion of an unmediated, non-

ideological representation of the world. *Vraisemblance* was both an aesthetically and politically charged concept from roughly the first quarter
of the seventeenth century onward. Generally speaking, it signaled, as
Gérard Genette has argued, not what readers believed could have happened, but what *should* have happened in a given narrative context.[5] Since
a reader's notions of how the world ought to be arranged imply a determinate political position, it follows that despite its rhetorical claim to formal transparency, verisimilitude harbors explicit ideological dimensions.
It would of course be absurd to attempt a detailed chronicle of the major
moments in the French novel here; I simply want to sketch out the principal aesthetic and political forces that shaped prose fiction during the eighteenth century in order to examine the inscription of a verisimilar violence
on the female body in Sade's *Justine*.

During the middle years of the eighteenth century, prose fiction, despite
an already considerable history in France, remained a marginal literary
genre. Bereft of classical ancestry, it was generally considered the bastard
child of literary history. Thought dangerous because they might inspire
untoward passions in their readers, novels nevertheless sometimes seemed
to possess didactic potential. Aubert de la Chesnaye des Bois did not
particularly approve of prose fiction but he did admit that "novels, when
they are well constructed and when they conform to the rules that good
sense has had to prescribe, are far from being a school for libertinism;
rather, they show virtue crowned and vice punished."[6] It is true that during the seventeenth century, and particularly throughout the popularity of
the gargantuan novels collectively referred to as heroic fiction, readers
would have entertained little doubt concerning precisely what constituted
vice and virtue. Whatever the aristocratic classes favored was, by and
large, what one read about in fiction. During the middle years of the
eighteenth century, however, competing political forces and a modification of the concept of aristocracy added a new and complex political
dimension to the philosophies of virtue.

After the death of Louis XIV and the removal of the court from Versailles, aristocrats struggled to shake off the yoke of absolutism and to
reaffirm their value to the nation. Since they had been relieved during the
previous century of their traditional privilege of bearing arms, aristocrats
began filling a large number of administrative posts, thus further blurring
the distinction between sword and robe. The ideology of aristocracy consequently subtly shifted from an abstract notion of virtue and birth to one
of institutional service. As if in response, eighteenth-century fiction dis-
continued the practice of depicting noble characters in grandiose actions,

and it abjured the overwrought conventions associated with those characters. Marginalized figures — in particular, women and folks of the middle
and lower classes — began to people eighteenth-century novels, and their
stories were told without the aid of traditional narrative convention.
What resulted was a new realism in eighteenth-century fiction that took as
fundamental and unquestionably natural the models of truth and behavior that derived not from absolutist politics but from the *embourgeoise-
ment* accompanying the rise to dominance of France's administrative
class. At the same time, however, the concomitant rejection of previous
generations' standardizing global narratives introduced Enlightenment
conceptions of reason into fiction, and with them the recognition that
narrative has a capacity to create — and consequently to contest — models
of truth.

The social and material elements underwriting the production of fiction
in the eighteenth century changed dramatically, but one of the elemental
catalysts responsible for its endurance remained constant: the desire to
represent or read about social stability. With the continued blurring of the
lines separating the *noblesse de robe* and the upper bourgeoisie, along
with the increased emphasis on administrative service and the protection
of money and property, the narrative subjects providing credible but nevertheless provocative defamiliarizations of reality had to change. Problematic feminine virtue seemed to offer writers a new lowest common
denominator of plausibility in fiction, since female characters either submitted to the patriarchal order or were harshly punished for their transgressions. In both cases, the bourgeois order of paternal name, legitimacy,
and property provided the normative stability from which narrative disruption proceeded.

By constituting the female protagonist as the figure of social disruption
in a narrative that contested the formal conventions of aristocratic fiction,
novelists provided prose fiction the means for negotiating new and complex social configurations, and translated class conflict into gender terms.
Because the social order the new political economy commanded was sym-
bolized by control of the woman's body, a particular ideological concern
could appear to be a natural one. The disposition of women in fiction
became, consequently, symptomatic of the social order, and female protagonists were charged with an overdetermined political significance: the
integrity of their bodies correlated with the stability of the bourgeois
patriarchy. Female characters whose bodies and desires were properly
contained and confined to the service of family, reproduction, property,
and exchange thus figured a bourgeois social ideal. Women who were

unrestrained represented, in their impugning of patriarchal property and its transmission, not merely gender instability but the precariousness of an entire complex of political, economic, and social systems. Thus, when prose fiction depicted the imposition of an alienated and class-based virtue on the woman's body, it did not simply represent a resistance able to generate narrative interest; it demonstrated that the incipient social order was able to negotiate and surmount political opposition. Rhetorically loaded female characters consequently had a new mode of *vraisemblance* written across their bodies in the form of virtue and social and sexual control.

Sade's novel transacts the ideological conflict between a profligate and decadent aristocracy and a constraining and repressive bourgeoisie. Making Justine herself the spokesperson for the virtue that alienates her both from the bourgeois merchant class whose interest it presumably guards and from the aristocratic libertines who refuse to recognize it, the novel depicts a struggle for hegemony.[7] Before he hands the narration over to Justine, Sade's omniscient narrator claims that the events in the poor woman's tale are offered up as "examples of virtue" and that the provocative story's principal value is its didactic rehearsal of specific philosophical positions. Both Justine and her libertine tormentors scramble to build a discursive framework capable of sustaining the ideological positions they explicitly endorse, but as I will now show, the forms of narration they are forced to adopt foreclose the possibility of achieving the political identities they advocate.

Justine consists primarily of the title character's narrative of the physical violence she experienced at the hands of a dozen or so libertines. Justine is spotted by Mme de Lorsange and M. de Corville while she is being taken to Paris for the confirmation of the death penalty she received in Lyon for having accidentally murdered a baby. When the two libertines engage Justine to tell them the story of her life, however, they probably do not expect the epic *récit* that follows. Full of repetitive and formulaic scenes, Justine's story is of her heroic struggle to maintain her virtue when everyone around her has other ideas. Although nearly any of Justine's descriptions of the violent episodes she underwent might emblematize her plight as well as her narrative style, one in particular, which occurs near the end of her tale, encapsulates particularly well her situation.

I am the center of abominable orgies, I am their object and their end. Already, four times each, La Rose and Julien have paid homage to their cult at my altars, while Cardoville and Saint-Florent, less robust, perhaps, or more dissipated, content themselves with a sacrifice to the altars of my lovers [*amants*]. This one is the last: it was high time — I was ready to faint.

"My comrade caused you great pain, Thérèse," Julien says to me. "I will repair everything."

Armed with a vial of spirits, he rubs some of it on me several times over. The traces of the atrocities my executioners committed start to fade, but nothing can diminish my agony: I never experienced any so sharp. (pp. 307–8)

Repetition, violence, blasphemy, resistance, memory, pain, and healing dominate this passage and, except for the last term in the list, most passages in the novel. As I will show in greater detail below, it is curious that both the libertines and Justine depend upon these things in order to form their identities; striking as well is the extent to which the novel itself relies on them. What demands consideration first, however, is the nature of the encounters between Justine and her tormentors. Understanding the outlandish practices they engage in and how they relate to the philosophies the libertines espouse will help situate the relationship of narrative, *vraisemblance*, and the inscription of political antagonism on the woman's body.

Justine's encounters with the various people who torment and abuse her proceed in remarkably similar fashion. First, since she is alone in the world and helpless, she narrates to them the story of her misfortunes in the hope, explicitly stated on several occasions, that she might move one of them to come to her aid. After she apprises her audience — presumably unwittingly — that since she has no protector they can do with her whatever they like, they proceed to do just that. What typically follow are the long descriptions of sexual violence that characterize Justine's encounters with the libertines and for which Sade is famous. Consisting of protracted portrayals of horrendous rapes, beatings, and mutilations, they seem all the more outrageous because those inflicting the violence derive more pleasure as the victim's pain increases. In general, as the descriptions progress, they become more detailed and more grotesque, and acts that could surely never be performed, much less with the victim's surviving, are recounted. In the passage cited above, for example, Justine has just been infibulated and then raped, impaled with some sort of metallic, expandable hot egg, and sodomized; thanks to the libertine talent of being able to "heal wounds in less time than it took to inflict them" (pp. 304–5), however, she not only survives the ordeal but seems, finally, strangely unaffected by it.

The libertines generally conceive the body of their victims to be nothing more than an instrument of their own pleasure, but it is an instrument that each of them is remarkably adept at playing. This is because the libertines are by and large excellent physiognomists: they can read a body the way most people read texts. Clément, one of the malignant monks at Ste.

Marie-des-bois, longs for the perfection of the science of anatomy because he believes it will effectively wipe out the subjective imponderables of human existence: "When the science of anatomy is perfected, we will be able to demonstrate quite simply through it the relationship between human organization and the proclivities that affect it. . . . What then will become of your laws, your morals, your religion . . . when we can demonstrate that a given flow of humors, a particular kind of nerve . . . suffice to make of a man the object of your punishments or your rewards?" (p. 170). Clément values such a science because it will teach him how better to manipulate the body of his subordinates and consequently how to derive more pleasure from them. His dispassionate litany of the body's instrumentality comes to its icy close when he describes the connection between the man who takes pleasure and the woman he uses: "There is truly no relationship whatsoever between that object and him" (p. 171).

Clément's remark about the radical disconnection between the libertine subject and his tormented object reveals that physical and philosophical or political violations of victims are interrelated. As many have already pointed out, these latter forms of violation are primarily discursive in nature. Since the 1960s, when Roland Barthes and Philippe Sollers first observed the intimate connection between libertine pleasure and the speech act, critics from perspectives as varied as Alice Laborde's and Jane Gallop's have commented on the violators' use of language.[8] Barthes remarks that "except for murder, there is only one characteristic that the libertines alone possess and that they never share, in whatever form: speech. The master is the one who speaks, who disposes of language in its entirety; the object is the silent one who remains separated, through a mutilation more absolute than any erotic torture, from any access to speech" (p. 32). Sollers concurs, writing that "the Sadian monster — who is, we must remember, a written monster — presents himself as the realization of an integral literalism: he is the one who says what he does and does what he says *and never anything else*" (p. 43). The libertines narrate each of their acts to their victims, explaining the scene before acting it out. In addition, they always take care to expound each aspect of their philosophies, as if to ensure that no dimension of their crime remains unclear or, worse, misunderstood. "I would be quite unhappy," Rodin the vivisector tells Justine, "if you misunderstood my method of thinking" (p. 107).

The philosophical debate normally inaugurates Justine's confrontations with the libertines. They bombard Justine with their lengthy invectives as a means of invalidating the ideology of virtue to which she clings. They undo whatever political or moral security she may have experienced when they show that the discourse and behavior normally associated with virtue might also be put in service to sustain vice. Consequently, the philosophical systems the libertines propose cease to be purely intellectual enterprises — they become, in fact, acts of violence themselves because they ravish the discursive structure of reason as the Enlightenment traditionally conceived it. Reason in the hands of the libertines is no longer a stable and easily categorized product like its eighteenth-century progenitor liberal education, a product which rapidly acquired the status of cultural capital; it is, rather, a volatile and dangerous weapon. The libertines deploy this weapon not only to expound their philosophies to their victims, but to make manifest the differences that separate them at the most fundamental level. They show their victims that what they take to be trans-historically and irreducibly human is nothing but a construction of bourgeois ideology. Violence in the libertine scheme of things is thus violation of and by language. Saying equals doing, for the libertines ("Cœur-de-Fer became aroused by disclosing his perfidious maxims" [p. 49]), and they attempt to effect a one-to-one correspondence between word and referent, halting the metonymic slippage of signifiers. In short, they try to be the masters in control of truth.

The libertine search for pleasure can properly be described as an inscription or writing of violence performed not just on the victim's body but on her entire subjectivity. Repeated violent scenes establish an iterable ideological complex based upon the transgression of existing cultural codes. Throwing their victims' moral and ideological beliefs into complete disarray, libertines proceed to tear their bodies asunder, inscribing upon them in their vicious attacks the marks of their own physical and ideological dominance. Rodin reveals that inflicting physical pain does not suffice in his search for pleasure; he needs to inflict a more lasting suffering. He remarks as he prepares to brand Justine with the *lettre ignomineuse* of the thief, "Let's punish her a thousand times more than if we took her life. Let's mark her, let's brand her! That disfigurement, together with all the other evil things she's got on her, will get her hanged or make her die of hunger. At least she'll suffer up until then and our continued vengeance will be all the more delicious" (p. 120).

Inflicting pain and suffering on Justine even long after he loses contact with her — up until the moment of her death, in fact — is Rodin's erotic fantasy, and this can help establish the parameters of the libertines' pleasure: they require the victim's complete annihilation, physically, politically, and spiritually. The libertines strive, in fact, to attain a state of phallic *jouissance* predicated on the obliteration of subjectivity. Phallic *jouissance,* we recall from Lacan and Leclaire, refers to the sensory experience of difference; perceived as the pleasure of unification and incorporation, phallic *jouissance* temporarily annuls the pain and anxiety caused by subjective separation or division.[9] Here, libertines strive to annihilate their victims totally, and by affecting a difference so radical between themselves and their victims they recreate the experience of unity and self-identity. Clément explains why a victim's pain causes him pleasure:

No sensation is as vivid as pain: its manifestations are sure, unlike those of pleasure, which women constantly feign and almost never experience. What egotism, youth, strength, and health you need to be sure to give a woman this doubtful and unsatisfying impression of pleasure! . . . He who can bring about in a woman the most tumultuous impression, he who can most upset the entire organization of this woman, will have decidedly succeeded in giving himself the greatest dose of voluptuousness possible. (pp. 173–74)

The point Clément makes is that libertine pleasure depends as much on inflicting physical pain on victims as it does on upsetting their social and psychic organization. Along with his colleagues of the cloth, Clément does what he can to upset his victims' belief structures, to the point of making them participate in a mock apparition of the Virgin Mary originally designed merely to con the gullible into contributing more money to the parish, but then inflicted on Justine and her cohorts as an involuntary blasphemous act. Thus, when he calls for the destruction of "the entire organization of this woman" (*bouleverser l'organisation de cette femme*), he effectively demands her subjective destruction by separating her from the social and discursive structures that constitute her self.

Libertine pleasure derives in part from the annihilation of victims' subjectivity, but it seems to require the demolition of libertine subjectivity as well. Cœur-de-Fer tells Justine, "Nature suffices unto itself" (p. 56), and he and his comrades continually strive to achieve the sort of self-plenitude normally attributed to Nature or whatever else one calls that which lies beyond the realm of signification. Escaping the limits of their own subjective organizations, freeing themselves from the confines imposed by bodily and subjective integrity, the libertines seem to achieve *jouissance* by approximating the self-plenitude they construe in Nature. At Ste. Marie-des-bois, the standard practice for choreographing one of the monks' orgasms is as follows: "Whenever a monk climaxed, in whatever fashion, all the girls were to surround him in order to ignite his senses from all quarters and so that voluptuousness could, if one can express it this way, more surely penetrate him through each of his pores" (p. 158). In a similarly regulated orgy, Justine describes the dissipation of individuality by remarking that "there were moments in which all of these bodies seemed to combine to form one" (p. 305). Libertines strive for total sensory awareness: La Dubois avers that "the only thing that is real is physical sensation" (p. 50), and as the above passages show, libertines seem to derive some of that awareness from the senses of those surrounding them. Geoffrey Bennington concludes, in fact, that the libertines desire to experience everything.[10]

Libertines draw their pleasure from the annihilation of their victims' subjectivities and from the dissolution of their own physical and psychical boundaries that results. Implicitly affirming their own integrity in their rejection of a common human bond, libertines deny all attempts to forge links that would construe them as anything but radically other. This is why they abuse their victims' bodies as well as their beliefs. Despite their shared proclivity for sophistry, however, libertines do not have a positive philosophy, since there are no principles or beliefs peculiar to them all. Except for a tendency to reject all attempts to make them part of a larger cultural order, libertines have nothing in common. Libertine philosophy, consequently, is a philosophy of the moment, premised on negation. It is based on determining victims' area of greatest resistance and then bludgeoning them with sophistry. Yet it is for this very reason that libertines are doomed to approaching their goal of total sensory plenitude and coincidence with Nature only asymptotically. Speaking the truth about their philosophy and explaining it to their victims are necessary parts of their violation, but that renders them dependent on their victims and hence not autonomous. It frustrates *jouissance* because it reaffirms subjectivity. Libertine destabilization of language thwarts their own desire to be absolutely other, revealing that the language of vice is as tenuous as that of virtue. Unable to be absolutely other, the libertines can only *say* that they are other; they consequently affirm that their position is not self-same and unique, but part of an antagonism requiring the participation of another. Since they rely on a victim to demonstrate their own ascendancy, and especially since they rely primarily on language to accomplish this, libertine pleasure demands an other capable of reflecting their desire.[11]

The libertines' urgent need for an other is the paradox constituting their subjective limit and prohibiting them from attaining the state of identity they crave. Their predilection for accumulating bodily experience of whatever sort (even that normally deemed painful), along with the need to demonstrate the factitious nature of bourgeois virtue, leads the libertines to try to detach themselves from the experience of their own bodies as ideologically determined. Libertines search, in fact, for the end of meaning; they seek the foreclosure on interpretation marking a nonsymbolic relationship to reality, what we might call an identity or adequation with the Real.[12] Desiring complete physical sensation totally removed from the confines of representation, the libertines strive to effect a liberation from human identity. Their absolute dependence on language, however, construes bourgeois virtue as their antagonizing limit. Since they nevertheless require elaborate philosophical justification to accompany their inscriptions of violence on their victims' bodies, libertines' accession to the Real can never be unmediated, and they must instead content themselves with *vraisemblance*.

It is on the body of the other, the victim, that the libertines inscribe their *vraisemblance*, and the more fully they are able to reduce her to pure instrumentality, the better she is able graphically to encode and represent to them their mastery. Justine appears to be the perfect victim. Described by all she meets as extraordinarily beautiful, she also manifests a remarkable tenacity in defending the precepts of virtue, and these two characteristics make her ripe for physical and philosophical violation. Justine registers the requisite amount of horror at the libertine's thoughts and activities, and in each instance her resistance simply eggs them on. No one is stauncher than Justine in refuting libertine philosophy, and if there seems to be no positive definition of libertinism, Justine's version of virtue consists as well in nothing but negation. That is, at each exposition of libertine beliefs Justine can only counter with contradiction. She never offers her own views on what it means to be virtuous, and she never performs a single virtuous act. Justine's dialectical self-definition causes her to be as radically other from the libertines as she possibly can; it leads her so far, in fact, to define herself not just as virtuous but also as victim. When she attempts to flee the chateau of Gernande, the mad blood-letter, she manages to reach the courtyard, only to find the walls impossible to climb. When the count mistakes her for a phantom and retreats in fright, Justine responds: "Oh! monsieur, punish me. . . . I am guilty and have no excuse" (p. 221). Similarly, Roland places his life in Justine's hands by giving her the end of the rope he uses to hang himself to increase his masturbatory pleasure. When he falls to the ground unconscious, Justine concludes: "I run to untie him, he falls to the ground insensible; but through my ministrations I soon succeed in bringing him back to his senses" (p. 260).

The libertines seem to have found in Justine precisely what they need to violate absolutely in their quest for self-identity through *jouissance*. She makes herself the other of libertinism and hence the ideal victim both through her speech and through her acts. That is, she impugns each of their beliefs, ostensibly to further the cause of virtue, and she acts — as in the scenes above — to maintain the balance of power in the libertines' favor and to continue the repetition of violence. If, however, her speech and her acts define her as the ideal other of libertinism and hence the perfect victim, her speech act itself — the novel's *récit* — does not instantiate her position but, rather, reverses it. Barthes and Sollers identify the libertine master as the one endowed with speech. Except for fifteen paragraphs, *Justine* is composed of Justine's own narrative to Corville and Lorsange. When the two libertines engage Justine to tell the story of her life, calling herself Thérèse ostensibly in order to protect her family name, she begins:

> To tell you the story of my life, madame, . . . is to offer you the most striking example of the misfortunes of innocence; it is to accuse the hand of God; it is to deplore the will of the supreme Being; it is a revolt against His sacred intentions . . . I wouldn't dare . . .
>
> Tears flowed abundantly from the eyes of this captivating girl, and after having given them course for a while, she began her story in these terms. (p. 25)

It is obvious from the first words she speaks that Justine has appropriated the tricks of libertine narration. We have seen that libertine discourse forces a contamination of speech and act, such that the *récit* becomes the instantiation of a violent speech act capable of producing outrage. In the first sentences she utters, Justine accomplishes a similar transgression through her use of language. Averring that telling equals accusing and deploring, she indicates that the mere recounting of her story is a rebellion against God's sacred intentions. Like the libertines, she turns an otherwise mundane speech situation into a transgressive speech act.

Barthes calls Justine "an ambiguous victim endowed with narrating speech" (p. 32). Given that he defines libertinism as the exercising of speech, this characterization of Justine seems singularly unsatisfying. Although it is certainly true that Justine is on the receiving end of a great many violent crimes, I would argue that her use of language casts her in a somewhat undecidable light. Justine does not attempt to upset the ideological ground from which her interlocutors speak, but she does quite clearly engage in violence by and of language. As we have just seen, Justine turns her narrative into a violent speech act by affirming that telling her tale is a blasphemous act. Although she does register the modicum of reluctance that propriety demands before beginning her story, her frequent hesitations at the seamier aspects of her tale point to a more calculated effect on her listeners. Justine's narrative strategies resemble the libertines' to the extent that she always informs her listeners that transgression is about to occur, and she ensures her listeners' full participation in the telling through well-timed pauses. " 'Have I not already soiled your imagination far too much with these infamous tales? Must I risk new ones?' 'Yes, Thérèse,' said M. de Corville, 'yes, we require these details from you' " (p. 241). Securing her audience's rapt attention, Justine then goes on to make them active participants in the violation of Thérèse: "You will permit me . . . to keep from you some part of the obscene details of this disgusting ceremony; let your imagination represent all that debauchery can dictate in such a situation to scoundrels such as these . . . and even then you will only most likely have but a vague idea of what happened next" (p. 133). Justine gives them all the material they need to complete her story, but by cannily withholding crucial information, she gets them to supply for themselves the erotic details, forcing them to inscribe their own marks of violence on the hapless Thérèse.

Justine projects Thérèse as a sign of herself, and the story in which Thérèse figures as central character seems designed to show her as the apotheosis of virtue. Thérèse is a purely textual manifestation of the narrator Justine; it is upon her that the libertines and the listening audience inscribe their marks of violence. Thérèse registers and retains for Justine's audience the memory of every act of violence performed against her. Nothing but an accumulation of repeated scenes of violence, Thérèse is a writerly text whose only purpose is to be the locus of pathos and abjection for her narrator. Thérèse knows no truth and voices no theory. Serving only as pure resistance to the libertines' inscriptions of defilement, her narrated body retains every violent trace and she appears more virtuous in her abiding adherence to virtue and hence all the more exquisitely transgressable.

Thérèse's resistance to the libertines is, as mentioned above, nothing but contradiction. Never refuting a libertine argument with anything more than a puerile gainsaying, she does nevertheless furnish a dialectical field of resistance, and this lies in the dimension in which her body is narrated. That is, as Justine tells it, Thérèse can be violated any number of times, but she still remains beautiful and virginal in appearance. Her body has the superhuman resilience and elasticity to survive all manner of beatings, brandings, and infibulations without producing the slightest scar; she is so recuperative, in fact, that it seems her hymen grows back after she is raped (p. 121). Thérèse's peculiar malleability is alone responsible for her status as the apotheosis of virtue: the more the libertines violate her and the more she refuses to abandon her virtuous beliefs, the stauncher she appears in sustaining virtue's principles. Thérèse would not be infinitely defilable, however, if her body were not unable to retain a mark of libertine transgression.[13]

Consequently, Justine inscribes on the narrated figure Thérèse verisimilar marks of violence attesting to the latter's virtue, and she incites her audience, as we have already seen, to do the same. Like the libertines, she must resort to the telling of a merely verisimilar tale in order to cover the holes in her own political and ideological position, in this case the appearance of virtue. In other words, since in Justine's narrative there appears to be no such thing as a virtuous act, she can only inhabit the virtuous position by saying that she does, and this entails narrating herself as vice's radical other.

Both Justine and the libertines want to be absolutely other, but they are in fact very much the same. They are constantly embattled, each incessantly attempting to become the absolute antithesis of the other. They both rely on narrative to suture the gaps that make it impossible to inhabit the positions they advocate, and they both rely on the figure of Thérèse, the narrated body that cannot retain a trace of the violence inscribed on it, as the principal character in a verisimilar tale illustrating their ideological positions. Both as well try to annihilate, physically or discursively, their antitheses in order better to occupy their positions. If Justine lacks the physical strength to overcome her oppressors, neither can the libertines annihilate Justine. This is because they cannot permanently inscribe their marks of violence on her—it is only Justine's narrated self Thérèse who retains the traces of transgression—and because Justine is too much like them: attempting, as they do, to become the other's antithesis, Justine fascinates them and mirrors their desire.

Justine and her libertine tormentors are effectively doomed to tell their stories, to continue to explain and to chronicle their pasts and presents, because it is only narrative construction that is capable of fixing their identities. Neither the libertines' nor Justine's position is a fully integrated stance whose self-evident identity obviates linguistic supplement. In both cases, the narratives that each must tell in order to constitute full integrity construe their opponents not as differentially other but as negatively antagonistic. That is, it is not simply the case that we know Justine is virtuous because she is not at all a libertine, or that a given libertine takes his identity from his radical opposition to virtue. Rather, the two positions— libertinism and virtue, at least as they contend in *Justine*—find their self-identities blocked precisely by that which they strive so vehemently to annihilate and in the very moment when they represent their positions.

Non-oppositional difference, the hallmark of Saussurean linguistics generally construed as the limit of empirical and positive meaning, is absent here. Instead, we find what Ernesto Laclau terms antagonism, "the limit of all objectivity" and "that which prevents the constitution of objectivity itself."[14] Because linguistic representation plugs the discontinuities inherent in any social structure, antagonism — the denial of identity — remains outside language.[15]

The antagonism that Justine narrates is that between virtue and vice, but what is particularly striking about this opposition is that both positions can achieve ascendancy only by seizing control of the woman's body. Since the goal of these ostensibly opposing ideologies is the same — the regulation of feminine sexuality — they differ only in their relative success at promoting their own specific partisan versions of the phenomenon. Consequently, the antagonism that Justine narrates forces the production of narrative: because one antagonistic position emanates from a source whose integrity is denied by the other, narrative serves the purpose of suturing the gaps that this other creates. The struggle in Justine is thus over the control of representation as both Justine and her libertine tormentors, using nearly identical narrative strategies, steadfastly attempt to tell their whole stories and gain recognition of their positions. Both work toward definitively inscribing the body of Thérèse with the proof of the ascendancy of their positions and both do so in the apparent belief that once the story is complete in all its details, then its philosophical position will achieve self-evident identity — it will achieve, that is, the end of meaning associated with a transparent and ideologically neutral position. Justine and the libertines seem to abide by the precept proclaimed by Justine's sister Juliette in the story of her own life that "philosophy must tell everything."[16]

Justine opens with the narrator's hesitations concerning the possibility of ever saying everything or of ever achieving the end of meaning associated with the formal transparency and the ideological neutrality of representation. Throughout the story of Thérèse and her misfortunes, the libertines portrayed and the narrator portraying use the female body to supplement the ideological positions from which they speak. It is as though their perpetual struggle revolved around the question of who would be permitted to mark definitively the female body — of who would, in other words, attain the power to anchor meaning and establish the specific ideological parameters of vraisemblance. The libertines use pain in order to verify their victim's resistance to annihilation and, consequently, their own mastery; Justine uses Thérèse as a mystic writing pad who retains for her listeners all memory of violence yet remains able to receive new marks. In both cases the control over the woman's body and over the discursive structures pertaining to it constitute political hegemony. The instability of the writing on Thérèse's body correlates with the instability of the expressly advocated ideological positions in the tale, since neither libertinism nor virtue occupies a stable, self-identical position.

The end of Justine's story, however, instantiates a permanent mark on the young woman. Concluding her long narrative to Mme de Lorsange and M. de Corville, Justine discovers that the former is her long-lost sister. She returns with her to her chateau, receiving the recompenses to virtue her story seemed always designed to elicit. One evening a storm develops:

Lightning flashes, hail falls, the winds kick up, the fire in the skies unsettles the clouds, shaking them horribly. It seemed that nature, tired of its works, was ready to confound the elements and cause them to take on new forms. Frightened, Mme de Lorsange begs her sister to close everything up as quickly as possible. Thérèse, hurrying to calm her sister, flies to the windows, which are already breaking; she struggles a moment against the wind: in an instant a clap of thunder flattens her out in the middle of the chamber. (p. 316)

Significantly, Justine is permanently marked ("It turned your stomach to look at this miserable creature") only after she finishes her narrative; the narrator, we might also note, continues to refer to her as Thérèse, despite the fact that her true identity is now revealed, thus retaining her identity as the locus of inscribability. Thérèse, the narrated character whose body received but failed to retain the marks of ideologically invested tales, is indelibly inscribed by a natural agent completely outside any symbolic order. As though an ironic response to the libertines who longed for total coincidence with the Real as nonsymbolic, the final mark on Justine is beyond the purview of traditional exegesis and finally puts an end to the woman's meaning.

Although the lightning bolt that permanently disfigures and kills Justine emanates from a purely nonsymbolic source, this does not prevent Juliette from inserting it into a narrative context and interpreting it as a sign that she should adhere to the principles of virtue.[17] Nevertheless, the novel's absurd ending on a *deus ex machina* is the only way of concluding on an uncommitted note a work whose principal thematic proposition entails the impossibility of fixing meaning except temporarily through narrative construction. That is, both Justine and the libertines try to inscribe Thérèse with their own ideologically invested form of *vraisemblance*: since their rhetorical strategies include the same moves, only a decisive and radically illegible stroke from a nonsymbolic source can conclude this struggle for hegemony. Emanating from the Real, the lightning bolt that finally inscribes Justine radically removes her from either of the ideologically informed narrative structures that had been competing for her possession. If it is a force from the Real that permanently inscribes Thérèse, however, it is that same force that dis-figures her as a device of narrative verisimilitude; when Thérèse is marked definitively and by a natural, nonsymbolic power, what comes to an end is her tropological nature — that which encodes or figures the competing versions of *vraisemblance* with which Justine and the libertines attempt to write her.

The conclusion of *Justine* returns to the nonsymbolic Real a body that sustained the agonistic attempts of antagonistic rivals to inscribe their discursive ascendancy on it. Revealing that opposing ideological positions nevertheless make use of the same rhetorical moves to cause their representation of the world to appear natural and uncontrived — in short, to appear realistic — the novel not only emphasizes narrative's capacity to create and contest models of truth, it dismisses any attempt to understand the world in any other way. It repudiates the libertines' endeavor to experience their bodies in a manner uninformed by the dominant ideological dictates concerning pleasure and property, and it rejects the concomitant intimation that contesting the reigning social order amounts to a demystification able to bring forth the end of meaning.

It is in this respect that Sade uses a model of the body as a heuristic device onto which he can map competing models of verisimilitude. The human body and the sensations of pleasure and pain it experiences seem to be irreducibly real, far removed from the social institutions and customs governing symbolic interaction. And yet, it is precisely this unrepresentable aspect of the body — its status as a non-discursive thing — that Sade reappropriates as an element of social contention, for he refuses to allow any movement or impression to fall outside the scope of articulation. Elaine Scarry has analyzed the manner in which pain as an archtypically unrepresentable personal phenomenon unreal to others translates into objectification and hence into power for the pain's inflicter.[18] Sade makes the pain and pleasure his characters experience the object and the point of his work; even normally unrepresentable bodily experiences are subsumed into the discursive, and hence ideological, structures that frame them. Thus, when Justine's body defies logic and science and fails to register a trace of the violence done to her, it does not violate the work's *vraisemblance*: rather, it reaffirms the preeminence of narrative in the social and political ordering of the individual. The simple fact that *Justine* tends to provoke outrage over the sexual violence the title character undergoes, rather than, say, laughter over its very implausibility, demonstrates that the human body is as much subject to the conventions of verisimilitude — and, of course, its ideology as well — as are character and plot.

It is of course ironic that a novel dealing with problematic political inscriptions of hegemony on the female body would make its point precisely by subjecting the woman to violence, degradation, and death. There is certainly no way of defending the marquis' peculiar method of attempting to undermine what he felt to be a repressive political structure with this sort of annihilating sexual violence. Curiously, the often overpowering images that one finds in Sade's work prompt either a complete detachment on the reader's part or an investment in and identification with what Thérèse is experiencing. This is the nefarious realism I alluded to earlier, a realism which, despite the patent absurdity of what it describes, nevertheless causes one to focus on Thérèse and to read her story without observing Justine's methodology. Consequently, the novel, like its title character, engages in a discursive subterfuge designed to conceal the ideological interrogations it performs and emphasize instead the physical — and not the discursive or political — transgressions it engages in.

The success of the buffer of violence Sade creates in *Justine* has been apparent in the criticism greeting the work since its publication. In 1792, for example, the *Journal général de France*, highlighting the tale's violent nature and its inappropriateness for women, selectively summoned its readers: "You, mature men, whom experience and the quiescence of all passions have placed outside of all danger, read [*Justine*] in order to see how far the delirium of human imagination can go; but immediately afterward throw it into the fire. This is advice you will give yourselves if you have the strength to read it entirely."[19] The point of *Justine* seems to be that one should forgo the idea of reaching the end of interpretation, the point at which body and mind, nature and culture intersect in a self-identical unity in which the concept of meaning is empty. Even the bodily experience of pleasure is a social and political phenomenon, the tale warns. Given the libertines' efforts to annihilate their victims' as well as their own subjectivities in order to heighten their perception of pleasure, it seems not only unbecoming but downright dangerous to read such a work "entirely."

Mrs. Robinson and the Masquerade
of Womanliness

CHRIS CULLENS

The "real" and the "sexually factic" are phantasmatic constructions—illusions of substance—that bodies are compelled to approximate, but never can. What, then, enables the exposure of the
rift between the phantasmatic and the real whereby the real admits
itself as phantasmatic? Does this offer the possibility for a repetition that is not fully constrained by the injunction to reconsolidate
naturalized identities? Just as bodily surfaces are enacted as natural, so these surfaces can become the site of a dissonant and de-
naturalized performance that reveals the performative status of the
natural itself.

— Judith Butler, *Gender Trouble*

Sometimes she'd play the Tragic Queen,
Sometimes the Peasant poor,
Sometimes she'd step behind the Scenes,
And there she'd play the W——.

— "Florizel and Perdita" (1780)

On 1780 the young Prince of Wales (later George IV) saw and became enamored from afar with the older actress Mary Robinson when she
was playing the role of Perdita in *The Winter's Tale.* Their ensuing affair
destroyed Robinson's successful career as an actress and her name. In fact,
she was rechristened by the public and forever after tarred with the romantic notoriety of being known as "Perdita," the lost one.

When the prince's passion cooled as rapidly as it had commenced, Robinson found herself truly living a winter's tale. Doubly humiliated, facing
poverty, banished from polite English society, separated from her dis-

solute husband, supporting a daughter, and chronically ill with the rheumatic fever that finally left her paralyzed, she turned to a literary career, churning out poetry, plays, and novels until her death in 1800. Although most of her works enjoyed a moderate popular success, Robinson's literary reputation in her lifetime and after rested primarily on her poetry. Very little attention has been paid to her novels, although M. Ray Adams, grouping her with the Jacobin writers of the 1790s whose political tenets she shared, devoted a chapter to her in his pioneering work on English radicalism.[1]

This neglect is unfortunate because Robinson's last novel contains what is not only one of the wildest plots in eighteenth-century fiction but also one which plays out that script of the exposure and multiple losses by which the female body fixed in the public gaze is threatened, a script Robinson herself enacted in exemplary fashion for her contemporaries. For Robinson's trouble was clearly, to invoke the title of Judith Butler's recent study, specifically "gender[ed] trouble." Caught in the double bind endemic to the "masquerade of womanliness," she paid for her unmasking by being nominally reassigned another demanding cultural role of embodiment. For flaunting the rift between the phantasmatic construction of desirable femininity she incarnated repeatedly as an actress and the "real" or "sexual factic" of an apparently irrepressible female sexuality, "the lost one" ended up functioning as a publicly identified sign of lost womanhood (see the epigraph from Butler). The Robinson affair stayed firmly lodged in the mass cultural imagination, not just because of the masses' traditional fondness for tales of dalliance between royalty and pretty commoners, but because of precisely this gratifyingly symmetrical representational alignment pertaining between Perdita's text, her initially coveted and finally crippled body, and her iconic significance. Robinson herself added another textual layer to her own legend with the life story retailed in her *Memoirs*, in which she set out to defend herself: "I know that I have been sufficiently the victim of events, too well to become the tacit acquiescer where I have been grossly misrepresented."[2] But, before that, she responded to the drama of misrepresentation she found herself living by writing a novel that itself represents, in Butler's words, a partial "exposure of the rift between the phantasmatic and the real whereby the real admits itself as phantasmatic."

On the one hand, *Walsingham, Or the Pupil of Nature* (1796) accomplishes this in the most spectacularly literal way: I know of no other eighteenth-century novel featuring a male protagonist who, at the end of four volumes, is revealed to narrator and readers to be a female transvestite. On the other hand, the author of *The Pupil of Nature* did indeed ultimately "bow to the injunction to reconsolidate naturalized identities," precisely through this unmasking revelation, which identifies the exposure and belated acceptance of womanliness with a string of accepted losses (of title, fortune, and, nearly, life) and which appears, moreover, to posit this situation as a necessary precondition for the restabilization of an epistemological order based, in the first instance, on binary sexual difference. We can label this a subvertingly grim exposé, a foreclosed fantasy, or an ideologically enforced capitulation. At any rate, it dramatically recapitulated the script of female coming-of-age that Robinson had lived.

In what follows, I propose to read *Walsingham* against both Robinson's own *Memoirs* and the historical context in which she constituted a readable sign and popular culture event herself. In doing so, I would like to look most closely at how the novel "discourses" masquerade, maternity, and what Butler has explored as "the melancholia of gender" by which both female and male subjectivities are bodily "inscripted" and achieve, or fail to achieve, textual representation via language — a medium that, for Robinson, itself seems marked by an originary melancholia. Furthermore, this reading will also be carried out against the backdrop of the thesis that the eighteenth century produced a crucial paradigm shift in the model of the body, a shift by which bodies came to be figured and categorized first and foremost on the basis of a universalized, essentialized sexual dimorphism. This thesis has recently been supported by the work of Tom Laqueur, who, in *Making Sex*, posits that precisely this period witnessed the rise of "a biology of incommensurability in which the relationship between men and women was not inherently one of equality or inequality but rather of difference that required interpretation."[3] In the view of this scholar, an older "one sex" biological model, which presented the female body as the anatomically inverted but otherwise not dissimilar version of the male body, was gradually superseded by a two-sex model. "As the natural body itself became the gold standard of social discourse, the bodies of women — the perennial other — thus became the battleground for redefining the ancient, intimate fundamental social relation: that of woman to man" (p. 152).

However, as Laqueur points out, the consolidation of this model did not proceed evenly or unchallenged. Moreover, it initially had less to do with key discoveries in anatomy, histology, and embryology (many of which did not take place until the mid-nineteenth century) than with the political, economic, and cultural agendas of the Enlightenment and post-revolutionary decades. Rather, it "*was* produced through endless micro-confrontations over power in the public and private spheres" (p. 193). Mary Robinson's *Pupil of Nature* is so fascinating precisely because it allows us to trace, in bizarre detail, how one such micro-confrontation was played out and dubiously resolved in the public and private sphere of popular fiction. As even the barest plot summary makes clear, the novel does indeed undeniably contribute to the construction of a social discourse in which the natural body and sexual otherness become the defining standard. But it could also be said to gesture back, almost nostalgically, to an older model of gender as theatrical construct or masquerade. It likewise makes clear that the biology of incommensurability, in spite of its own rhetoric, remains intimately tied up with material inequality, and testifies to the high price exacted, in the form of psychic trauma and residual melancholy, by the cultural mandate to produce sexed bodies.

At the outset, it should be noted that the general figure type of the cross-dressed female featured in *Walsingham* was by no means the invention of the author. *Walsingham*'s transvestite character has literary roots in such scandalous eighteenth-century treatments as Charlotte Cibber Charke's autobiographical *Narrative* and Fielding's *The Female Husband*, as well as in the English theater's old and uniquely popular tradition of both male and female cross-dressing (just as Robinson's own autobiography belongs to a popular genre of sometimes scurrilous, sometimes sentimental accounts of actresses' lives and loves that goes back to the Restoration).[4] Robinson herself had played male roles with notable success on stage, and even came near to playing that role privately at a crucial point in her life. As she recalls in her *Memoirs*, the Prince of Wales was kept on such a short leash by his disapproving father that his desire to bring about an initial private meeting with her hatched some wild plots: "A proposal was now made that I should meet his Royal Highness at his apartments, in the disguise of male attire. I was accustomed to perform in that dress, and the Prince had seen me (I believe) in the character of 'the Irish Widow.' The indelicacy of such a step, as well as the danger of detection, made me shrink from the proposal" (*Memoirs*, 2:50). The underlying rationale here is amusing: It's wrong, and besides it wouldn't work. But the ambiguity of this response runs through the novel Robinson wrote fifteen years afterward: Is drag unnatural because it constitutes a crime against nature, or because it is simply over the long haul an unsustainable and hence dangerous act?

The Pupil of Nature suggests that such an act can at least be sustained for eighteen years, not to mention four volumes. Specifically, the novel's eponymous hero and narrator, Walsingham Ainsworth, loses both his rightful inheritance and his future bride through the machinations of his cousin Sir Sidney Aubrey, a girl brought up and presented to the world as a boy. Her mother, Lady Aubrey, did this to keep the Welsh family estate, Glenowen, under their control. The girl's father, having died shortly before the birth of his only child, had stipulated that if the child was female, the bulk of his estate was to pass to the next living male relative. Lady Aubrey, by raising the girl abroad, in isolation, and with the help of a conniving governess, Mrs. Blagden, and then extracting an oath from her adolescent daughter to maintain the male disguise indefinitely, on pain of her own and her parent's disgrace, thus manages to hold on to her husband's fortune for a further eighteen years. But her plot begins to unravel when mother and daughter finally return to England, where Sir Sidney meets and falls helplessly in love with a man — her own supplanted and hostile cousin Walsingham, to be exact.

Walsingham, already smarting at the effects of Lady Aubrey's dislike (a dislike dictated by a guilty conscience over her treatment of her only sister's orphaned child), resents the dazzling impression that the Continental polish and education of the newly returned family heir make on everyone. Walsingham is an individual of brooding personality and awkward behavior, and he reacts with puzzled distrust to the affection his cousin shows him. His worst suspicions, and his own firm conviction that he is destined to be the continual object of inexplicable family persecution, are finally confirmed: he flees the estate in fury and embarks on a catastrophic series of adventures in Bristol, London, and Bath, when he discovers Sidney interfering repeatedly to alienate the affections of, first, his tutor's sister, Isabella Hanbury, whom he has grown up expecting to marry, and then of other women he encounters in the course of his ill-fated peregrinations. The narrator is naturally unable to understand this behavior as Sidney's desperate attempt to make sure that, if she cannot have Walsingham, no one else will. When Isabella, who has been let in on Sidney's secret and gladly resigns any interest she might have had in the narrator, announces her intention to travel alone with "Sir Aubrey" to the Continent, Walsingham can only interpret this as proof that his libertine cousin has made her his mistress. The life-threatening illness of Lady Aubrey, and then of Sidney, brings all the characters back to the estate, ushering in the denouement that reestablishes the natural order through Sidney's unmasking. Mrs. Blagden, the governess who started out as Lady Aubrey's domestic accomplice and has since become her blackmailer, dies a grotesque death at Walsingham's hands, leaving the remorseful Lady Aubrey free to renounce her claims on her daughter, rather than watch

Sidney waste hopelessly away as the result of a psychosomatic illness caused by her guilt and frustrated passion.

"Hear, hear it then, Walsingham, and let the agonizing confession touch your heart to pity — I have no son! the wretched, the ill-fated Sidney is my daughter!"[5] Lady Aubrey then immediately proceeds with commendable sangfroid to practical matters: "The amiable Sidney has been educated in masculine habits; but every affection of her heart is beautifully feminine; heroic though tender; and constant, though almost hopeless. She will, nevertheless, demand some time to fashion her manners to the graces of her sex" (4: 388). This "refashioning" is subsequently effected with such promptness as to raise once again the possibility the novel has just gone to extraordinary lengths to discredit: taking on an unaccustomed sex is more or less akin to assuming another fashion or learning a new role. And within ten pages, Walsingham, reunited with his cousin on the Continent, is singing "the virtues, the heroic virtues of my transcendent Sidney!" (and soon-to-be wife). "Indeed, so completely is she changed, so purely gentle, so feminine in manners; while her mind still retains the energy of that richly-treasured dignity of feeling which are the effects of a masculine education, that I do not lament past sorrows, while my heart triumphs" (4: 398). Nature has finally triumphed along with the narrator, vanquishing "dissimulation" and representational vertigo through the apparently irrepressible instincts of maternal resignation and heterosexual desire. This victory having been effected, the novel then quickly pairs off or otherwise benevolently settles its whole supporting cast in the last two pages.

The plot by itself is remarkable enough; but the temporality and the narrative structure of the fiction's *sujet* lend it even odder twists. *The Pupil of Nature* is technically an epistolary novel: a short correspondence between Walsingham and Rosanna, an acquaintance he has made in Germany, prompts him to send her an account of his strange life, to explain to her the sources of the mysterious "dejection of mind" and "poisonous melancholy" that she and others have observed in him (1:10–11). The genesis of the account is thus rooted in the emotional dynamic of sentimental confidentiality, but also in an act of grotesque bodily violence. For Walsingham composes it while under the impression that the misfortunes of his life have culminated in his inadvertent murder of his cousin. Immediately after Lady Aubrey's revelation, which should have cleared everything up, the already gravely ill Sidney falls unconscious after Walsingham, instead of delivering to Sidney's attendant a requested vial of medicine, distractedly gives her the unmarked bottle of laudanum he has procured and kept with him for his own self-destruction. Curiously, rather than sticking around the estate to see if his cousin actually dies, the near-mad narrator is precipitously hustled to the Continent, where he is wandering gloomily around in ignorance of Sidney's miraculous recovery when Rosanna meets him. Meanwhile, Sidney is in Switzerland, undergoing her feminizing metamorphosis, upon completion of which Walsingham is informed of her survival and reunited with her.

In other words, the text of the novel, which is also the story of the narrator's life, is fashioned during precisely that interval in which Sidney's refashioning as female occurs offstage — and whether Sidney is actually alive during this interval seems oddly irrelevant to narrator and author. Indeed, in terms of the novel's psychosexual dynamics, this state of suspended animation her character is placed in during the stage of narrative generation literalizes the physical finality of gender assumption: the transvestite Sidney must "die" as a male, or at least be confined to the passivity of unconscious immobility, in order to be reborn female.

Furthermore, this near-death effected by Walsingham's vengefully operating unconscious places his cousin under a condition of double erasure: during the temporal interval of the text's composition, her physical existence is uncertain, and narratively the crucial story of her refashioning, the transcendent Sidney's traumatic *Aufhebung* into adult female subjectivity, remains *untold*. What we get is a kind of Portrait of a Lady, or What It Takes to Make a Lady — without the Lady, as if the essence of womanliness, and the process required to refine this raw material into the finished product "Woman," were not finally textualizable from the inside.[6] Womanliness makes itself felt precisely through its effects on observers. Hence, when a female body refuses to represent femininity, that refused assignment triggers a general crisis of apprehension in the empire of signs that gender differentiation underwrites. This is the moral of the story we *are* told.

The master plot of *Walsingham* is thus the plot of a belatedly won male mastery. The narrator, presenting his own life story in the spirit of an exemplary case study, starts with infancy: "As it is to the events of my childhood that I owe those indelible prejudices which have attended me, from hour to hour, each darker than the former, I will not omit the slightest incident that may serve to prove, how strongly the earliest impressions take hold on the senses" (1: 21). What Walsingham's account "proves" is how effectively the natural powers of prehension are indeed steered by "prejudice" or social construction. Even in looking at another body, we see what we expect to see, reading that body not just through its attire and deportment but, even more tellingly, through the name, title, education, property, and past invested in it. Even before her birth, Sidney's existence is completely overcoded, for everyone, by one socially crucial signifier, namely, that of the long-awaited and overdue family "heir." Indeed, the narrator recounts his childhood as the story of a traumatic expulsion from Paradise into a brutish world of inequality and indifference, an expulsion occasioned not so much by his cousin's actual birth as by his own prior introduction to the material significance of this one crucial term, and to how social processes of denomination and entitlement operate to class and classify even infant bodies.

As long as Lady Aubrey and her husband remain childless, Walsing-ham, the only child of Lady Aubrey's dead sister, reigns unchallenged as His Majesty the Baby: "I became the little sovereign of Glenowen; every wish was anticipated, every word was law: I traversed the domains of my patron, uncontrolled, exulting, happy!" (1: 50). But the child's traumatic dethronement commences with his aunt's anxiously awaited pregnancy, and is completed after his kindly uncle has died in a riding accident, his aunt has departed to bear and raise Sidney in France, and he has been left, isolated and neglected, to the care of the estate's loutish domestics. "Noth-ing was [now] talked of but the little stranger, the young Lord of Glen-owen, who was expected to be more wise and more beautiful than any thing mortal. . . . My little bosom swelled with grief, while the bath, the paddock, the plantations, and the ponies, were by anticipation bestowed on the expected heir of Glenowen, and, for the first moment in my life, I began to feel the miseries of dependence" (1: 56–57). Such laments dra-matize an originary infant encounter with lack: the first perceived experi-ence of maternal insufficiency coincides with a rudely abrupt introduction to a social order organized around the conjunction of male body, family name, and inherited property that Sidney is predestined to incorporate. For the narrator, this traumatic encounter together with the ensuing ne-glect "implanted the first roots of that melancholy which has never ceased to be the prominent characteristic of my nature" (1: 70).

This resentful melancholy reinforces in the narrator that curious astig-matism which renders him unable really to *see* the cause of his misery. As early as his ninth year, when he meets his cousin for the one and only time during his childhood, the narrator receives intimations from a suspicious domestic that all is not as it seems in the Aubrey household; but it simply never occurs to him, then or later, to view his rival's confusing behavior as anything other than the use and abuse of the prerogatives to which Sidney's status as "heir" entitles "him." The only close physical description of Sidney is given of him/her as an infant, at a point when flowing dark ringlets and a soft complexion are sexually undifferentiated traits. Later, when Walsingham encounters the adult Sidney, his description is mediated through others' laudatory reports ("Born to embellish society, Sir Sidney comes among us like a constellation") and steered by his own jealous interest in whether his cousin has acquired the education and character that would make him worthy of the high station he was "born to."

To his own chagrin, he must concede that his rival does indeed conform to all preconceived expectations (preconceived inasmuch as they literally predate and supersede the biological outcome of Sidney's conception): "Sir Sidney Aubrey was exactly the being whom Isabella had described — handsome, polite, accomplished, engaging, and unaffected. He sang, he danced, he played on the mandolin, and spoke the Italian and French languages with the fluency of a native." But in addition to displaying these graces, which could be ascribed to either a male or a female education, Sidney also proves to be "expert at all manly exercises; a delightful poet; and a fascinating companion" (1: 269). The narrator views and presents his cousin to readers not in terms of physical appearance (other than "handsome") but rather in terms of "polish" and self-assured sociability, the lack of which seals his own marginalization. Hence, even after Sidney begins behaving with inexplicable inconsistency, alienating the affections of the women Walsingham covets and making them his own confidantes and allies, the narrator accounts for this ambiguity, not without satisfaction, by exchanging one descriptive category of conventional, recognizable masculinity for another: the perfect young gentleman has turned out after all to be a "gay, capricious, trifling *libertine*." Sidney's revealing declaration, "Wherever I go, I make a woman my companion; whatever I meditate, I consult a woman: in short, when I abandon the sex, I must cease to live" (1: 275), though nothing less than the literal truth, can thus only be interpreted by Walsingham as a typical rake's credo.[7]

In short, what the narrator's astigmatic occlusion of physical detail makes clear is that it is not bodies in the flesh, described in their corporeal specificity, that are the object of inspection in this novel; rather, it is the significatory categories that they embody, by which they are invested, predicated, and assigned a social place in "the eyes of the world." The existence of a Sidney questions all these categories precisely because "he" challenges the conventional terms of what Michael Moon and Eve Sedgwick, in an article on celebrity and transvestism, have called "*the representational contract* between one's body and one's world."[8] Transvestism, as Moon and Sedgwick point out, offers one potential means for the individual to renegotiate that contract. But Walsingham (the character, as opposed perhaps to *Walsingham* the text) is interested not in renegotiation, but rather in reconfirmation of *his* fixed place as recognized, entitled man among men in a world already marked by a lethal representational flux. Although Walsingham (echoing Robinson's sentiments) argues vehemently for the abolition of class and hierarchical distinctions and for the precedence of merit over birth, he cannot dispense with the fundamental organizing distinction of incommensurable sexual difference. In this respect, the novelist follows the pattern of other liberal polemicists and writers of the revolutionary and postrevolutionary decades, for whom the classic social contract argument for the revision of the old order did not countermand but rather dovetailed with this new "biology of incommensurability."[9] *La petite différence* turns out to be the big difference, the difference par excellence that underwrites the narrator's ability to distinguish, to distinguish himself, and to assume a distinguished position within a social and semiotic field in which both he and the now-identified object of his desire can finally be accommodated as bivalent terms that complement, rather than cancel out each other.

Prior to this felicitous resolution, however, Walsingham wanders cluelessly through a world pervaded by a creeping miasma of misrecognition, of which his own blindness is only one element. From the hidden nucleus of Sidney's secret a virus of contagious destabilization seems to spread out, for the use of the transvestite motif in the novel is directly linked to the more general epistemological breakdown of social semantics portrayed in it. Walsingham labels himself "the victim of appearances," and in a sense this appellation could be applied to most of the work's figures. In the world of this text, simulation is inseparable from dissimulation and "personality" gets read as a variety of strategic impersonations. The only character in the novel endowed with the status of infallible moral arbiter is named Mr. Optic, whose moniker underscores the equation of corporeal clear-sightedness and ethical perspicacity. But Optic is an allegorical fragment, as out of place in *Walsingham* as Squire Allworthy would be in *Vathek*, because he constitutes an isolated trace of that dream of semiotic transparency the text can invoke but, given the ubiquitous scotomization the rest of its characters labor under, not itself envision.

Although Sidney constitutes the epitome of corporeal impersonation, the narrator's story, too, once he has left his Welsh home, unfolds primarily in the mode of a tragicomedy of mistaken identities: he is repeatedly arrested or suspected as a result of being taken for someone else. He in turn compounds the confusion by continually committing the same mistakes with others (or with other things, as in the case of the laudanum he hands on to Sidney) and then absconding from a compromising situation before he can explain himself. This confusion climaxes in fratricide when, at the end of the novel, Walsingham fatally injures a mysterious highwayman who has been dogging his steps, and for whom he himself has been mistaken, only to discover that the man is his own illegitimate half-brother, the product of a short-lived affair between his father and the hated Mrs. Blagden (see 4: 348–69). Walsingham's remorse over this death is explicable in terms of the novel's psychodynamic structure, for Edward Blagden is clearly his own double, an even more dispossessed, marginalized, and hence more dangerously peripatetic and rootless version of himself. Walsingham may be a poor relation and Sidney a transvestite heir, but neither of them must live out the stigma of incorporating that particular clash of fleshly facticity and patriarchal social order signified by the word "bastard," and by the ensuing denial of access to the name of the father. In this sense the legitimate/illegitimate opposition constitutes a cultural moment of corporeal differentiation prior perhaps even to compulsory sexual differentiation — the "first cut" inflicted by a social system in the ongoing process of inscribing naturally fungible individual bodies by granting or refusing to grant them recognition. Given the operation of this imperative, as it is reproduced in the text, Edward Blagden, a character who seems to be hastily inserted into the novel only to have his doubly disgraceful existence revealed on his deathbed, functions structurally as a scapegoat for the ongoing tension between social signification and recalcitrant bodies that would otherwise discharge itself on both Walsingham and Sidney.

The historical prototype for the sort of dizzying interpretational disequilibrium *The Pupil of Nature* incorporates is of course the masquerade (a social and literary locus that, as Terry Castle has shown, is linked to eighteenth-century transvestite subcultures). Hence, it is not surprising that the work contains two major masquerade episodes, even though, by the mid-1790s, the popularity of organized masquerades had long since peaked. Castle has examined how, in some eighteenth-century novels, the masquerade, with the carnivalesque freedom it provides to act out and try on unfamiliar identities, functions as a crucial site of *éclaircissement*.[10] However, in Robinson's hands the masquerade motif has grown not just superannuated but morbid, and even sadistic, since its setting condenses the malice and corruption of the urban beau monde, as well as the threat of corporeal dissimulation and of the communal crisis of indifferentiation to which the novel's characters are continually subjected. To the disgusted narrator, commenting on the masked balls, the majority of celebrants, cloaked in their basic black dominoes, "presented a sombre similarity, which levelled all forms and features to one gloomy mass of insipidity" (3: 39), and those participants who can be identified are recognizable precisely because they have selected disguises grotesquely out of keeping with their true character and appearance. Furthermore, in *Walsingham*, masquerades, far from contributing to improved understanding or resolution, intensify frustration or usher in tragedy. For instance, the narrator's first masked ball ends when his frantic pursuit through the crowd of a figure he thinks is Isabella is arrested by the "most unzephyr-like hand" of a loud and portly Venus who proceeds to make laughingstocks of them both by berating him for tearing off one of her tinfoil wings in passing. After this, the narrator recovers his self-respect by foiling a dissolute nobleman's attempt to abduct the innocent Amelia Woodford, Walsingham's London landlady's daughter, whom he has accompanied to the ball — but with the result that he must go into hiding the next morning to escape the nobleman's wrath (see 3: 28–50).

In addition, his good deed proves to have even more uncomfortable consequences. Amelia, to whom Walsingham has been attracted primarily because she reminds him uncannily of Isabella, has fallen in love with her mother's romantically melancholy boarder. Shortly thereafter, she accompanies him to another masked ball, where Walsingham has again gone in search of Isabella. Instead, he meets an insultingly persecuting figure, who turns out to be Sidney; although the narrator is not in a position to appreciate the ironies of encountering a disguised transvestite, Sidney's provoking assurance that, even if he should find Isabella, she will never be his, drive him mad. Furious (as well as drunk), he again glimpses the costumed female figure whom he had earlier taken for Isabella. Catching up with her, he discovers that the lovely lady will neither unmask nor speak to him. But she does not refuse his attentions. Bundling her into a coach, he dashes with her to his lodgings, where they fall into bed together (the lady still apparently veiled). When he wakes up to find that the face on the pillow belongs to a wretched and remorseful Amelia Woodford — who, in a rash attempt to wring some soft words out of the object of her hopeless attachment, has exchanged her disguise at the second masked ball for the costume of the female figure she observed Walsingham pursuing at the first masquerade — morning-after chagrin acquires a new meaning (3: 72–95).

It is an extraordinary episode, one that would not be out of place in, say, a medieval fabliau or even in earlier eighteenth-century satire, but it contrasts jarringly with the generally decorous tonal and descriptive range characteristic of later eighteenth-century women's fiction. Of course, a novel featuring a transvestite protagonist has already clearly placed itself beyond that range. In addition, the episode does nothing more than "flesh out" the century's fears and fantasies about the masquerade's transgressive appeal, the putative encouragement the setting offered to "forget oneself" temporarily, throw the usual behavioral constraints overboard, and, at worst, embark on an orgy of anonymous coupling. However, more than anything, the incident functions to foreground once again to what an extent bodies are phantasmatically fungible, marked by the place they have been preassigned in the beholder's representational economy, even (or precisely) in a moment that seems to guarantee the maximum of unmediated corporeal transparency.

The episode also suggests specifically to what an extent the masquerade of womanliness makes women interchangeable units in the eyes of the paradigmatically male beholder — even one operating within a representational economy that has been turned upside down by the forces of dissimulation and destabilization. Amelia, who finally dies, constitutes the quintessential female victim of this destabilized significatory economy. And yet, this World Turned Upside Down, whose exemplary locus is the masked ball and whose exemplary figure is the transvestite Sir Sidney, also takes on the aspect of a *paradis des femmes*, in which events are generally precipitated by the force of female desire. Indeed, the novel portrays women as more masculinely rakish than men; during his brief, disastrous sojourns in Bath and London, the narrator is thoroughly fleeced by a circle of female gamblers, and subjected to the aggressive attentions of old and young female admirers. One, the aged Lady Amaryllis, after inviting him with a leer back to her estate to enjoy "the sporting season," even tries later at the first masked ball to bundle *him* off in her coach. In addition to bearing the brunt of Sidney's lovingly active persecution, which determines the whole course of his wanderings, Walsingham must also cope with Amelia Woodford's fall into manipulative wantonness, with Isabella's apparently hardened pride in being Sidney's "companion," and with the lively Lady Arabella, who, in the last volume, alternately taunts and blandishes him into a half-hearted, strangely befuddled proposal. Unable to protect himself against the sex he desperately wants to believe requires his protection, the narrator is continually placed in a frustrating and comical position of prudish passivity that might be characterized as more typically feminine.

The narrator's overdetermined vulnerability is connected to a general breakdown of masculine, and specifically paternal, authority at work in *The Pupil of Nature*. In this vacuum, women rule. And the rule of women, both within and outside the domestic sphere, is connected, as already shown, to that carnivalesque disordering of semantic, sexual, and social axioms characteristic of the World Turned Upside Down that the masquerade emblematizes.[11] Although paternal authority is to a certain extent represented by benevolent tutors and advisers, fathers themselves are practically absent from the novel. Sir Edward Aubrey's death sets up the preconditions for his daughter's parodic fulfillment of his last wishes, and Walsingham's own father, finally revealed to be Mrs. Blagden's seducer, simply abandons him after his mother's death. Mothers, on the other hand, are very much present, even if the power they exercise, especially within kinship systems, has been inherited or usurped from men. The text valorizes an ideal of self-sacrificing maternity which its characters fail spectacularly to live up to, since its plot is actually steered by the machinations of a matched set of monstrous mothers, Lady Aubrey and her accomplice and ultimate blackmailer, the governess Mrs. Blagden, through whose perverse pedagogy Sidney is formed in the requisite male mold.

Indeed, in the novel, female power is inseparable from, and ultimately seems to rest on, the potentially monstrously absolute and abusable power of the mother as the primary formative agent of the infant body and psyche. Walsingham himself, as already mentioned, associates that traumatic early experience of social marginalization, which has left him locked in a depressive position with insufficient maternal solicitude: "I had never known a mother: I had been thrown on the wide world, like a garden flower, transplanted to a desert; all around me was barren, or overrun with weeds! . . . I had never tasted the balmy kiss of maternal fondness, except when I was incapable of appreciating its value" (1: 145). As this and other similar narratorial laments attest, *The Pupil of Nature* incorporates a contemporary pedagogical discourse in which motherhood is invested with a new importance, as a force of (at the very least, preliminary) acculturation and individuation. Through the initial maternal intervention the child can be decisively placed or displaced in relation to the larger paternal symbolic order that underwrites the stability of representation, lines of inheritance, and sexual identity. And woe to the child that has been placed, through maternal neglect, illegitimacy, or systematic inculcation, at odds with that order.

At this point, we might pause to consider what motivates the curiously schizophrenic structure of this text. *The Pupil of Nature* obeys the imperative, loosely inscribed in its own subtitle, of enforcing a realignment of body and sign, nature and culture, invoking, at its outer limits, the utopia of a paternal *but* benevolent representational economy that can assign every body its rightful, differentiated place without that assignment inscribing itself in the individual flesh and psyche as wound, stigma, exclusion, or lack. The major portion of the narrative, however, unleashes, with undeniable *Schadenfreude* and manic relish, a patently unnatural dystopia of semantic instability, female misrule, and perpetual masquerade. The novel's split structure of aggression — figured by a female who usurps and uses a male persona and privileges, primarily against men — and belated deference to the need for containment itself in fact mimics the structure of the "masquerade of womanliness," as first described in Joan Reviere's classic case study.[12] According to Reviere, such a masquerade occurs when a woman uses an exaggerated display of femininity — coquettishness, helplessness, deference, maternal solicitude — to fend off the retribution she fears for desiring and acting out the prerogatives of masculinity — professional competency, aggression, the chance to compete with and triumph over men. As Reviere admitted, this phenomenon complicates any attempt to "draw the line between genuine womanliness and the 'masquerade'" (p. 37), i.e., to distinguish between substantive sexual identity and the mimicry of a social construct. Theorists working in Reviere's wake have continued to develop the thesis that the masquerade figures the constitutive aporetic structure of femininity itself. They suggest that femininity takes shape first and foremost as spectacle (its privileged register that of the visual, of *Schein*), as a dramatization, aimed at both entrapping and securing the male gaze, of "the sexual division [that] is the crucial articulation of symbolic division. . . . The masquerade is a representation of femininity but then femininity is representation, the representation of the woman."[13]

Measuring this equation against the roles Robinson played in her own life and in the public life of her era, we can see more clearly how this particular author could have written a text riven with the very contradictions of bodily constitution and representation that it explores. Moon and Sedgwick have underscored how "our puritanical rage against representation itself" redounds on those who do the work, "the wearing, wasting, perhaps necessary, in any case *exacted* labor," of representing culture to itself, specifically through embodying (or, as in the case of the fat woman, embodying the opposite of) a culture's normative body types (p. 29). In her earlier life Robinson belonged to one category that has, to a disproportionate extent, borne the brunt of that puritanical rage. Actresses have historically been lavishly rewarded but also stigmatized for making the masquerade of womanliness their business, thereby flaunting both the hold the display of desirable femininity has on the gaze and the artificial, manipulable, reproducible nature of that display as precisely "unnatural" representation. In turn, they pay for the resentment their de-essentializing role-playing arouses by being subjected to a re-essentializing refusal to distinguish between the public and the private female self, when the professional versatility displayed on stage is equated with offstage promiscuity. Robinson's career was caught and ruined by a particularly vicious application of this equation. This left her painfully well situated to appreciate both the penalties as well as the rewards of publicly representing womanliness.

On the one hand, the *Memoirs* attests strikingly to what a desperately needed source of narcissistic gratification, as well as income, acting offered Robinson. When she discusses her profession in the *Memoirs*, Robinson generally sounds like the pro she was, one who learned swiftly to master opening-night jitters and a huge range of roles, and to glory in contact with colleagues of Garrick's and Sheridan's caliber. On the other hand, her autobiography also shows, much more ambiguously, how its author both gloried in and shrank from being in the public eye. In fact, the *Memoirs* has been derided for displaying traces of ridiculously disingenuous personal vanity. That derision attests to the uneasiness aroused by a woman whose awareness and management of her appearance were obviously so keen as to often seem to verge on a dispassionate appraisal of herself as visual object.

For instance, Robinson seems intensely sensitive to how even everyday dress functions as costume, and how costume, in turn, functions on- *and* offstage as *the* signifying metonymy of the individual female's substance. The author of the *Memoirs*, with a corporeal specificity so notably lacking in *Walsingham*, repeatedly includes extended descriptions of her own dress on important occasions. Nothing more clearly illustrates the sometimes dizzying possibilities of phantasmatic emancipation from one's natural state that costume holds out than the fact that, as Robinson delicately commented to her readers, she made her debut in the role of Juliet, wearing "pale pink satin, trimmed with crepe, richly spangled with silver, . . . some months advanced in that situation which afterwards . . . made me a second time a mother" (1: 189). But to play to the prying gaze, albeit in order to deceive or subdue it, entails the risk of inciting it. Even innocuousness can backfire: "The first time I went to Ranelagh my habit was so singularly plain and quaker-like, that all eyes were fixed upon me" (1: 95). It is difficult to determine whether consternation, gratification, or simple detached appraisal shapes such a statement. In a later episode, when Robinson remembers how, at the Pantheon, she was "disconcerted" by the "fixed stare" of several "men of fashion" who followed her about, asking bystanders who she was, she reports: "My manner and confusion plainly evinced that I was not accustomed to the gaze of impertinent high breeding" (1: 98). Clear evidence of having made an impression coexists with discomfort; but, most tellingly, the author herself describes her response from the exterior, the point of view of a spectator, in terms of the effect it produced.

Robinson spent the rest of her life as the victim and prisoner of that gaze of high breeding she had not only played to but internalized. Never did it operate more destructively than in the wake of the scandal that left her marked as Perdita, and inaugurated her career as author under the sign of "lost" womanhood. Journalists and satirists, as well as common gossip, reveled, with an avidity anything other than "high-bred," in the spectacle of this celebrity's fall. For instance, a contemporary satire, entitled "Florizel and Perdita" (meant to be sung to the tune of "O Polly Is a Sad Slut") proclaims:

> A tender Prince, ah, well-a-day!
> Of years not yet a Score,
> Had late his poor Heart stol'n away
> By one of many more;
>
> As many more (at least) she is,
> As might have been the Mother
> (You'd say it if you saw her Phiz)
> Perhaps of such an other.
>
> Her Cheeks were vermeil'd o'er with Red,
> Her Breast Enamelled White,
> And nodding Feathers deck'd her Head,
> A Piece for Candle Light.
>
> Sometimes she'd play the Tragic Queen,
> Sometimes the Peasant poor,
> Sometimes she'd step behind the Scenes,
> And there she'd play the W——.
>
> Two Thousand Pounds, a princely Sight
> For doing just no more,
> Than what is acted every Night
> By ev'ry Sister W——.[14]

This endearing squib is interesting precisely because it aims to hit the public nerve by activating most of the anxieties about female power, inherently theatrical womanliness, and the at once pathetically exposed and diabolically dissimulating female body that Robinson herself later incorporated in *Walsingham*. The actress, though in actuality only twenty-one when she met the prince, is nonetheless presented as a predatory, even incestuous crone. Belittled for displaying signs of age, she is subsequently belittled for resorting to artificial means to efface them. Her profession likewise tells against her: the common cosmetics and ornaments she uses to participate in the masquerade of womanliness are also the tools of her trade — the actress's trade, but also the prostitute's. The satire implies that the two businesses are fundamentally coextensive, since both are based on the ability to enact over and over a charade of enhanced, submitting femininity. Among the woman judged guilty of wanting to appeal to (or simply appealing to) the male gaze, the professional actress, and the "working girl," the distinctions blur, because "playing the W — [hore]" clearly entails some of the same performative skills and the same double bind that "playing the W — [oman]" does.

In the print sold to accompany this satire, Robinson is shown standing grandly in the middle of a circle of boxes labeled "carmine," "whitewash," "pomatum," and "dentifrice." The actress is clad in Welsh national costume (born in Bristol of Welsh parentage, Robinson favored this garb). With a tall crowned hat perched on her already impressive tower of powdered hair, she looms over an enamored prince, who looks no less foolish for being clothed in classical armor. Overtones of the dominatrix and the hypocritical woman of letters, who uses her intellectual pretensions to cloak her amorous knowledgeability, merge in the female figure that grasps what looks like a long staff in one hand while with the other she holds out to her adorer a book entitled *Essay on Man*. Other scurrilous prints circulated at the time likewise emphasize the specter of unnatural female domination and petticoat government that the figure of Mrs. Robinson seemed to conjure up in the public eye. In one, Robinson is shown riding in a carriage drawn by a pair of goats, to which the prince plays driver, and Lord North, who should have prevented this demeaning arrangement, snores obliviously atop the vehicle. In another, which comments on the actress's supposed later affair with Charles Fox, the lovers are pictured driving in a chaise; she holds the reins and flourishes a whip, and he leans back wearing a stuporous, vaguely tormented expression.

But another penny print circulated at the time furnishes perhaps the oddest and, for the purposes of this analysis, most intriguing testimony to the role of virulent phobic object women like Robinson took on in the English mass-culture imagination during the revolutionary decades (see

illustration). In what may well be intended to mimic the layout of a playing card, say, the king or queen of hearts, it features a central figure, split
and conjoined in the middle, compounded of the half-face portraits of a
bare-breasted Robinson and the Prince of Wales. Down on one side a
coroneted George III comments, "Oh, My Son, My Son"; above him the
Hanoverian motto "Ich dien" ("I serve"), appended to the family's three-
plumed crest, comments ironically on the prince's amorous enthrallment.
On the lady's side, a tiny antlered face identified as "*King of Cuckolds
Robin-son*" supports, on its horns, another crest, consisting of a plate
bearing the heads of his wife's three most famous conquests.

Clearly, a public drama of the mourned wayward son is being icono-
graphically enacted here, one of a misled youth who, through his unwor-
thy entanglement, threatens to blight not just his own future, but the
country's as well. Likewise, in robbing the monarch of his son, the Robin-
sons, commoners and habitués of the demimonde, are challenging not just
paternal but national authority. What really lends the print its crudely
effective charge, however, is the transgressive sexual amalgamation of the
hermaphroditic central figure, its power to affront condensed and inten-

sified in the ample female breast that protrudes above the otherwise fully clothed lady's ruffled bodice. This defrocking of course works in the first instance to expose Robinson as a woman who will defrock herself for the highest bidder. However, the dominant sexual feature, the breast, also hints at the power of the enthralling, infantilizing phallic mother. Moreover, the men's heads piled on the plate associate Robinson with another exhibitionistic female performer and, not coincidentally, traditional prototype of the castrating woman, Salome. The print thereby suggests (and suggests all the more fearfully by not providing explicit captions for this part of its message) that the prince, rather than being viewed as having "come into his manhood" with this his first affair, has surrendered some portion of it. At any rate, the illustration's at once desexed and bisexed central figure manifestly incorporates those anxieties about the breakdown of the cosmic order, which included a powerful latent hysteria over the blurring of gender roles, as well as about the distinctions upon which the class order, lines of inheritance, and the separation of public and private interests are based, that the publicly flaunted mésalliance of royal heir and actress obviously triggered.

In looking at this print, as well as at the masquerade milieu and transvestite protagonist of *The Pupil of Nature*, one could choose to insist on its transgressive appeal. For it would certainly be tempting to remain with the kind of currently popular reading by which (in the critical summation of Moon and Sedgwick) the "understanding of transvestism can take on a utopian tinge: as a denaturalizing and defamiliarizing exposure of the constructed character of *all* gender; as a translation of what are often compulsory gender behaviors to a caricatural, exciting, *chosen* plane of arbitrariness and free play" (p. 16). But in *Walsingham* the masquerade of gender simply does not transpire in a mode of the exuberantly carnivalesque, much less of the titillatingly bawdy.[15] This particular World Turned Upside Down presided over by a duo of monstrous mothers and a crossdressed Princess of Misrule ultimately constitutes not a funfair but a gothic nightmare for all of its participants, and most signally for its narrator, for whom the displacement, disorder, and disorganization that world celebrates represent merely the continuation of his own "natural" condition. Thus, to redress this prevailing disorder the transvestite's transgression, which epitomizes this disorder, is neither valenced as unilateral liberation nor simply dismissed as punishable perversion. Rather, it is *psychologized* as blockage — that is, as a temporary liberation purchased at the price of prolonged infantilization, a maternally imposed arrested development for *both* male and female.

Sidney's renunciation of masculine privilege thus anticipates the script of ontogenetic sexual development elaborated by the human sciences in the course of the nineteenth century, and given programmatic formulation by Freud in the *Three Essays on Sexuality*. In fact, the literary account prefigures the medico-psychiatric account in the most radical way, by grotesquely literalizing it. The pubescent girl, caught in a phase of development that, for males and females alike, is undifferentiatedly "phallic," confidently assumes the role of her mother's "little man," until adult femininity emerges via what is "actually a type of regression" — *Rückbildung* — "characterized by a new wave of repression." Freud concludes: "Es ist ein Stück männlichen Sexuallebens, was dabei der Verdrängung verfällt" ("It is a piece of masculine sexual life which thereby yields to repression").[16] In *Walsingham* femininity is likewise figured as a reversion entailing a necessary surrender — of unthinkingly assumed but nonetheless inappropriate prerogatives. The threateningly undifferentiated sexuality of the maiden must be fixed in adult femininity so that the female little man does not make permanently infantilized, impotent, displaced little men of the adult males around her.[17] Her loss, literalized in this novel in the near-death, disentitlement, and disentailment that accompany Sidney's belated accession to womanhood, constitutes their libidinal and financial gain, by reinstating that "signifying economy of masculinity" enforced by the exclusionary terms of her late father's will.[18]

The female power represented by maternity in *The Pupil of Nature* is, through a similar strategy, punitively checked and then positively revalenced in terms of the capacity for submissive resignation. The structural pairing of the two monstrous mothers, Lady Aubrey and Mrs. Blagden, allows this symmetrical resolution. At the end, the scheming governess is punished for her crimes against the class and "natural" order by a grotesquely carnal death, reminiscent of the brothel keeper Sinclair's end in *Clarissa*. In the same encounter that leads to her son's demise, she is panicked by Walsingham's pistol shot and jumps out a window. The narrator's last sight of her dwells on the spectacle of the corporeal disorder that she has disseminated and now graphically incorporates: "Almost every bone in her body was shattered by the concussion; — her arm and leg were broken — her skull fractured, and her flesh bruised, while the agonies of a violent death wrong her heart in every fibre" (4: 359–60). Lady Aubrey, by contrast, is belatedly rehabilitated by her decision to let her daughter drop her male persona, rather than see her waste hopelessly away. Hence, she is allowed to escape with a mere confession: "I am criminal, dreadfully criminal; — but I will lay open my heart, bleeding with contrition, before the tribunal of my Maker, and bow to the chastening scourge, till I have expiated my offences" (4: 373). The "instinct" of mother love thus finally wins out, however impeded or absent it may have been during the course of the novel; and its triumph assumes the exemplary form of a resignation by which the mother, surrendering her hold on her female child, re-signs her in the very act of designating her as not-male and reassigning her the roles of soon-to-be woman and wife.[19]

So, by the end of the novel, the hasty unveiling and reveiling of Sidney as the absent but systemically crucial Key Signifier of sexual difference have epistemologically stabilized the universe of misrecognition in which the novel's characters have wandered. And yet nature itself, the work's master sign, somehow remains a slippery and bivalent notion. It is never made completely clear in *Walsingham* whether the novel's subtitle implies an originary condition or a pedagogical project. Sometimes it seems to function as a shorthand reference to Jacobin determinism's emphasis on how the individual will be decisively shaped by environmental factors, especially during the formative periods of infancy and adolescence. Hence, Walsingham can lament his lack of "that resisting quality, which imposes self-denial, even where our passions and our interests impel us on to mischief. But I was the pupil of nature: my mind was permitted to form its bent, before I had judgment to discriminate the paths which led to reputation or dishonour. . . . I had no prospect of happiness; and a perpetual scene of sorrow disheartened me, till fortitude and hope seemed weary of the contest" (1: 252). On this level, the author actually denaturalizes an older concept of nature.

Yet Robinson obviously stops short of a complete deconstruction of the terms she sets out to problematize. By the end of the novel, "nature," formerly annexed to a "perpetual scene of sorrow," has, like maternity, apparently been rehabilitated. Taking leave from "those trifling vicious reptiles whom you have met with during the progress of my disastrous story," Walsingham proclaims: "If they continue to triumph over the children of worth and genius, it will only prove that, in this undefinable sphere, where the best and wisest cannot hope for happiness, the *demons of art* are permitted to oppress with wrongs, while they lift the empty brow of arrogance and pride above the illustrious pupils of GENIUS, TRUTH, and NATURE!" (4: 401). Fittingly, the character who has presented his life story as one exemplifying the trials of the doubly motherless child remains in his own words a "pupil" and "child," but one who can finally define his place within "this undefinable sphere" through a strategy of affiliation that makes both nature and him members of an abstract family of personified symbolic values.

By the terms of the narrator's final judgment, "NATURE" has belatedly taken its place on the side of the angels by being pitted against the worldly *"demons of art"* — meaning apparently, in the first instance, hypocrisy, social pretension, falsity. Where, however, does this antinomy leave this text qua work of art? The category of "art" it belongs to may be debatable, but *it* surely has some demons driving it: can we therefore employ the description its transvestite heroine applies to herself, and label it a "monster of dissimulation"? If nothing else, the narrative has certainly carried on its own pronominal masquerade with the reader, pending the hasty terminological tidying-up that re-predicates Sir Sidney as "daughter" and apotheosizes "nature" as "NATURE." Linked, moreover, to this rather malicious if entertaining masquerade are the spectacular, and sometimes seemingly gratuitous, violence of the novel, as well as an excess of melancholia that it cannot finally completely absorb.

This disfiguring excess of both violence and melancholia remains as symptom of the text's irresolvable uneasiness about figuration — as a process by which the raw material of bodies takes on socially and sexually recognizable contours, and by which linguistic articulation is aligned with modes of representation. For in this text language itself seems to serve as the carrier of a primal desolation and isolation it inscribes in its user: Walsingham's depressive subjectivity is shaped by his traumatic childhood lesson in what the word "heir" means for those to whom it does not apply, and in turn shapes a narrative that pendulates largely within an affective range extending from sullen dejection to suicidal frenzy. Robinson's *Memoirs* in fact contains a scene of primal language acquisition which is in keeping with this view, when the author describes how her own daughter first "blessed [her] ears with the articulation of words."

The circumstance made a forcible and indelible impression on my mind. It was a clear moonlight evening; the infant was in the arms of her nursery maid; she was dancing her up and down, and was playing with her; her eyes were fixed upon the moon, to which she pointed with her small fore-finger; — on a sudden a cloud passed over it, and the child, with a slow falling of her hand, articulately sighed, "all gone!" This had been a customary expression with her maid, whenever the infant wanted any thing which it was deemed prudent to withhold or to hide from her. These little nothings will appear insignificant to the common reader; but to the parent whose heart is ennobled by sensibility, they will become matters of important interest. (1: 169–70)

This elegiac scenario invokes, however sentimentally, an entry into language that marks the elegiac mode itself as the founding form of linguistic expressivity, since this entry is activated by the recognition and internalization of lack.[20] The natural world naturally withholds; the social world also, whether protectively or punitively, withholds. Operating in tandem, they imprint in the child an understanding of loss, of authority as the agency of deprivation, that is acknowledged in the first articulate sigh. Growing up — at least as one grows up in *The Pupil of Nature* — the child will find this primal loss consolidated by a series of deprivations, dependences, resignations, and confrontations with the lethal reality of "all gone." The body count in *Walsingham* is simply horrific — perhaps not surprising in a narrative that climaxes in an act of bodily self-abandonment. One character accedes to the position of being cut out, "dis-incorporating" the masculine identity she has grown up with, so that another may finally be enabled to "cut a figure" as full-fledged gentleman. But learning to cut a figure in this text always appears to involve some infliction of loss on someone. For, whatever brief moment of triumph the narrator may enjoy at its end, *The Pupil of Nature*, taken in total, also consists of an articulate sigh, as well as an at times numbingly monotonous howl of rage, directed against a world in which representation itself finally seems to be a no-win game.

REFERENCE MATTER

Notes

KELLY AND MÜCKE; *Body and Text in the Eighteenth Century*

1. Jean Starobinski, "The Natural and Literary History of Bodily Sensation," in *Fragments for a History of the Human Body*, ed. Michel Feher (New York: Zone Books, 1983), pt. II, p. 369.

2. Jacques Lacan, "The Mirror Stage as Formative of the Function of the I as Revealed in Psychoanalytic Experience," in idem, *Ecrits*, trans. Alan Sheridan (New York: Norton, 1979), pp. 1–7.

3. Julia Kristeva, "L'abjet d'amour," *Tel Quel* 91 (Summer 1982): 17–32; and idem, *The Powers of Horror: An Essay on Abjection*, trans. Leon S. Roudiez (New York: Columbia University Press, 1982).

4. Judith Butler, *Gender Trouble: Feminism and the Subversion of Identity* (New York: Routledge, 1990), p. 68.

5. Peter Stallybrass and Allon White, *The Politics and Poetics of Transgression* (Ithaca, N.Y.: Cornell University Press, 1986), p. 10.

6. Elaine Scarry, *The Body in Pain: The Making and Unmaking of the World* (Oxford: Oxford University Press, 1985), p. 161.

7. John Locke, *An Essay Concerning Human Understanding*, ed. Peter H. Nidditch (Oxford: Clarendon Press, 1975), IV, xxi, 1–4.

8. Barbara Maria Stafford has explored and richly documented how during the eighteenth century the human body and particularly its anatomical studies became the guiding metaphor for the exploration and representation of the "unseen" and new territories of knowledge. See her *Body Criticism: Imaging the Unseen in Enlightenment Art and Medicine* (Cambridge, Mass.: MIT Press, 1991).

9. See Michel Foucault, *The Order of Things: An Archeology of the Human Sciences* (New York: Vintage Books, 1973); Jurij M. Lotman, "Problèmes de la typologie des cultures," in *Essays in Semiotics/Essais de sémiotique*, ed. Julia Kristeva, Josette Rey-Debove, and Donna Jean Umiker (The Hague: Mouton, 1971), pp. 46–56; and David E. Wellbery, *Lessing's Laocoon: Semiotics and Aesthetics in the Age of Reason* (Cambridge, Eng.: Cambridge University Press, 1984).

10. See, e.g., Laura Brown and Felicity Nussbaum, eds., *The New Eighteenth Century* (London: Methuen, 1987); and Leopold Damrosch, Jr., ed., *Modern Essays in Eighteenth Century Literature* (Oxford: Oxford University Press, 1988).

COOK; *The Limping Woman and the Public Sphere*

1. For example, Richardson's *Clarissa* directs Anna's attention, and ours, to the material evidence of her anguish, making her letter bear witness in multiple ways: "You will not wonder to see this narrative so dismally scrawled. It is owing to different pens and ink, all bad, and written by snatches of time: my hand trembling too with fatigue and grief" (*Clarissa*, Vol. II [London: Dent, 1984], p. 371). The trope is already conventional in Ovid's *Heroides*, which makes artful use of it in Sappho's letter to Phaon.

2. Although this representation of subjectivity as bound up in the body is clearest in those letter-fictions that purport to record the fluctuating psychosomatic temperature of the lovesick woman, it is inherent to a greater or lesser degree in all narratives in letter form. Criticism attending specifically to the gendered implications of this aspect of the genre includes Susan Lee Carrell's *Le Soliloque de la passion féminine, ou le dialogue illusoire* (Paris: Jean-Michel Place, 1982), Peggy Kamuf's *Fictions of Feminine Desire: Disclosures of Heloise* (Lincoln: University of Nebraska Press, 1982), and Linda Kauffman's *Discourses of Desire: Gender, Genre, and Epistolary Fiction* (Ithaca, N.Y.: Cornell University Press, 1986).

3. Michel Foucault, *Discipline and Punish*, trans. Alan Sheridan (New York: Vintage Books, 1979), p. 28.

4. On Enlightenment fictions of contract, see Louis Althusser's *Montesquieu, Rousseau, Marx: Politics and History*, trans. Ben Brewster (London: Verso, 1982), pp. 113–34; and Carole Pateman's *The Sexual Contract* (Stanford, Calif.: Stanford University Press, 1988), esp. chap. 4.

5. This discussion of the epistolary novel as mediating between what Walter Benjamin calls auratic and mechanically reproducible textual forms draws on Benjamin's essays "Unpacking My Library: A Talk About Book Collecting" and "The Work of Art in the Age of Mechanical Reproduction," in his *Illuminations*, ed. Hannah Arendt, trans. Harry Zohn (New York: Schocken Books, 1969), pp. 59–68, 217–52.

6. Translations of the *Persian Letters* are my own from the 1964 Garnier-Flammarion edition, and parenthetical references give the number of the letter in this edition.

7. Discussions of the eunuchs include Aram Vartanian's "Eroticism and Politics in the *Lettres persanes*," *Romanic Review* 60 (1969): 23–33; and Michel Delon's "Un monde d'eunuques," *Europe* 55 (1977): 79–88. Exceptional in its attention to the wives' letters is Suzanne Rodin Pucci's "Letters from the Harem: Veiled Figures of Writing in Montesquieu's *Lettres persanes*," in *Writing the Female Voice: Essays on Epistolary Literature*, ed. Elizabeth C. Goldsmith (Boston: Northeastern University Press, 1989), pp. 114–34. On Roxane's last letter, see Jean Starobinski, "Les *Lettres persanes*: Apparence et essence," *Neohelicon* 3–4 (1974): 83–112, to which I return below.

Of course, to identify the "chaîne secrète" with a single character or group of characters requires a totalizing reading of a very flexible and highly ironized text; such claims necessarily remain in competition, often revealing more about the biases of their champions than about the text they purport to explain.

8. The Republic of Letters, that favorite metaphor of Enlightenment print culture, seems to have been understood in the first half of the eighteenth century as something like a transnational discursive network whose citizens exchange ideas freely and openly through more and more widely circulated print-forms: newspapers, periodicals, broadsides, pamphlets, and books. The metaphor is, of course, an ancient one, but I am concerned here with the Enlightenment version of the ideal, which was distinctively shaped by the proliferation of print (although such non-written discursive exchanges as speeches, sermons, and public rituals are also relevant to it). This ideal of the public sphere is definitively described in Jürgen Habermas's *Structural Transformation of the Public Sphere: An Inquiry into a Category of Bourgeois Society*, trans. Thomas Burger with Frederick Lawrence (Cambridge, Mass.: MIT Press, 1989).

9. Alvin Kernan describes this as the shift from the world of "polite or courtly letters . . . primarily oral, aristocratic, amateur, authoritarian, court-centered" into the technology and logic of a "print-based, market-centered, democratic literary system" supplied by a burgeoning publishing industry (*Samuel Johnson and the Impact of Print* [Princeton, N.J.: Princeton University Press, 1989], p. 4). Elizabeth Eisenstein notes that the "romantic figure of the aristocratic or patrician patron has tended to obscure the more plebeian and prosaic early capitalist entrepreneur who hired scholars, translators, editors, and compilers, when not serving in these capacities himself" (*The Printing Press as an Agent of Change* [Cambridge, Eng.: Cambridge University Press, 1979], p. 153). Thinking of Montesquieu as involved in the material production of his text, if not precisely as an "early capitalist entrepreneur," allows us to make sense of the print-culture allusions that engage me here.

10. The designation of Amsterdam is Eisenstein's (p. 138). The Maison Desbordes also published Calvinist-identified books and periodicals, including one significantly entitled *L'Histoire critique de la République des Lettres*.

11. For a brief account of the mechanism of French governmental censorship, see Daniel Roche's essay "Censorship and the Publishing Industry," in *Revolution in Print: The Press in France 1775–1800*, ed. Robert Darnton and Roche (Berkeley: University of California Press, 1989), pp. 3–26. Darnton's *The Literary Underground of the Old Regime* (Cambridge, Mass.: Harvard University Press, 1982) documents the foreign printing shops, the international smuggling networks, and the internal distribution systems for unauthorized or forbidden literature. Together these formed a counterstructure to the privileged, government-protected French printing and booksellers' guilds, whose relatively few members obtained copyrights by purchasing *privilèges*. See also his essay "Philosophy Under the Cloak," in *Revolution in Print*, pp. 27–49.

12. In a later edition of the *Persian Letters*, Montesquieu employs the metaphor of paternal abandonment explicitly in commenting on textual inconsistencies: "These errors, in subsequent editions, have multiplied innumerably because this

work was abandoned by the author from its birth" (Paris: Gallimard, 1973), p. 420. The image of the text as orphan reappears, of course, in the epigraph to the *Esprit des lois*: "Prolem sine matre creatam," referring to the motherless Erichthonius, fostered by Athena.

For a reading of anonymity or the "negation of persons" as precisely what enables the colonial and revolutionary American public sphere, see Michael Warner's *Letters of the Republic: Publication and the Public Sphere in Eighteenth-Century America* (Cambridge, Mass.: Harvard University Press, 1990), pp. 39–43. Obviously, the limping woman of Montesquieu's preface motivates my negative reading of anonymity in the *Persian Letters*.

13. In later editions, these attributes are identified as "Persian," effectively modifying the implicit universalism of the original text, but my argument here has to do specifically with the print-culture contexts of the 1721 edition. Textual changes across the editions are tracked in Vernière's edition of the *Lettres persanes* (Paris: Garnier, 1960).

14. The word also echoes Barthes's "Sinicism," another term that describes a discursive code for the production and representation of otherness. The editor's claim to have de-Orientalized the Persians' letters by translating them according to French *moeurs* encourages the reader to infer that "Frenchness," like "Persianness," is also a matter of coding.

15. Scholarly editors of the *Lettres persanes* assign this sentence a footnote stating that Montesquieu's wife limped. This does not, of course, explain the *symbolic* function of the limping woman in relation to the thematics of the public, publication, and publicity around which the "Introduction" is built, but I have found no critical discussion of this figure.

16. My use of the term "gaze" refers primarily to a historically specific redefinition of spectacularity from a Renaissance class-based model (the spectacular body is the source of power) to a gendered model (feminized spectacle/masculine gaze). In comparing despotic and absolutist spectacularity with the gaze of the master of the harem, the *Persian Letters* suggests how the former was discursively translated into the latter.

The psychoanalytic connotations of the term are also relevant, though I do not appeal to them rigorously here. In the complex understanding of the word deriving from Jacques Lacan's work, the concept of the gaze refers not to the seeing subject's mistaken assumption of full self-consciousness (the definitive instance of *méconnaissance*), but rather to the inherently inaccessible mastery implicit in the desiring gaze of the Other. Such an understanding is relevant to Montesquieu's subtle analysis of the self-undermining structures of despotism. See *The Four Fundamental Concepts of Psycho-Analysis*, trans. Alan Sheridan (New York: Norton, 1981), pp. 105–9.

17. Studies of the distinctively inflected iconologies of female rulers, which necessarily problematize the traditional phallic metaphorics of power, have made us aware of the gendering of all political representations. For example, see Louis Adrian Montrose's analyses of representations of Queen Elizabeth, including "The Elizabethan Subject and the Spenserian Text," in *Literary Theory/Renaissance Texts*, ed. Patricia Parker and David Quint (Baltimore: Johns Hopkins University

Press, 1980), pp. 303–40; and his " 'Shaping Fantasies': Figurations of Gender and Power in Elizabethan Culture," *Representations* 1 (1983): 61–94.

18. Recalling her sexual triumph, Zachi wishes for witnesses: "Had heaven only given my rivals the courage to remain as witnesses of all the marks of love I received from you!" (III).

19. Grosrichard analyzes a Western traveler's account of the blinding of a harem child to explore the European thematics of the despotic gaze. He concludes, "Etre le maître, donc, c'est voir. Ignorant, ivre, malade, qu'importe: il voit" (*Structure du sérail: La Fiction du despotisme asiatique dans l'Occident classique* [Paris: Seuil, 1979], p. 73). See also the related discussion on pp. 26–33.

20. Norbert Elias, *The Court Society*, trans. Edmund Jephcott (Oxford: Basil Blackwell, 1983), pp. 81–82. As Elias points out, the relocation of the royal apartments at Versailles to a more retired courtyard by Louis's successors is a significant index of the changes in symbolic strategies of subsequent reigns. Other suggestive discussions of absolutist semiotics include Ernst Kantorowiscz's *The King's Two Bodies: A Study in Mediaeval Political Theology* (Princeton, N.J.: Princeton University Press, 1957); and Louis Marin's *Portrait of the King*, trans. Martha M. Houle (Minneapolis: University of Minnesota Press, 1988).

21. This point is well argued in Joan B. Landes's *Women and the Public Sphere in the Age of the French Revolution* (Ithaca, N.Y.: Cornell University Press, 1988), pp. 20–21. Landes's perceptive and important feminist revision of Habermas's public sphere theory, and specifically her interest in the instrumental gendering of eighteenth-century politics, helped shape this discussion. See also Carolyn C. Lougee's *Paradis des femmes: Women, Salons, and Social Stratification in Seventeenth-Century France* (Princeton, N.J.: Princeton University Press, 1976).

22. Here the *Persian Letters* takes up one of the central principles of the seventeenth-century *thèse nobiliare*, which argued that the nobility were the ideal citizens and the king's proper advisers, counterbalancing the encroaching interests of the *bourgeoisie* and of the Crown. For a discussion of the *thèse nobiliare* and its counterpart the *thèse royale*, see Nannerl Keohane's *Philosophy and the State in France* (Princeton, N.J.: Princeton University Press, 1980), pp. 346–50.

Montesquieu has sometimes been associated with the philosophes who supported the *thèse royale*, which called for an enlightened absolute monarch to protect the people against a domineering, luxurious nobility. Such a reading might make the *Persian Letters* part of a slowly rising tide of democratic revolutionary consciousness, with Roxane's "revolt" proleptically figuring the fall of the Bastille. The teleological bias of such a reading obviously discredits it, and as I suggest below, its conversion of an enslaved woman's suicide into a figure for national revolution should trigger our suspicion. Louis Althusser has authoritatively demolished this Whig reading of Montesquieu, properly placing him with such ideologues of the *noblesse de robe* as Fénelon and Saint-Simon. See *Montesquieu, Rousseau, Marx*, pp. 65–74, 83–86, 98–106.

23. Because their gatherings centered on Paris rather than Versailles and promoted the careers of nonaristocratic males, both aristocratic and bourgeois *salonnières* were attacked for undermining the social hierarchies of the nation. This analysis makes it plain that the rise of a new ideology of the family in the eigh-

teenth century was not, as it is sometimes described, a "natural" side effect of the rise of a bourgeois class seeking to promote its own values. As Landes and Lougee point out, the ideal of the "domestic republic" was first articulated not by Rousseau or the philosophes but by seventeenth-century aristocrats with very specific political interests, many of which Montesquieu shared. In the *Esprit des lois*, Montesquieu follows Fénelon and Saint-Simon in arguing for a "domestic republic" in which women hold their proper subordinate places as the primary condition of a stable sociopolitical order (see Landes, *Women and the Public Sphere*, pp. 35–38).

24. The idealization of masculine civic virtue as a counter to absolutism underlies much eighteenth-century political philosophy, which was fascinated by the Roman republic's separation of *oikos* from *polis*. States so organized were thought to be virile, founded on and reinforcing "masculine" attributes in their citizens, in contrast to both absolutist and despotic forms of government. On the eighteenth-century discourse of civic virtue in general, see J. G. A. Pocock's *The Machiavellian Moment: Florentine Political Thought and the Atlantic Republican Tradition* (Princeton, N.J.: Princeton University Press, 1975). Iris Marion Young offers a feminist reading of related issues in her essay "Impartiality and the Civic Public: Some Implications of Feminist Critiques of Moral and Political Theory," in *Feminism as Critique*, ed. Seyla Benhabib and Drucilla Cornell (Minneapolis: University of Minnesota Press, 1987), pp. 57–76.

25. Peter de Bolla's analysis of the changes in the discourse on the British national debt in the 1750s and 1760s concentrates on a set of corporeal images similar to those I discuss here, although of course they are deployed differently in the later British context. See *The Discourse of the Sublime: Readings in History, Aesthetics, and the Subject* (Oxford: Basil Blackwell, 1989), pp. 103–39. Of particular relevance here is his concept of how "defiguration" works in the discourse on debt: by de-figuring the body, bodily metaphors were intended "to return to the body its lost literality" so that it could serve as "a site of literal meaning, or semantic purity" (p. 112). This purity served those condemning the manipulation of public credit by private profiteers: "Money must be returned to its literal status, as coin, material and diverted from its use as trope, the generator of endless 'paper' money" (p. 121). Such a strategy of defiguration is at work in the images of the diseased feminine body of France and the hyperphallic body of the false Ibrahim (discussed below), as well as in the mobilization of gender in the harem letters — although, as I will suggest, Montesquieu's view of semantic purity is ironic.

26. Law (1671–1729) promoted the circulation of paper notes only partially supported by specie reserves to generate wealth. In 1716 the French government permitted him to establish a modest private bank issuing such notes. When it succeeded, the Crown took it over as the Banque Royale, the king's name thenceforth appearing as guarantor on the notes. Law's various companies were granted vast monopolies, eventually including the slave trade, the colonization of Louisiana, lucrative tax-farming contracts, and the reorganization of the immense national debt. The sale of shares in his various companies reached madly inflated heights by early 1720. Law converted to Catholicism to become controller-general of France, and the credit of the government was effectively conflated with that of

his Compagnie des Indes. Its fall ruined many and, perhaps worse, instilled a lasting national distrust of all financial innovations that can be contrasted with British attitudes after the almost contemporary South Sea Bubble. For further discussion of these issues, see P. G. M. Dickson's magisterial *The Financial Revolution in England* (Oxford: Oxford University Press, 1967).

27. As the ironization of Zulema's tale and Usbek's theory of the origin of society suggest, Montesquieu disagreed profoundly with the implications of social contract theory; see Althusser, *Montesquieu, Rousseau, Marx*; and Lougee, *Paradis des femmes*, for discussions of this point.

28. The date of the first harem letter locates it chronologically between Letters CIV and CV. The sequence and dating of these letters were carefully reworked by Montesquieu in later editions to heighten the contrast between Usbek's philosophical liberalism and his domestic despotism; here I follow the last edition. See Robert Shackleton's "The Moslem Chronology of the *Lettres persanes*," *French Studies* 8 (1954): 17–27.

29. Foucault's analysis of confessional sexuality as disciplinary instrument comes to mind here, but Montesquieu frames the effect ironically. See Part III, "Scientia Sexualis," in *The History of Sexuality*, Vol. 1, *An Introduction*, trans. Robert Hurley (New York: Vintage, 1980), pp. 53–73.

30. Gayatri Chakravorty Spivak notes the frequency of such allegorizations of narratives about third-world women and suggests what is at stake: "By the rules of a parable the logic of the connection between the tenor and the vehicle of the metaphor must be made absolutely explicit. Under the imperatives of such a reading, the 'effect of the real' of the vehicle must necessarily be underplayed. The subaltern must be seen only as the vehicle of a greater meaning. . . . What must be excluded from the story is precisely the attempt to represent the subaltern as such" ("A Literary Representation of the Subaltern," in idem, *In Other Worlds: Essays in Cultural Politics* [New York: Routledge, 1988], p. 244).

31. When Starobinski writes of this moment, "Dans l'imminence de la mort s'ouvre la perspective d'une raison universellement libératrice" ("Les *Lettres persanes*," p. 103), he ignores the fact that universal reason cannot liberate the dead Roxane. Keohane makes the same point about this letter: despite its "heartening affirmation of the indomitable well-springs of human liberty," Roxane is dead by her own hand when we read it, and is thus permanently excluded from reason's beneficial effects (*Philosophy and the State*, p. 402).

It was briefly fashionable to propose that the wives could be seen as freed by the walls of the harem to express a non-phallic sexuality, perhaps something like the eunuchoid sexuality of the "third sense," and that the effects of *jouissance* deconstruct the phallic economy of the harem from within. It seems to me that such a reading is forestalled by the fundamentally "masculist" structure of the text, which appropriates and consumes all its sexual discourses voyeuristically.

32. Indeed, the epistolary genre itself has been assessed as a "failed" form by teleological literary criticism, since it does not achieve what is accepted to be the transparent "realism" of third-person narrative. For this very reason, however, as I have suggested here, the epistolary novel is particularly well suited to Foucault's call for a political anatomy. Although the letter purports to anchor identity in a

conventional model of the body/subject, the authority of that model can be easily undermined through thematizations of textuality's absence, as the *Persian Letters* shows. In contrast, the nineteenth-century realist novel uses the narratological device of free indirect discourse to allow the reader to move in and out of a character's consciousness in an illusion of seamless textual transparency. This technology produces a very different model of representation that functionally dissolves the "natural" margins of the body. Authority is thus detached from any originary body and disseminated through a newly expanded field of the fiction as a unified whole. The mystification of power produced by this effect is expressed in Flaubert's description of the ideal author as the absent god of a text, "invisible and all-powerful . . . everywhere felt, but never seen." This analysis of the ideological effects of third-person narrative draws on John Bender's "Impersonal Violence: The Penetrating Gaze and the Field of Narration in *Caleb Williams*" (in *Critical Reconstructions: The Relationship of Fiction and Life*, ed. Robert M. Polhemus and Roger B. Henkle [Stanford, Calif.: Stanford University Press, forthcoming]). Reading backward from this postcorporeal dissemination of authority allows us to grasp the specific defigurative/disembodying possibilities of epistolary narrative.

33. As Dena Goodman has argued, the philosophes' writings manifest their belief that rhetoric is a form of action, politically efficacious through its capacity of transforming readers' opinions and their actions. The *locus classicus* for this point is Diderot's definition of a good dictionary as one that will "change the common way of thinking." Goodman links the political project of the *Encyclopédie* to works by Montesquieu, Rousseau, and Diderot in her *Criticism in Action: Enlightenment Experiments in Political Writing* (Ithaca, N.Y.: Cornell University Press, 1989), to which I return below.

34. Discussing Montesquieu's exploitation of epistolary temporality and of the polyphonic form, Laurent Versini asserts that he was "le premier à composer véritablement un roman par lettres" (*Laclos et la tradition: Essai sur les sources et la technique des "Liaisons dangereuses"* [Paris: Librairie C. Klincksieck, 1968], p. 275).

35. I take the in/of opposition from Tzvetan Todorov's essay "Le Sens des lettres," in his *Littérature et signification* (Paris: Larousse, 1967), pp. 47–49. Janet Altman's neologism is defined in her *Epistolarity: Approaches to a Form* (Columbus: Ohio State University Press, 1982), p. 189.

36. While Goodman recognizes that Montesquieu's critical question concerns not only the story told in the letters but also the construction of the extra-textual reader as a political critic, she too concludes that the "comparative critical method" of Montesquieu's work is a failure, leaving his readers impotent: "Not only Usbek but Montesquieu has failed to bridge the gap between knowledge and action, criticism and change." She takes this to be a result of the narratological form of the *Persian Letters*. Polyphonic epistolary narrative employs as its central principle not plot development, "the dynamics of the action narrated from letter to letter," but instead "thematic echoes, parallels, and antitheses" between letters, thus creating a rich but ultimately "static" image of society (*Criticism in Action*, p. 103). While I disagree to some extent with this assessment, I prefer to redefine the problem

altogether. By reframing the *Persian Letters* in the context of print culture, I extend the scope of analysis beyond the plot contained *in* the letters to a consideration of the *Letters* itself in the context of Enlightenment print culture. I thus arrive at a different conclusion about the significance and efficacy of Montesquieu's text.

SACCAMANO; *Wit's Breaks*

1. Because of dangerous "accessory ideas," "Noses ran the same fate some centuries ago in most parts of *Europe*, which Whiskers have now done in the kingdom of *Navarre*." " 'Twas plain to the whole court the word [whiskers] was ruined: *La Fosseuse* had given it a wound" (Laurence Sterne, *The Life and Opinions of Tristram Shandy, Gentleman*, ed. Ian Watt [Boston: Houghton Mifflin, 1965], p. 263).

2. Paul de Man, "The Epistemology of Metaphor," *Critical Inquiry* 5 (1978): 21.

3. Joseph Addison and Richard Steele, *The Spectator*, ed. Donald F. Bond, 5 vols. (Oxford: Clarendon Press, 1965), 1: 244–45; hereafter cited by volume and page number, respectively. The series on wit spans numbers 58 to 63.

4. William H. Youngren ("Addison and the Birth of Eighteenth-Century Aesthetics," *Modern Philology* 79 [1982]: 267–83) has discussed Addison's stress on the temporal experience of readers.

5. David A. Hansen also notes Addison's restriction of this "any" as a revision of Locke. See "Addison on Ornament and Poetic Style," in *Studies in Criticism and Aesthetics, 1660–1800: Essays in Honor of Samuel Holt Monk*, ed. Howard Anderson and John S. Shea (Minneapolis: University of Minnesota Press, 1967), pp. 94–127, esp. pp. 105–6. In "Addison's Theory of the Imagination as 'Perceptive Response' " (in *Papers of the Michigan Academy of Science, Arts, and Letters*, ed. Eugene S. McCartney and Alfred H. Stockard [Ann Arbor: University of Michigan Press, 1935], 21: 509–30), Clarence Dewitt Thorpe discusses how Addison enlarged on Locke's conception of imagination.

6. John Sitter has recently noted that Addison and Matthew Prior "question Locke's devaluation of wit and the opposition of wit to judgment" in order to treat them as "different manners" or modes of the same cognitive operation, "not distinct actions": "If we can have right and wrong judgments we can have right and wrong — or true or false — wit as well" ("About Wit: Locke, Addison, Prior, and the Order of Things," in *Rhetorics of Order/Ordering Rhetorics in English Neoclassical Literature*, ed. J. Douglas Canfield and J. Paul Hunter [Newark: University of Delaware Press, 1989], pp. 156, 153). Although Sitter astutely reads the way that Locke's epistemological problems with wit indicate more general difficulties with the *Essay's* theories of language and knowledge, he does not investigate the complementary move in Addison to protect the truth of figural language by constructing false wit as its rhetorically debased other. Sitter does acknowledge that neoclassical poetics remains "grounded in 'logocentrism' " (p. 156), but this means that Addison legitimates figural language within a representational model of linguistic signification — hence, as we shall see, the need to exclude linguistic materiality and to identify the wit of truth with metaphor. In this respect, neo-

classical poetics serves the aims of Lockean philosophy; as Jacques Derrida has noted, "Each time that a rhetoric [or, we might add, a poetics] defines metaphor, not only is *a* philosophy implied, but also a conceptual network in which philosophy *itself* has been constituted" ("White Mythology: Metaphor in the Text of Philosophy," in idem, *Margins of Philosophy*, trans. Alan Bass [Chicago: University of Chicago Press, 1982], p. 230).

7. Dominique Bouhours, *La manière de bien penser dans les ouvrages d'esprit*, 3d ed. (Amsterdam, 1705), p. 17. The citations that follow occur on pp. 17–18.

8. In the Old Testament, Scarry writes, "the activity of creating becomes conflated with the activity of wounding" because wounding "re-enacts the power of alteration that has its first profound occurrence in creation"; what Scarry calls the "deconstruction" of production ("bodily reproduction" as well as "the production of material and verbal artifacts") is "rescued" in the New Testament, where "creating and wounding are once more held securely in place as separable categories of action" (*The Body in Pain: The Making and Unmaking of the World* [Oxford: Oxford University Press, 1985], p. 184). I want to argue, however, that both bodies and poetic artifacts depend on the possibility of an enabling break—a contingent material force that makes possible signifying relations but that humanist discourse can only abhor as a wound. As Mark Seltzer has remarked: "The overlapping of the terms of creation and the terms of power can only indicate an absolute difference because deconstruction, for Scarry, can have nothing to do with construction; the questioning of difference, the exigencies of reference, the relays that establish relations between apparently opposed registers—all are synonymous with destruction" and require vigilant ethical surveillance ("Statistical Persons," *Diacritics* 17 [1987]: 88).

9. *A Tale of a Tub*, ed. A. C. Guthkelch and D. Nichol Smith (Oxford: Clarendon Press, 1958), p. 149.

10. In *The Powers of Horror: An Essay on Abjection* (trans. Leon S. Roudiez [New York: Columbia University Press, 1982]), Julia Kristeva notes that the uncertainty of boundaries, especially corporeal limits, "represents for the subject the risk to which the very symbolic order is permanently exposed, to the extent that it is a device of discriminations, of differences." This risk issues from "the prohibitions that found the inner and outer borders in which and through which the speaking subject is constituted—borders also determined by the phonological and semantic differences that articulate the syntax of language" (p. 69). In the borderline case of abjection, the patient's speech "keeps breaking up to the point of desemantization," becoming notes, music, rhythm, while its themes are dislocated "like the limbs of a fragmented body" (p. 49).

11. *Essay on Criticism*, in *The Poems of Alexander Pope*, ed. John Butt (New Haven, Conn.: Yale University Press, 1963), ll. 88–91.

12. *Virgil's Georgics*, in *The Poems of John Dryden*, ed. James Kinsley, 4 vols. (Oxford: Clarendon Press, 1958), 3: bk. 1, ll. 81–93; Virgil, *Georgics*, bk. 1, ll. 54–61. Hereafter, Dryden's translation of the *Georgics* in the third volume of this edition will be cited by book and verse number, followed by the corresponding reference to the Latin text.

13. *Virgil's Georgics*, bk. 1, ll. 75, 79–80 (bk. 1, ll. 50, 53).

14. Ibid., bk. 1, ll. 185–88 (bk. 1, ll. 121–23).

15. Ibid., bk. 1, ll. 191, 195–96 (bk. 1, ll. 125, 127–28).

16. Ibid., bk. 1, ll. 239, 232–33 (bk. 1, ll. 160, 155).

17. *The Prose Works of Alexander Pope*, ed. Norman Ault and Rosemary Cowler, 2 vols. (vol. 1 — Oxford: Basil Blackwell, 1936; vol. 2 — Hamden, Conn.: Archon Books, 1986), 2: 192, 191.

18. *The Miscellaneous Works of Joseph Addison*, ed. A. C. Guthkelch, 2 vols. (London: G. Bell and Sons, 1914), 2: 6.

19. Jean Baudrillard, *The Mirror of Production*, trans. Mark Poster (St. Louis: Telos Press, 1975), pp. 59, 61.

20. J. G. A. Pocock, *The Machiavellian Moment: Florentine Political Thought and the Atlantic Republican Tradition* (Princeton, N.J.: Princeton University Press, 1975), p. 431. Pocock contends that "Defoe and Addison do not seem to have reified the world of speculation and exchange by alluding to the labor that gave it value, and the substitution of *homo faber* for *homo politicus* was not effected"; instead, they validated "the commercial world by appeal to conceptions of public virtue" (p. 458). Although it may be the case that such a historical succession of paradigms did not take place in the early eighteenth century, there are allusions enough to the value of labor and labor-producing value in Addison to warrant the kind of analysis I undertake here. For justification, one need not go as far as Baudrillard, who argues that bourgeois political economy only actualizes a "revolution of the rational calculus of production" begun much earlier: "The ideological form most appropriate to sustain the intensive rational exploitation of nature takes form within Christianity during a long transition: from the 13–14th century, when work begins to be imposed as a value, up to the 16th century when work is organized around its rational and continuous scheme of value — the capitalist productive enterprise and the system of political economy, that secular generalization of the Christian axiom about nature" (*Mirror of Production*, pp. 64–65).

21. Defoe's *Review*, ed. Arthur Wellesley Secord (New York: Columbia University Press, 1938), 3 [no. 2]: 8. Addison's *Spectator* 69 (May 19, 1711) seems to paraphrase this number of the *Review* (Jan. 3, 1706), in which Defoe admires the "Wisdom and Direction of *Nature Natureing*" for producing different species in different climates and thus "insensibly preserv[ing] the Dependance, of the most Remote Parts of the World upon one another" (p. 8).

22. Aristotle, *Rhetoric*, trans. W. Rhys Roberts (New York: Modern Library, 1954), 1371b21–26.

23. Jean-Joseph Goux, *Symbolic Economies: After Marx and Freud*, trans. Jennifer Curtiss Gage (Ithaca, N.Y.: Cornell University Press, 1990), p. 98.

24. Addison, *The Freeholder*, ed. James Leheny (Oxford: Clarendon Press, 1979), pp. 225, 224.

KELLY; *Locke's Eyes, Swift's Spectacles*

1. Sigmund Freud, *The Standard Edition of the Complete Psychological Works of Sigmund Freud*, 24 vols., ed. James Strachey (London: Hogarth Press, 1953–74), 5: 611.

2. See Jacques Derrida, "Freud and the Scene of Writing," in idem, *Writing and Difference*, trans. Alan Bass (Chicago: University of Chicago Press, 1978), pp. 196–231.

3. Johnson shows a preoccupation with Swift's "spectacles" elsewhere as well. He quotes a passage from "Stella's Birthday (1727)" under the entry for "spectacles" in the *Dictionary*, and Boswell reports him quoting the same passage in their trip to Oxford in 1784: "He soon dispatched the inquiries which were made about his illness and recovery, by a short and distinct narrative; and then assuming a gay air, repeated from Swift, —

> 'Nor think on our approaching ills,
> And talk of spectacles and pills.' "

See Boswell's *Life of Johnson* (Oxford: Clarendon Press, 1934), 4: 285, Thursday, June 3, 1784.

4. *The Life of Swift*, in *Samuel Johnson: Selected Poetry and Prose*, ed. Frank Brady and W. K. Wimsatt (Berkeley: University of California Press, 1977), p. 465. All references to *The Life of Swift* are to this edition.

5. In his *Observations upon Lord Orrey's Remarks on the Life and Writings of Dr. Jonathan Swift* (London, 1754), Patrick Delany attributes Swift's failed memory to his isolation, an isolation that Delany understands to have been caused equally by Swift's habitual and antisocial avarice and by a stubborn whim:

> To this end [the unfurnishing of Swift's memory], another cause also contributed; an obstinate resolution, which he had taken, never to wear spectacles. A resolution, which the natural make of his eyes, (large and prominent) very ill qualified him to support. This made reading very difficult to him: and the difficulty naturally discouraged him from it: and gradually drew him, in a great measure, to decline it. And as he was now at a loss how to fill up that time which he was before wont to employ in reading, this drew him on to exercise, more than he ought: for that he over-exercised himself is out of all doubt. (pp. 145–46)

The same detail appears in Hawkesworth's "Account of the Life of the Reverend Jonathan Swift" (London, 1755). Hawkesworth borrows heavily from Orrey and, like Orrey, depicts Swift as a morbid psychology:

> His solitude which has been already accounted for, prevented the diversion of his mind by conversation from brooding over his disappointments, and aggravating every injury that he had suffered from all the circumstances which ingenious resentment, if it does not find, is apt to create: a resolution which he had taken, and to which he obstinately adhered, not to wear spectacles, precluded the entertainment which he might otherwise have found in books, and his giddiness, though it was a mere corporal disorder, prevented the employment of his mind in composition. In this situation his thoughts seem to have been confined to the contemplation of his own misery which he felt to be great, and which in this world he knew to be hopeless; the sense of his present condition was necessarily complicated with regret of the past, and with resentment both against those by whom he had been banished, and those who had deserted him in his exile. A fixed attention to one object long continued is known to destroy the ballance of a mind, and it is not therefore strange that Swift should by degrees become the victim of outrageous madness. (p. 29)

For an account of Swift's early biographers, see Wayne Warnocke, "Samuel Johnson on Swift: *The Life of Swift* and Johnson's Predecessors in Swiftian Biography," *Journal of British Studies* 7 (1968): 56–64.

6. John Boyle, Earl of Orrey, *Remarks on the Life and Writings of Dr. Jonathan Swift* (London, 1752), p. 266.

7. Sir Walter Scott continues this tradition, writing of Swift's death: "At length, when this awful moral lesson had subsisted from 1743, until the 19th October 1745, it pleased God to release the subject of these Memoirs from his calamitous situation" (*Memoirs of Jonathan Swift, D.D.*, in *The Miscellaneous Prose Works of Sir Walter Scott, Bart.* [Edinburgh, 1827], 2: 451–54).

8. Paul J. Korshin writes that "Johnson's well-known dislike of Swift presents . . . a critical problem: Johnson's friends and contemporaries either assumed that there were personal factors at the root of it all, made suppositions that Johnson was jealous of Swift's great reputation, or ignored an increasingly embarrassing situation; modern scholarship, when not ignoring the problem, tends to resolve the issue by seeking, or postulating, psychological and temperamental affinities between the two men as a basis for Johnson's negative attitude toward Swift" ("Johnson and Swift: A Study in the Genesis of Literary Opinion," *Philological Quarterly* 48 [1969]: 464–65).

9. Johnson, "The Vanity of Human Wishes," in *The Poems of Samuel Johnson*, ed. David Nichol Smith and Edward L. McAdam (Oxford: Clarendon Press, 1974), p. 130.

10. See Leopold Damrosch, Jr., *The Uses of Johnson's Criticism* (Charlottesville: University Press of Virginia, 1976); and Robert Folkenflick, *Samuel Johnson, Biographer* (Ithaca, N.Y.: Cornell University Press, 1978), for discussions of Johnson's use of anecdotal detail in biography. W. B. C. Watkins discusses Johnson's identification with Swift as an aspect of their need for trifles (see *Perilous Balance: The Tragic Genius of Swift, Johnson, & Sterne* [Princeton, N.J.: Princeton University Press, 1939], pp. 25–48).

11. A similar situation arises in *The Life of Dryden*, when Johnson describes at great length the spectacle surrounding Dryden's burial. Scott extends Johnson's association between untimely death and moral spectacle to the macabre: "The curiosity of strangers sometimes led them to see this extraordinary man in this state of living death" (*Memoirs of Jonathan Swift*, p. 454).

12. *Rambler* 60, in *The Yale Edition of the Works of Samuel Johnson* (New Haven, Conn.: Yale University Press, 1969), p. 184. All references to *The Rambler* are to this edition.

13. It would of course be possible and really quite easy to collapse this distinction back into Johnson's "private" anxieties simply by understanding Johnson's biographical work as an extension of his private fears about mortality and madness. Johnson's obsessive remarks about scheduling various aspects of his life, including his writing, come quickly to mind, as does his tendency to procrastinate so that he had to write hurriedly, behind time. My primary concern here is that we move our analysis of these connections beyond Johnson's hypothetical psyche, and then we can read the relationship between Johnson and Swift as part of the history of biography and of the relation between constructions of genre and subjectivity in the eighteenth century.

14. "We shall speak of a fully 'perspectival' view of space not when mere isolated objects, such as houses or furniture, are represented in 'foreshortening,' but rather only when the entire picture has been transformed . . . into a 'window,' and when we are meant to believe we are looking through this window into a space. The material surface upon which the individual figures or objects are drawn or painted or carved is thus negated, and instead reinterpreted as a mere 'picture plane'" (Erwin Panofsky, *Perspective as Symbolic Form*, trans. Christopher S. Wood [New York: Zone Books, 1991], p. 27).

15. The best resource for detailed analyses of the rhetorical features of Johnson's prose is still W. K. Wimsatt, Jr., *The Prose Style of Samuel Johnson* (New Haven, Conn.: Yale University Press, 1941).

16. Martin Maner treats a similar configuration in Johnson in *The Philosophical Biographer: Doubt and Dialectic in Johnson's Lives of the Poets* (Athens: University of Georgia Press, 1988): "When seen from an empirical perspective, biography takes on new importance and dignity. If induction from experience is the basis for evaluating probability, and if probable knowledge is the basis for human conduct, then a literary form based on induction from particulars may be the most philosophical of literary forms rather than the least" (p. 7).

17. I am indebted to the following works for my understanding of perspective: Peter de Bolla, "Of the Distance of the Picture, the Viewing Subject," in idem, *The Discourse of the Sublime: Readings in History, Aesthetics, and the Subject* (Oxford: Basil Blackwell, 1989); Samuel Y. Edgerton, Jr., *The Renaissance Rediscovery of Linear Perspective* (New York: Harper & Row, 1975); William M. Ivins, Jr., *The Rationalization of Sight* (New York: DaCapo Press, 1973); Francis Jenkins and Harvey White, *Fundamentals of Optics* (New York: McGraw-Hill, 1976); Erwin Panofsky, *Perspective as Symbolic Form*, trans. Christopher S. Wood (New York: Zone Books, 1991); David W. Tarbet, "Reason Dazzled: Perspective and Language in Dryden's *Aureng-Zebe*," in *Probability, Time, and Space in Eighteenth-Century Literature*, ed. Paula Backscheider (New York: AMS Press, 1979), pp. 187–205; and John White, *The Birth and Rebirth of Pictorial Space* (London: Faber & Faber, 1987).

18. John Locke, *An Essay Concerning Human Understanding*, ed. Peter H. Nidditch (Oxford: Clarendon Press, 1975), I, i, 7, p. 47. All references to Locke's *Essay* are to this edition.

19. Compare Locke's definition of space as "lasting distance" and time (duration) as "perishing distance" (*Essay*, II, xv, 12) to Claudio Guillen's conclusion that, in perspective, "the most important relational structure is distance, and things are seen in depth *with regard to the point of view*, that is to say, as more or less remote from the spectator" (Claudio Guillen, "On the Concept and Metaphor of Perspective," in idem, *Literature as System* [Princeton, N.J.: Princeton University Press, 1971], pp. 283–371).

20. Guillen makes general remarks on the application of the metaphor of perspective to cognition and judgment by "precise minds" in the seventeenth century. See "Metaphor of Perspective," p. 314.

21. Lawrence Lipking, "Johnson and the Meaning of Life," *Harvard Studies 12*, ed. James Engell (Cambridge, Mass.: Harvard University Press, 1984), p. 9.

22. Swift, "Stella's Birthday [1725]," in *Jonathan Swift: The Complete Poems*, ed. Pat Rogers (New Haven, Conn.: Yale University Press, 1983), pp. 286–87.

23. See Irvin Ehrenpries, *Swift: The Man, His Works, and the Age* (Cambridge, Mass.: Harvard University Press, 1983), on Swift's attack of orbital cellulitis (p. 916) and on Swift's death (pp. 918–20).

24. See de Bolla, "Of the Distance of the Picture," for a discussion of anamorphosis as the negative aspect of perspective. For a general discussion, see Jurgis Baltrusaitis, *Anamorphic Art* (Cambridge, Eng.: Chadwyck-Healey, 1977).

25. Jonathan Swift, *A Tale of a Tub*, ed. A. C. Guthkelch and D. Nichol Smith (Oxford: Clarendon Press, 1958), p. 277.

DE BOLLA; *The charm'd eye*

1. This larger project, *The Education of the Eye*, examines three overlapping contexts in which the spectator is produced, regimented, and liberated. These contexts, the viewing of gardens, houses, and pictures, are all sites for the social and historical investigation of the visual domain. The present essay forms one part of the segment on gardens.

2. Of course it is impossible to speak about vision without recourse to figurative language; in this sense we, individuals of the late twentieth century, are no better off than the eighteenth-century spectators I shall go on to discuss. The obverse of vision mapped onto visuality could be said to be the quintessentially post-Freudian post-empirical form of the model.

3. This range of competing discourses would include, among others, the division of painting into distinct genres, estate portraiture, social and economic local history, husbandry and farming manuals, the picturesque, and geological and topographical tours.

4. This has, in fact, begun to change. See, e.g., Tom Williamson and Liz Bellamy, *Property and Landscape: A Social History of Land Ownership and the English Countryside* (London: George Philip, 1987); and Sue Farrant, "The Development of Landscape Parks and Gardens in Eastern Sussex c. 1700–1820 — A Guide and Gazetteer," *Garden History* 17 (Autumn 1989): 166–80.

5. See G. E. Fussell, *The Exploration of England: A Select Bibliography of Travel and Topography 1570–1815* (London: Mitre Press, 1935); and Edward Geoffrey Cox, *A Reference Guide to the Literature of Travel*, vol. 3, *Great Britain* (Seattle: University of Washington, 1949).

6. See, e.g., Arthur Young, *A Six Months Tour Through the North of England*, 4 vols. (London, 1770); and idem, *A Six Weeks Tour Through the Southern Counties of England and Wales* (London, 1768).

7. This is not to suggest that the leisure activity of looking is disinterested but that it is less complexly determined; we do not have to sort out the interconnections between the range of skills and observational criteria of the local historian and the grammar of looking as it develops over time and through specific motivations of the looker (i.e., gender or class).

8. For an account of the internal design history of the garden, see Tom Turner, *English Garden Design* (Woodbridge: Antique Collectors' Club, 1986).

9. Horace Walpole, "The History of the Modern Taste in Gardening," in I. W. U. Chase, *Horace Walpole, Gardenist* (Princeton, N.J.: Princeton University Press, 1943), p. 35. William Kent can only be considered as one of the founders of the English layout of gardens. Much recent work has investigated the continuity of early eighteenth-century gardens with seventeenth-century models and has looked to Kent's contemporaries Addison and Shaftesbury as co-founders of the English style. See John Dixon Hunt, *Garden and Grove* (London: Dent, 1986); Charles Hinant, "A Philosophical Origin of the English Landscape Garden," *Bulletin of Research in the Humanities* 83 (1980): 292–306; David Leatherbarrow, "Character, Geometry and Perspective: The Third Earl of Shaftesbury's Principles of Garden Design," *Journal of Garden History* 4 (1984): 332–58. It should also be pointed out that this coupling of the garden to explicit political concerns, and to the differences between the look of England (its countryside) and its constitutional organization and the look of France, say, and its political system, was a common feature of late eighteenth-century discussions of landscape. Such was the power of Walpole's "History" that overtly political readings filtered into the picturesque debates engaged in by Uvedale Price, Humphrey Repton, and Richard Payne Knight. Repton, for example, writes in his *Letter to Uvedale Price*: "I cannot help seeing great affinity betwixt deducing gardening from the painters' studies of wild nature, and deducing government from the uncontrolled opinions of man in a savage state" (*Sir Uvedale Price on the Picturesque* [Edinburgh, 1842], p. 413). For a discussion of Walpole's politicization of landscape history, see Richard E. Quaintance, "Walpole's Whig Interpretation of Landscape History," *Studies in Eighteenth-Century Culture* 9 (1979): 285–300; and Samuel Kliger, "Whig Aesthetics: A Phase in Eighteenth Century Taste," *ELH* 16 (1949): 135–50.

10. John Dixon Hunt, "Emblem and Expressionism in the Eighteenth-Century Landscape Garden," *Eighteenth-Century Studies* 4 (1971): 294–317. Hunt's distinction has become a commonplace of the standard literature on eighteenth-century gardens. For other influential accounts, see Ronald Paulson, *Emblem and Expression: Meaning in English Art of the Eighteenth Century* (London: Thames and Hudson, 1975), esp. pp. 19–34; and H. F. Clark's pioneering study, "Eighteenth-Century Elysiums," *Journal of the Warburg and Courtauld Institutes* 6 (1943): 165–89.

11. The best account of the rise of domestic tourism can be found in Esther Moir, *The Discovery of Britain: The English Tourists, 1540–1840* (London: Routledge & Kegan Paul, 1964); but see also Ian Ousby, *The Englishman's England* (Cambridge, Eng.: Cambridge University Press, 1990); Adrian Tinniswood, *A History of Country House Visiting* (Oxford: Basil Blackwell & The National Trust, 1989); and for a detailed account of the picturesque, see Malcolm Andrews, *The Search for the Picturesque: Landscape Aesthetics and Tourism in Britain* (Stanford: Stanford University Press, 1989).

12. I mean to signal here that the investigation of changes in design only goes so far. What is left out of such internal histories of the garden form is how the constitution of the visual field itself changes over time. It is these changes together which impinge upon the individual viewer, making certain kinds of demands on the form and social status of the viewing subject. The present essay attempts to

enlarge upon this complex of historically mutating forms in and around the garden experience.

13. The taste for such gardens began to change by mid-century. Horace Walpole remarked of his visit to Stowe in 1753: "I have no patience at building and planting a satire" (*The Yale Edition of Horace Walpole's Correspondence*, 48 vols., ed. W. S. Lewis [London: Oxford University Press, 1937–83], pp. xxxv, 76).

14. Stowe of course combines different styles, as it evolved over a long period of time. The literature on the garden is voluminous; for helpful accounts, see Peter Willis, *Charles Bridgeman and the English Landscape Garden*, Studies in Architecture 17 (London, 1977); George Clarke, "The Garden at Stowe," *Apollo* 97 (June 1973): 110–15; idem, "William Kent: Heresy in Stowe's Elysium" in *Furor Hortensis: Essays on the History of the English Landscape Garden* (Edinburgh: Elysium Press, 1974); and John Martin Robinson, *Temples of Delight* (London: George Philip, 1990).

15. Remarking of the Temples of Ancient and Modern Virtue at Stowe, Kames says: "The temples of Ancient and Modern Virtue in the garden of Stowe, appear at first view emblematical; and when we are informed that they are so, it is not easy to gather their meaning: the spectator sees one temple in full repair, another in ruins; but without an explanatory inscription, he may guess, but cannot be certain, that the former being dedicated to Ancient Virtue, the latter to Modern Virtue, are intended a satire upon the present times. On the other hand, a trite emblem, like a trite smile, is disgustful" (*Elements of Criticism*, 3d ed. [London, 1765], p. 474).

16. The name of Capability Brown is of course most often linked with this kind of sequential response as one moves through the extent of the park. In many cases Brown's clients appropriated vast tracts of land to create this aesthetic experience. For a good account of the significant increase in estate sizes, see Joan Bassim, "The English Landscape Garden in the Eighteenth Century: The Cultural Importance of an English Institution," *Albion* 11 (Spring 1979): 15–33; and on Brown, see Roger Turner, *Capability Brown and the Eighteenth Century English Landscape* (London: Weidenfeld & Nicolson, 1985); and Dorothy Stroud, *Capability Brown* (London, Faber & Faber, 1975).

17. There are problems in taking the Leasowes as an example of the second type of garden, since it was substantially created at a time when the emblematic garden is generally held to have been still in the ascendant, and its owner and creator had died before the expressionistic had really become the dominant mode.

18. Here the nuances of the division between the public and the private need to be rehearsed, since for the period in question the "public" domain was constituted as a political concept which operated most often as one of the ways in which elitist culture maintained its social domination. Although this is generally the case, it is also worth stressing that the area in question, the public domain, was fiercely contested by rival and opposing factions within the social realm. For some of these factions the "public" needed to be opened up more fully to a "republic of taste." There are complex issues involved in this which are most succinctly signaled through reference to what has become known as the "discourse of civic humanism." Indeed, the depth and penetration of this discourse into the further reaches of eighteenth-century culture are a matter of contemporary debate and investiga-

tion. The most extensive use of this idea, though not without its critics, can be found in John Barrell, *The Political Theory of Painting from Reynolds to Hazlitt: "The Body of the Public"* (New Haven, Conn.: Yale University Press, 1986).

19. Dreams or fantasy experience often figure in eighteenth-century discussions of rural retirement and gardens. Perhaps the earliest of significant influence is Addison's dream in *Tatler* 123 (Jan. 21, 1710), which has been said to have provided the prompt for Stowe's Grecian Vale; see George Clarke, "Grecian Taste and Gothic Virtue: Lord Cobham's Gardening Programme and Its Iconography," *Apollo* 97 (June 1973): 566–71. It is also significant that Shenstone's "Unconnected Thoughts on Gardening" is preceded in *The Works in Verse and Prose of William Shenstone*, 2 vols. (London, 1764) by "A Vision"; see also Goldsmith's "Reverie," which was stimulated by thinking of the Leasowes (discussed below).

20. Other kinds of discussion of the garden can be found in David Jacques, *Georgian Gardens: The Reign of Nature* (London: B. T. Batsford, 1983); Christopher Thacker, *The History of Gardens* (London: Croom Helm, 1979); and John Dixon Hunt, *The Figure in the Landscape* (Baltimore: Johns Hopkins University Press, 1976).

21. Details of Shenstone's life may be found in Marjorie Williams, *William Shenstone: A Chapter in Eighteenth-Century Taste* (Birmingham: Cornish Bros., 1935); and E. Munro Purkis, *William Shenstone: Poet and Landscape Gardener* (Wolverhampton: Whitehead Bros., 1931).

22. Discussions of the "circuit" can be found in Ronald Paulson, "The Pictorial Circuit and Related Structures in Eighteenth-Century England," in *The Varied Pattern: Studies in the Eighteenth Century*, ed. Peter Hughes and David Williams (Toronto: A. M. Hakkert, 1971), pp. 165–87; and Max F. Shulz, "The Circuit Walk of the Eighteenth Century Landscape Garden and the Pilgrim's Circuitous Progress," *Eighteenth-Century Studies* 15 (1981): 1–25. The literature on Stourhead is substantial; see, e.g., Kenneth Woodbridge, *Landscape and Antiquity: Aspects of English Culture at Stourhead, 1718 to 1838* (Oxford: Clarendon Press, 1970); Michael Charlesworth, "On Meeting Hercules in Stourhead Garden," *Journal of Garden History* 9 (1989): 71–75; and Edward Malins, *English Landscaping and Literature, 1660–1840* (New York: Oxford University Press, 1966), esp. pp. 51–55.

23. See Oliver Goldsmith, "The History of a Poet's Garden," *Westminster Magazine*, Jan. 1, 1773 in Oliver Goldsmith, *Collected Works*, 5 vols., ed. A. Friedman (Oxford: Oxford University Press, 1966).

24. For details, see Robert Williams' introduction to Dalrymple's essay in *Journal of Garden History* 3 (1983): 144–56.

25. James Turner has argued for a specific program of response: "I suggest . . . that Shenstone tried to design a system in which sex, land, morality, and their economic structure combine in such a way that we forget their mutual inapplicability, and come to feel that each can only be fully understood in combination with the others; for example, sex becomes moral when converted into thrifty landscape" ("The Sexual Politics of Landscape: Images of Venus in Eighteenth-Century English Poetry and Landscape Gardening," *Studies in Eighteenth-Century Culture* 11 [1982]: 360). Turner's argument is committed to a reading of Shen-

stone's garden in terms of both literary expression and garden design and attempts to construct a composite form or text of the garden itself. His emphasis on reading, however, departs from the present focus of attention on the activity of looking, thereby diminishing the visual in favor of the readerly. This difference aside, Turner's argument requires careful consideration as the most adventuresome discussion to date concerning the contemporary eighteenth-century experience of the garden.

26. There are other contemporaneous accounts in manuscript; see John Riely, "Shenstone's Walks: The Genesis of the Leasowes," *Apollo* 110 (Sept. 1979): 202–9.

27. Art and *"Nature"* are continuously investigated in the garden literature of the period. See David C. Streatfield and A. M. Duckworth, *Landscape in the Gardens and Literature of Eighteenth Century England* (Los Angeles: University of California Press, 1981).

28. Robert Dodsley, quoted in Shenstone's *Works*, 2: 334. References in the text are to page numbers in this edition.

29. Later toward the end of the century not only had the garden changed in material form, what it represented and how one responded to that representation had also changed. Thus, John Aikin, in his *Letters from a Father to His Son*, 3d ed. (London, 1796), complained: "The tumbling rills of the Leasowes were such miniature cascades, that they appeared more like stage scenery than objects of romantic nature" (p. 150).

30. It is interesting to note here that R. Patching in his visit to the garden in 1757 had no such trouble with the "fairy"; he writes: "Two cascades are here remarkable for their Beauty and Simplicity; exceeding many Things of more Costly Workmanship, having the Advantage of unaffected Nature on their Side, and are indeed so elegantly rude, so rural and romantic, as must inspire the Beholder with a Notion, that the poetic Description of *Arcadia* and *Fairyland* are not altogether Fictions" (*Four Topographical Letters* [London, 1757], pp. 57–58).

31. Many guidebooks demonstrate the same fact by their translations from the classics. Perhaps the most overt example of this phenomenon is Joseph Baretti's *A Guide through the Royal Academy* (London, n.d. [1781]), which is explicitly aimed at those who do not "know the design, the history, and the names of the various Models that stand before them" (p. 3).

32. Oliver Goldsmith, *Collected Works*, 3: 206.

33. A corrective account of the garden and how it changed is given by G. Lipscombe in his *Journey into South Wales* (London, 1799). Lipscombe makes it clear that the real had impinged only too forcefully within the arcadian idyll. He comments in a rather deadpan way that the view from a particular seat has undergone some changes: "The view it formerly commanded of the valley near *Hales Owen*, is now excluded by the high banks of the *Stourbridge* canal" (p. 300).

34. For a discussion of the country/city pairing, see Maren-Sofie Rostvig, *The Happy Man: Studies in the Metamorphoses of an Ideal*, 2d ed., 2 vols. (Oslo and New York, 1962 and 1971); and Raymond Williams, *The Country and the City* (London, 1973).

35. There are instances of female characters taking on masculine stereotypes

within the civic humanist tradition. See, e.g., Joseph Spence's figuration of virtue as feminine with manly characteristics. John Barrell discusses this, in " 'The Dangerous Goddess': Masculinity, Prestige, and the Aesthetic in Early Eighteenth-Century Britain," *Cultural Critique* 12 (1989): 101–31.

36. The classic discussion of society's effeminacy can be found in John Brown, *An Estimate of the Manners and Principles of the Times*, 2d ed. (London, 1757).

37. Heely is here echoing a well-grounded sense of the benefit of the countryside, namely, that it provide "retirement." The contemplative benefits of this have been advertised at least since ancient Rome; there are, however, closer eighteenth-century examples which furnish the immediate context for Heely's prescription. See, e.g., Robert Morris, *Lectures on Architecture* (London, 1736):

> Noblemans Seats, besides Grandeur, are erected for a Retirement, or as a Retreat from Publick Cares, perhaps in some silent unfrequented Glade, where Nature seems to be lull'd into a kind of pleasing Repose, and conspires to soften Mankind into solid and awful Contemplation, especially a curious and speculative Genius, who in such distant and remote Recesses, are free from the Noise and Interruption of Visitors or Business, or the Tumult of the Populace, which are continually diverting the Ideas into different Channels. (p. 88)

38. One summer, for example, Shenstone writes that he had been "exhibiting himself" to 150 people in his walks, and likens this situation to that of a "turk in a seraglio." See *The Letters of William Shenstone*, ed. Marjorie Williams (Oxford: Basil Blackwell, 1939), p. 183.

39. The political and ideological dimensions of garden design have been explored most fruitfully by Carole Fabricant in her "Binding and Dressing Nature's Loose Tresses: The Ideology of Augustan Landscape Design," *Studies in Eighteenth-Century Culture* 8 (1979): 109–35.

40. The literature on this "painterly" mode of looking at the landscape is substantial. The best account, however, remains Elizabeth Manwaring, *Italian Landscape in Eighteenth Century England: A Study Chiefly of the Influence of Claude Lorrain and Salvator Rosa on English Taste, 1700–1800* (New York: Oxford University Press, 1925).

41. In this way the landscape comes to look at us, returning our gaze in a supportive reflection of our own self-construction. This sense of the gaze is developed most suggestively in the French twentieth-century philosophical tradition, and most clearly in the work of Merleau-Ponty, Sartre, and Lacan. It is Lacan, however, who develops the idea in ways coincident with the current argument. See Jacques Lacan, *The Four Fundamental Concepts of Psycho-Analysis* (Harmondsworth, Eng.: Penguin, 1979), p. 95.

42. It was William Chambers, the royal architect, who formulated this leveling and educative experience most clearly:

> But Gardening is of a different nature: its dominion is general; its effects upon the human mind certain and invariable; without any previous information, without being taught, all men are delighted with the gay luxuriant scenery of summer, and depressed at the dismal aspect of autumnal prospects; the charms of cultivation are equally sensible to the ignorant and the learned, and they are equally disgusted

at the rudeness of neglected nature; lawns, woods, shrubberies, rivers and mountains, affect them both in the same manner; and every combination of these will excite similar sensations in the minds of both. (*A Dissertation on Oriental Gardening* [London, 1779], p. ii)

43. For a discussion of the emergence of a viewing public for high art, see David Solkin, "Portraiture in Motion: Edward Penny's *Marquis of Granby* and the Creation of a Public for English Art," *Huntington Library Quarterly* 49 (Winter 1986): 1–23.

44. On contemporary accounts of visits to the pleasure gardens of London, see Pierre Grosley, *A Tour to London*, 2 vols. (London, 1772); *London and its Environs Described* (London, 1761); *A Description of the Vaux-Hall Gardens* (London, 1767); and *A Sketch of the Spring Gardens, Vauxhall* (London, [1750]). For later accounts, see Warwich Wroth, *The London Pleasure Gardens of the Eighteenth Century* (London, 1896); J. G. Southworth, *Vauxhall Gardens* (New York: Columbia University Press, 1941); *Vauxhall Gardens* (New Haven, Conn.: Yale Center for British Art, 1983).

45. See Andre Rouquet, *The Present State of the Arts in England* (London, 1755): "Portraiture is the kind of painting most encouraged, and consequently the most followed in England; it is the polite custom, even for men, to present one another with their pictures" (p. 33).

46. Descriptions of experiences of the visual constantly have recourse to the trope "all who have eyes," as if the minimum qualification in order to be a viewer is merely the fact of being human. For a good example of this, see *The Ambulator*, 2d ed. (London, 1782), p. 205.

LYNCH; *Overloaded Portraits*

1. Laurence Sterne, *The Life and Opinions of Tristram Shandy*, ed. Graham Petrie (Harmondsworth, Eng.: Penguin, 1967), p. 74. Subsequent citations are to this edition and appear in the text.

2. See Terence Cave, *Recognitions: A Study in Poetics* (Oxford: Clarendon Press, 1988), esp. chap. 4, "The Decline of Recognition: Eighteenth-Century Variants."

3. See Jayne Elizabeth Lewis's argument about the uses of the body in English print culture: "Swift's Aesop/Bentley's Aesop: The Modern Body and the Figures of Antiquity," *The Eighteenth Century: Theory and Interpretation* 32 (1991): 99–118.

4. I am indebted here to Richard W. F. Kroll, *The Material Word: Literate Culture in the Restoration and Early Eighteenth Century* (Baltimore: Johns Hopkins University Press, 1991), and to Douglas Lane Patey, *Probability and Literary Form: Philosophic Theory and Literary Practice in the Augustan Age* (Cambridge, Eng.: Cambridge University Press, 1987). See also Dorothea E. von Mücke, "The Project of Anschaulichkeit in the Mid-eighteenth Century," chap. 1 of her *Virtue and the Veil of Illusion: Generic Innovation and the Pedagogical Project in Eighteenth-Century Literature* (Stanford: Stanford University Press, 1991).

5. Third Earl of Shaftesbury (Anthony Ashley Cooper), *Second Characters, or,*

The Language of Forms, ed. Benjamin Rand (Cambridge, Eng.: Cambridge University Press, 1914), p. 99.

6. Compare Richard Brilliant, *Portraiture* (Cambridge, Mass.: Harvard University Press, 1991), pp. 47, 106.

7. John Donaldson, *The Elements of Beauty* (Edinburgh: Elliot & Cadell, 1780), p. 47; Johann Georg Sulzer, *Allgemeine Theorie der schönen Künste* (Biel, 1777), cited in Barbara Maria Stafford, *Body Criticism: Imaging the Unseen in Enlightenment Art and Medicine* (Cambridge, Mass.: MIT Press, 1991), p. 84. Eighteenth-century definitions of character are helpfully elucidated by Paul J. Korshin, "Probability and Character in the Eighteenth Century," in *Probability, Time, and Space in Eighteenth-Century Literature*, ed. Paula Backscheider (New York: AMS Press, 1979), pp. 63–77; and Patrick Coleman, "Character in an Eighteenth-Century Context," *The Eighteenth Century: Theory and Interpretation* 24 (1983): 51–63.

8. John Locke, *An Essay Concerning Human Understanding*, ed. Peter H. Nidditch (Oxford: Clarendon Press, 1975), II, i, 2. Subsequent citations are to this edition and appear in the text. I am indebted to the discussion of Locke's model of the rational mind in Nancy Armstrong and Leonard Tennenhouse, "The Interior Difference: A Brief Genealogy of Dreams, 1650–1717," *Eighteenth-Century Studies* 23 (1990): 458–78. See especially their comments on how closely Locke "identified the production of human understanding with his own act of writing.... We can regard the world that develops inside the mind as sensation becomes subject to reason as the other half and complement to the world of property. Consciousness begins as an empty space 'void of all Characters' and acquires knowledge according to the same principle of appropriation by which the body acquires property" (p. 468).

9. Tellingly, John Evelyn's *Numismata: A Discourse on Medals, Antient and Modern* (London: Tooke, 1697) concludes with a chapter entitled "A Digression Concerning Physiognomy."

10. Compare Joel Weinsheimer, "Theory of Character: *Emma*," *Poetics Today* 4 (1979): 190: "Novelistic characters are envisioned, even by the sometime playwright, Fielding, as marks in a book; they are characters, not persons ... not masks, which the word person deriving from (*dramatis*) *persona* would have implied."

11. Henry Fielding, *The History of the Adventures of Joseph Andrews*, ed. Douglas Brooks-Davies (Oxford: World's Classics, 1970), p. 79. Subsequent citations are to this edition and appear in the text.

12. Samuel Butler, *Characters*, ed. Charles W. Daves (Cleveland: Case Western Reserve University Press, 1970), pp. 185–86, 219.

13. The term "characteristic writing" is Henry Gally's designation in 1725 for the Theophrastan character (*A Critical Essay on Characteristic-Writings* [Los Angeles: William Andrews Clark Memorial Library, 1952]). Subsequent citations of Gally are to this edition and appear in the text. Gally is speaking of writings we would now call character *sketches*, but "characteristic writing" is also a term Sarah Fielding uses to describe fictional *narratives*, like those she and her brother wrote (see her Introduction to *The Cry: A New Dramatic Fable* [London: Dodsley, 1754], p. 18).

14. I draw my examples of "characters" available at printshops from *Sayer and Bennett's Catalogue of New and Valuable Prints* (London, 1775; rpt. London: Holland Press, 1970).

15. Jerome Christensen illustrates the place of the copy theory of knowledge in the political economy and the career practices of Enlightenment intellectuals. See *Practicing Enlightenment: Hume and the Formation of a Literary Career* (Madison: University of Wisconsin Press, 1987), chap. 5.

16. Samuel Person, *An Anatomical Lecture of Man, Or a Map of the Little World* (London, 1664), cited in J. W. Smeed, *The Theophrastan 'Character': The History of a Literary Genre* (Oxford: Clarendon Press, 1985), p. 263; Ralph Johnson, *The Scholar's Guide* (London, 1665), quoted in Daves' Introduction to Butler, *Characters*, p. 5.

17. E. H. Gombrich, "The Experiment of Caricature," in idem, *Art and Illusion: A Study in the Psychology of Pictorial Representation* (Princeton, N.J.: Princeton University Press, 1960), p. 343.

18. Julie Stone Peters, *Congreve, the Drama, and the Printed Word* (Stanford: Stanford University Press, 1990), pp. 136–38.

19. Chandra Mukerji, *From Graven Images: Patterns of Modern Materialism* (New York: Columbia University Press, 1983), p. 21.

20. This changeling's persisting presence renders him in effect a "character" in the *Essay*. Our sense that Locke is not in control of the pathos or sensationalism of his examples contributes to our sense of this "monster's" autonomy or, as we say with reference to novelistic characters, our sense of this monster's life of his own. This is surely what Paul de Man had in mind when, discussing Locke, he called attention to the ineluctable excessiveness of the bit of text that is supposed merely to exemplify: "Examples used in logical arguments have a distressing way of lingering on with a life of their own." De Man's essay continues, fittingly, with a consideration of prosopopoeia, the trope of the giving of figure or face — the trope that, as a classic case of the swelling figure, figures things into life. Prosopopoeia casts a spell on language and conjures up anthropomorphic entities, "potential ghosts and monsters," who come to dwell within it. See "The Epistemology of Metaphor," in *On Metaphor*, ed. Sheldon Sacks (Chicago: University of Chicago Press, 1979), pp. 18n4, 19.

21. Susan Stewart discusses fine description in terms that clarify the political stakes of the empiricist's championing of the nuance and the detail: "Refinement has to do with not only the articulation of detail, but also the articulation of difference, an articulation which has increasingly served the interests of class. . . . The sign itself is dissolved into its differences from other signs within a system of signs: the material world is made symbolic according to the signifying practices of class" (*On Longing: Narratives of the Miniature, the Gigantic, the Souvenir, the Collection* [Baltimore: Johns Hopkins University Press, 1984], p. 29).

22. As John Barrell notes, eighteenth-century writers came to believe that economic progress depended on an ever-increasing variety of trades: thus Tobias Smollett's *Roderick Random* represents over one hundred practitioners of different occupations. See *English Literature in History, 1730–80* (New York: St. Martin's Press, 1983).

23. Warton's comments appeared in the periodical *The Adventurer*, no. 49, and are cited in Smeed, *The Theophrastan 'Character,'* p. 65.

24. See Louise Lippincott, *Selling Art in Georgian London: The Rise of Arthur Pond* (New Haven, Conn.: Yale University Press, 1983); and Diana Donald, "'Calumny and Caricatura': Eighteenth-Century Political Prints and the Case of George Townshend," *Art History* 6 (1983): 44–68.

25. *Baratariana, a select collection of fugitive political pieces* (Dublin, 1773), quoted in Donald, "'Calumny and Caricatura,'" p. 57. My information about etymologies for "caricature" comes from Ernst Kris, *Psychoanalytic Explorations in Art* (New York: International Universities Press, 1952), p. 189.

26. Fuseli's lectures to the Royal Academy are cited in John Barrell, *The Political Theory of Painting from Reynolds to Hazlitt: "The Body of the Public"* (New Haven, Conn.: Yale University Press, 1986), p. 286.

27. Stafford, *Body Criticism*, p. 152.

28. Joshua Reynolds, *Discourses on Art*, ed. Robert R. Wark (New Haven, Conn.: Yale University Press, 1975), discourse 3, p. 44. Subsequent citations are to this edition and appear in the text, where I cite discourse and page numbers.

29. For an extensive discussion of the place of character in Barry's lectures, see Barrell, *Political Theory of Painting*, pp. 173–82.

30. As the Academicians knew, Du Bos and Montesquieu had both opined that the characteristically inferior bodily structure of the English (product of the dreadful weather) would impede the nation's success in the arts of design. I quote Johann Joachim Winckelmann, who in 1755 compared the classical Greek face with the modern European face, much to the disadvantage of the latter: "Modern works are distinguished from those of the Greeks by numerous little hollows, by too many conspicuous dimples. Where these do occur in the works of the ancients, they are employed with wise economy. . . . In the physical beauty of the Greeks and in the works of their masters, there was a greater unity of construction, a nobler integration of the parts, and a higher degree of completeness" (*Thoughts on the Imitation of the Painting and Sculpture of the Greeks*, trans. H. B. Nisbet, in *German Aesthetics and Literary Criticism*, ed. H. B. Nisbet [Cambridge, Eng.: Cambridge University Press, 1984], p. 37). Winckelmann moves, intriguingly, from an account of the Greeks' superior beauty to the notion that the Greeks also possessed a better sense than the moderns of the requisite economy in line drawing: "The dividing line between completeness and superfluity in nature is a fine one, and the greatest of modern masters . . . who have tried to avoid an emaciated contour have erred on the side of corpulence, while others have made their figures excessively lean" (pp. 39–40).

31. See Marcia Pointon, "Portrait-Painting as a Business Enterprise in London in the 1780s," *Art History* 7 (1984): 187–205.

32. My sources here are Sean Shesgreen, ed., *Engravings by Hogarth: 101 Prints* (New York: Dover, 1971); Ronald Paulson, *Hogarth: His Life, Art, and Times*, 2 vols. (New Haven, Conn.: Yale University Press, 1971); idem, *Hogarth*, vol. 2, *High Art and Low, 1732–1750* (New Brunswick, N.J.: Rutgers University Press, 1992); and William Hogarth, *Analysis of Beauty*, ed. Joseph Burke (Oxford: Clarendon Press, 1953). Subsequent citations of the *Analysis* and also of Hogarth's "Autobiographical Notes" (included in Burke's edition) appear in the text.

I also draw on Lance Bertelsen's account of Hogarth's participation in "a pattern of response to the institutions and symbols of both sophisticated and popular English culture, a pattern . . . representative of the confluence of cultural phenomena at the level of middling culture" (*The Nonsense Club: Literature and Popular Culture, 1749–1762* [Oxford: Clarendon Press, 1986], p. 4).

33. B. Walwyn, *Essay on Comedy* (London, 1782), cited in Devin Burnell, "The Good, the True, and the Comical: Problems Occasioned by Hogarth's *The Bench,*" *Art Quarterly* n.s. 1 (1978): 29. In his interesting discussion of *Characters and Caricaturas*, Paulson argues that the engraving does indeed depict one female character, and that the head growing out of the back of Hogarth's head is that of the artist's wife, Jane. This punning depiction of Janus (or "Jane-Us") may be, as Paulson contends, Hogarth's ironic way of introducing *Marriage A-la-mode* with an allusion to his own happy marriage; it also seems an apt emblem for the ambiguity of Hogarth's position in the debates about the overloading of faces. See Paulson, *Hogarth*, 2: 208.

34. Martin Battestin was the first modern scholar to recognize Fielding. See "Pictures of Fielding," *Eighteenth-Century Studies* 17 (1983–84): 1–13.

35. Barrell remarks of Reynolds' system of species and classes, "The difficulty of this position . . . is that there is no limit to the number of classes we can invent . . . ; and the more we do invent, the more we seem to shatter the uniformity of human nature which a public art exists to represent" (*Political Theory of Painting*, pp. 105–8). Note also the problems Joshua Reynolds has in dealing with the painter's need to depict the expressions of the passions: "If you mean to preserve the most perfect beauty *in its most perfect state*, you cannot express the passions, all of which produce distortion and deformity, more or less, in the most beautiful faces" (*Discourses on Art*, 5, p. 78 [emphasis in the original]).

36. *The Monthly Review* (Sept. 20, 1758), cited in Burnell, "The Good, the True, and the Comical," p. 18.

37. Francis Grose, *Rules for Drawing Caricaturas, with An Essay on Comic Painting* (London: Samuel Bagster, 1788), pp. 5, 4.

38. In his discussion of the formation of critical and theoretical canons for the stage, Shearer West relates how acting theory "appropriated the formulae and critical methods of art theory"; "the actor became an image, . . . analysed like a work of art" (*The Image of the Actor: Verbal and Visual Representation in the Age of Garrick and Kemble* [London: Pinter, 1991], p. 89).

39. I am indebted here to Patey's discussion in *Probability and Literary Form*, chap. 4, of the display of the passions; and to Alan T. McKenzie, " 'The Countenance You Show Me': Reading the Passions in the Eighteenth Century," *Georgia Review* 32 (1978): 758–73.

40. James Beattie, *Essays on Poetry and Music* (London, 1776), cited in Patey, *Probability and Literary Form*, p. 86.

41. Warton's praise of Garrick's "little touches of nature" is cited in George Winchester Stone, Jr., and George M. Kahrl, *David Garrick: A Critical Biography* (Carbondale: Southern Illinois University Press, 1979), p. 39.

42. For the conversation with Burney, see James Boswell, *The Life of Johnson*, ed. R. W. Chapman (Oxford: World's Classics, 1980), p. 663. Johnson's remarks to Thrale are cited in Cecil Price, *Theatre in the Age of Garrick* (Totowa, N.J.:

Rowman & Littlefield, 1973), p. 18. For a brilliant account of the public's scrutiny of the player's person, see Kristina Straub, *Sexual Suspects: Eighteenth-Century Players and Sexual Ideology* (Princeton, N.J.: Princeton University Press, 1992).

43. Aaron Hill, *An Essay on the Art of Acting* (London, 1746), cited in George Taylor, " 'The Just Delineation of the Passions': Theories of Acting in the Age of Garrick," in *The Eighteenth-Century English Stage*, ed. Kenneth Richards and Peter Thomson (London: Methuen, 1982), p. 65. This semaphoric language of the body had been codified by Charles Le Brun in his *Method to Learn to Design the Passions*, introduced into England in 1701. Le Brun was one of the first to offer European cultural producers detailed physiognomic information — to illustrate a practical application of the theory of the passions.

44. Samuel Foote, *A Treatise on the Passions, So Far as They Regard the Stage* (London, 1747; rpt. New York: Benjamin Blom, 1971), p. 1. Subsequent citations are to *Treatise on the Passions* and appear in the text.

45. Denis Diderot, "Le paradoxe sur le comédien," cited in McKenzie, " 'The Countenance You Show Me,' " p. 766. I have drawn on the sophisticated account of Garrick's "naturalism" that Leigh Woods offers in *Garrick Claims the Stage: Acting as Social Emblem in Eighteenth-Century England* (Westport, Conn.: Greenwood Press, 1984).

46. On the demonizing of "low" entertainment during Garrick's lifetime, see Peter Stallybrass and Allon White, "The Grotesque Body and the Smithfield Muse," chap. 2 of *The Politics and Poetics of Transgression* (Ithaca, N.Y.: Cornell University Press, 1986).

47. *Theophilus Cibber to David Garrick, Esq.* (London, 1759), cited in Woods, *Garrick Claims the Stage*, p. 18; see the same page for Charles Macklin's normative sense of how " 'the restless abundance of [Garrick's] action and his gestures . . . exceeded the fair business of character.' "

48. Abbé Le Blanc, *Letters on the English and French Nations* (London, 1747), cited in Price, *Theatre in the Age of Garrick*, p. 15.

49. Shaftesbury, *Second Characters*, p. 131. On the gender of the detail in neoclassical aesthetics, see Naomi Schor, *Reading in Detail: Aesthetics and the Feminine* (New York: Methuen, 1987), esp. pp. 42–47. Garrick's use of accessories is censured in F. B. L.'s *The Rational Rosciad* (London, 1767): "His over frequent turning round about, / His handkerchief forever in and out, / His hat still moulded in a thousand forms, / His pocket clapping when his passion storms" (cited in Price, *Theatre in the Age of Garrick*, p. 25).

50. Charles Le Brun, *A Method to Learn to Design the Passions*, trans. John Williams, ed. Alan T. McKenzie (Los Angeles: William Andrews Clark Memorial Library, 1980), p. 31. On Hamlet's wig, see Woods, *Garrick Claims the Stage*, p. 121.

51. The *London Chronicle*'s review of *Harlequin Skeleton* is cited in Price, *Theatre in the Age of Garrick*, p. 74; Horace Walpole is cited in Woods, *Garrick Claims the Stage*, p. 18. Stone and Kahrl trace Garrick's involvement with the pantomimic tradition throughout their biography of the actor. See chap. 2 of *David Garrick*, "Garrick and the Acting Tradition," and chap. 7, "Garrick's Own Plays."

52. Wesley is cited in Peter de Bolla, *The Discourse of the Sublime: Readings in History, Aesthetics, and the Subject* (Oxford: Basil Blackwell, 1989), p. 155.

53. De Bolla, *The Discourse of the Sublime*, pp. 161, 131.

54. Tobias Smollett, *The Adventures of Roderick Random*, ed. Paul-Gabriel Boucé (Oxford: World's Classics, 1981), p. 395; idem, *The Adventures of Peregrine Pickle*, ed. James L. Clifford (Oxford: World's Classics, 1983), p. 273.

55. Hogarth appears in Smollett's *Peregrine Pickle* as Mr. Pallet, a painter who is touring the artistic treasures of the Continent. Smollett shows us how contemptuously he views Hogarth's claim to have invented comic history painting by having Pallet wax rhapsodic over Flemish art's closeup views of Nature's particularity. Pallet's own work replays the pursuit of the verisimilar associated with the primitive origins of mimesis and with, in particular, the legend of how Zeuxis deceived the birds with a hyper-real painting of a bunch of grapes. Pallet boasts to his fellows travelers that "in execution he had equalled, if not excelled, the two ancient painters who vied with each other in the representation of a curtain and a bunch of grapes; for he had exhibited the image of a certain object so like to nature that the bare sight of it set a whole hogsty in an uproar" (p. 335).

56. Tobias Smollett, *The Adventures of Ferdinand Count Fathom*, ed. Paul-Gabriel Boucé (Harmondsworth, Eng.: Penguin, 1990), p. 43.

57. Isaac D'Israeli, *A Dissertation on Anecdotes* (London, 1793), cited in Patey, *Probability and Literary Form*, p. 124; on Alison, see Patey, p. 257. In this short exposition of psychological fiction I draw on Frances Ferguson, "Rape and the Rise of the Novel," *Representations* 20 (Fall 1987): 88–112. See as well Mary Poovey's account of how the heroine of early nineteenth-century fiction is consistently the victim of false appearances and others' misreadings: *The Proper Lady and the Woman Writer: Ideology as Style in the Works of Mary Wollstonecraft, Mary Shelley, and Jane Austen* (Chicago: University of Chicago Press, 1984), esp. pp. 21–26.

58. *The Works of Thomas Chatterton*, ed. Donald S. Taylor (Oxford: Clarendon Press, 1971), 1: 593–94. The Pinchbecks are featured in the Fillinham collection of print ephemera, vol. 5, British Library, London.

59. See the entries for "queer card," "rum fellow," and "quiz" in E. Cobham Brewer, *The Dictionary of Phrase and Fable* (New York: Avenel, 1978).

60. I am grateful for the assistance of the staffs of the British Library and of the Theatre Museum, London, as well as for the financial support I received from the Mellon Fellowship program during the research stage of this project. For simultaneously demanding and encouraging readings of early drafts, I am also indebted to John Bender, Bliss Carnochan, Terry Castle, Stacy Hubbard, Jim Holstun, Tom Keirstead, Roy Roussel, Katie Trumpener, and Bill Warner. For assistance with the illustrations, I am grateful to John Chaimov; the Department of Special Collections, University of Chicago Library; and the Julian Park Publication Fund at SUNY/Buffalo.

GWILLIAM; *Cosmetic Poetics*

1. For a remarkable discussion of the links between femininity and "overly made-up representation" in rhetoric and painting, see Jacqueline Lichtenstein,

"Making Up Representation: The Risks of Femininity," *Representations* 20 (1987): 77–87.

2. [Antoine Le Camus], *Abdeker: Or the Art of Preserving Beauty* (London: Printed for A. Millar, 1754). Martha Pike Conant, in *The Oriental Tale in England in the Eighteenth Century* (New York: Columbia University Press, 1908), calls *Abdeker* "unimportant but curious—an awkward combination of an Eastern love-story with recipes and lectures on hygiene" (p. 103).

3. Courtney Melmoth [Samuel Jackson Pratt], *The New Cosmetic, or the Triumph of Beauty, A Comedy* (London, 1790).

4. For a summary of the philosophical and early Christian history of the bias against cosmetics, see Marcia L. Colish, "Cosmetic Theology: The Transformation of a Stoic Theme," *Assays: Critical Approaches to Medieval and Renaissance Texts*, 1, ed. Peggy Knapp and Michael Stugrin (Pittsburgh: University of Pittsburgh Press, 1981), pp. 3–14.

5. See Neil McKendrick, John Brewer, and J. H. Plumb, *The Birth of a Consumer Society: The Commercialization of Eighteenth-Century England* (Bloomington: Indiana University Press, 1982).

6. *The Gentleman's Magazine: and Historical Chronicle* 6 (1736): 377.

7. François Bruys, *The Art of Knowing Women: or, The Female Sex Dissected* (London, 1730), p. 112.

8. Dr. John Gregory, *A Father's Legacy to His Daughters* (New York: Shober & Loudoun, 1775), p. 14.

9. Roy Porter, "Making Faces: Physiognomy and Fashion in Eighteenth-Century England," *Etudes Anglaises* 38 (1985): 389. For more on the blush, see Ruth Bernard Yeazell, "Modest Blushing," in idem, *Fictions of Modesty: Women and Courtship in the English Novel* (Chicago: University of Chicago Press, 1991), pp. 65–80.

10. Jefferson quoted in Winthrop Jordan, *White over Black: American Attitudes Toward the Negro, 1550–1812* (Chapel Hill: University of North Carolina Press, 1968), p. 458.

11. Wylie Sypher, in *Guinea's Captive Kings: British Anti-Slavery Literature of the XVIIIth Century* (Chapel Hill: University of North Carolina Press, 1942), identifies the period from 1787 to 1791 as the high tide of literary antislavery (p. 10). Sypher describes in some detail (although derisively) Samuel Jackson Pratt's poetic contributions to antislavery, but does not mention *The New Cosmetic*. Sypher clearly considers Pratt an opportunist and a hack; for a more sympathetic examination of Pratt's prolific career and ambiguous reputation, see Josephine Grieder, " 'Amiable Writer' or 'Wretch'? The Elusive Samuel Jackson Pratt," *Bulletin of Research in the Humanities* 81 (1978): 464–84. For discussions of Pratt as a novelist, see April London's entry in the *Dictionary of Literary Biography: British Novelists 1660–1800*, ed. Martin C. Battestin (Ann Arbor, Mich.: Gale Research, 1985); and J. M. S. Tompkins, *The Popular Novel in England, 1770–1800* (Lincoln: University of Nebraska Press, 1961). Tompkins uses a quotation from one of Pratt's novels as the epigraph for her book, and concludes with an invocation of him as a quintessential figure for her project.

12. The loss of complexion (or gaining of color) was a frequent source of anxiety for European women in the West Indies. Janet Schaw, in her journal of a trip to Antigua and elsewhere, notes the concern about fairness of skin that characterized the white "Creole" inhabitants of the islands: "In short, [the Creole women] want only colour to be termed beautiful, but the sun who bestows such rich taints on every other flower, gives none to his lovely daughters; the tincture of whose skin is as pure as the lily, and as pale. . . . From childhood they never suffer the sun to have a peep at them, and to prevent him are covered with masks and bonnets." [Janet Schaw,] *Journal of a Lady of Quality; Being the Narrative of a Journey from Scotland to the West Indies, North Carolina, and Portugal, in the Years 1774 to 1776*, ed. Evangeline Walker Andrews and Charles McLean Andrews (New Haven, Conn.: Yale University Press, 1939), p. 114.

As Winthrop Jordan remarks, and as *The New Cosmetic* bears out, "A tanned skin implied an affinity which [the white woman in the West Indies] had to deny" (*White over Black*, p. 148).

13. Oddly enough, Louisa's anathematized color is not itself stable. She is variously described as a "Mulatto," a "blackamore," "brown as a gipsey," "brown as a berry" — and, significantly, as something unnameable: "The poor girl herself looked like — . . . I won't tell you," says Lovemore. She also is said to have "*lost* a little color" and to be one of the things that has faded "in this climate."

14. Morris quoted in Sypher, *Guinea's Captive Kings*, p. 224. Sypher quotes a more luridly detailed description of the process from the anonymous novel *The Adventures of Jonathan Corncob* (p. 279). In "'And wash the Ethiop white': Femininity and the Monstrous in *Othello*," Karen Newman discusses the meaning and history of the proverb, although without reference to the West Indian twist. In Jean E. Howard and Marion F. O'Connor, eds., *Shakespeare Reproduced: The Text in History and Ideology* (New York: Methuen, 1987), pp. 141–62.

15. "The basic question was: of the myriad observable differences between people — in skin, hair, or bones — which are significant, actually differentiating one race from another?" (Londa Schiebinger, "The Anatomy of Difference: Race and Sex in Eighteenth-Century Science," *Eighteenth-Century Studies* 23 [1990]: 387–405). Some of the eighteenth-century anatomists Schiebinger quotes find skin color "an unreliable measure of racial difference," and seek to locate difference in the skeleton and the skull.

16. If the sun has caused Louisa's change of race, the alteration is presumably purely or primarily facial; thus the question arises whether the actress playing Louisa would appear in some form of blackface, which would then be washed off for her transformation. This possibility, added to the presence of Quacou and another slave, also probably white actors in blackface, further destabilizes the representation of race in the play.

17. In an uncontrollable display of racial scapegoating, Schaw goes on to accuse these women of being insolent and licentious and of procuring abortions. [Schaw,] *Journal*, pp. 112–13.

18. *Abdeker*, for example, offers the following (notably unhealthy) recipe for "*An excellent White Paint for the Face*": "Take of the white Part of Hartshorn a

Pound, of the Flour of Rice two Pounds, of White Lead half a Pound, of Cuttle-Fish Bone two Ounces; Frankincense, Mastich, Gum *Arabic*, of each an Ounce; dilute the Whole in a sufficient Quantity of Rose-Water. Wash the Face therewith" (p. 81).

MÜCKE; *Horror and Euphemism in Lessing*

1. For Lessing's poetics of the fable and bourgeois tragedy, see chaps. 1 and 2 of my *Virtue and the Veil of Illusion: Generic Innovation and the Pedagogical Project in Eighteenth-Century Literature* (Stanford: Stanford University Press, 1991). See esp. pp. 96–114 for a discussion of Lessing's poetics and Julia Kristeva's notion of "abjection" as it is developed in her "L'abjet d'amour," *Tel Quel* 91 (Summer 1982): 17–32; and idem, *The Powers of Horror* (New York: Columbia University Press, 1982). If I use the terms "horror" and "disgust" almost interchangeably, I am aware that this can only be justified in the context of eighteenth-century theories of the "mixed sentiments" (*Theorie der "vermischten Empfindungen"*). These theories attempt to explain how pain can be turned into pleasure and vice versa. The two texts by Lessing I am analyzing in this essay belong also to this context. Within the history of aesthetics this discourse on the mixed sentiments constitutes both the predecessor and larger field for the discourse on the sublime. One distinguishing feature of the discourse on the mixed sentiments is the constant shifting of the boundaries between moral and aesthetic categories. Thus the term "horror," which usually connotes moral outrage, can also be used interchangeably with "disgust." See, e.g., Lessing's discussion on the affect evoked by wild beasts and corpses in chap. 24 of the *Laokoon*. I thank Arnold Davidson for an interesting comment on this point.

2. Carol Jacobs, "The Critical Performance of Lessing's *Laokoon*," *Modern Language Notes* 102 (Apr. 1987): 483–521; for a good comparatist overview of eighteenth-century positions (Boileau, Batteux, Addison, Hume, Burke, Diderot, Mendelssohn, and Lessing) on ugliness and disgust, see Herbert Dieckmann, "Das Abscheuliche und Schreckliche in der Kunsttheorie des 18. Jahrhunderts," in H. R. Jauss, *Die nicht mehr schönen Künste: Grenzphänomene des Ästhetischen* (Munich: Fink, 1968), pp. 271–317. For a discussion of disgust in Kant's aesthetics, see Jacques Derrida, "Economimesis," *Diacritics* 11 (1981): 3–25.

3. See Johann Joachim Winckelmann's treatise *On the Imitation of Greek Works in Painting and Sculpture* (1755).

4. Gotthold Ephraim Lessing, "Laokoon: Oder über die Grenzen der Malerei und Poesie," in idem, *Werke in drei Bänden* (Munich: Hanser, 1982), 3: 13. All translations are mine; page references will be given in parentheses, and all refer to vol. 3 of this edition.

5. For a detailed analysis of Lessing's *Laokoon*, see David Wellbery, *Lessing's Laocoon: Semiotics and Aesthetics in the Age of Reason* (Cambridge, Eng.: Cambridge University Press, 1984), and p. 105 (for this particular issue).

6. In this particular case the operation of interpreting, molding, and transforming the affective charge associated with a vision is accomplished by narrative focalization, through the differentiation between the vision through which the

elements are presented and the identity of the voice that is verbalizing that vision — more simply, between those who see and those who speak. On narrative focalization, see Mieke Bal, *Narratology: Introduction to the Theory of Narrative* (Toronto: University of Toronto Press, 1985), p. 101.

7. "Not that I did not think that our contemporary audience is a bit too disgusted by anything that is called or resembles a pamphlet. The contemporary audience seems to want to forget that it owes the Enlightenment over so many important issues merely to the spirit of contradiction, and that men would not have been able to agree on anything in this world had they never disputed anything" (p. 190).

8. "Dispute [*Streit*] has always nourished the spirit of examination, has always maintained prejudice and prestige in a state of commotion; in brief, it has prevented the painted [*geschminkte*] untruth from establishing itself in the place of truth" (p. 190). In order to become part of Enlightenment discourse we need to control our gut-level responses and disengage ourselves from the vicissitudes of our personal lives (see p. 191).

9. See *Iliad*, bk. 5, ll. 681–82.

10. "The reason is clear: without this general uniformity no universal recognizability is possible" (p. 195).

11. For the eighteenth-century experience of death, see John McManners, *Death and the Enlightenment* (London: Oxford University Press, 1985), esp. chap. 1, "Death's Arbitrary Empire," pp. 5–23.

12. See Elaine Scarry's reading of Sartre's "Wall" in her *The Body in Pain* (Oxford: Oxford University Press, 1985), pp. 30–33.

13. See Peter Stallybrass and Allon White, *The Politics and Poetics of Transgression* (Ithaca, N.Y.: Cornell University Press, 1986), pp. 8–26.

WELLBERY; *Morphisms of the Phantasmatic Body*

1. *Werther* was first published in 1774. A revised and slightly expanded edition appeared in 1787. In the following, I shall refer to the latter edition in the translation of Victor Lange: Johann Wolfgang von Goethe, *The Sorrows of Young Werther, Elective Affinities, Novella*, trans. Victor Lange and Judith Ryan, ed. David E. Wellbery, vol. 9 of *Goethe's Collected Works* (New York: Suhrkamp, 1987). Page references to this edition are given in parentheses. They are followed by page references to the German text in the seventh edition of Johann Wolfgang von Goethe, *Werke*, vol. 6, ed. Benno von Wiese (Hamburg: Christian Wegner, 1968).

2. Psychologists, phenomenologists, and psychoanalysts have emphasized that the human body cannot be described as an objective material entity located in neutral geometric space. Introception and extroception, not to speak of haptic behavior, occur from a situated incarnate perspective that itself develops across an intricate ontogenesis. The literary evocation of the phantasmatic body draws its resources from this history of incarnate subjectivity. Psychology: Henri Wallon, *Les Origines du caractère chez l'enfant* (Paris: Boivin, 1933); phenomenology: Maurice Merleau-Ponty, *The Primacy of Perception*, ed. James M. Edie (Evanston:

Northwestern University Press, 1964), esp. "The Child's Relations with Others," pp. 96–155; psychoanalysis: Jacques Lacan, "Le Stade du miroir comme formateur de la fonction du Je," in idem, *Ecrits I* (Paris: Seuil, 1966), pp. 89–97. Relations of influence and, in Merleau-Ponty's case, explicit reference link the three texts cited here.

3. The theoretically most powerful and historically most detailed discussion of this reorientation is Friedrich A. Kittler's *Discourse Networks, 1800/1900,* trans. Michael Metteer with Chris Cullens, Foreword by David E. Wellbery (Stanford: Stanford University Press, 1990), pt. 1, pp. 3–173, which includes references to the pertinent historical literature. For a treatment of the generic changes that accompany the historical shift in structures of socialization, see Dorothea E. von Mücke, *Virtue and the Veil of Illusion: Generic Innovation and the Pedagogical Project in Eighteenth-Century Literature* (Stanford: Stanford University Press, 1991). The significance of the historical reorganization of the family for *Werther* is discussed in Reinhart Meyer-Kalkus, "Werthers Krankheit zum Tode: Pathologie und Familie in der Empfindsamkeit," in *Urszenen: Literaturwissenschaft als Diskursanalyse und Diskurskritik,* ed. Friedrich A. Kittler and Horst Turk (Frankfurt: Suhrkamp, 1977), pp. 76–138.

4. Rudolf Braun, "'The Invention of Tradition': Wilhelm II. und die Renaissance der höfischen Tänze," *Zeitschrift für Volkskunde* 82 (1986): 227–49, esp. pp. 234–41. Braun refers to further literature on the subject.

5. Thus, in Sophie La Roche's *Miss Sternheim (Das Fräulein von Sternheim, 1771),* the major sentimental epistolary novel written in German prior to *Werther,* the hypermoralized Seymour must look on as the lascivious prince dances with the novel's heroine: "The deepest pain was in my soul when I heard her sing and saw her dance the minuet with the Prince and with others. But when he embraced her around her body, pressed her to his breast and bounced along at her side in the amoral, obscene German whirlwind dance with an intimacy that ripped apart all bonds of decorum—my quiet melancholy was transformed into burning rage" (Sophie von La Roche, *Geschichte des Fräulein von Sternheim,* ed. Fritz Brüggemann [Leipzig: Reclam, 1938], pp. 166–67).

6. In the poem "An Christel," composed probably in the same year as *Werther,* Goethe exploits this sexual connotation to achieve a naughtily burlesque effect: twirling about with Christel in the "airy German dance," the speaker of the poem confesses, indirectly but unmistakably, to getting an erection. See Goethe, *Sämtliche Werke,* vol. 1, *Gedichte, 1756–1799,* ed. Karl Eibl (Frankfurt: Deutscher Klassiker Verlag, 1987), pp. 221–22.

7. Prior to the cited passage, Werther describes the waltz in cosmic terms as dancers whirling around each other "like the planets" ("wie die Sphären") (p. 17; p. 25).

8. Where the English translation I have cited has "lost sight of everything else" the German text reads: "alles rings umher verging," which can be given more literally as "everything round about passed away." This figure of 'world-loss' is insistent in the novel, sometimes rendered in terms of 'disappearance' ("verschwinden"), sometimes actively as a 'forgetting' ("vergessen") of the world, sometimes as a visual 'dimming' or 'becoming dusk' ("dämmern").

9. See the rich descriptions in Norbert Elias, *Die höfische Gesellschaft* (Frankfurt: Suhrkamp, 1981).

10. On the accusation of pansexualism leveled against Freud and on the specific legitimacy of the term as regards Freud's work, see Jean Laplanche, *Life and Death in Psychoanalysis*, trans. Jeffrey Mehlman (Baltimore: Johns Hopkins University Press, 1976), p. 26.

11. Meyer-Kalkus, "Werthers Krankheit zum Tode," pp. 90–97.

12. In the poem "Ganymed," which bears many similarities to the passage in question, Goethe designates this embrace with the phrase "umfangend umfangen" ('embracing embraced') (*Gedichte, 1756–1799*, p. 205). The point I want to stress here is that the 'total embrace' is not merely a mutual embrace on the part of two finite entities, but is a paradoxical (impossible) structure in which the subject at once encircles totality and is encircled by that same totality, in which, in other words, defining limits are eradicated.

13. Critics, including Meyer-Kalkus, tend to read Werther's incapacity to "express" what he feels as a symptom of his artistic inability, his lack of self-distance, his essential passivity. This psychologizing reading of the passage often leads to a contrast between the novel's protagonist and its author, the latter succeeding where the former fails. See, e.g., Peter Pütz, "Werthers Leiden an der Literatur," in *Goethe's Narrative Fiction: The Irvine Symposium*, ed. William J. Lillyman (Berlin: de Gruyter, 1983), pp. 55–68, esp. p. 59. But such a reading effaces the poetological innovation of the novel, the project of taking novelistic discourse into domains that cannot be fixed within a representational order. The structures of infinite crossing and total embrace are characterized precisely by the fact that they cannot be pictured, that every attempt to lend them some sort of objectival mooring collapses. Thus, Werther's closing lament does not so much bear on his personal failure as an artist as it does on the absolute heterogeneity between the 'mirror' (visual representation) *of* his soul that a drawing would be and the 'mirror' that his soul, as infinite crossing and total embrace, *is*. This structural heterogeneity, and not a merely idiosyncratic failing, is the source of Werther's suffering.

14. Note that Spinoza's concept of *amor dei intellectualis* differs from Werther's experience in at least two respects. First, it exists in the mode of intuitive knowledge of the sort involved in the cognition of mathematical truths, whereas the passage from *Werther* stresses feeling as the mode of ecstatic apprehension. Second, Spinoza's love of God is imperfect, only a "part of the infinite love with which God loves himself." Such an awareness of the deficiencies of finitude seems to me entirely absent from Goethe's text. See Benedict de Spinoza, *Ethics*, ed. James Gutman (New York: Hafner, 1949), p. 274.

15. This formulation is influenced by the analysis of Freud's *Three Essays on the Theory of Sexuality* developed in Laplanche, *Life and Death in Psychoanalysis*, esp. pp. 8–24. To radicalize the nonsubstitutional aspect of the definition, one might restate it as follows: sexuality is the originary becoming-catachresis of incarnate subjectivity.

16. It would require more space than I can afford here to show that 'tears' in Goethe's novel, far from being an unmotivated residue of sentimentalism, occupy a systematic position within a maternally centered economy of gift and debt (here,

'gratitude'). This economy can be studied *in nuce* in the early ballad "Der König in Thule," in *Gedichte, 1756–1799*, pp. 1222–23. In a forthcoming study of Goethe's lyric poetry I discuss the system of exchange that organizes this text.

17. Werther's last written words prior to his suicide return to this first scene, tying together, as if with a ribbon, the beginning and end of his love for Charlotte:

> This pink bow which you wore the first time I saw you, surrounded by the children—Oh, kiss them a thousand times for me, and tell them the fate of their unhappy friend! I think I see them playing around me. The darling children! How they swarm [wimmeln] about me! How I attached myself to you, Charlotte! From the first moment I saw you. I knew I could not leave you! Let this ribbon be buried with me; it was a present from you on my birthday. How eagerly I accepted it all! [Wie ich das alles verschlang!] (p. 86; p. 123)

Note that the vision of the 'swarming' children picks up the verb employed for the 'blurring' of the natural world in the May 10 letter. Note further that Charlotte gives Werther the ribbon on his birthday, the day that commemorates the maternal gift of life. And note finally that the verb Werther uses to indicate his acceptance of everything that has come to him from Charlotte and that is summed up or condensed in the ribbon—the verb "verschlingen"—designates a form of eager, oral consumption. At the same time, an alternative sense of the verb—'to twist, interlace, intertwine, entangle'—makes itself felt in this context defined by the 'ribbon.' Orality ties the knot of Werther's love for Charlotte, of the destiny of his desire. I shall return to the word "verschlingen" in another, related context.

18. On the reading of this scene as baptism, see Caroline E. Wellbery, "From Mirrors to Images: The Transformation of Sentimental Paradigms in Goethe's *The Sorrows of Young Werther*," *Studies in Romanticism* 25 (1986): 231–49. As the author points out, the baptism enacted in the passage effects a matrilinear recoding of Christian religious symbolism. This transformation corresponds to the maternal figuration of the Spinozist *amor dei intellectualis* discussed above. A parallel but differently accentuated reading of the scene is developed by Friedrich A. Kittler, "Autorschaft und Liebe," in *Austreibung des Geistes aus den Geisteswissenschaften*, ed. F. A. Kittler (Paderborn: Schöningh, 1980), pp. 142–73.

19. One of the historical innovations of the eighteenth century, of course, is the replacement of the harpsichord, which only allows the production of discrete, articulate tones, by the pianoforte, which is capable of producing tonal glides and elisions. Thus, the piano becomes the instrument of the ebbs and flows of emotionality, an uninterrupted extension of the interior body. See, in this connection, the informative historical analysis by Wolfgang Scherer, " 'Aus der Seele muss man spielen': Instrumentelle und technische Bedingungen der musikalischen Empfindsamkeit," in *Materialitäten der Kommunikation*, ed. Hans Ulrich Gumbrecht and Karl Ludwig Pfeiffer (Frankfurt: Suhrkamp, 1988), pp. 295–309.

20. I have thus far ignored connections between *Werther* and other texts by Goethe from the same period. At this point, however, a reference to the *Urfaust* seems unavoidable. Since the lexical and imagistic (e.g., the 'cave mouth' as site of a "schweben") relevance of the passage is patent, I cite it without further commentary:

Ach könnt ich doch auf Berges Höhn
In deinem lieben Lichte gehn
Um Bergeshöhl mit Geistern schweben
Auf Wiesen in deinem Dämmer weben
Von all dem Wissensqualm entladen
In deinem Thau gesund mich baden.

Johann Wolfgang von Goethe, *Urfaust*, ed. Robert Petsch, rev. ed. (Stuttgart: Reclam, 1987), p. 4, ll. 39–44. Prose translation: "Oh, if I could only on mountain heights / Walk in your [the moon's] dear light / Float about mountain caves with spirits / Weave on meadows in your dusk / Unburdened of all knowledge-smoke / Bathe myself healthy in your dew."

21. I mentioned in connection with the first letter of the novel that one of the varieties of 'liquidity' the novel employs is that of a 'healing balm' ("Balsam"). In the semantic system of Goethe's poetry, this "balm" is intimately related to its opposite, 'poison' ("Gift"). Moreover, both varieties of 'liquidity' are figures for 'love,' which is to say that the 'liquid love' that circulates through Goethe's *oeuvre* is intrinsically ambivalent. Thus, the disappointed lover in the poem "Harzreise im Winter" ("Journey to the Harz Mountains in Winter") is said to be one, "dem Balsam zu Gift ward" ('for whom balm became poison') and "Der sich Menschenhass / Aus der Fülle der Liebe trank" ('Who drank hate of mankind / Out of the fullness of love'). Note also that this disappointed lover is absorbed by a natural barrenness that orally consumes him: "Die Öde verschlingt ihn" ('The barrenness swallows him up') (Goethe, *Gedichte, 1756–1799*, p. 323). But the most remarkable example of this semantic ambivalence inherent in the complex of 'liquid love' is provided by the poem "An den Geist des Johannes Secundus" ("To the Spirit of Johannes Secundus"), a poem addressed to the author of the *Basia* (*Kisses*) and entirely focused on the sphere of orality. The poem concludes with the lines: "Denn von der Liebe alles heilendem / Gift Balsam ist kein Tröpfgen drunter" ('For of love's all-healing / Poison balm not a drop is there') (Goethe, *Gedichte, 1756–1799*, p. 233). For a detailed discussion of both these texts, I must refer to the study-in-preparation on Goethe's poetry mentioned in note 16 above.

22. Jacques Lacan, *Les Complexes familiaux dans la formation de l'individu* (Paris: Navarin Editeur, 1984), pp. 28–30. My attention was drawn to this passage by Mikkel Borch-Jacobsen. See his commentary in *Le Lien affectif* (Paris: Aubier, 1991), pp. 246–47. Clearly there are aspects of Lacan's speculation that contravene certain points in my analysis of *Werther*. Apparently, my remarks on orality, the maternal breast, and the autoerotic structure of Werther's wish mix the complex of severance organized by the maternal imago with structures established only later, during oedipalization. Orthodoxy, however, is not my concern here, and since the maternal imago in any case, according to Lacan, continues to inform these later phases with its essential ambivalence, exhibiting its force even in "the most highly evolved forms of love," this confusion of levels on my part seems hardly a grave transgression.

23. The passage is reproduced in the critical apparatus of the Hamburg edition (see note 1), p. 531.

24. John Bender's investigations in *Imagining the Penitentiary: Fiction and the*

Architecture of Mind in the Eighteenth Century (Chicago, 1987), although applying for the most part to English material, suggest that the morphism of the incarcerated body is more than an idiosyncrasy of Werther's. Patterns of social discipline emergent in the eighteenth century place the individual body, as it were,
within an optic of imprisonment, submit it to an observational and regulating gaze
that is itself related to mechanisms of impersonal narration. On the basis of Bender's analysis, the speculation seems warranted that Werther's self-projection as
incarcerated body derives from the internalization of institutional mechanisms of
surveillance; that, in sensing his existence as incarceration, he metaphorizes himself from the perspective of a social other. This also applies to his self-projection as
absolute body which, as the following remarks attempt to show, rests on the
internalization of an other (echoic) voice. Whether this otherness can be localized
in specific institutions, however, is open to question.

25. Johann Gottfried Herder, *Sämmtliche Werke*, ed. B. Suphan (Berlin: Weid-
mannsche Buchhandlung, 1877–1913), 25: 314–15.

26. Johann Gottfried Herder, *Werke in zwei Bänden*, ed. Karl-Gustav Gerold
(Munich: Hanser, 1953), 1: 809.

27. Ibid., 1: 809–10.

28. G. W. F. Hegel, *Enzyklopädie*, par. 351, addendum, cited from *Werke* X, ed.
E. Moldenhauer and K.-M. Michel (Frankfurt: Suhrkamp, 1986).

29. "Just to look into her black eyes is a source of happiness for me! And what
grieves me is that Albert does not seem so happy as he — hoped to be — as I —
thought I would be — if — I don't like to use these dashes, but here I can't express
myself in any other way; and I am probably explicit enough" (p. 58; p. 82). It
should be noted that the dash is conventionally used in the German text of the
novel in situations of quoted dialogue, where it functions to distinguish the speech
of one speaker from that of another. This use of the dash as a kind of parti-
tioning device peculiar to the written rendition of oral discourse is effaced in the
translation.

30. The relationship between orality and writing that characterizes the novel as
a whole is dramatized in Werther's conflict with his supervisor at court, the ambas-
sador: "I like to do work quickly and, when the job is finished, leave it at that. But
he [the ambassador] is likely to return my papers to me, saying, 'They will do, but
you might look them over again. One can always find a better word or a more
appropriate particle.' I completely lose my patience. Not a single 'and' or any other
conjunction must be omitted: he hates the inversions which I sometimes employ;
and if we don't tune our sentences to the official key, he can't understand a word"
(p. 43; p. 61). The passage cites commonplaces of the late eighteenth-century
discussion (Rousseau, Herder) of writing as the grammaticalization and rigidify-
ing regulation of oral spontaneity. Writing is the entrance of convention and law
into a language originally poetic and musical.

31. In addition to this retribution fantasy as an attack on the throat, the text
deploys a number of corporeal figures that bear on the register of liquidity so
prominent in the morphism of the absolute body. Thus, near the end of the novel
Werther imagines his heart, brain, or senses as so compressed that they no longer
produce any soothing liquid. A typical example: "And this heart is now dead; no

delight will flow from it. My eyes are dry, and my senses, no longer freshened by soft tears, cause an anxious constriction of my brow" (p. 60; p. 84). The corporeal figuration, in all such cases, involves a blockage of flow, an interruption of the circulation of liquidity.

32. Herder, *Werke in zwei Bänden*, 1: 741.

33. Hegel, *Enzyklopädie*, par. 358. Werner Hamacher's commentary on the passage is particularly apposite to my concerns in this essay: "The voice is the ideal movement of the body in space, its death, which in sound is immediately heard and returns to the interior of the body; the form, in which the exteriority of body space negates itself and brings itself to the abstract unity of self-feeling" (*Pleroma: zu Genesis und Struktur einer dialektischen Hermeneutik bei Hegel*, in G. W. F. Hegel, *Der Geist des Christentums: Schriften 1796–1800*, ed. (Frankfurt, Berlin, Vienna, 1978), p. 268. Giorgio Agamben, commenting on some of the same passages in Hegel (and referring also to Herder), argues similarly: "Thus, the animal voice is the *voice of death*. Here the genitive should be understood in both an objective and a subjective sense. 'Voice (and memory) *of death*' means: the voice is death, which preserves and recalls the living as dead, and it is, at the same time, an immediate trace and memory of death, pure negativity" (*Language and Death: The Place of Negativity*, trans. Karen E. Pinkus with Michael Hardt, vol. 78 of *Theory and History of Literature* (Minneapolis: University of Minnesota Press, 1991), p. 91. The original Italian edition was published in 1982.

SCHNEIDER; *Deconstruction of the Hermeneutical Body*

1. For a representative traditional interpretation, see Benno von Wiese, "Das verlorene und das wieder zu findende Paradies: Eine Studie über den Begriff der Anmut bei Goethe, Schiller und Kleist," in *Kleists Aufsatz über das Marionettentheater: Studien und Interpretationen*, ed. Helmut Sembdner (Berlin: Erich Schmidt, 1967), pp. 196–220. Two early ironic readings are Wolfgang Binder, "Ironischer Idealismus: Kleists unwillige Zeitgenossenschaft," in idem, *Aufschlüsse: Studien zur deutschen Literatur* (Zurich and Munich: Artemis, 1976); pp. 311–29; and Beda Allemann, "Sinn und Unsinn von Kleists Gespräch 'Über das Marionettentheater,'" *Kleist-Jahrbuch*, 1981–82: 50–65. The most important and influential recent analysis is Paul de Man, "Aesthetic Formalization: Kleist's 'Über das Marionettentheater,'" in idem, *The Rhetoric of Romanticism* (New York: Columbia University Press, 1984), pp. 263–90.

2. For the English translation of Kleist's text, I rely mostly on an unpublished manuscript by Carol Jacobs, with friendly permission of the author. I have only occasionally altered her version. This is by far superior to the standard translation. The German original can be found in Heinrich von Kleist, *Sämtliche Werke und Briefe*, ed. Helmut Sembdner, 2 vols. (Munich: Hanser, 1984), 1: 338–45. Since the text is rather short, I will not reference the pages.

3. De Man's article "Aesthetic Formalization" is the decisive document for this tendency. Other studies include William Ray, "Suspended in the Mirror: Language and the Self in Kleist's 'Über das Marionettentheater,'" *Studies in Romanticism* 18 (1979): 521–46; Cynthia Chase, "Mechanical Doll, Exploding Machine: Kleist's

Models of Narrative," in idem, *Decomposing Figures: Rhetorical Readings in the Romantic Tradition* (Baltimore: Johns Hopkins University Press, 1986), pp. 141–56; a Lacanian analysis by Bernhard Greiner, " 'Der Weg der Seele des Tänzers': Kleists Schrift 'Über das Marionettentheater,' " *Neue Rundschau* 98 (1987): 112–31; on the importance of the theater, see the excellent last chapter in Ingeborg Harms, *Zwei Spiele Kleists von Trauer und Lust: 'Die Familie Schroffenstein' und 'Der Zerbrochene Krug'* (Munich: Fink, 1990). My own approach is closest to Brittain Smith's in the following article, which I only received in manuscript form after I had essentially finished this essay: " 'Es ist ein Schrecken, es zu sehen': The Dance of Dialogue in Kleist's 'Über das Marionettentheater.' "

4. Mikhail Bakhtin, *Rabelais and His World*, trans. Helene Iswolsky (Bloomington: Indiana University Press, 1984), esp. chap. 5. For the general background of the process of civilization as the disciplining of the body, see the extensive work of Norbert Elias, esp. *The Civilizing Process*, trans. Edmund Jephcott (New York: Pantheon, 1982).

5. Friedrich Schiller, "Über Anmut und Würde" (1793), in idem, *Sämtliche Werke*, ed. Gerhard Fricke and Herbert G. Göpfert (Munich: Hanser, 1960), 5: 437 ("Anmut ist eine Schönheit, die nicht von der Natur gegeben, sondern von dem Subjekte selbst hervorgebracht wird") and 477 ("Die Anmut lässt der Natur da, wo sie die Befehle des Geistes ausrichtet, einen Schein von Freiwilligkeit").

6. Grace as internalization of violence becomes particularly clear in a footnote to Schiller's essay, which could well have provided Kleist with a clue to his parody on the dance teacher.

7. For the principal constellation in the context of the aesthetic perception of nature in the eighteenth century, see Helmut J. Schneider, "The Staging of the Gaze: Aesthetic Illusion and the Scene of Nature in the 18th Century," forthcoming in *Appearances: Essays in Culture, Perception and the Arts*, ed. Frederick Burwick and Walter Pape.

8. Schiller, *Sämtliche Werke*, 5: 483

9. See Alexander Weigel, "König, Polizist, Kasperle . . . und Kleist: Auch ein Kapitel deutscher Theatergeschichte, nach bisher unbekannten Akten," in *Impulse: Aufsätze, Quellen, Berichte zur deutschen Klassik und Romantik*, ed. W. Dietze and P. Goldammer, 4th series (Berlin and Weimar: Aufbau Verlag, 1982), pp. 253–77. And see idem, "Der Schauspieler als Maschinist: Heinrich von Kleists 'Über das Marionettentheater' und das 'Königliche Nationaltheater,' " in *Heinrich von Kleist: Studien zu Werk und Wirkung*, ed. Dirk Grathoff (Opladen: Westdeutscher Verlag, 1988), pp. 263–80. A cabinet order of Friedrich Wilhelm III from November 17, 1809, started a police action against marionette presentations in pubs and "Tabagien," citing the damaging influence on the morals of the simple people. The action reached its peak at exactly the same time that Kleist published his essay in four sequential issues of his daily *Berliner Abendblätter*. Brittain Smith, " 'Es ist ein Schrecken, es zu sehen,' " drew my attention to these interesting historical articles.

10. Greiner, " 'Der Weg der Seele des Tänzers,' " p. 122, mentions that traveling actors' and artists' groups often consisted exactly of these three attractions.

11. The excellent essay by Brittain Smith, " 'Es ist ein Schrecken, es zu sehen,' "

takes the dancer's "exposure" by the narrator as its point of departure for the reading of Kleist's text as a dialogic dance in which the partners try to hide and cover themselves up as they continually expose themselves to the other.

12. E.g., shortly after this quote: "This remark seemed to me at first to throw some light on the pleasure that he had alleged to find in the theater of the marionettes. In the meantime I did not suspect by far the consequences that he would draw from this later." "Vorgeben," "allege," articulates literally the "pretense" or facade behind which to hide, which keeps the dialogue going; just as the logical operation of "Folgerungen ziehen," "to draw (pull) consequences (sequences, something that follows)," corresponds on the literal level to the pulling of strings of the puppets.

13. "Da diese Äusserung, *durch die Art, wie er sie vorbrachte, mehr, als ein blosser Einfall schien,* so liess ich mich bei ihm nieder, um ihn über die Gründe, auf die er eine so sonderbare Behauptung stützen könne, näher zu vernehmen." "Vorbrachte," cf. "vor-geben" in the preceding note.

14. "Nehmen," "to take," has a natural association with the hand which, as we shall see, plays an important role in the text. E.g., later when the dancer in the fencing anecdote is led to the bear where he experiences his defeat, "the brothers took me by the hand," in a gesture of superiority and of "taking somebody in," as in the German word "einvernehmen." The procedure of "literalization of metaphor" is generally prominent in Kleist's work. It forms the central thesis of Ilse Graham, *Word into Flesh: A Poet's Quest for the Symbol* (Berlin: de Gruyter, 1977). See also Clayton Koelb, *Inventions of Reading: Rhetoric and the Literary Imagination* (Ithaca, N.Y.: Cornell University Press, 1988).

15. It is something, of course, that the German language particularly lends itself to, which makes this feature to a certain extent untranslatable. This must be taken into account if we analyze it as an intentional strategy. But the text exploits this possibility of the language rather consistently, as I will try to point out as I go along.

16. "Sehen Sie nur die P——an, fuhr er fort, wenn sie die Daphne spielt, und sich, verfolgt vom Apoll, nach ihm umsieht; die Seele sitzt ihr in den Wirbeln des Kreuzes; sie beugt sich, als ob sie brechen wollte, wie eine Najade aus der Schule Bernins. Sehen Sie den jungen F——an, wenn er, als Paris, unter den drei Göttinnen steht, und der Venus den Apfel überreicht: die Seele sitzt ihm gar (es ist ein Schrecken, es zu sehen) im Ellenbogen."

17. In Luther's translation: "dass er nicht ausstrecke seine Hand, und breche auch von dem Baum des Lebens, und lebe ewiglich!" (Gen. 3: 22).

18. Interestingly, contemporary historico-philosophical rewritings of the biblical story by Kant and Schiller liked to compare man's state of innocence with that of children held by the "Gängelband" or the "Leitband des Instinkts" (the guiding leash). Schiller at one point even speaks directly of an "Automat" (p. 767). This may have inspired Kleist to pick the marionette for his state of grace whose meaning in *Geschichtsphilosophie*, however, was of course negative: only after breaking loose from his tutelage and falling, man had to stand up on his own feet; he grew, in Schiller's words, "from a happy instrument to an unhappy artist" (p. 767)—in our terms, to a creator and splitter of himself, who had to continue on his road of

autonomous self-creation (dis- and re-embodiment). Perfection would occur if we regained the felicitous security of the child or puppet without its dependence; if we became the happy instrument again, but now the instruments of ourselves as the *happy* artists; we would, to stay in the image, become marionettes pulling our own strings with full freedom *and* in strict conformity with the law of nature. Of course, this is Kleist's and not Schiller's image, and it describes the process between the puppeteer and the puppet which Kleist and his dancer use to bring out the paradoxical (if not absurd) character of this utopian thought. But the mechanical character of the marionette whose construction conforms (by necessity) with nature not only parodies the reconciliation of reason and nature celebrated in Schiller's concept of grace but also replaces it with a *constructivist* artistic utopia, as we shall see. Friedrich Schiller, "Etwas über die erste Menschengesellschaft nach dem Leitfaden der mosaischen Urkunde" (1790), in *Sämtliche Werke,* 4: 767–80. Immanuel Kant, "Mutmasslicher Anfang der Menschengeschichte" (1786), in *Werkausgabe,* ed. Wilhelm Weischedel (Frankfurt: Suhrkamp, 1977), 11: 83–102.

19. If the contrast is between the last fraction of spirit about which the dancer had "spoken" before, as distinct from the merely mechanical side of the puppeter's business as the narrator had thought, pictured, "imagined" it ("es mir gedacht"), then we can read this as causally related. The spirit comes *through* language and is dependent on it, in contrast to other means of more immediate representation (if they exist, witness the automatic dance which can only be produced "by means of a crank," "vermittels"). Compare the phonetic assonance in "Bruch" and "gesprochen" — language produces the fraction/fracture of "Geist."

20. This connection has been demonstrated especially in Rilke research, i.e., the figure of the doll in the fourth "Duineser Elegie." See Eva M. Lüders, "Rilke und der Tänzer: Zu einer ästhetischen Frage der modernen Dichtung," *Deutsche Vierteljahresschrift für Literaturwissenschaft und Geistesgeschichte* 42 (1968): 515–52; Jacob Steiner, "Das Motiv der Puppe bei Rilke," in Sembdner, ed., *Kleists Aufsatz über das Marionettentheater,* pp. 132–70; Rainer Nägele, *Theater, Theory, Speculation: Walter Benjamin and the Scenes of Modernity* (Baltimore: Johns Hopkins University Press, 1991), chap. 1. See also Brigitte Peucker, "German Cinema and the Sister Art: Wegener's 'The Student of Prague,'" in Nancy Kaiser and David E. Wellbery, eds., *Traditions of Experiment from the Enlightenment to the Present: Essays in Honor of Peter Demetz* (Ann Arbor: University of Michigan Press, 1992), pp. 167–85.

21. "Hervorbringen" is the same word that was used for producing the movements of the puppets with a crank.

22. Compare "before my eyes"; the ambiguous German word "Bemerkung" contains both elements, the visual and the linguistic.

23. A brilliant interpretation of this middle narrative is found in de Man, "Aesthetic Formalization." De Man was the first to see this theme (used as the title of his essay) in the context of classicism, which he contrasts with the association of blood suggested by the splinter and the "blushing" of the youth at the remark of his elder.

24. Gerhard Kurz refers to the article "Dornauszieher" in the *Reallexikon zur*

deutschen Kunstgeschichte, for the iconographical information that the foot represented the seat of the affections (*affectiones*), for which the thorn served as punishment—another example of spiritualization. " 'Gott befohlen': Kleists Dialog 'Über das Marionettentheater' und der Mythos vom Sündenfall des Bewusstseins," *Kleist-Jahrbuch* 1981–82: 270.

25. The *"blosse* Bemerkung" associates "bare" and exposure ("entblössen"), as Brittain Smith, " 'Es ist ein Schrecken, es zu sehen,' " has most recently pointed out.

26. The split between outside and inside is repeated on the level of the text's organization into halves. The argumentative exchange of the first part, in which the narrator elicits and questions the cryptic and desultory remarks of Herr C., is followed by the exchange of the two anecdotal stories, which establishes a kind of agreement between the two men. This division even shows in the appearance of the printed pages: the many short paragraphs of the first half, containing the rivals' back-and-forth questions and answers, attacks and defenses, give way to the larger blocks of the narratives, which, as it were, solidify the chopped-up pages and pacify the contestants. But the reassuring coherence of the stories is as deceptive as it is rhetorically efficacious.

27. For a detailed interpretation of this gesture, which a little later is repeated by Herr C., see Brittain Smith, " 'Es ist ein Schrecken, es zu sehen.' "

28. De Man, "Aesthetic Formalization," p. 281.

GUSTAFSON; *Goethe's 'Clavigo'*

1. Johann Wolfgang von Goethe, *Clavigo*, in *Hamburger Ausgabe*, vol. 4 (Munich: C. H. Beck, 1982), p. 288. All subsequent references are to this edition and appear in the text. All translations are my own.

2. No earlier study of *Clavigo* focuses on the issues of writing or, more specifically, of the "writing" and "reading" of the body in the play. Other studies concentrate on biographical and philological concerns. See Osman Durrani, "Die Diskussion über Goethes 'Clavigo': Ein Beitrag zur Abgrenzung der biographisch orientierten Goetheforschung," *Goethe Jahrbuch* 96 (1979): 84–100; Albert Bielschowsky, *The Life of Goethe, 1749–1778* (New York: Putnam, 1905); Georg Grempler, *Goethes Clavigo: Erläuterung und literarhistorische Würdigung* (Halle: Max Niemeyer, 1911); Regina Otto, "Clavigo," *Goethe Jahrbuch* 90 (1973): 22–36; Inge Strohschneider-Kohrs, "Goethes Clavigo," *Goethe Jahrbuch* 90 (1973): 37–50; Edward Dvoretzky, "Lessingsche Anklänge in Goethes Clavigo: Ein Prolegomenon zu einer sprachlichen und stilistischen Untersuchung," *Lessing Yearbook* 4 (1972): 37–58; and Peter Burgard, "Emilia Galotti und Clavigo: Werthers Pflichtlehre und unsere," *Zeitschrift für deutsche Philologie* 104 (1985): 481–94.

3. For detailed studies of these broader issues, see Friedrich Kittler, "Erziehung ist Offenbarung: Zur Struktur der Familie in Lessings Dramen," *Jahrbuch der Schillergesellschaft* 21 (1977): 111–37; Albert M. Reh, "Wunschbild und Wirklichkeit: Die Frau als Leserin und als Heldin des Romans und des Dramas der Aufklärung," in *Die Frau als Heldin und Autorin: Neue Kritische Ansätze zur deutschen Literatur*, ed. Wolfgang Paulsen (Munich: Francke, 1979), pp. 82–95; Kay Goodman and Susan Cocalis, *Beyond the Eternal Feminine: Critical Essays*

on Women and German Literature (Stuttgart: Hans-Dieter Heinz, 1982); Andreas Huyssen, "Das leidende Weib in der dramatischen Literatur von Empfindsamkeit und Sturm und Drang: Eine Studie zur bürgerlichen Emanzipation in Deutschland," *Monatshefte* 69 (Summer 1977): 159–73; and Inge Stephan, "Frauenbild und Tugendbegriff im bürgerlichen Trauerspiel bei Lessing und Schiller," *Lessing Yearbook* 17 (1985): 1–20.

4. Wolfgang Martens, "Leserezepte für Frauenzimmer: Die Frauenzimmerbibliotheken der deutschen Moralischen Wochenschriften," in *Archiv für Geschichte des Buchwesens* 15 (1975): 1145–1146.

5. Sara Etta Schreiber, *The German Woman in the Age of Enlightenment* (New York: King's Crown Press, 1948), p. 13.

6. *The Spectator* 7, no. 490 (London, 1797), p. 65.

7. Wolfgang Martens, *Die Botschaft der Tugend: Die Aufklärung im Spiegel der deutschen Moralischen Wochenschriften* (Stuttgart: J. B. Metzerlersche, 1968), p. 369.

8. Jacques Derrida, *Spurs: Nietzsche's Styles*, trans. Barbara Harlow (Chicago: University of Chicago Press, 1978), p. 47.

9. Martens, "Leserezepte," p. 1153, points out that the writers of moral weeklies in Germany, like Hagedorn and Bodmer, felt that to encourage women's desire to read they needed to avoid an abstract, dry style. The style of their weeklies ought to be "light, entertaining, conversational and engaging."

10. Martens, "Leserezepte," p. 1153.

11. Durrani suggests that Marie's "sickness becomes the theme of the work." Moreover, he asserts (accepting the position of Clavigo) that Marie's sickness indicates a type of moral infirmity: "Goethe has used this motif repeatedly in his works and it serves most often to mark or establish a transgression" ("Die Diskussion über Goethes 'Clavigo,' " p. 98).

12. Derrida suggests in *Spurs* that stylistic distancing is necessary because "woman is not a determinable identity" (p. 39).

13. Bielschowsky writes: "But surely as the faithless one has wounded her, she loves him still. This is an exact picture of Friederike after Goethe's departure" (*Life of Goethe*, p. 236). In contrast, Grempler acknowledges Marie's hatred for Clavigo, but like the characters in the play, he dismisses its significance: "The sympathetic feelings of Marie prove to be much stronger than hate or jealousy" (*Goethes Clavigo*, pp. 86–87).

14. Grempler accepts Sophie's interpretation of Marie's symptoms: "This Sophie sees in Marie's passionate resistance, in the embarrassment which overwhelms her sister's senses — not the effects of hate and disgust — and rightly so — but a lack of confidence in herself. Marie's fearful anxiety is an expression of the innermost love" (*Goethes Clavigo*, pp. 90–91).

15. Eve Kosofsky Sedgwick, *Between Men: English Literature and Male Homosocial Desire* (New York: Columbia University Press, 1985), pp. 25–26, maintains that "in any male dominated society there is a special relationship between male homosocial (including homosexual) desire and the structures for maintaining and transmitting patriarchal power." Moreover, "patriarchal heterosexuality can best be discussed in terms of one or another form of the traffic in women: it is the use of

women as exchangeable, perhaps symbolic property for the primary purpose of cementing the bonds of men with men."

16. Julia Kristeva, *The Powers of Horror: An Essay on Abjection*, trans. Leon S. Roudiez (New York: Columbia University Press, 1982), pp. 82, 2.

17. The cannibalistic climax of Beaumarchais's visions of revenge (beginning with "If only I had him beyond the seas") is not included in the text as reproduced in the *Hamburger Ausgabe (HA)*. The passage is in the first published version of *Clavigo* (*Druck* E), which appeared through Weygand in Leipzig (1774). See the notes in *HA*, 4: 572.

18. Sigmund Freud, "Totem and Taboo," in *The Freud Reader*, ed. Peter Gay (New York: Norton, 1989), p. 503.

19. Kristeva, *Powers of Horror*, p. 118.

20. Julia Kristeva, "Novel as Polylogue," in idem, *Desire in Language*, trans. T. Gora, A. Jardine, and L. S. Roudiez (New York: Columbia University Press, 1980), p. 191.

21. Ibid., p. 195.

22. Saint George, who accompanies Beaumarchais to Madrid, says: "Promise me, my friend, once more that you will consider where you are. In a foreign land where all of your friends, where all of your wealth won't protect you against the secret machinations of a contemptible enemy" (p. 268).

23. Durrani reasserts the patriarchal position of the men in the play when he avers: "In this scene Marie is blinded by jealousy and completely misjudges the true character of her lover, for Clavigo lies (as we know from the first scene) at the feet of no other woman. He attempts indeed to manage without female companionship and grieves over his breach of faith." Her vision of revenge points to an "estrangement from life itself," Durrani observes, "and so we can determine that sickness and jealous love for Clavigo are her essential characteristics" ("Die Diskussion über Goethes 'Clavigo,'" p. 99).

24. Grempler maintains that "in his frenzy [Beaumarchais] misjudges Marie's psyche completely. He believes that she would experience joy and satisfaction at the sight of the dying Clavigo" (*Goethes Clavigo*, p. 81).

25. This moment of "unity" is described by Gerhard Sauder, ed., *Der Junge Goethe*, vol. 1.1 (Munich: Hanser, 1985), p. 997, as "the binding together of death and love." Grempler suggests that "in this manner Clavigo openly demonstrates his return to virtue, that is, to the morality of the middle-class world" (*Goethes Clavigo*, p. 58).

26. Compare the view of the death scene put forward in the notes in *HA*, p. 570: "Clavigo dies, but his death is welcomed by him and appears as the path to unity with the beloved, who awaits him. Deeper levels of significance arise here, as opposed to those in force earlier in the drama. The tie to the beloved is now no longer a question of loyalty, honor, or virtue, but a magical tie. The realm of middle-class community and of middle-class love recedes as does that of the greater world. The realm of a higher love opens which is shared only by these two particular souls — souls destined for each other. The world transforms, and the tragic demise of certain individuals is surmounted by the transfiguration of the lovers."

DIPIERO; *Disfiguring the Victim's Body*

1. Pierre Choderlos de Laclos, *Les Liaisons dangereuses* (Paris: Garnier-Flammarion, 1964), p. 376. All subsequent references are to this edition and appear in the text. Translations of this and succeeding French works are my own.

2. In the ostensible "Editor's preface," for example, we read: "The work's utility, which might yet be contested, nevertheless seems to me easy to establish. I believe that it is to pay service to morals to unveil the means by which the evil corrupt the good, and I believe that these letters can be effectively put to this service" (p. 17).

3. The classic critical work on realism in eighteenth-century French fiction is Georges May's *Dilemme du roman au dix-huitième siècle* (Paris: Presses Universitaires de France, 1963). But see also Vivienne Mylne, *The Eighteenth-Century French Novel: Techniques of Illusion* (Cambridge, Eng.: Cambridge University Press, 1981); English Showalter, *The Evolution of the French Novel* (Princeton, N.J.: Princeton University Press, 1972); and, more recently, William Ray, *Story and History: Narrative Authority and Social Identity in the Eighteenth-Century French and English Novel* (Cambridge, Eng.: Basil Blackwell, 1990).

4. Donatien Alphonse François, Marquis de Sade, *Justine ou les malheurs de la vertu* (Paris: 10/18, 1969), p. 13. All subsequent references to *Justine* are to this edition and appear in the text.

5. Gérard Genette, "Vraisemblance et motivation," in idem, *Figures II* (Paris: Seuil, 1969).

6. Aubert de la Chesnaye des Bois, *Lettres amusantes et critiques sur les romans en général* (Paris: Gissey, 1743), "Première lettre," p. 20.

7. The use of the word "libertine" is Sade's, and it might provoke some confusion regarding the relationship between the people who victimize Justine and the *libertins érudits* of the previous century. See Joan DeJean, *Libertine Strategies* (Columbus: Ohio State University Press, 1981); Antoine Adam, *Les Libertins au XVIIe siècle* (Paris: Buchet, 1964); and René Pintard, *Le Libertinage érudit dans la première moitié du dix-septième siècle* (Paris: Boivin, 1943).

8. Roland Barthes, "L'Arbre du crime," and Philippe Sollers, "Sade dans le texte," both in *Tel Quel* 28 (Winter 1967); Alice Laborde, *Le Mariage du marquis de Sade* (Paris: Champion-Slatkine, 1988); idem, *Sade romancier* (Neuchâtel: Baconnière, 1974); Jane Gallop, *Intersections* (Lincoln: University of Nebraska Press, 1981).

9. See Jacques Lacan, especially "Dieu et la jouissance de la femme," *Le Séminaire: XX* (Paris: Seuil, 1975); *Feminine Sexuality: Jacques Lacan and the école freudienne*, ed. Juliet Mitchell and Jacqueline Rose, trans. Rose (New York: Norton, 1982); "The Signification of the Phallus," *Ecrits: A Selection*, trans. Alan Sheridan (New York: Norton, 1977); the section entitled "Le Paradoxe de la jouissance," in *Le Séminaire: VII* (Paris: Seuil, 1986), pp. 197–285. And Serge Leclaire, esp. "Les Éléments en jeu dans une psychanalyse," *Cahiers pour l'analyse* 5.

10. Geoffrey Bennington, *Sententiousness and the Novel* (Cambridge, Eng.: Cambridge University Press, 1985), p. 180.

11. Josué Harari expands on this point by noting that discourse and activity not only inform one another but are mutually dependent and by extension mutually exclusive. He writes: "Sadian discourse exists on an equal footing with desire: both move within a single spiral, with one constantly opposed to the other, but with neither in a position to dominate or to comment on the other" (*Scenarios of the Imaginary: Theorizing the French Enlightenment* [Ithaca, N.Y.: Cornell University Press, 1987], p. 189).

12. If the libertines seek the end of meaning, Marcel Hénaff makes the counterpoint that interpretation is the realm of the victim. He writes: "Not only does [interpreting] prove that one does not know, that one is outside the game, but it is also necessarily erring on signs, it is misapprehending their function as lure and it is forgetting that they are by hypothesis conventional and hypocritical" (*Sade: L'Invention du corps libertin* [Paris: Presses Universitaires de France, 1978], p. 55).

13. For a different perspective on Justine's infinitely renewable body, see Slavoj Žižek, *The Sublime Object of Ideology* (New York: Verso, 1989), esp. pp. 134–35.

14. Ernesto Laclau, *New Reflections on the Revolution of Our Time* (London: Verso, 1990), p. 17.

15. See also Laclau and Chantal Mouffe: "For every language and every society are constituted as a repression of the consciousness of the impossibility that penetrates them. Antagonism escapes the possibility of being apprehended through language, since language only exists as an attempt to fix that which antagonism subverts" (*Hegemony and Socialist Strategy* [London: Verso, 1985], p. 125).

16. Sade, *Histoire de Juliette*, 3 vols. (Paris: 10/18, 1976), 3: 503.

17. The same event in the *Histoire de Juliette* provokes the opposite reaction, however. Toward the end of that novel, Juliette puts her sister out into a storm as a way of tempting fate. When she is killed and disfigured, the joyous crowd calls out: "Come contemplate the work of heaven, come see how it rewards virtue: is it worth the trouble to cherish it, when those who serve it best become such cruel victims of fate?" (3: 500).

18. Elaine Scarry, *The Body in Pain: The Making and Unmaking of the World* (Oxford: Oxford University Press, 1985), esp. pp. 51–59 and 218–20.

19. *Journal général de France*, Sept. 27, 1792, cited by Françoise Laugaa-Traut, *Lectures de Sade* (Paris: Colin, 1973), p. 38.

CULLENS; *The Masquerade of Womanliness*

1. See Stuart Curran's "The I Altered" (in Anne Mellor, ed., *Romanticism and Feminism* [Bloomington: Indiana University Press, 1988], pp. 185–207), which includes Robinson's poetry in the consideration of work by other female poets of the later eighteenth century. See also M. Ray Adams, *Studies in the Literary Backgrounds of English Radicalism* (London: Franklin and Marshall Press, 1947).

2. Mary Robinson, *Memoirs of the Late Mrs. Robinson*, completed and edited by Maria Robinson, 2 vols. (London, 1801), 2: 122. All subsequent references are to this edition and appear in the text.

3. Tom Laqueur, *Making Sex: Body and Gender from the Greeks to Freud* (Cambridge, Mass.: Harvard University Press, 1990), p. 154.

4. See Kristina Straub's *Sexual Suspects: Eighteenth-Century Players and Sexual Ideology* (Princeton, N.J.: Princeton University Press, 1992), for analyses both of Charke's *Narrative* and of the type of actress's autobiography that presents its subject as "sentimental victim." Straub also offers an excellent discussion of many issues relevant to Robinson's career and to *Walsingham*, most notably the eighteenth century's attempt to control and contain (while continuing to enjoy) the often untidy spectacle provided by actors and actresses on- and offstage. Straub summarizes:

> Up to the nineteenth century, discourse about players in Britain shows marks of a struggle to subject them to the decorous order of an idealized spectatorship; these marks make clear both the force of that order and its inability to totalize. Players in popular theatrical literature constitute a discursive site that complements — indeed, is necessary to — the epistemological authority of the spectator. At the same time, this discourse about players reveals the often less-than-effective cultural and linguistic means by which that authority is constructed and maintained as a "natural" category. (pp. 4–5)

Straub, together with Peter Stallybrass and Allon White (*The Politics and Poetry of Transgression* [Ithaca, N.Y.: Cornell University Press, 1986]), likewise emphasizes how the site of the theater presents a particularly disturbing challenge to the imposition of not just a politics of the gaze but also a politics of the gazed-upon, exhibited body — a body often figured, in the cases of both male and female players, as ambiguously classed, ambiguously or monstrously sexed, and suspiciously vagrant.

5. Mary Robinson, *Walsingham, Or the Pupil of Nature: A Domestic Story*, ed. Gina Luria, 4 vols. (New York: Garland Press, 1974), 4: 386. All subsequent references are to this edition, part of the Garland series The Feminist Controversy in England (1788–1810), and appear in the text.

6. See Jacques Lacan, "God and the *Jouissance* of the Woman" and "A Love Letter" (in *Feminine Sexuality: Jacques Lacan and the école freudienne*, ed. Juliet Mitchell and Jacqueline Rose, trans. Rose [New York: Norton, 1992], pp. 137–61), which employ the concept of erasure to explore the structural contradictions pertaining to the construct of femininity.

7. See Francette Pacteau, "The Impossible Referent: Representations of the Androgyne" (in *Formations of Fantasy*, ed. Victor Burgin, James Donald, and Cora Kaplan [London: Methuen, 1986], pp. 62–85), for an analysis relevant to the novel's presentation of Sidney, since in the attempt to visualize this character (an effort the text both discourages and teases the reader to undertake), one alternative that emerges is androgyny. For Pacteau, the androgyne paradigmatically figures both the fear and the fantasy of pre-oedipal sexuality, the disavowal of sexual difference, whereas the transvestite would figure the culturally more threatening refusal via parody of sexual difference — but the readerly attempt to imagine Sidney brings up some of the same issues of the impossible referent.

8. Michael Moon and Eve Kosofsky Sedgwick, "Divinity: A Dossier, a Perfor-

mance Piece, a Little-Understood Emotion," *Discourse* 13 (Fall/Winter 1990–91): 27.

9. See Laqueur, *Making Sex*, p. 152; as well as Gary Kelly, *The English Jacobin Novel, 1780–1805* (Oxford: Clarendon Press, 1976); and Patricia Meyer Spacks, "Energies of the Mind: Novels of the 1790s," in idem, *Desire and Truth: Functions of Plot in Eighteenth-Century English Novels* (Chicago: University of Chicago Press, 1990), pp. 175–202.

10. See Terry Castle, *Masquerade and Civilization: The Carnivalesque in Eighteenth-Century English Culture and Fiction* (Stanford: Stanford University Press, 1986).

11. For relevant background on the carnivalesque, see Stallybrass and White, *Politics and Poetry of Transgression*, esp. pp. 1–26; and Mary Russo, "Female Grotesques: Carnival and Theory," in *Feminist Studies/Critical Studies*, ed. Teresa de Lauretis (Bloomington: Indiana University Press, 1986), pp. 213–29.

12. Joan Reviere, "Womanliness as a Masquerade," reprinted in *Formations of Fantasy*, pp. 35–44.

13. Stephen Heath, "Joan Reviere and the Masquerade," in *Formations of Fantasy*, pp. 52, 53.

14. Quoted in Marguerite Steen, *The Lost One: A Biography of Mary (Perdita) Robinson* (London: Methuen, 1937). Unfortunately the only full biography of Robinson now in circulation, Steen's account does not consider her literary production at all and is gratingly condescending, sensationalistic, and silly as well. It does, however, contain interesting contemporary material pertaining to the various scandals of its subject's life, since that is clearly the biographer's primary interest. See pp. 122–23 for full text of the satire, as well as for illustrations of all the prints discussed later in this paper. See also the entry on Robinson in *The Dictionary of British and American Women Writers, 1600–1800*, ed. Janet Todd (Totowa, N.J.: Rowman & Allanheld, 1985).

15. This judgment is based heavily on the novel's dominant depressive affect and the recontaining operation carried out by its conclusion. And yet, to touch on an issue largely ignored in this essay, the reading experience of *Walsingham* does potentially extend an invitation to enjoy not only the spectacle of cross-dressing but also more than one transgressive scenario of same-sex desire, depending on what the individual reader may or may not suspect prior to finishing the book. Readers who take Sidney at face value as male are left to ponder the motivations for the mixed signals sent by "his" alternately kind and cruel, but clearly obsessive behavior toward his cousin; the two "men's" tormented pattern of flight from / pursuit of each other lends an implicitly eroticized impetus to their relationship, suggesting the classic uncanny configuration of homosocially bonded doubles. On the other hand, readers who suspect the truth about Sidney's gender have another field of potentially transgressive speculation opened up, namely, the nature of the attachment between her and her "companion," Isabella, and whether Isabella herself is a dupe, accomplice, or lover. At any rate, the novel plays actively with the responsive register of "knowingness," specifically knowing or bringing a "knowing" suspicion to bear on the secret of someone else's concealed sex and sexuality, that Moon and Sedgwick discuss in their article "Divinity" and that Sedgwick also

deals with more fully in *Epistemology of the Closet* (Berkeley: University of California Press, 1990). As Sedgwick notes, the appeal to this epistemological modality can either serve to consolidate homophobic condescension and control or, by contrast, usher in the possibility of readerly complicity and/or identification.

16. Sigmund Freud, *Drei Abhandlungen zur Sexualtheorie und verwandte Schriften* (Frankfurt: Fischer, 1985), p. 90, my translation.

17. Straub notes, likewise, the potential threat embodied in the figure of the cross-dressed actress in Charlotte Charke's *Narrative*, who "is also capable of holding a mirror up to masculinity that reflects back an image of castration which cannot be entirely controlled by the mechanisms of projection" (*Sexual Suspects*, p. 134).

18. See Judith Butler, *Gender Trouble: Feminism and the Subversion of Identity* (New York: Routledge, 1990), on the "politics of sexual discontinuity" characterizing the position of the hermaphrodite Herculine Barbin, in which Robinson's transvestite Sidney also ends up caught:

> Herculine's pleasures and desires are in no way the bucolic innocence that thrives and proliferates prior to the imposition of a juridical law. Neither does s/he fully fall outside the signifying economy of masculinity. S/he is "outside" the law, but the law maintains this "outside" within itself. In effect s/he embodies the law, not as an entitled subject, but as an enacted testimony to the law's uncanny capacity to produce only those rebellions that it can guarantee will — out of fidelity — defeat themselves and those subjects, who, utterly subjected, have no choice but to reiterate the law of their genesis. (p. 106)

19. Robinson's own *Memoirs* also furthers that discourse on the affective centrality of maternity that was emerging during her lifetime and has climaxed in the psychoanalytic (particularly object relation theory's) preoccupation with the mother-infant bond. The *Memoirs* testifies to her own belief in motherhood as the most rewarding of female experiences (1: 143–44) and to her maternal solicitude (emphasis on breast-feeding, caring for her children through their illnesses herself, keeping them by her constantly, and her desolation at the death of her second child). This emphasis on maternity may have served as one of the more powerful of the defensive strategies available to the author; as Robinson's biographer says, "Even her worst enemies could not deny her the two virtues which she possessed in extravagant degree: she was a devoted mother and a most courageous woman" (*Lost One*, p. ix). On the other hand, she did raise and support her one surviving child, Maria, alone, and that child stuck by her scandalous parent loyally, acting as her amanuensis, and in her work on the *Memoirs* added many testimonies to Robinson's maternal affection. The *Memoirs*, in other words, portrays the mother-daughter relationship, otherwise singularly absent in eighteenth-century women's fiction, as positive, enduring, and mutually protective, and *Walsingham* offers the negatively strong, pathologized version of this bond's endurance.

20. The many pieces of poetry scattered through *Walsingham* are themselves almost all of the elegiac or graveyard school. Usually dashed off by the narrator under the pressure of overwhelming emotion while the described events were unfolding, they are subsequently inserted into the chronicle he *later* assembles.

This body of poetry, commemorating isolated moments characteristically marked by feelings of abandonment, isolation, or desperation, thereby offers the only textual primary evidence left over from the actual interval in which the recounted events occurred. Indeed, the verses, given their frequently suicidal, hallucinatory, incoherent, or simply bathetic intensity, do serve to disjoint the chronological life story retrospectively imposed to order and contain that "kernal of the Real," the originary trauma, of which the poetry constitutes the most telling trace *within* the prose's master, albeit melancholic, narrative.

Index

In this index an "f" after a number indicates a separate reference on the next page, and an "ff" indicates separate references on the next two pages. A continuous discussion over two or more pages is indicated by a span of page numbers, e.g., "57–59." *Passim* is used for a cluster of references in close but not consecutive sequence. Entries are alphabetized letter by letter, ignoring word breaks, hyphens, and accents.

Library of Congress Cataloging-in-Publication Data

Body and text in the eighteenth century / edited by Veronica Kelly and
Dorothea von Mücke.
p.   cm.
Includes bibliographical references and index.
ISBN 0-8047-2269-2 (cloth : alk. paper) :
— ISBN 0-8047-2268-4 (pbk. : alk. paper) :
1. Literature, Modern — 18th century — History and criticism.
2. Body, Human, in literature.   I. Kelly, Veronica, 1955- .
II. Mücke, Dorothea E. von.
PN751.B65 1994
809'.9336—dc20
93-11547   CIP

⊗ This book is printed on acid-free paper

Designed, Engraved, and Published by Wm. Hogarth, March 5 1753, according to Act of Parliament.